The Knight Captain is the New Princess-to-Be

1

Story and art by Yasuko Yamaru

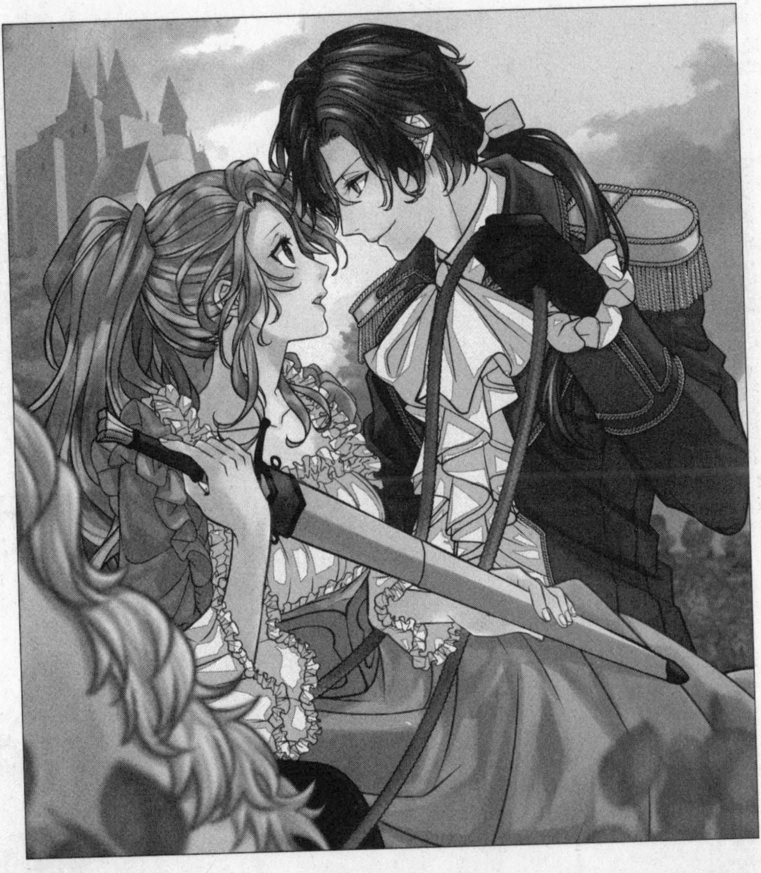

The Knight Captain is the New Princess-to-Be

1

CONTENTS

Chapter 1

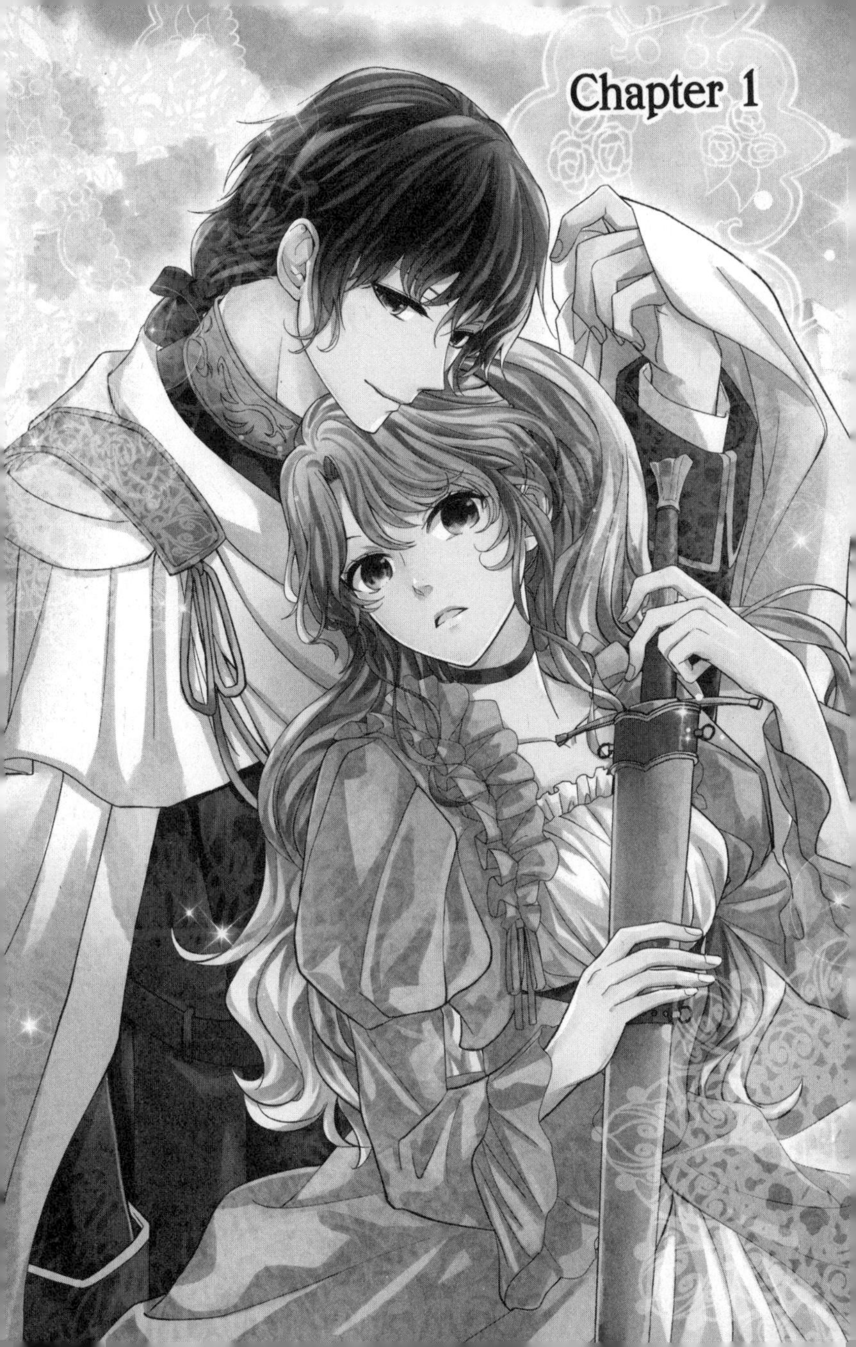

The Knight Captain is the New Princess-to-Be

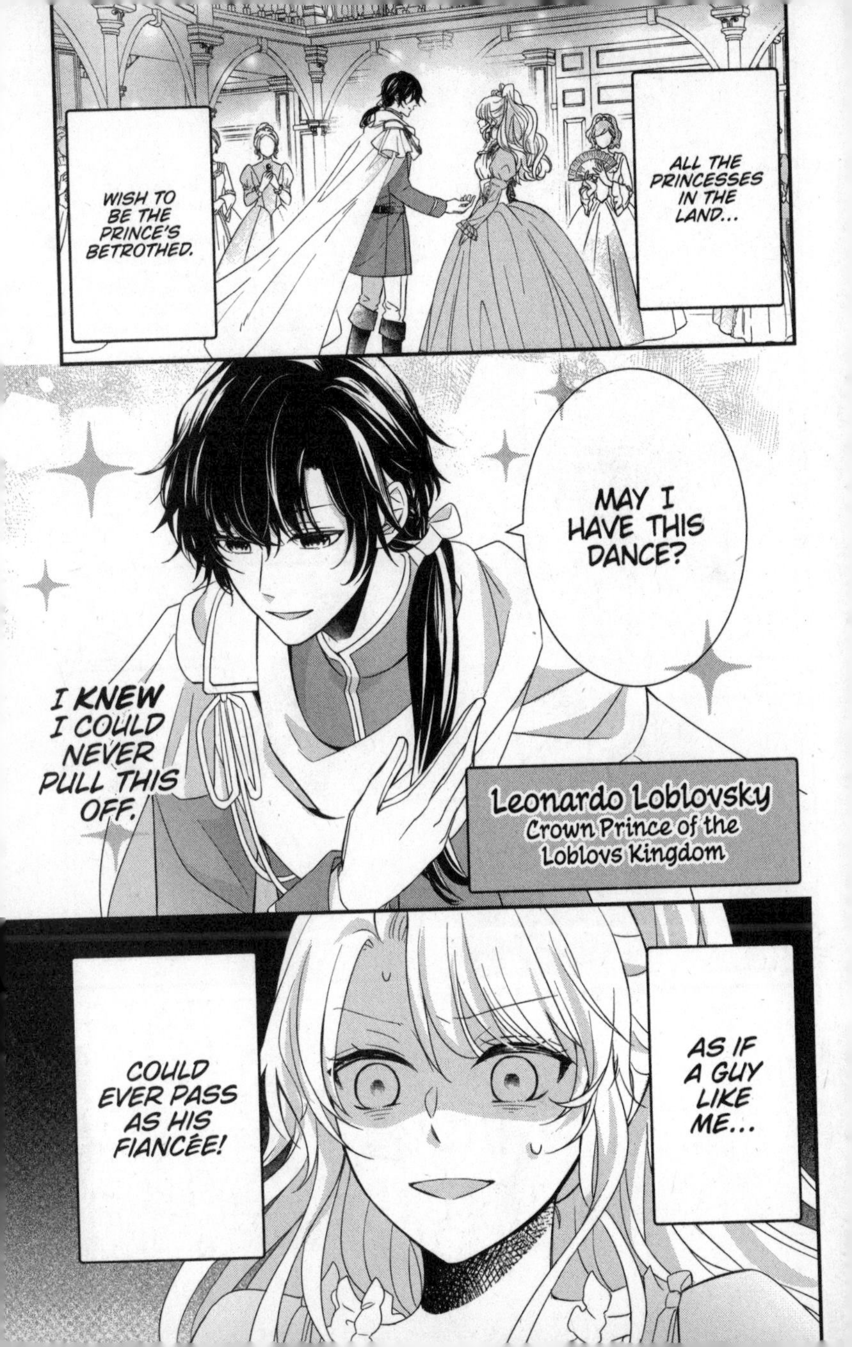
ALL THE PRINCESSES IN THE LAND...
WISH TO BE THE PRINCE'S BETROTHED.
MAY I HAVE THIS DANCE?
Leonardo Loblovsky
Crown Prince of the Loblovs Kingdom
I KNEW I COULD NEVER PULL THIS OFF.
AS IF A GUY LIKE ME...
COULD EVER PASS AS HIS FIANCÉE!

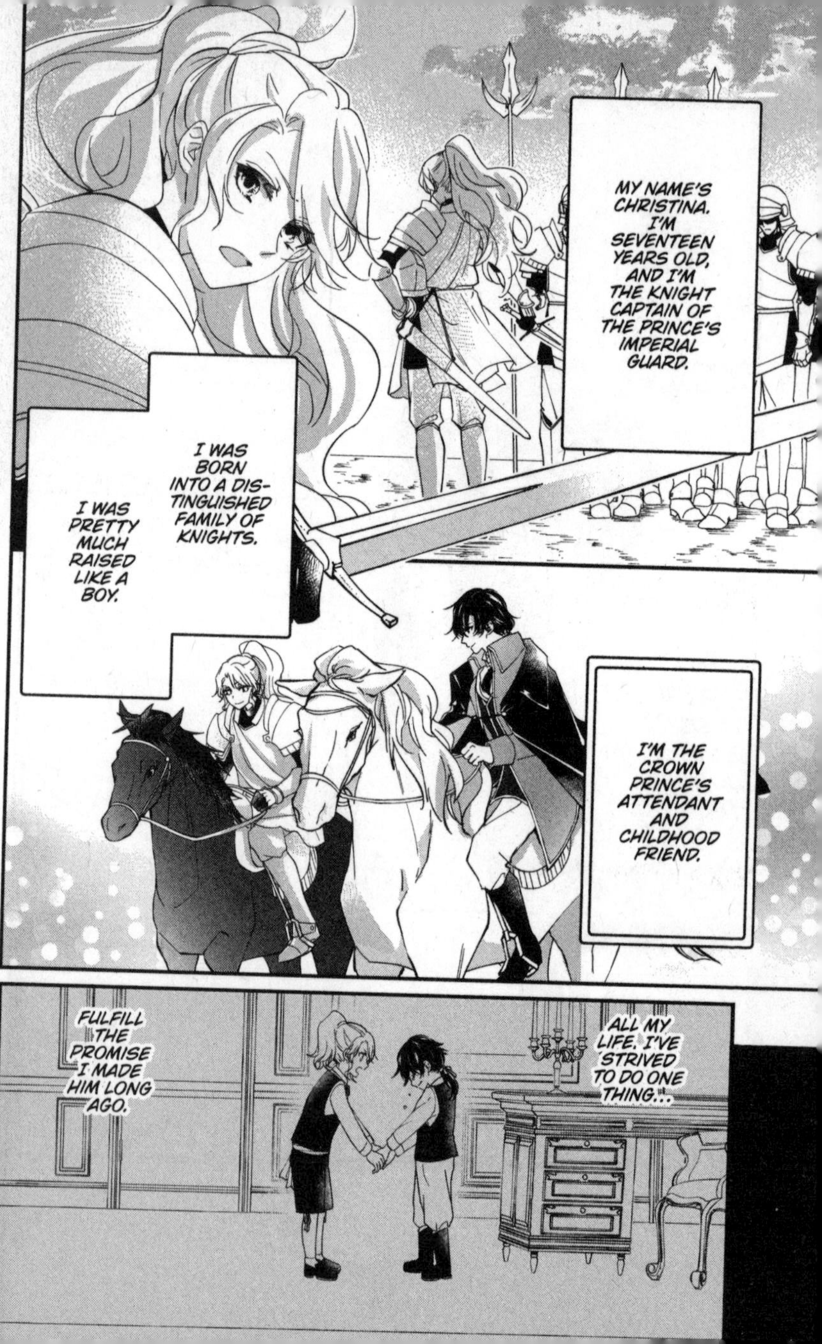
MY NAME'S CHRISTINA. I'M SEVENTEEN YEARS OLD, AND I'M THE KNIGHT CAPTAIN OF THE PRINCE'S IMPERIAL GUARD.
I WAS BORN INTO A DIS-TINGUISHED FAMILY OF KNIGHTS.
I WAS PRETTY MUCH RAISED LIKE A BOY.
I'M THE CROWN PRINCE'S ATTENDANT AND CHILDHOOD FRIEND.
ALL MY LIFE, I'VE STRIVED TO DO ONE THING...
FULFILL THE PROMISE I MADE HIM LONG AGO.

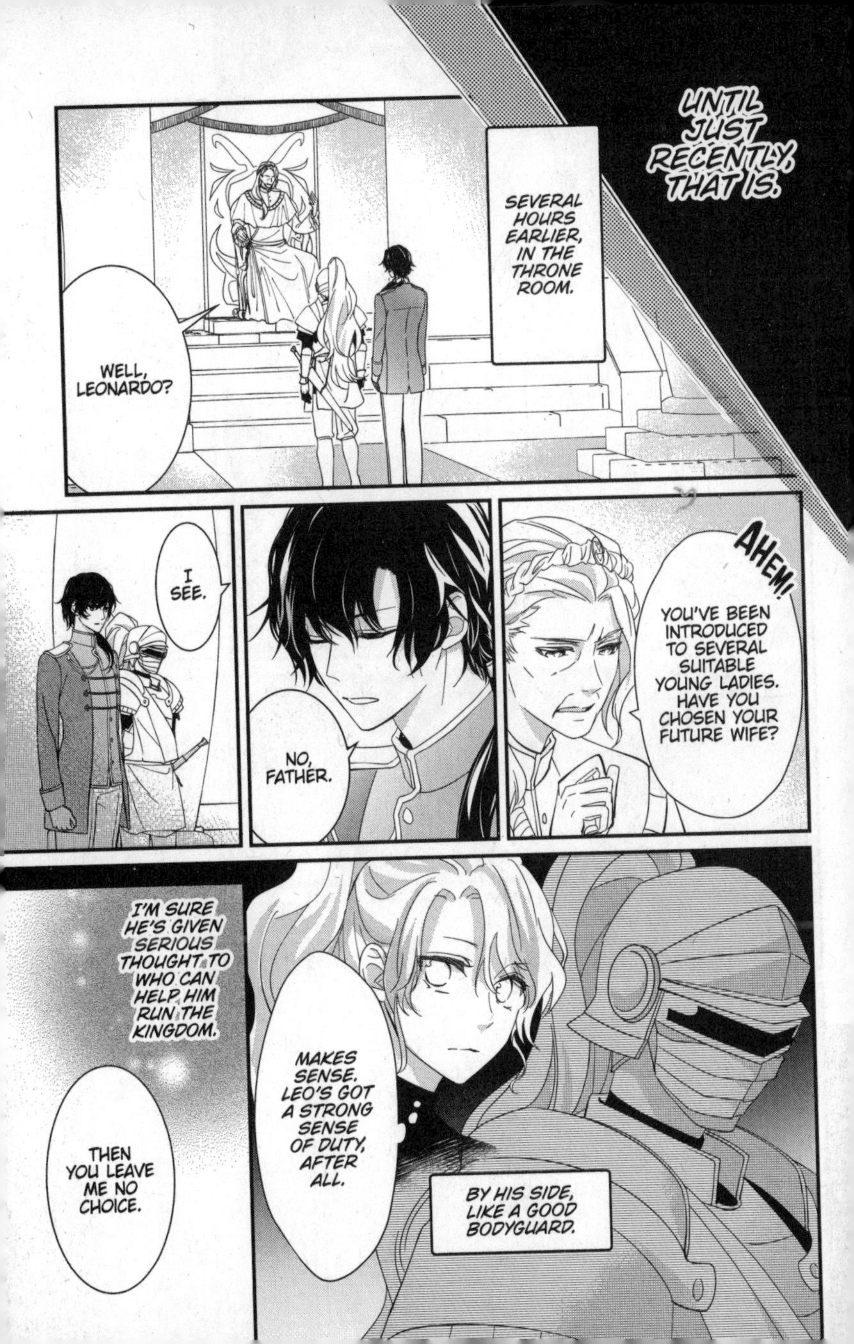
UNTIL JUST RECENTLY, THAT IS.
SEVERAL HOURS EARLIER, IN THE THRONE ROOM.
WELL, LEONARDO?
AHEM!
YOU'VE BEEN INTRODUCED TO SEVERAL SUITABLE YOUNG LADIES. HAVE YOU CHOSEN YOUR FUTURE WIFE?
NO, FATHER.
I SEE.
MAKES SENSE. LEO'S GOT A STRONG SENSE OF DUTY, AFTER ALL.
BY HIS SIDE, LIKE A GOOD BODYGUARD.
I'M SURE HE'S GIVEN SERIOUS THOUGHT TO WHO CAN HELP HIM RUN THE KINGDOM.
THEN YOU LEAVE ME NO CHOICE.

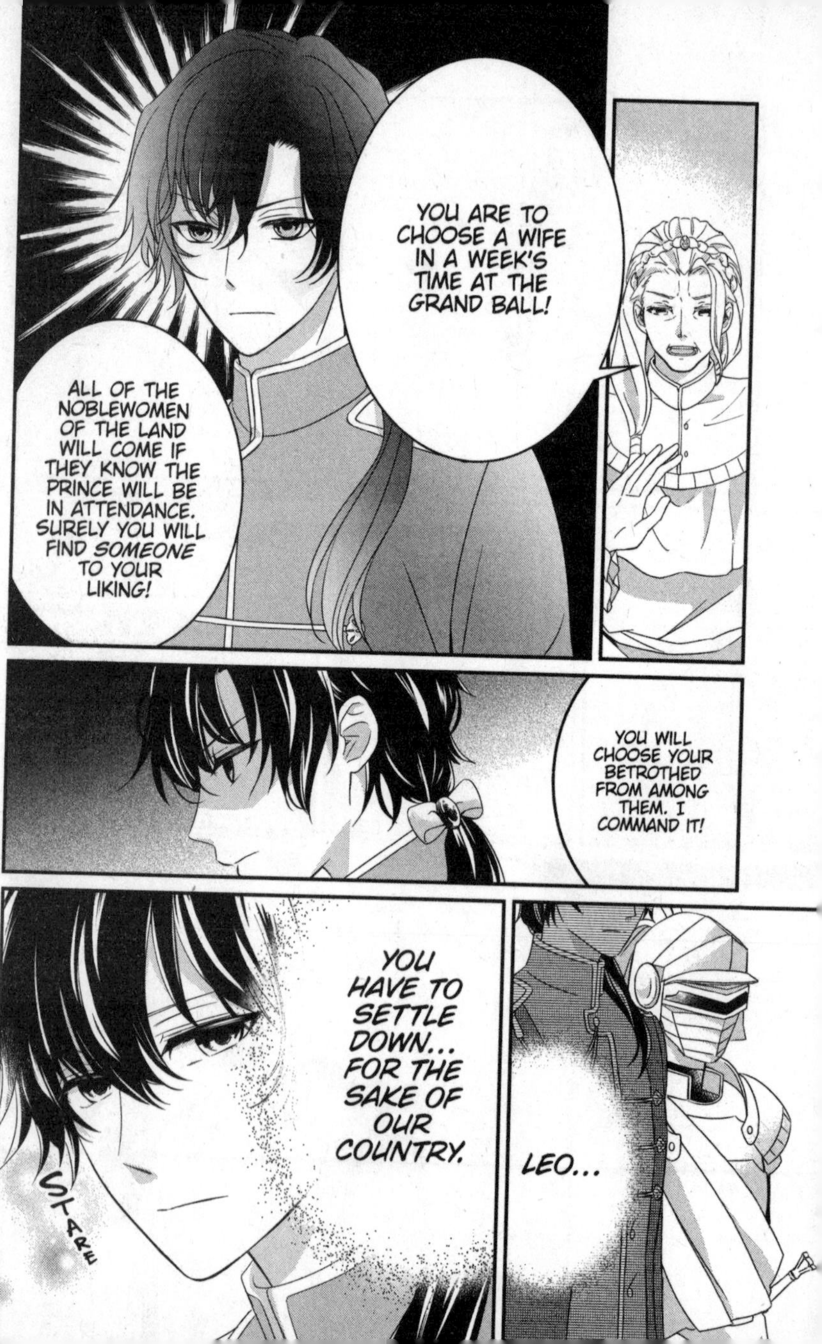
YOU ARE TO CHOOSE A WIFE IN A WEEK'S TIME AT THE GRAND BALL!
ALL OF THE NOBLEWOMEN OF THE LAND WILL COME IF THEY KNOW THE PRINCE WILL BE IN ATTENDANCE. SURELY YOU WILL FIND *SOMEONE* TO YOUR LIKING!
YOU WILL CHOOSE YOUR BETROTHED FROM AMONG THEM. I COMMAND IT!
LEO...
YOU HAVE TO SETTLE DOWN... FOR THE SAKE OF OUR COUNTRY.
STARE

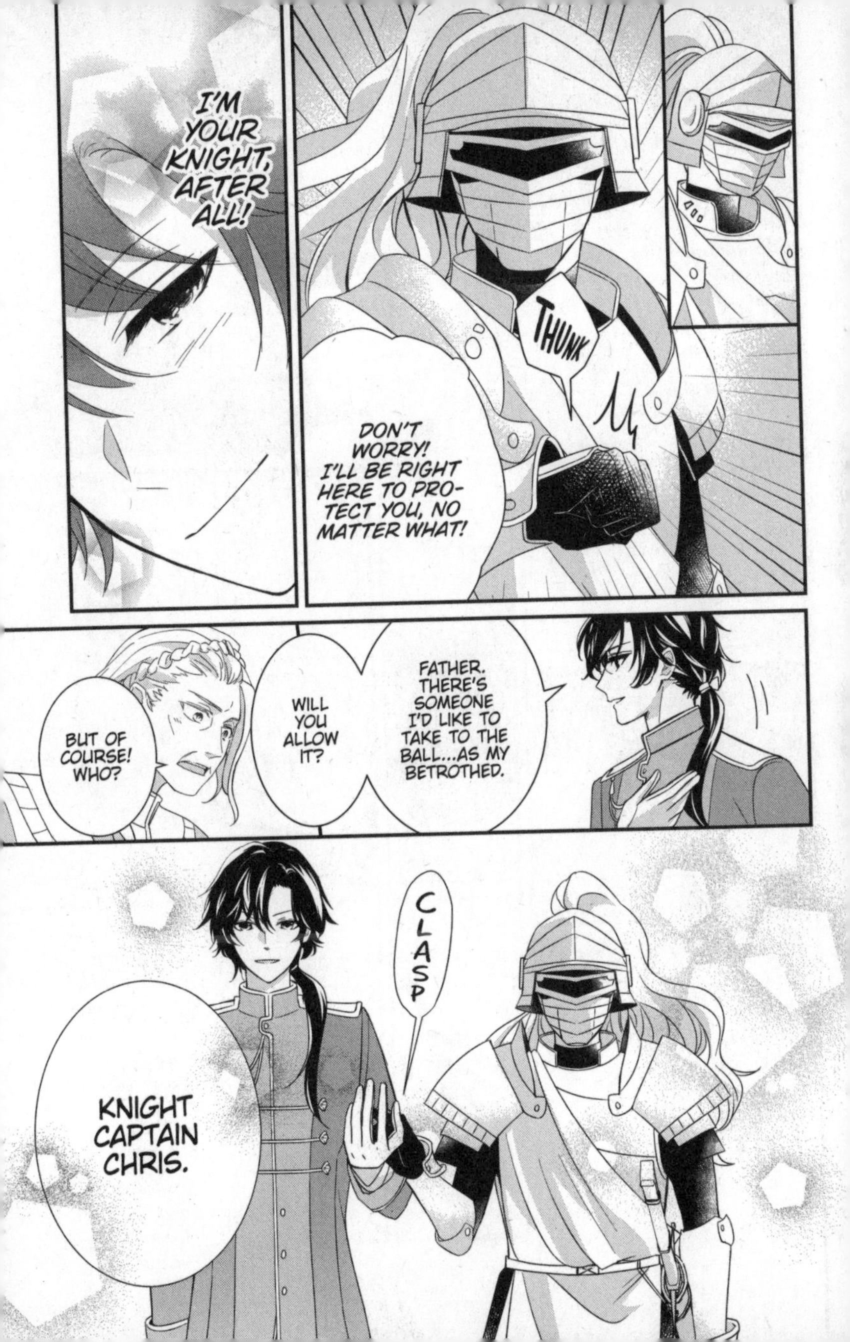
THUNK
DON'T WORRY! I'LL BE RIGHT HERE TO PRO-TECT YOU, NO MATTER WHAT!
I'M YOUR KNIGHT, AFTER ALL!
FATHER. THERE'S SOMEONE I'D LIKE TO TAKE TO THE BALL...AS MY BETROTHED.
WILL YOU ALLOW IT?
BUT OF COURSE! WHO?
CLASP
KNIGHT CAPTAIN CHRIS.

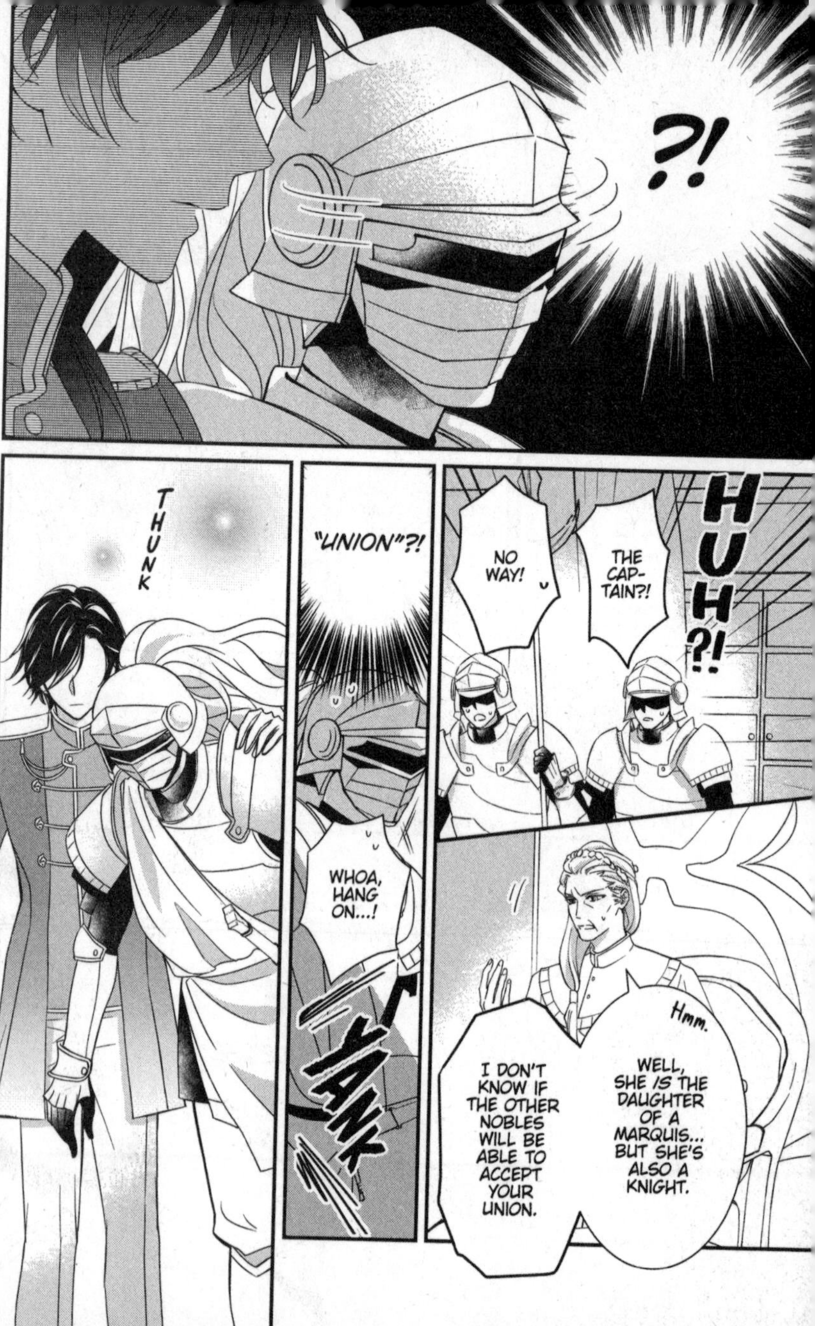
?!
HUH?!
THE CAP-TAIN?!
NO WAY!
Hmm.
WELL, SHE *IS* THE DAUGHTER OF A MARQUIS... BUT SHE'S ALSO A KNIGHT.
I DON'T KNOW IF THE OTHER NOBLES WILL BE ABLE TO ACCEPT YOUR UNION.
"UNION"?!
WHOA, HANG ON...!
YANK
THUNK

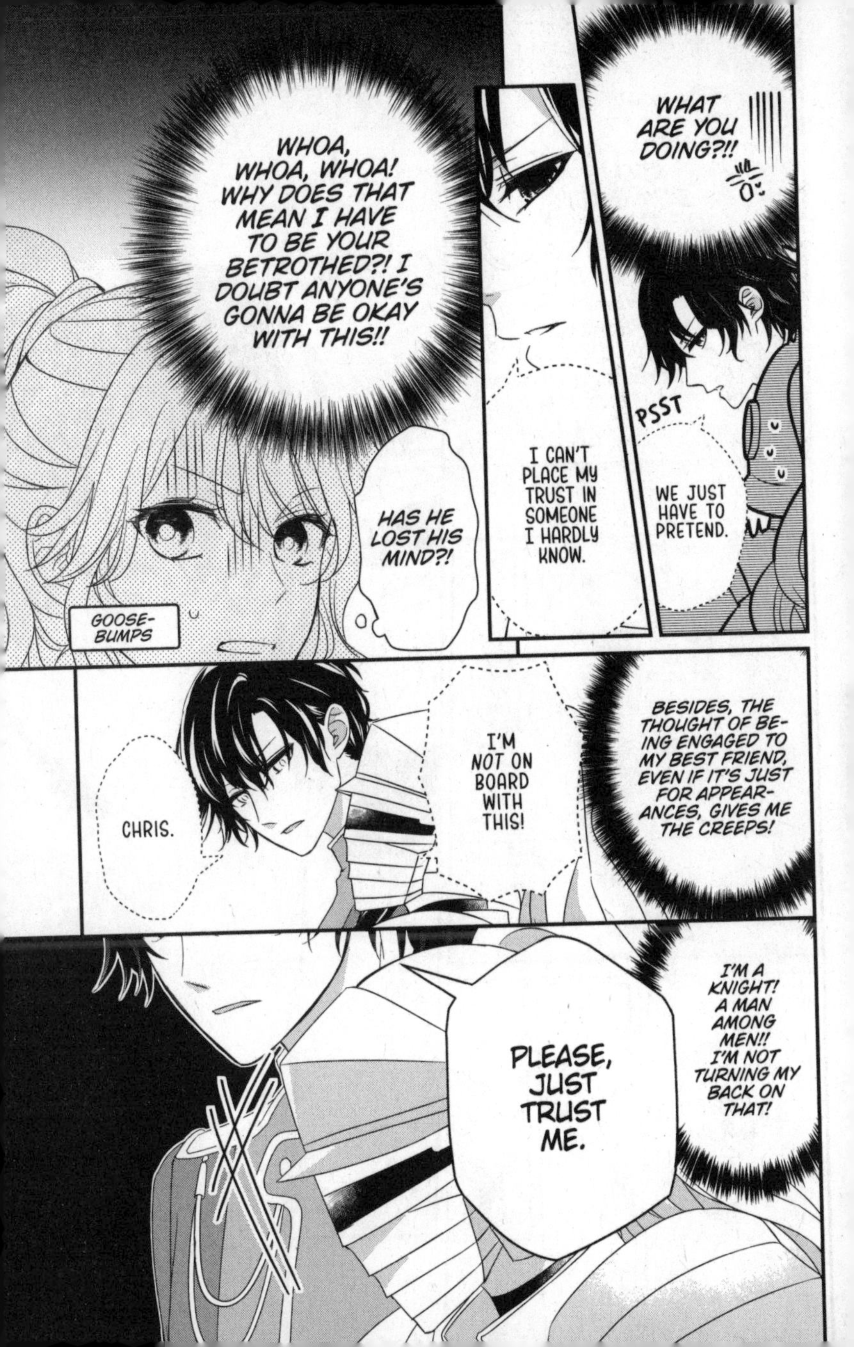
WHAT ARE YOU DOING?!!
PSST
WE JUST HAVE TO PRETEND.
I CAN'T PLACE MY TRUST IN SOMEONE I HARDLY KNOW.
WHOA, WHOA, WHOA! WHY DOES THAT MEAN I HAVE TO BE YOUR BETROTHED?! I DOUBT ANYONE'S GONNA BE OKAY WITH THIS!!
HAS HE LOST HIS MIND?!
GOOSE-BUMPS
BESIDES, THE THOUGHT OF BE-ING ENGAGED TO MY BEST FRIEND, EVEN IF IT'S JUST FOR APPEAR-ANCES, GIVES ME THE CREEPS!
I'M NOT ON BOARD WITH THIS!
CHRIS.
I'M A KNIGHT! A MAN AMONG MEN!! I'M NOT TURNING MY BACK ON THAT!
PLEASE, JUST TRUST ME.

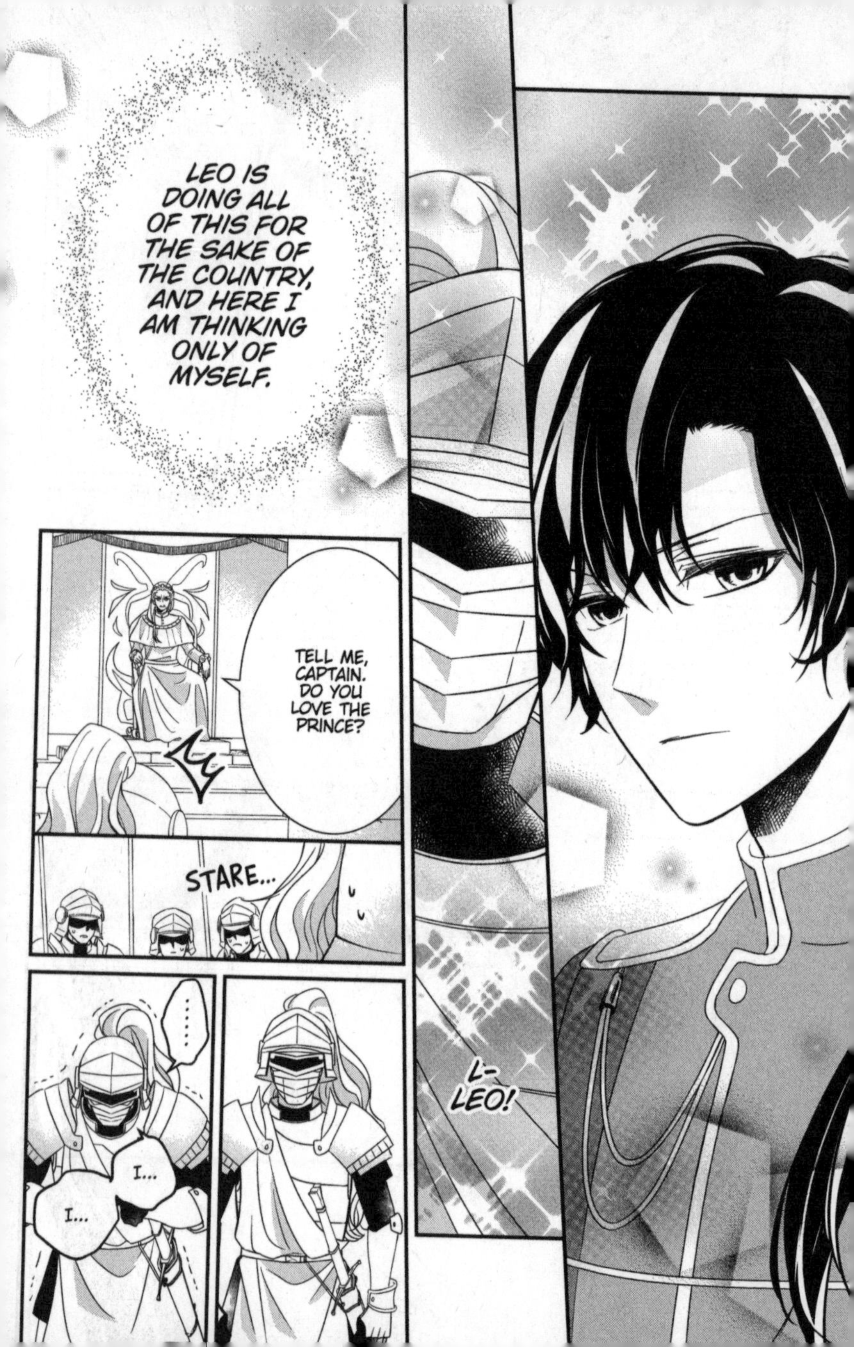
L-LEO!
LEO IS DOING ALL OF THIS FOR THE SAKE OF THE COUNTRY, AND HERE I AM THINKING ONLY OF MYSELF.
TELL ME, CAPTAIN. DO YOU LOVE THE PRINCE?
STARE...
......
I...
I...

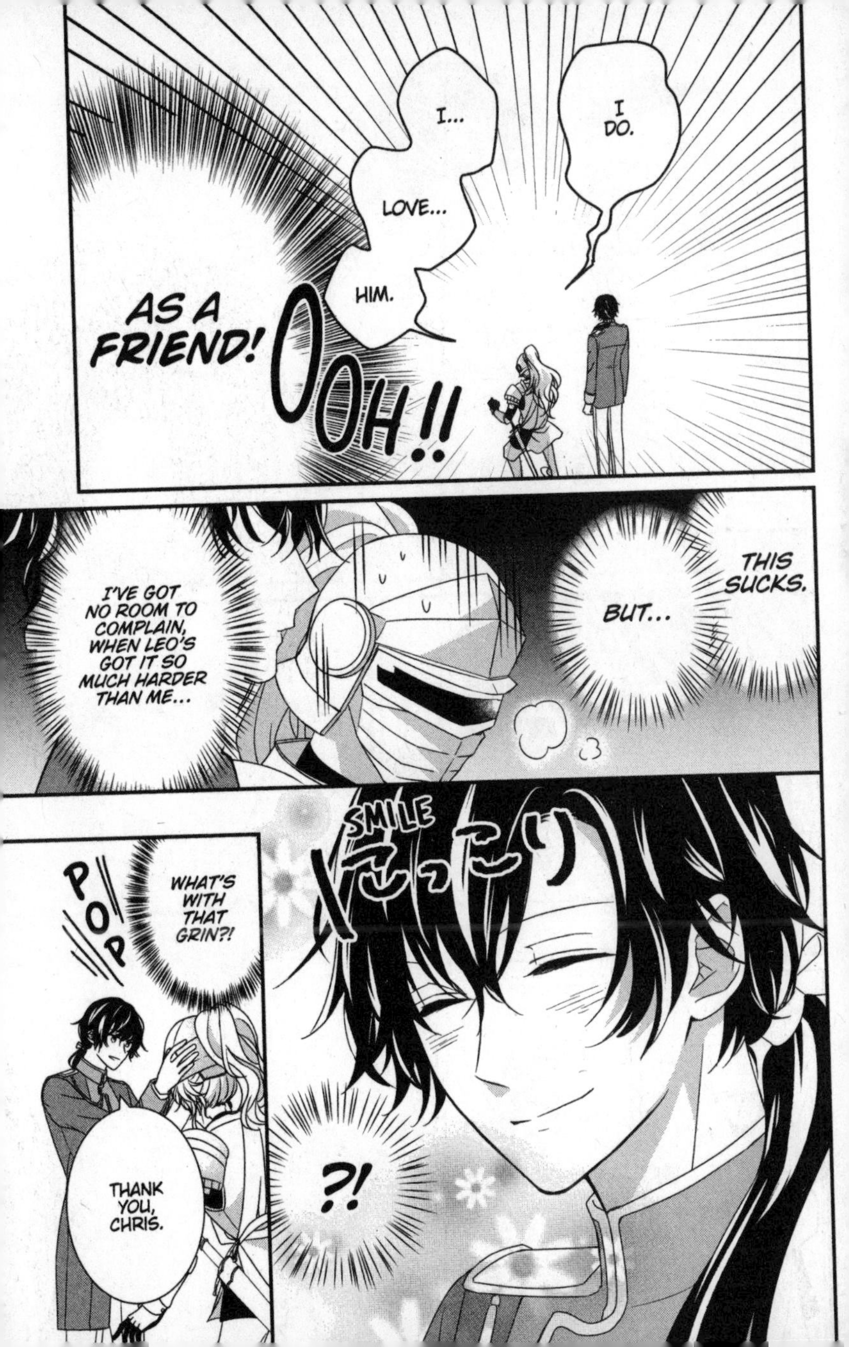
I DO.
I...
LOVE...
HIM.
OOOH!!
AS A FRIEND!
THIS SUCKS.
BUT...
I'VE GOT NO ROOM TO COMPLAIN, WHEN LEO'S GOT IT SO MUCH HARDER THAN ME...
SMILE
?!
POP
WHAT'S WITH THAT GRIN?!
THANK YOU, CHRIS.

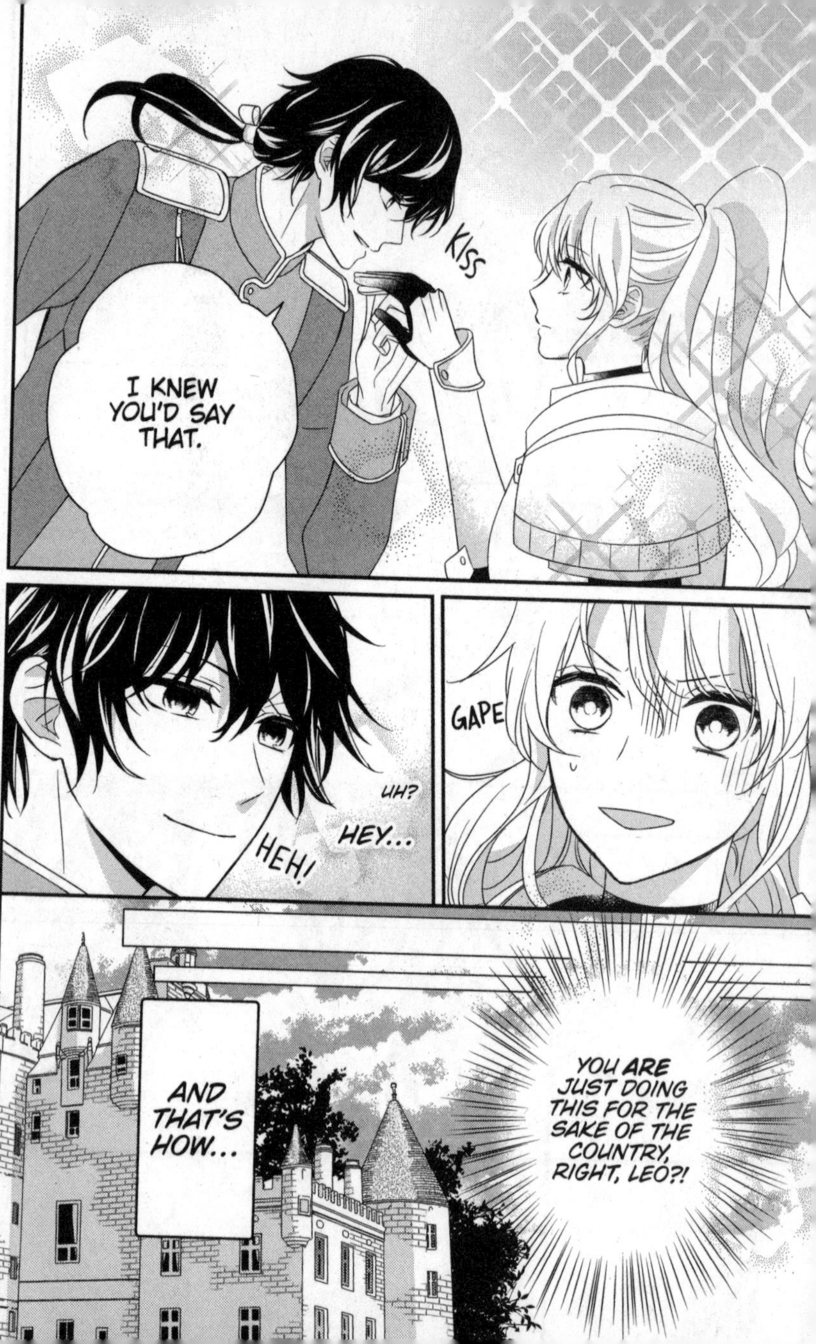
KISS
I KNEW YOU'D SAY THAT.
GAPE
UH?
HEY...
HEH!
YOU ARE JUST DOING THIS FOR THE SAKE OF THE COUNTRY, RIGHT, LEO?!
AND THAT'S HOW...

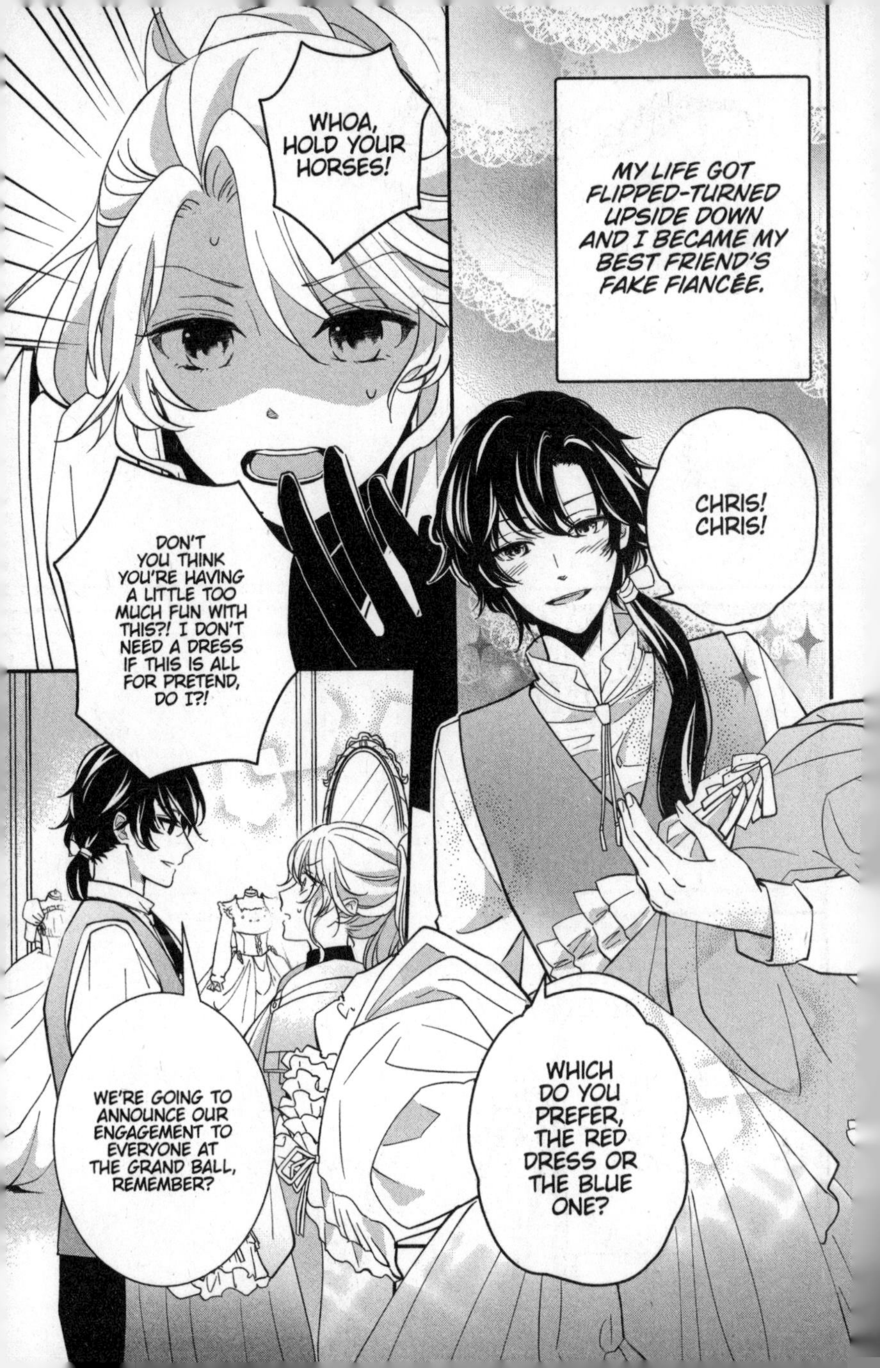
MY LIFE GOT FLIPPED-TURNED UPSIDE DOWN AND I BECAME MY BEST FRIEND'S FAKE FIANCÉE.
CHRIS! CHRIS!
WHICH DO YOU PREFER, THE RED DRESS OR THE BLUE ONE?
WHOA, HOLD YOUR HORSES!
DON'T YOU THINK YOU'RE HAVING A LITTLE TOO MUCH FUN WITH THIS?! I DON'T NEED A DRESS IF THIS IS ALL FOR PRETEND, DO I?!
WE'RE GOING TO ANNOUNCE OUR ENGAGEMENT TO EVERYONE AT THE GRAND BALL, REMEMBER?

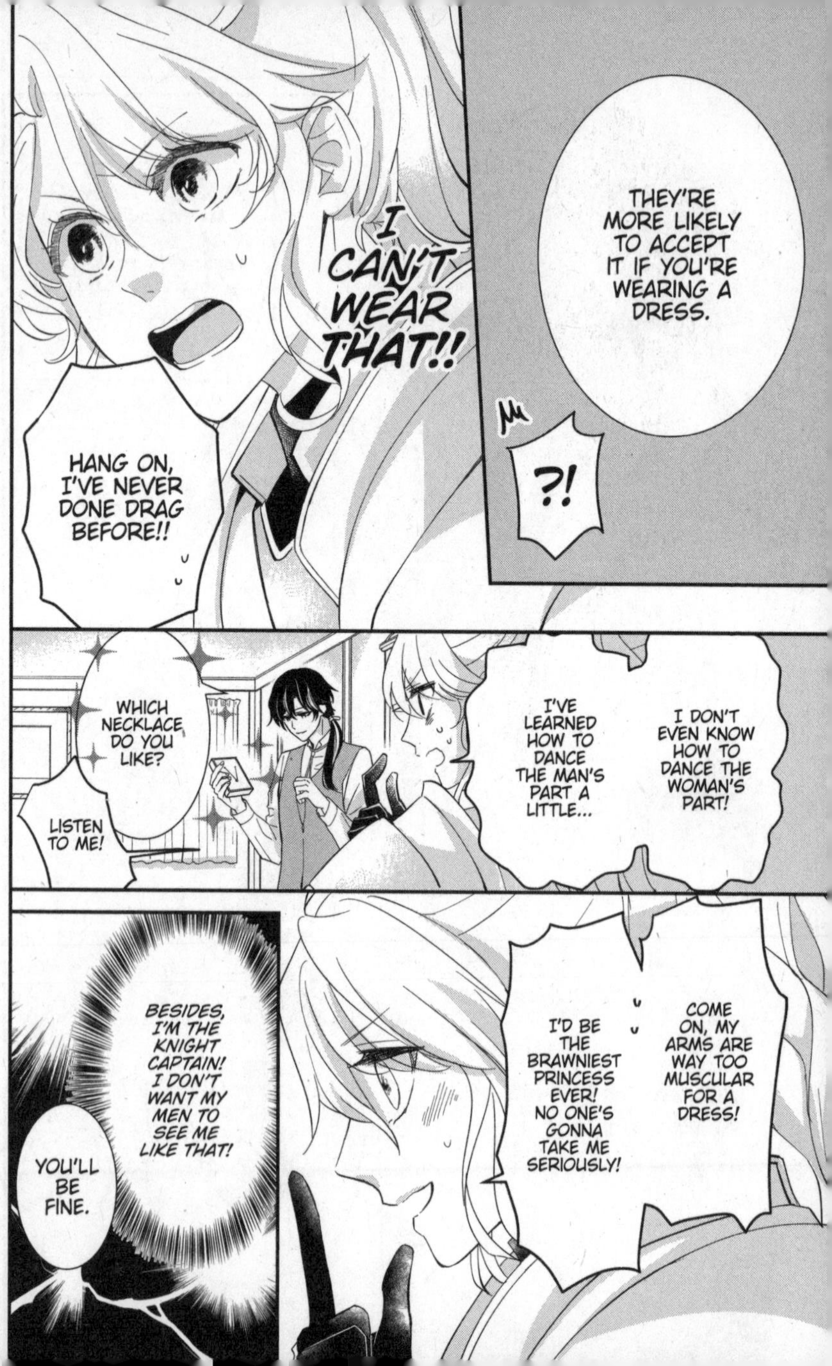
THEY'RE MORE LIKELY TO ACCEPT IT IF YOU'RE WEARING A DRESS.
?!
I CAN'T WEAR THAT!!
HANG ON, I'VE NEVER DONE DRAG BEFORE!!
I DON'T EVEN KNOW HOW TO DANCE THE WOMAN'S PART!
I'VE LEARNED HOW TO DANCE THE MAN'S PART A LITTLE...
WHICH NECKLACE DO YOU LIKE?
LISTEN TO ME!
COME ON, MY ARMS ARE WAY TOO MUSCULAR FOR A DRESS!
I'D BE THE BRAWNIEST PRINCESS EVER! NO ONE'S GONNA TAKE ME SERIOUSLY!
BESIDES, I'M THE KNIGHT CAPTAIN! I DON'T WANT MY MEN TO SEE ME LIKE THAT!
YOU'LL BE FINE.

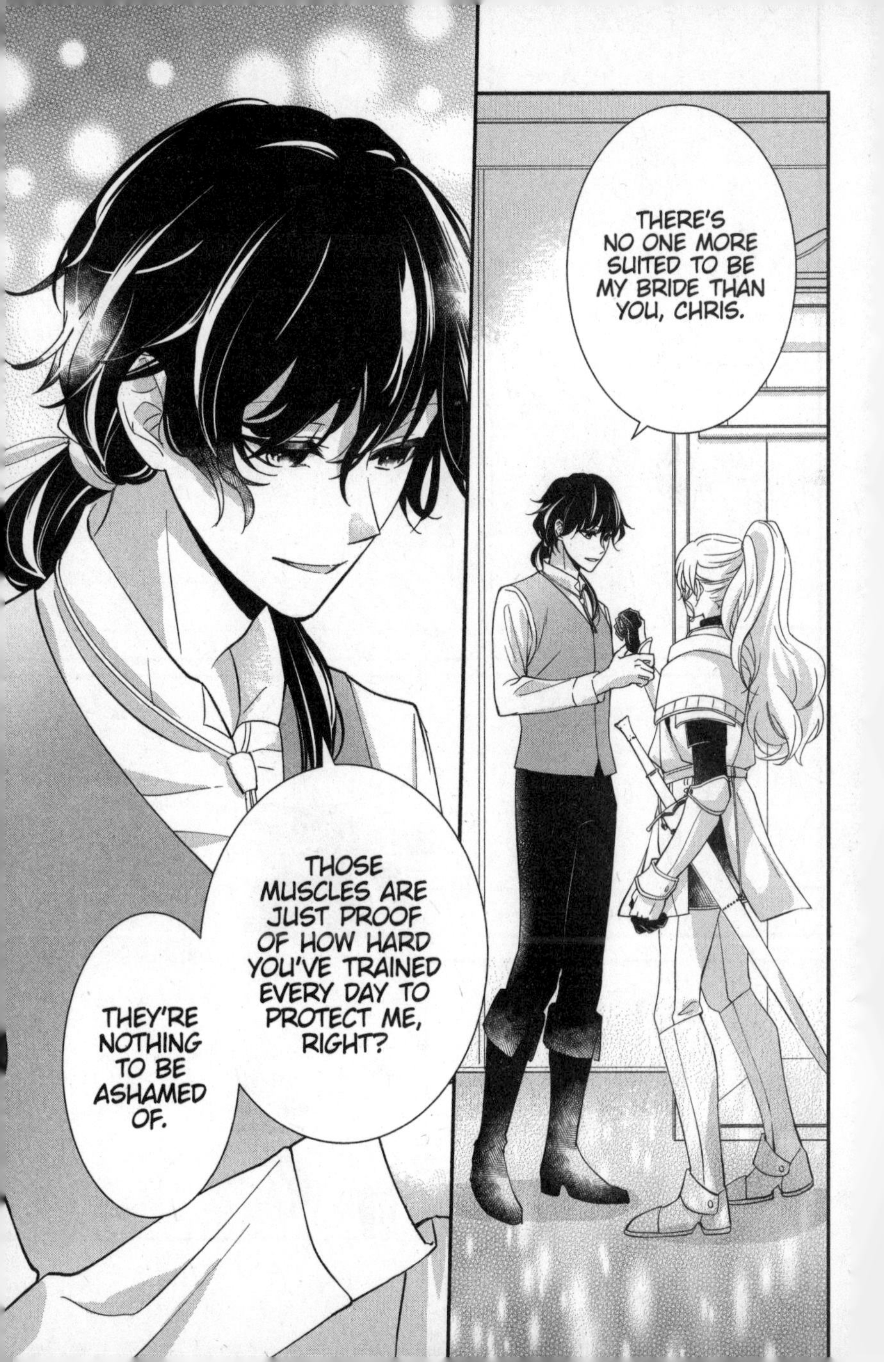
THERE'S NO ONE MORE SUITED TO BE MY BRIDE THAN YOU, CHRIS.
THOSE MUSCLES ARE JUST PROOF OF HOW HARD YOU'VE TRAINED EVERY DAY TO PROTECT ME, RIGHT?
THEY'RE NOTHING TO BE ASHAMED OF.

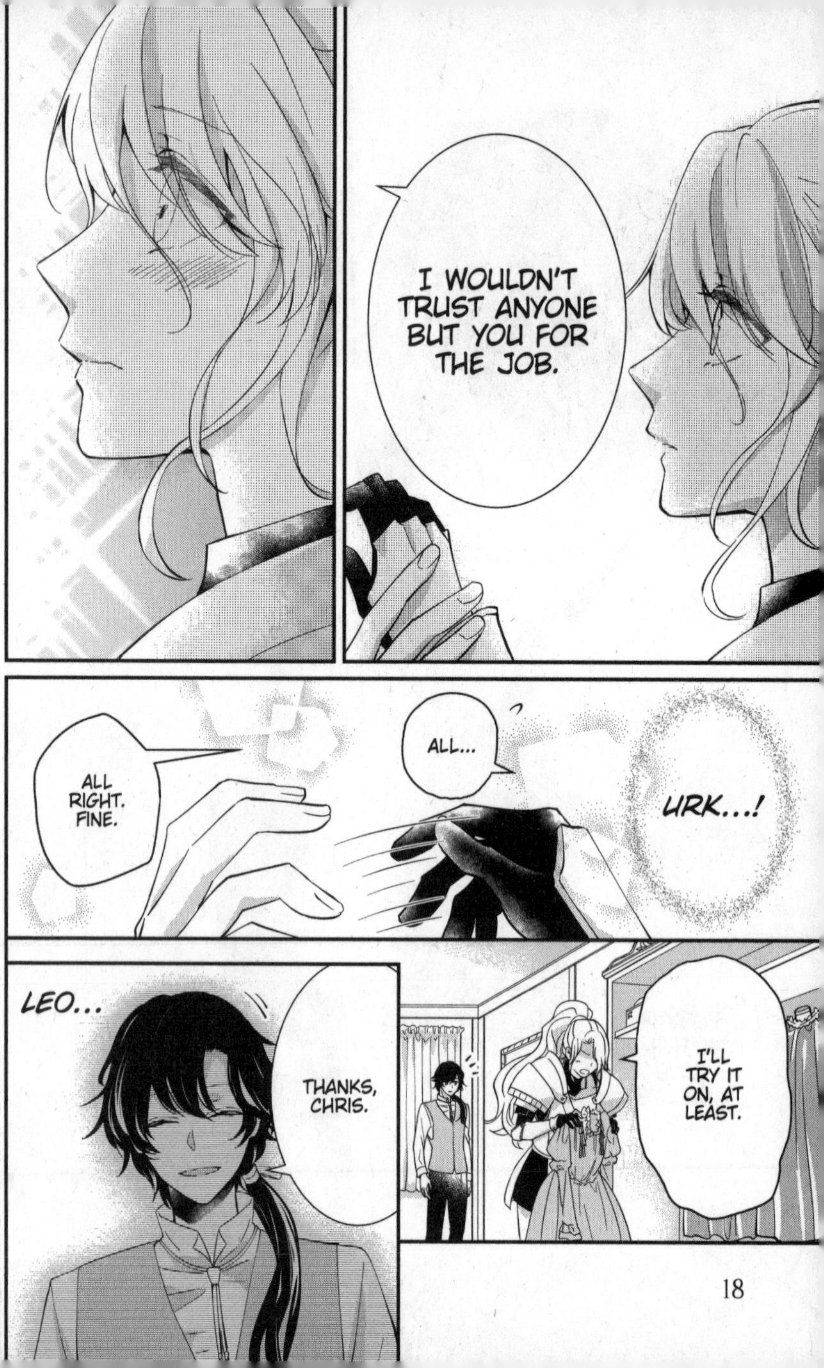
I WOULDN'T TRUST ANYONE BUT YOU FOR THE JOB.
URK...!
ALL...
ALL RIGHT. FINE.
I'LL TRY IT ON, AT LEAST.
THANKS, CHRIS.
LEO...

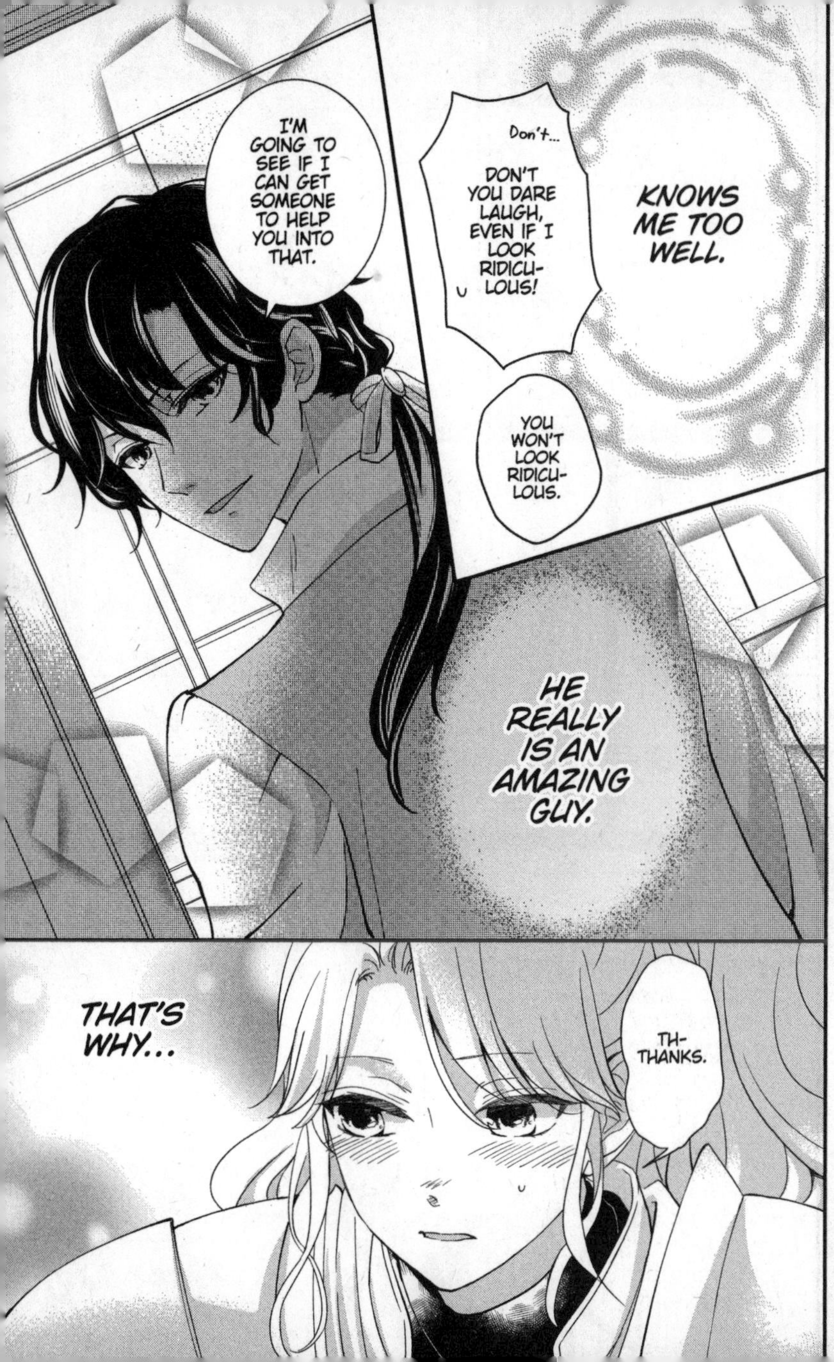
KNOWS ME TOO WELL.
Don't... DON'T YOU DARE LAUGH, EVEN IF I LOOK RIDICULOUS!
YOU WON'T LOOK RIDICULOUS.
I'M GOING TO SEE IF I CAN GET SOMEONE TO HELP YOU INTO THAT.
HE REALLY IS AN AMAZING GUY.
TH-THANKS.
THAT'S WHY...

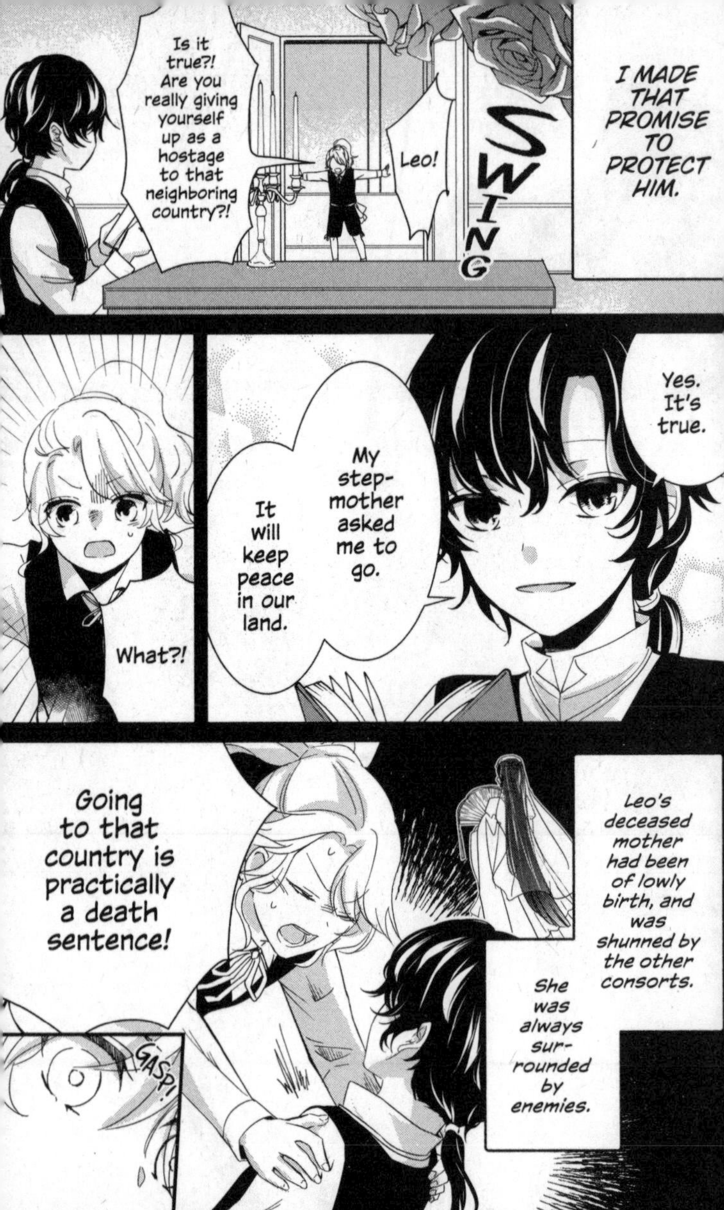
I MADE THAT PROMISE TO PROTECT HIM.
SWING
Leo!
Is it true?! Are you really giving yourself up as a hostage to that neighboring country?!
Yes. It's true.
My step-mother asked me to go.
It will keep peace in our land.
What?!
Leo's deceased mother had been of lowly birth, and was shunned by the other consorts.
She was always sur-rounded by enemies.
Going to that country is practically a death sentence!
GASP!

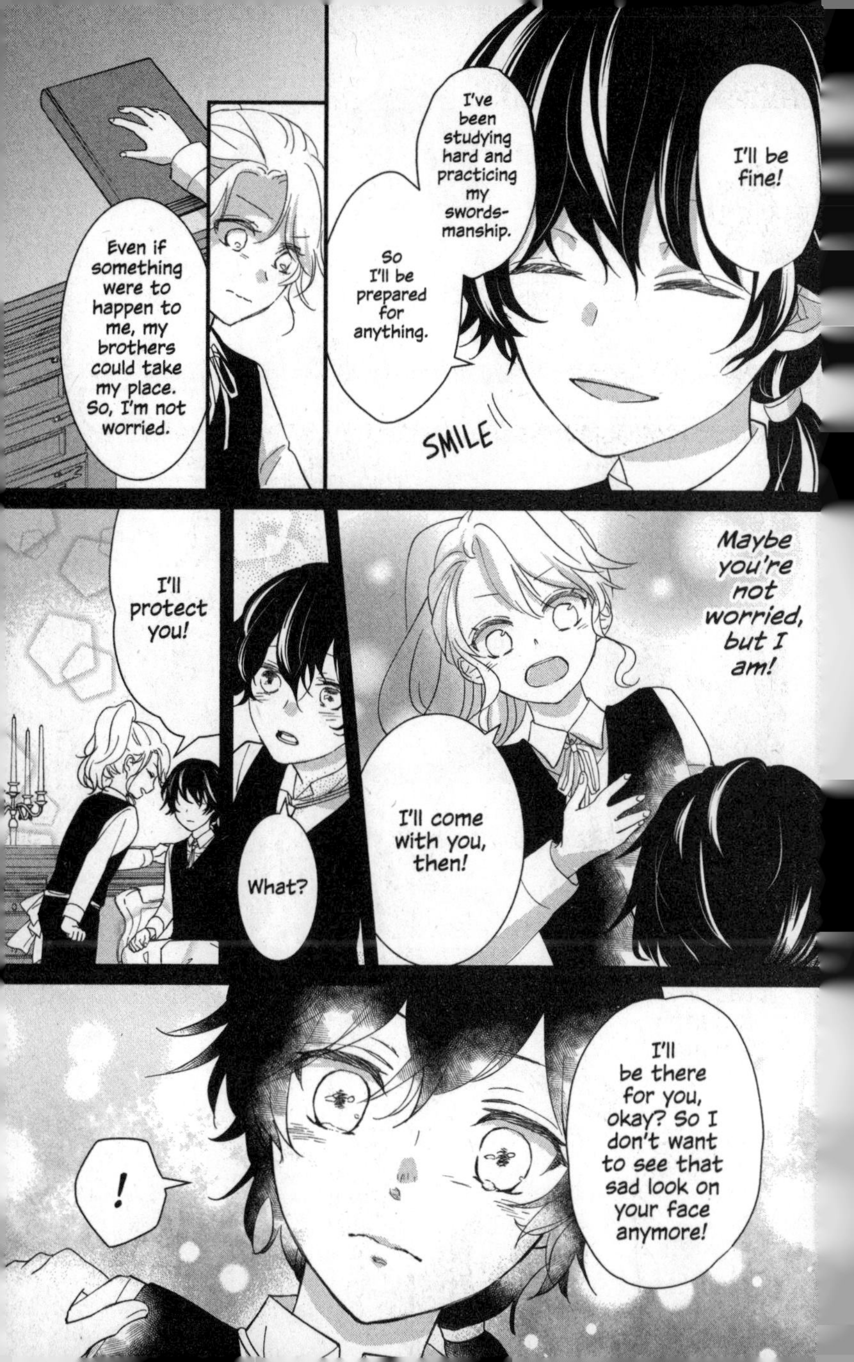
I'll be fine!
I've been studying hard and practicing my swordsmanship.
So I'll be prepared for anything.
SMILE
Even if something were to happen to me, my brothers could take my place. So, I'm not worried.
Maybe you're not worried, but I am!
I'll come with you, then!
What?
I'll protect you!
I'll be there for you, okay? So I don't want to see that sad look on your face anymore!
!

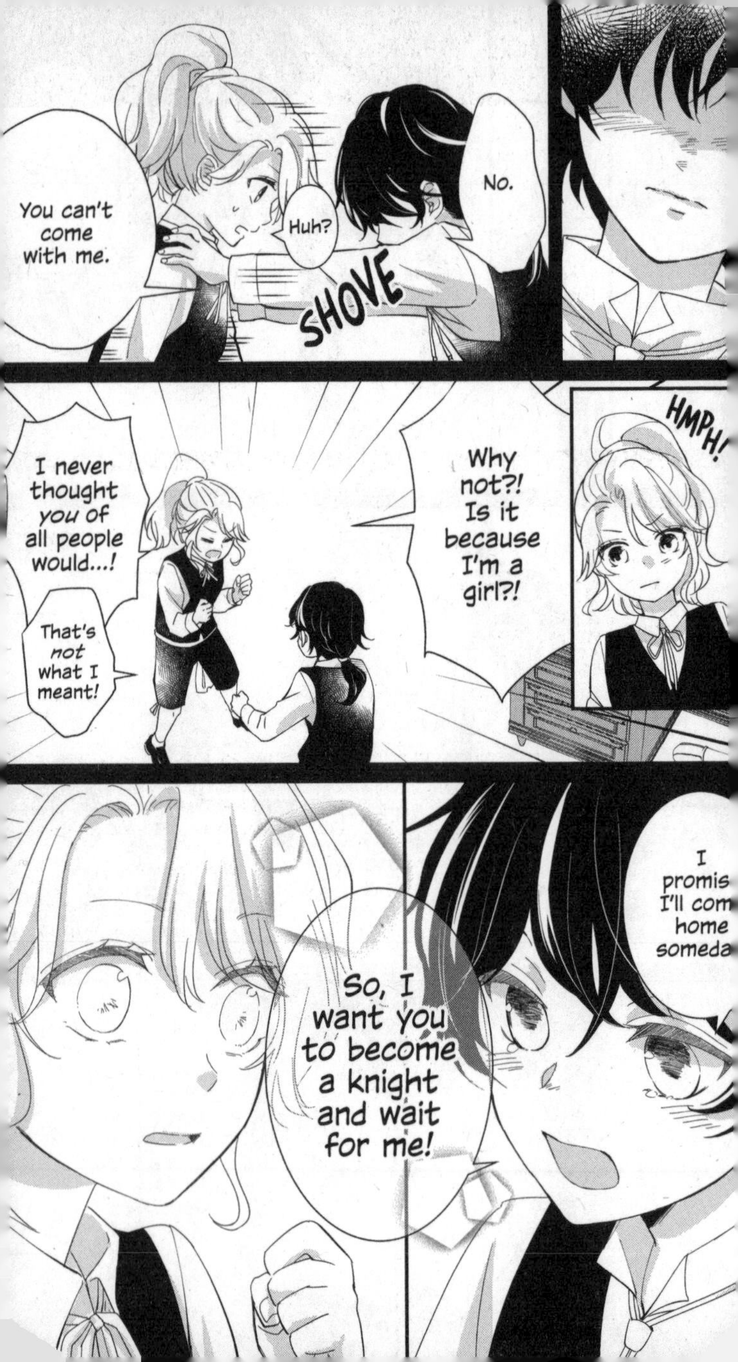
No.
Huh?
You can't come with me.
SHOVE
HMPH!
Why not?! Is it because I'm a girl?!
I never thought *you* of all people would...!
That's *not* what I meant!
I promis I'll com home someda
So, I want you to become a knight and wait for me!

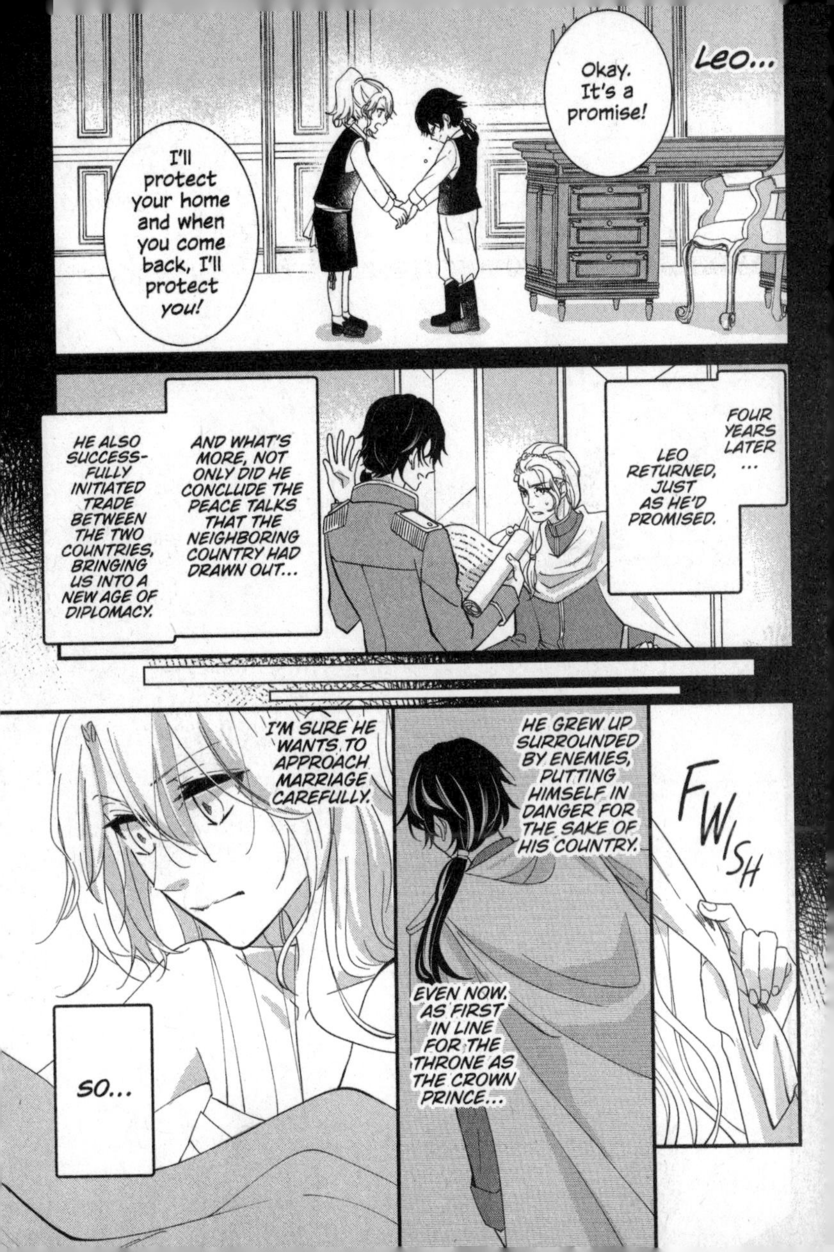
Leo...
Okay. It's a promise!
I'll protect your home and when you come back, I'll protect you!
FOUR YEARS LATER...
LEO RETURNED, JUST AS HE'D PROMISED.
AND WHAT'S MORE, NOT ONLY DID HE CONCLUDE THE PEACE TALKS THAT THE NEIGHBORING COUNTRY HAD DRAWN OUT...
HE ALSO SUCCESS-FULLY INITIATED TRADE BETWEEN THE TWO COUNTRIES, BRINGING US INTO A NEW AGE OF DIPLOMACY.
FWISH
HE GREW UP SURROUNDED BY ENEMIES, PUTTING HIMSELF IN DANGER FOR THE SAKE OF HIS COUNTRY.
EVEN NOW, AS FIRST IN LINE FOR THE THRONE AS THE CROWN PRINCE...
I'M SURE HE WANTS TO APPROACH MARRIAGE CAREFULLY.
SO...

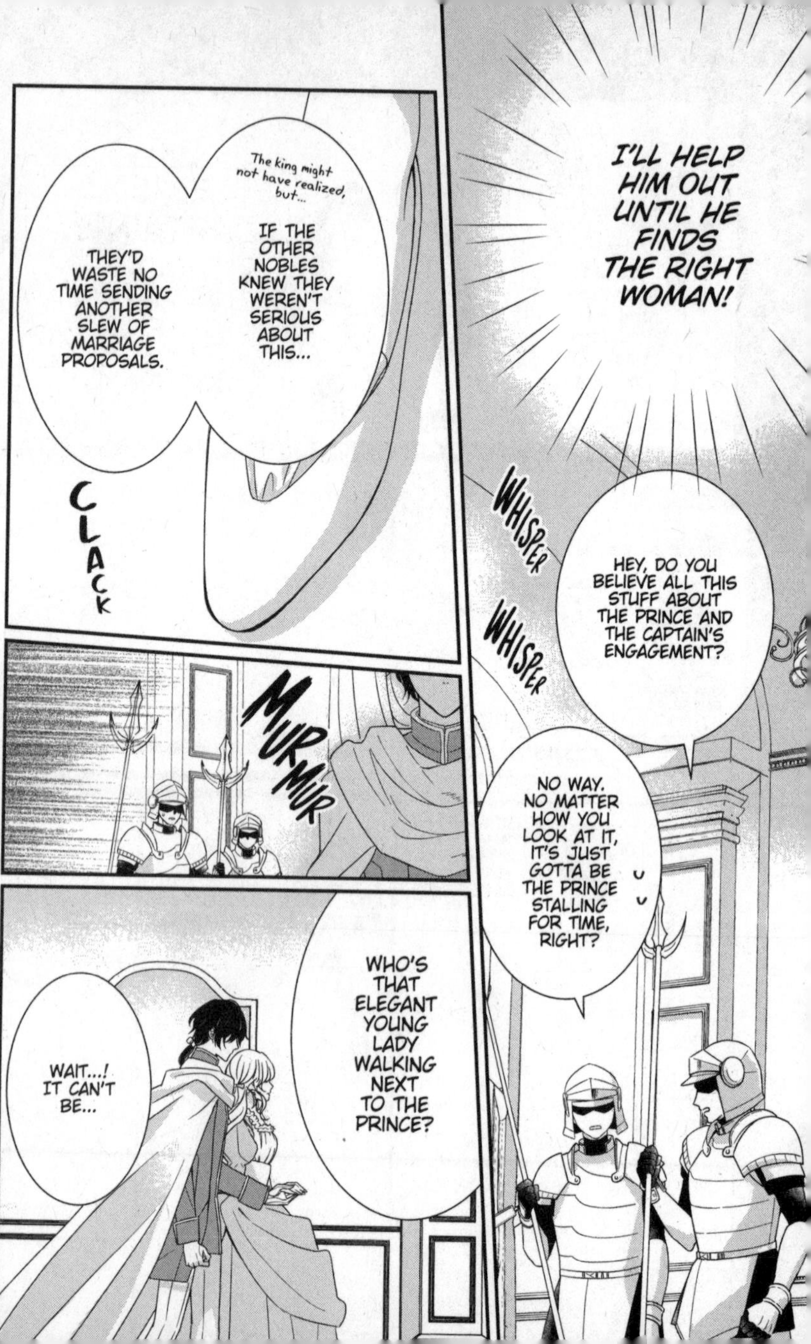
I'LL HELP HIM OUT UNTIL HE FINDS THE RIGHT WOMAN!
WHISPER
WHISPER
HEY, DO YOU BELIEVE ALL THIS STUFF ABOUT THE PRINCE AND THE CAPTAIN'S ENGAGEMENT?
NO WAY. NO MATTER HOW YOU LOOK AT IT, IT'S JUST GOTTA BE THE PRINCE STALLING FOR TIME, RIGHT?
The king might not have realized, but...
IF THE OTHER NOBLES KNEW THEY WEREN'T SERIOUS ABOUT THIS...
THEY'D WASTE NO TIME SENDING ANOTHER SLEW OF MARRIAGE PROPOSALS.
CLACK
MURMUR
WHO'S THAT ELEGANT YOUNG LADY WALKING NEXT TO THE PRINCE?
WAIT...! IT CAN'T BE...

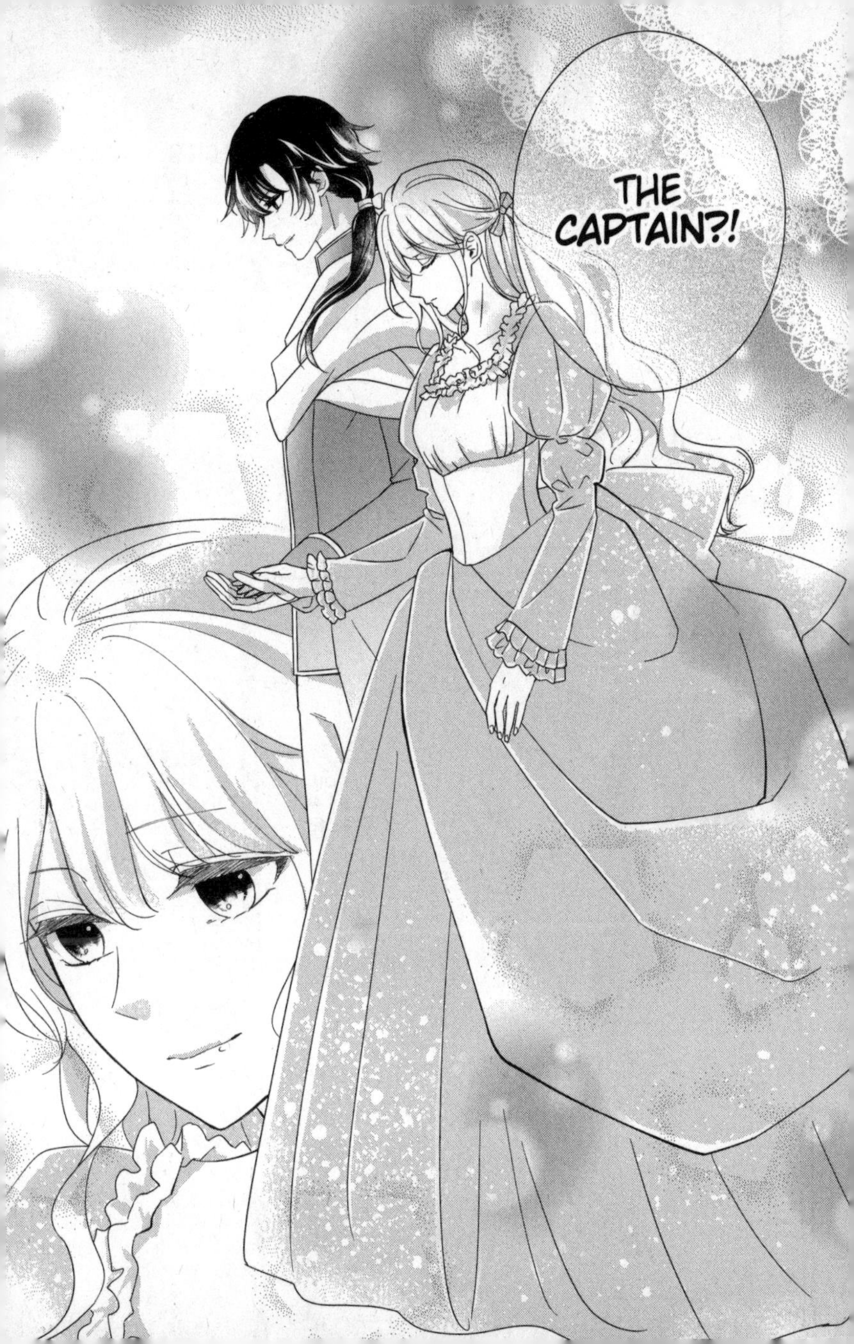
THE CAPTAIN?!

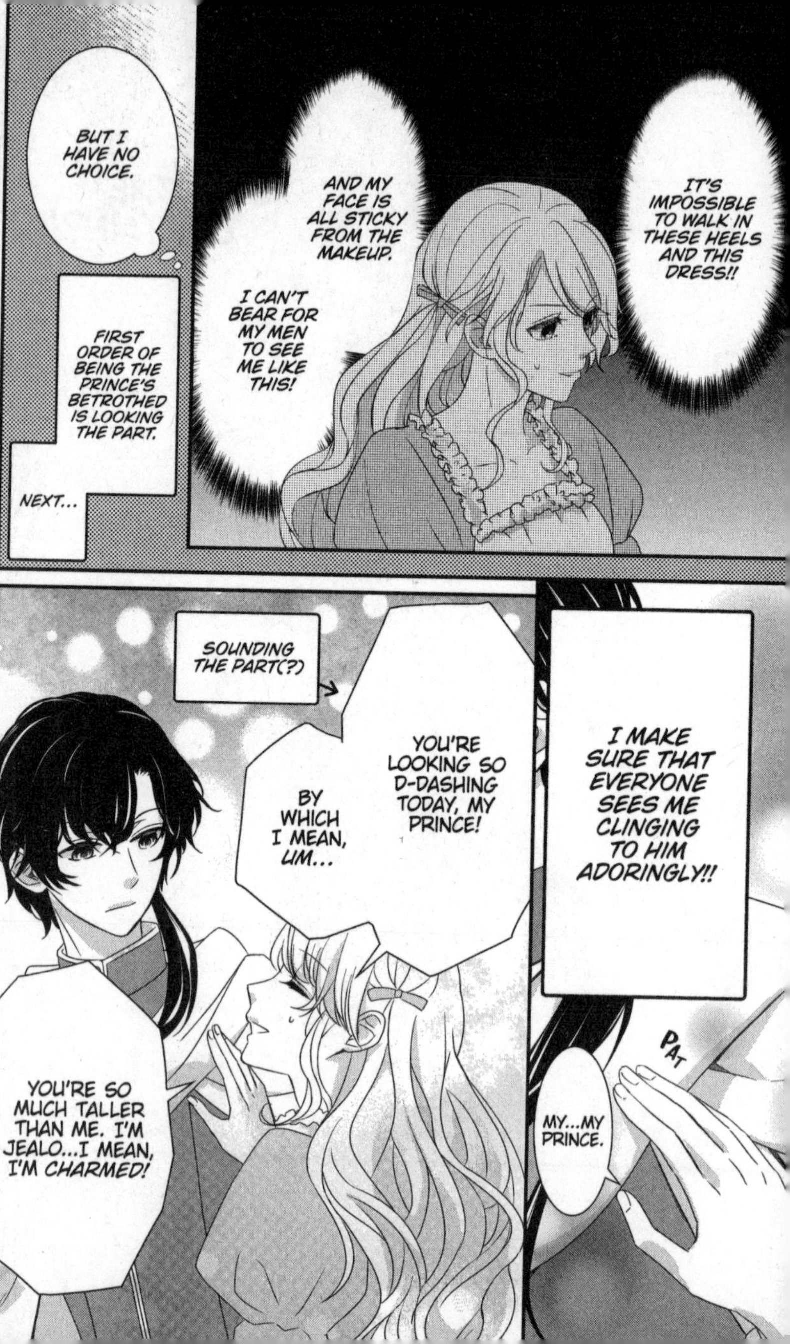
IT'S IMPOSSIBLE TO WALK IN THESE HEELS AND THIS DRESS!!
AND MY FACE IS ALL STICKY FROM THE MAKEUP.
I CAN'T BEAR FOR MY MEN TO SEE ME LIKE THIS!
BUT I HAVE NO CHOICE.
FIRST ORDER OF BEING THE PRINCE'S BETROTHED IS LOOKING THE PART.
NEXT...
I MAKE SURE THAT EVERYONE SEES ME CLINGING TO HIM ADORINGLY!!
PAT
MY...MY PRINCE.
SOUNDING THE PART(?)
YOU'RE LOOKING SO D-DASHING TODAY, MY PRINCE!
BY WHICH I MEAN, UM...
YOU'RE SO MUCH TALLER THAN ME. I'M JEALO...I MEAN, I'M CHARMED!

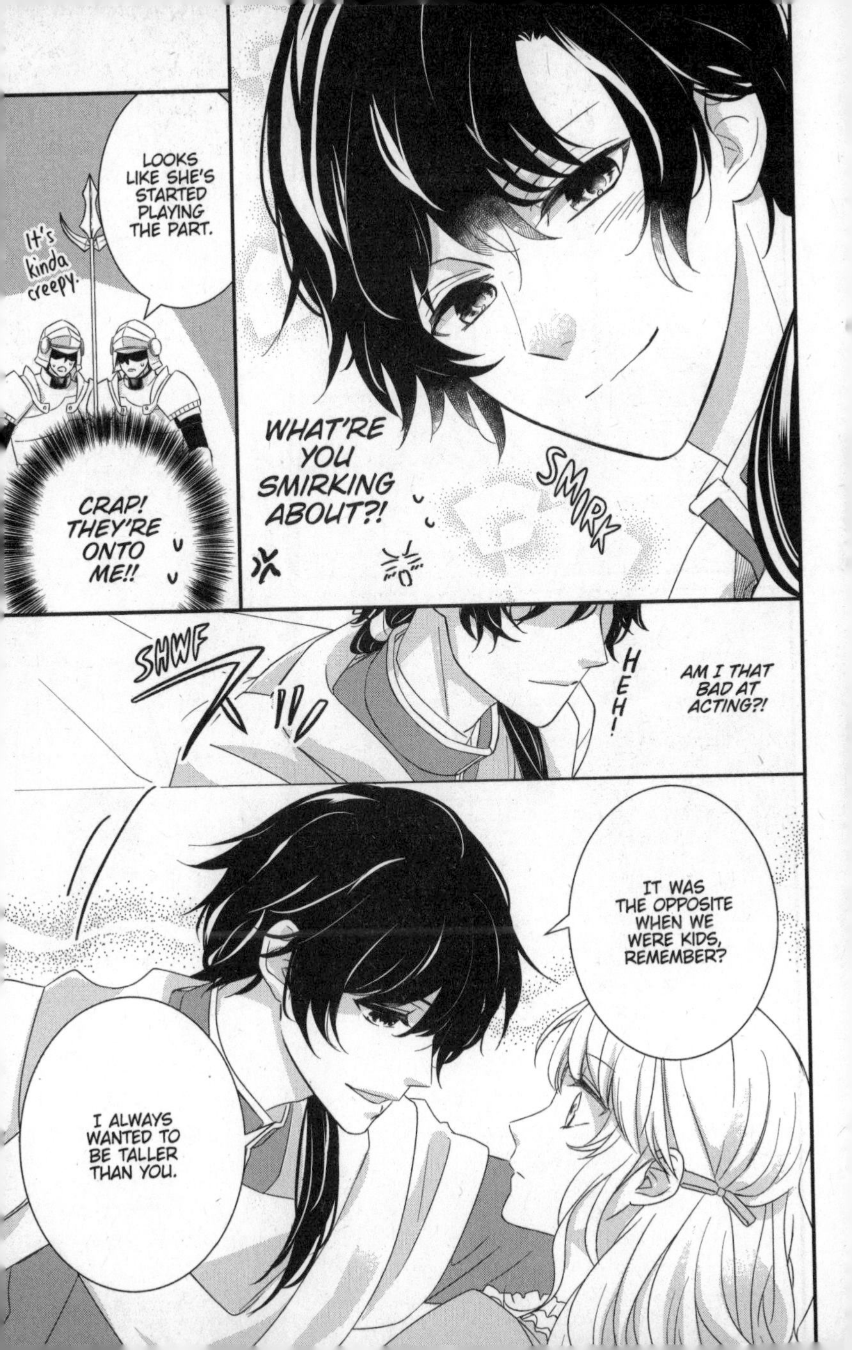
SMIRK
WHAT'RE YOU SMIRKING ABOUT?!
LOOKS LIKE SHE'S STARTED PLAYING THE PART.
It's kinda creepy.
CRAP! THEY'RE ONTO ME!!
AM I THAT BAD AT ACTING?!
HEH!
SHWF
IT WAS THE OPPOSITE WHEN WE WERE KIDS, REMEMBER?
I ALWAYS WANTED TO BE TALLER THAN YOU.

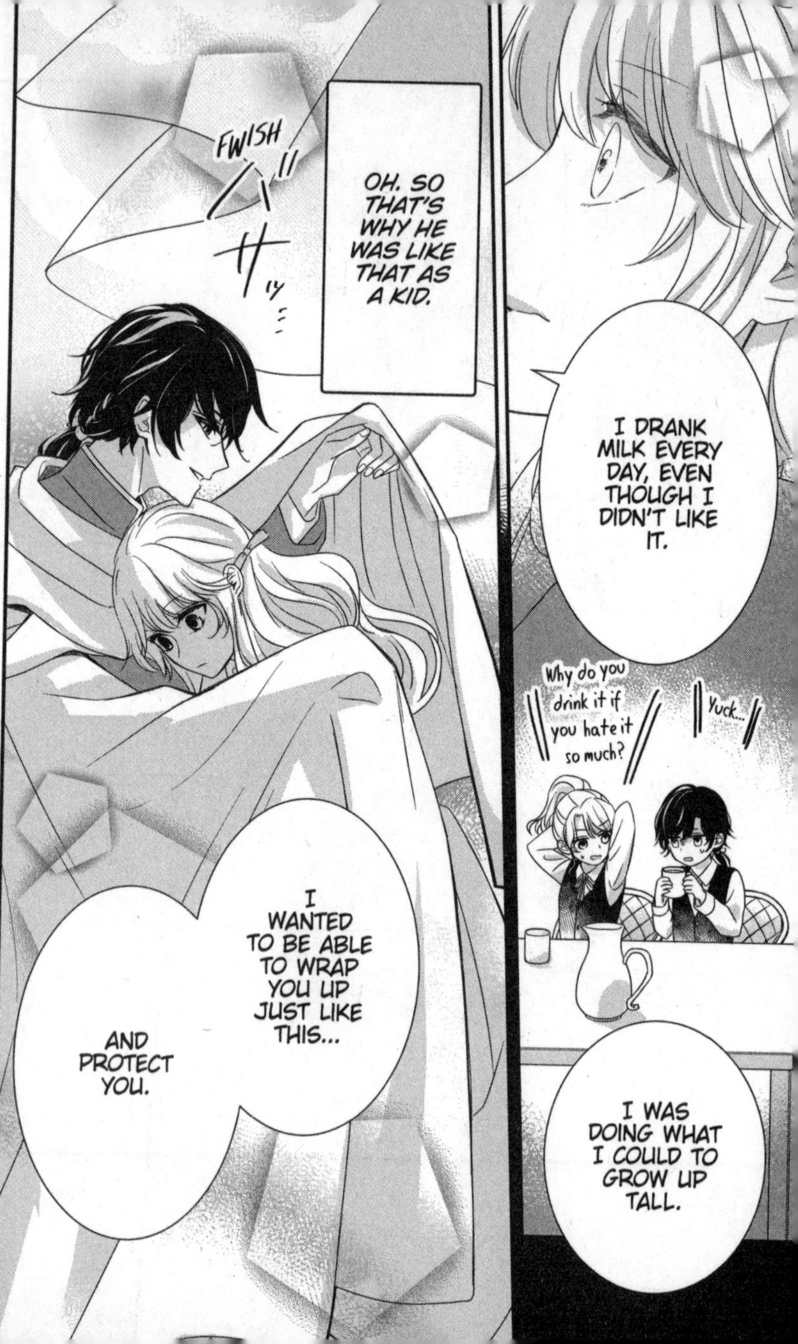
I DRANK MILK EVERY DAY, EVEN THOUGH I DIDN'T LIKE IT.
Yuck...
Why do you drink it if you hate it so much?
I WAS DOING WHAT I COULD TO GROW UP TALL.
OH. SO THAT'S WHY HE WAS LIKE THAT AS A KID.
FWISH
I WANTED TO BE ABLE TO WRAP YOU UP JUST LIKE THIS...
AND PROTECT YOU.

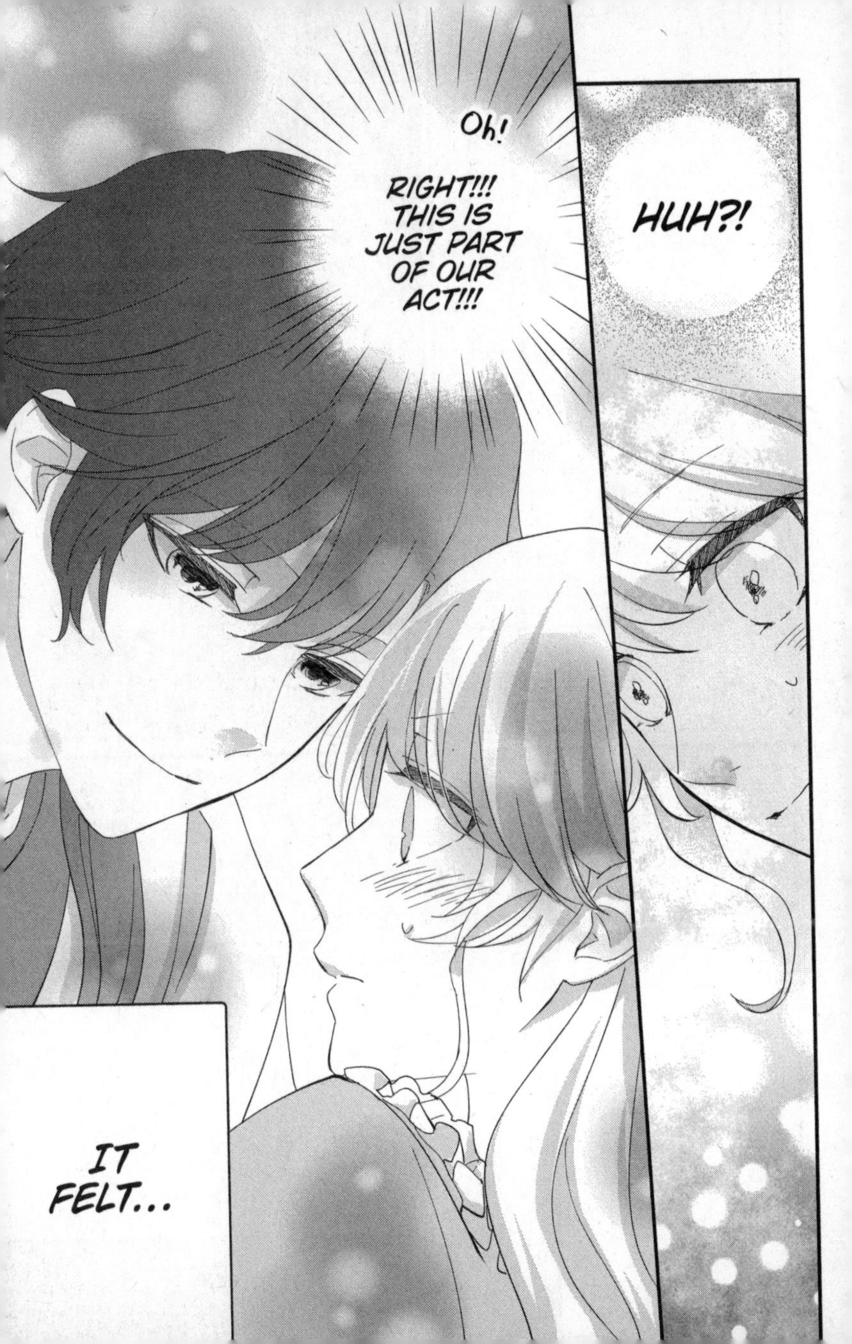
HUH?!
Oh!
RIGHT!!! THIS IS JUST PART OF OUR ACT!!!
IT FELT...

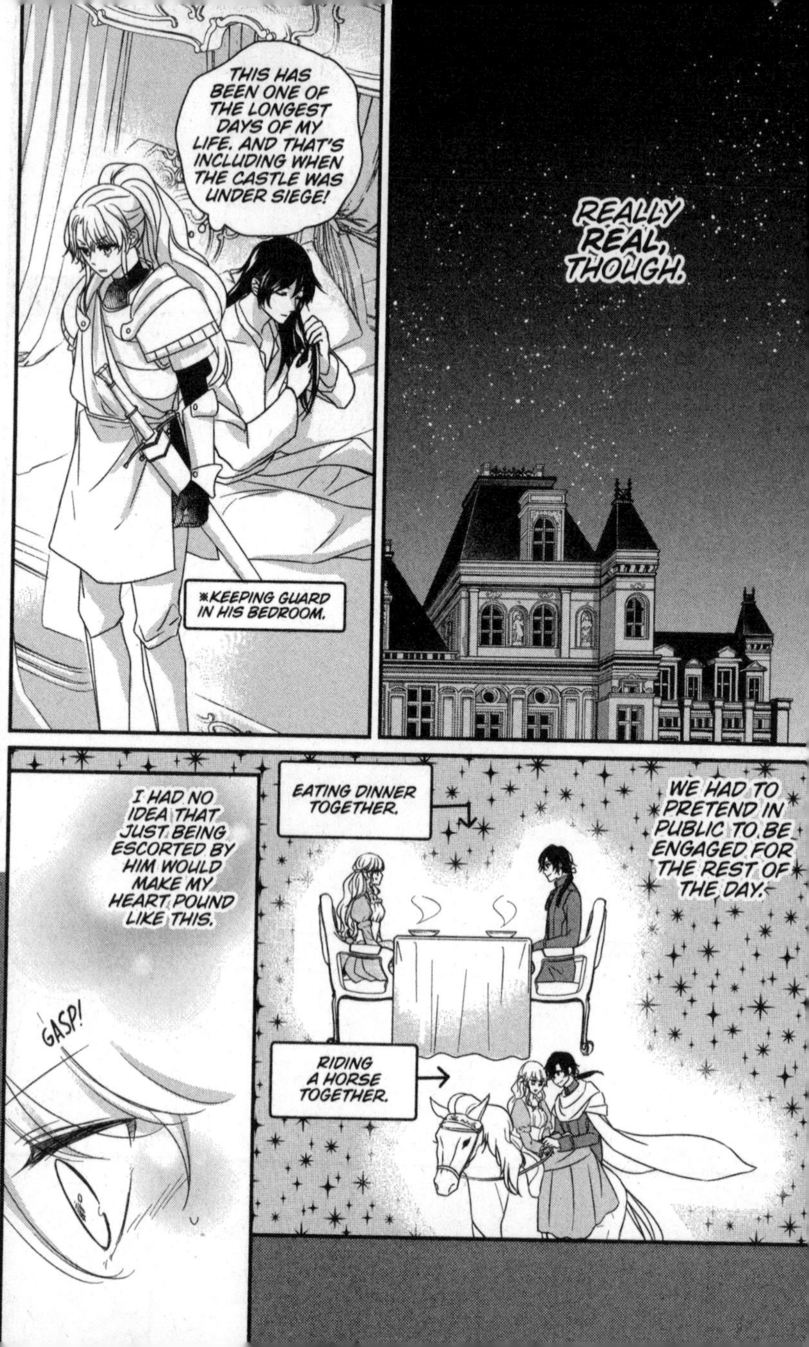
REALLY REAL, THOUGH.
THIS HAS BEEN ONE OF THE LONGEST DAYS OF MY LIFE. AND THAT'S INCLUDING WHEN THE CASTLE WAS UNDER SIEGE!
※KEEPING GUARD IN HIS BEDROOM.
WE HAD TO PRETEND IN PUBLIC TO BE ENGAGED FOR THE REST OF THE DAY.
EATING DINNER TOGETHER.
RIDING A HORSE TOGETHER.
I HAD NO IDEA THAT JUST BEING ESCORTED BY HIM WOULD MAKE MY HEART POUND LIKE THIS.
GASP!

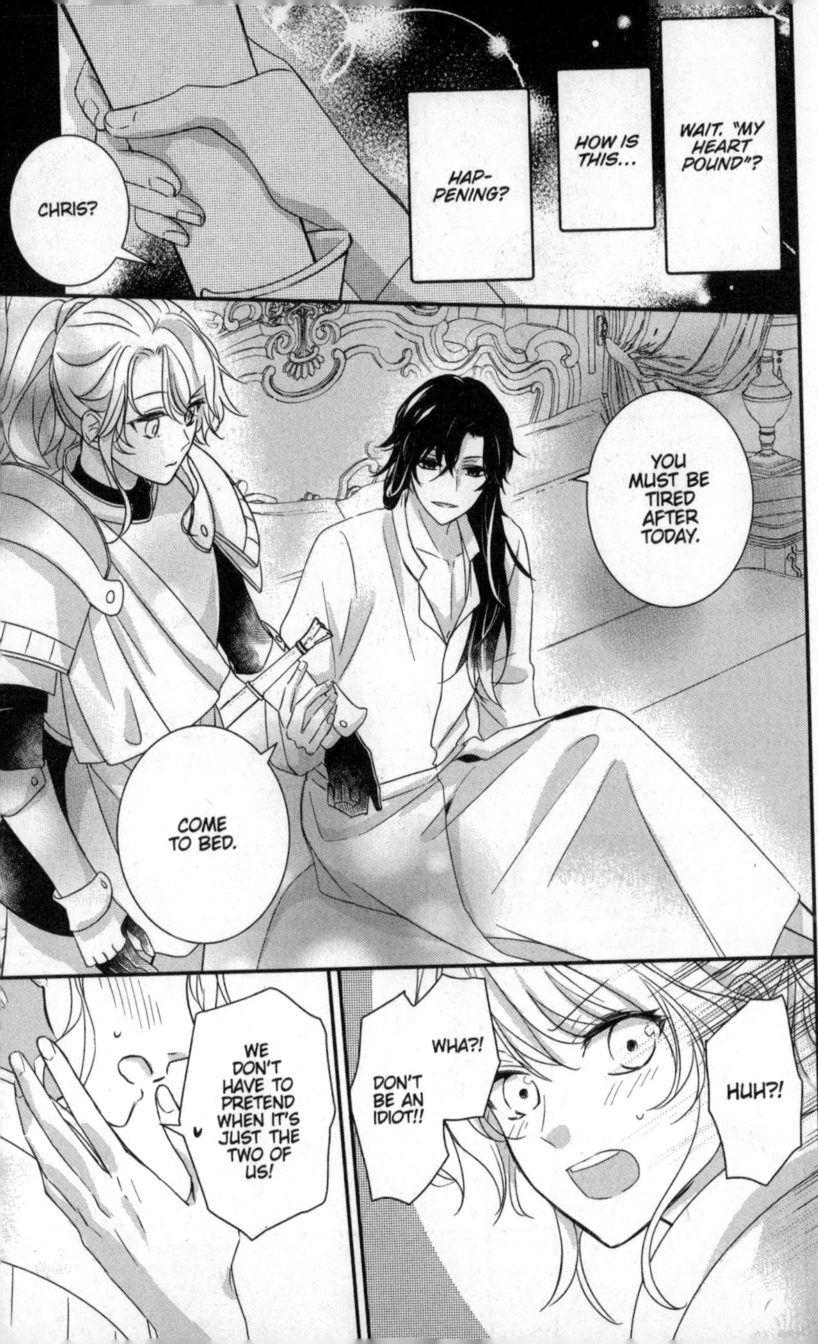
WAIT. "MY HEART POUND"?
HOW IS THIS...
HAP-PENING?
CHRIS?
YOU MUST BE TIRED AFTER TODAY.
COME TO BED.
HUH?!
WHA?!
DON'T BE AN IDIOT!!
WE DON'T HAVE TO PRETEND WHEN IT'S JUST THE TWO OF US!

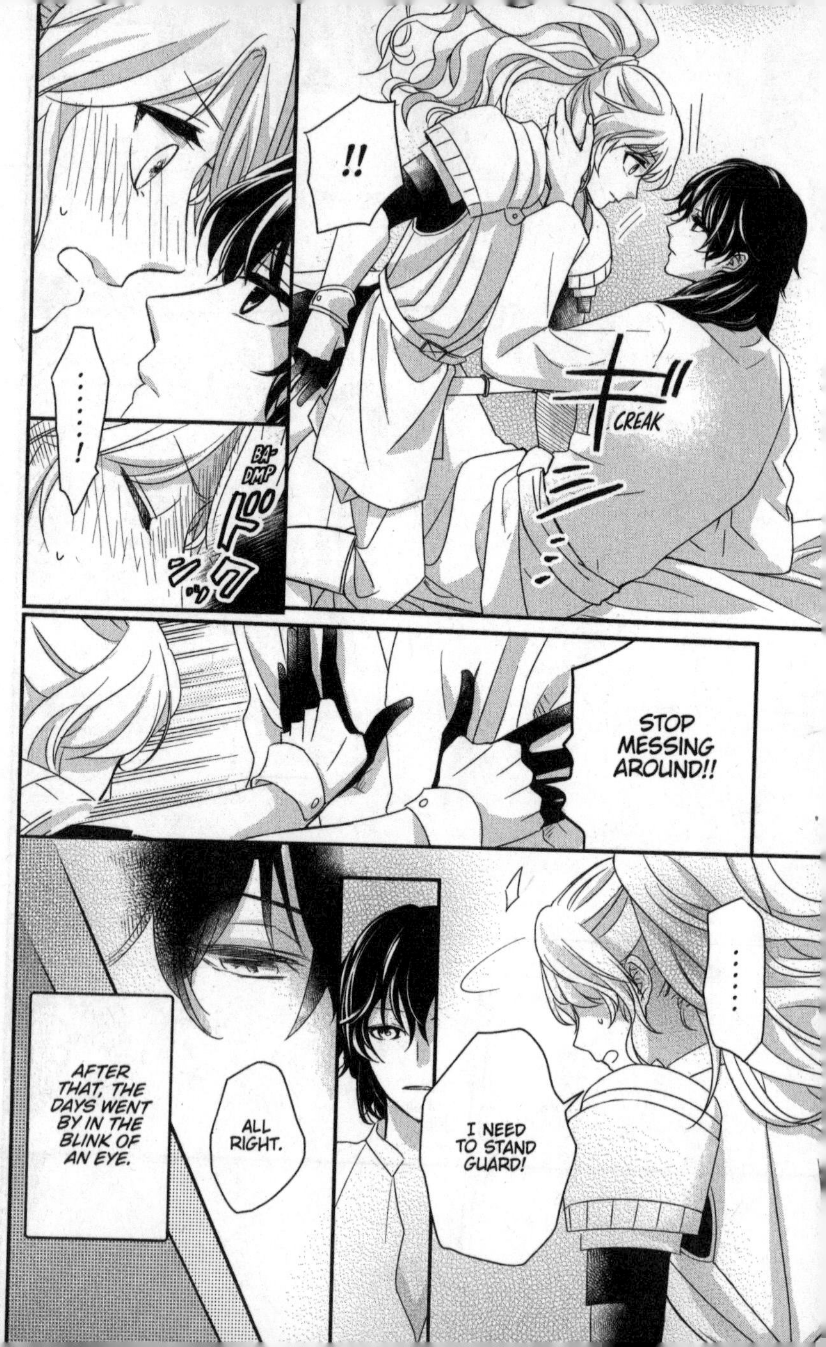
!!
CREAK
......!
BA-DMP
STOP MESSING AROUND!!
......
I NEED TO STAND GUARD!
ALL RIGHT.
AFTER THAT, THE DAYS WENT BY IN THE BLINK OF AN EYE.

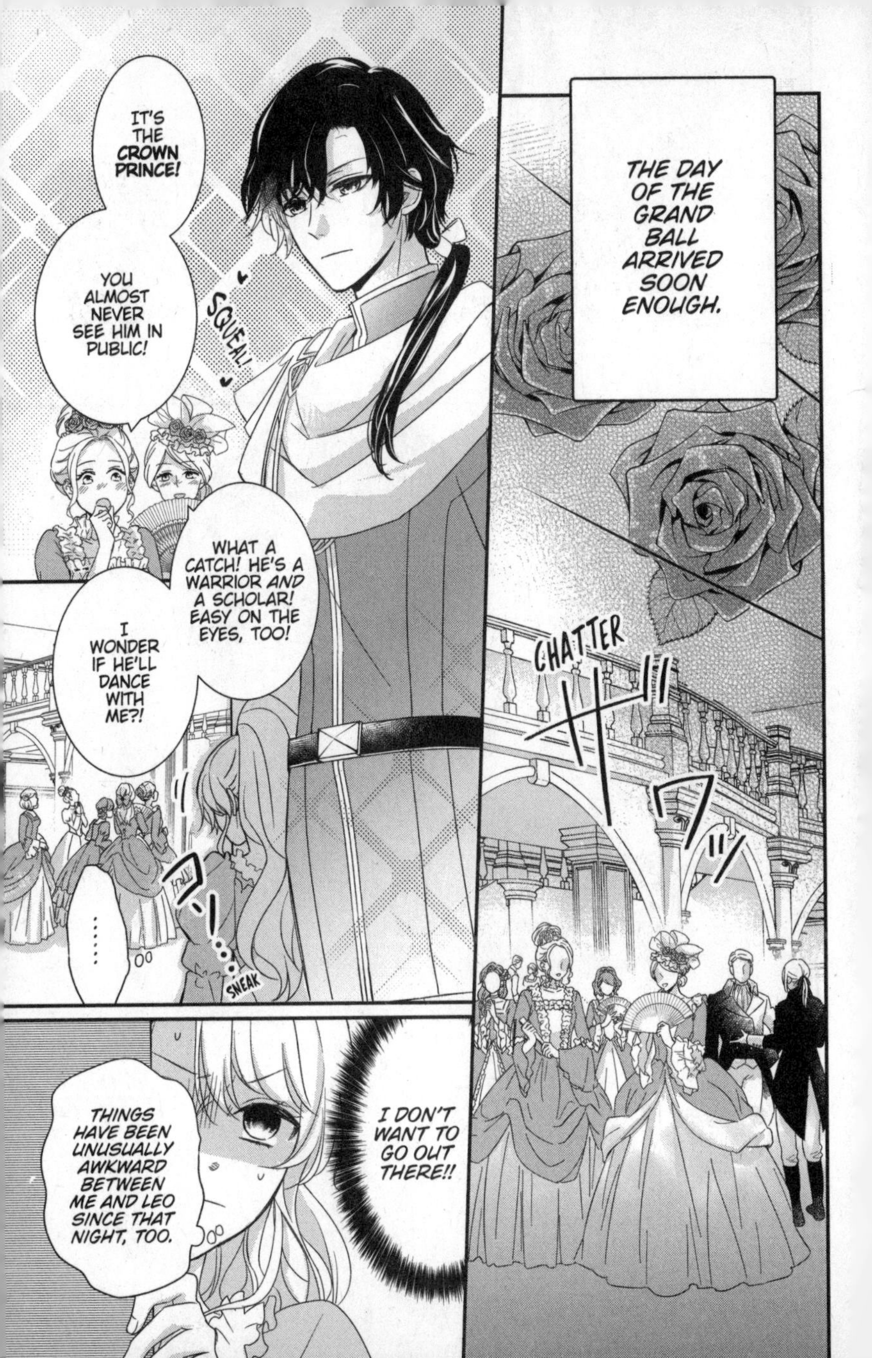
THE DAY OF THE GRAND BALL ARRIVED SOON ENOUGH.
CHATTER
IT'S THE CROWN PRINCE!
YOU ALMOST NEVER SEE HIM IN PUBLIC!
SQUEAL!
WHAT A CATCH! HE'S A WARRIOR AND A SCHOLAR! EASY ON THE EYES, TOO!
I WONDER IF HE'LL DANCE WITH ME?!
......
SNEAK
I DON'T WANT TO GO OUT THERE!!
THINGS HAVE BEEN UNUSUALLY AWKWARD BETWEEN ME AND LEO SINCE THAT NIGHT, TOO.

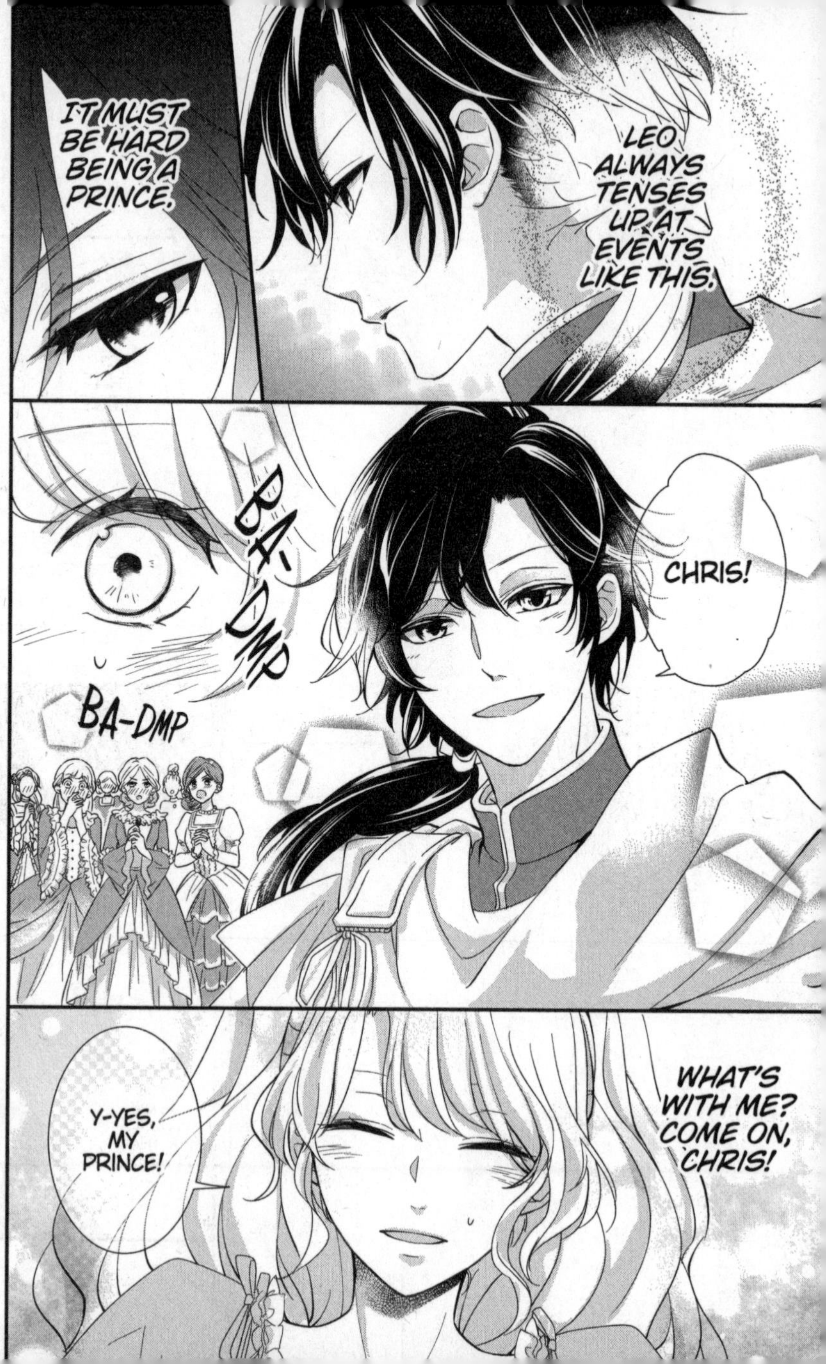
LEO ALWAYS TENSES UP AT EVENTS LIKE THIS.
IT MUST BE HARD BEING A PRINCE.
CHRIS!
BA-DMP
BA-DMP
WHAT'S WITH ME? COME ON, CHRIS!
Y-YES, MY PRINCE!

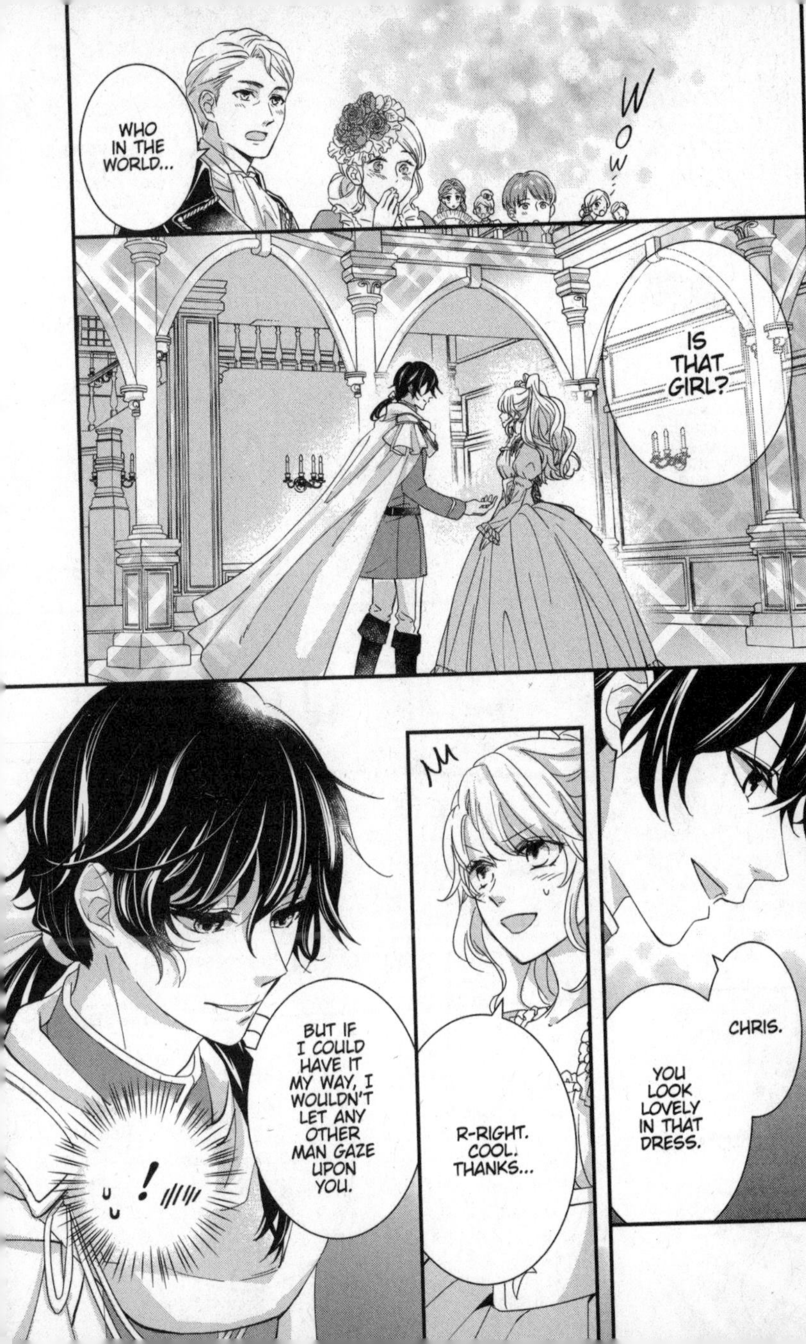
WOW...
WHO IN THE WORLD...
IS THAT GIRL?
CHRIS.
YOU LOOK LOVELY IN THAT DRESS.
MM
R-RIGHT. COOL. THANKS...
BUT IF I COULD HAVE IT MY WAY, I WOULDN'T LET ANY OTHER MAN GAZE UPON YOU.
!

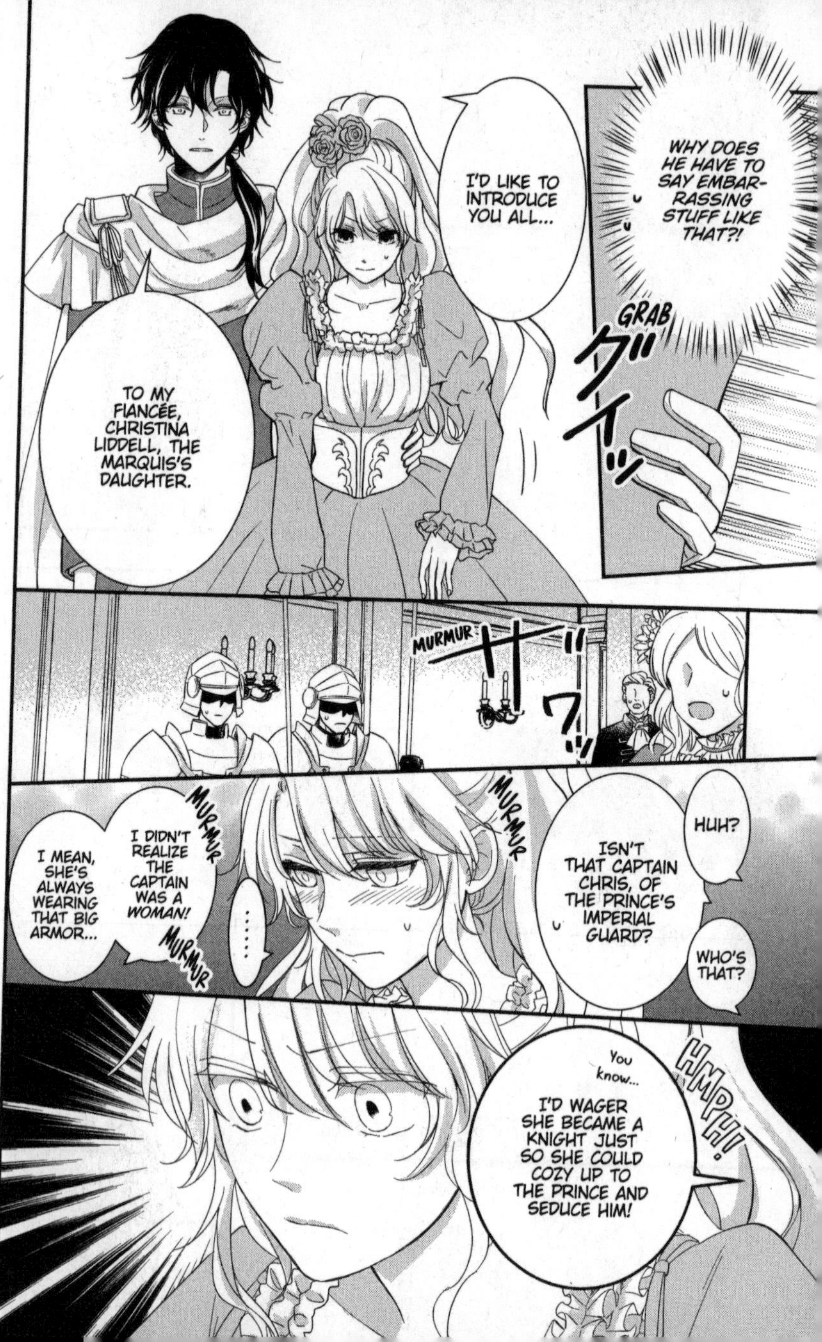
WHY DOES HE HAVE TO SAY EMBAR-RASSING STUFF LIKE THAT?!
GRAB
I'D LIKE TO INTRODUCE YOU ALL...
TO MY FIANCÉE, CHRISTINA LIDDELL, THE MARQUIS'S DAUGHTER.
MURMUR
HUH?
ISN'T THAT CAPTAIN CHRIS, OF THE PRINCE'S IMPERIAL GUARD?
WHO'S THAT?
MURMUR
I DIDN'T REALIZE THE CAPTAIN WAS A WOMAN!
......
I MEAN, SHE'S ALWAYS WEARING THAT BIG ARMOR...
MURMUR
MURMUR
HMPH!
You know...
I'D WAGER SHE BECAME A KNIGHT JUST SO SHE COULD COZY UP TO THE PRINCE AND SEDUCE HIM!

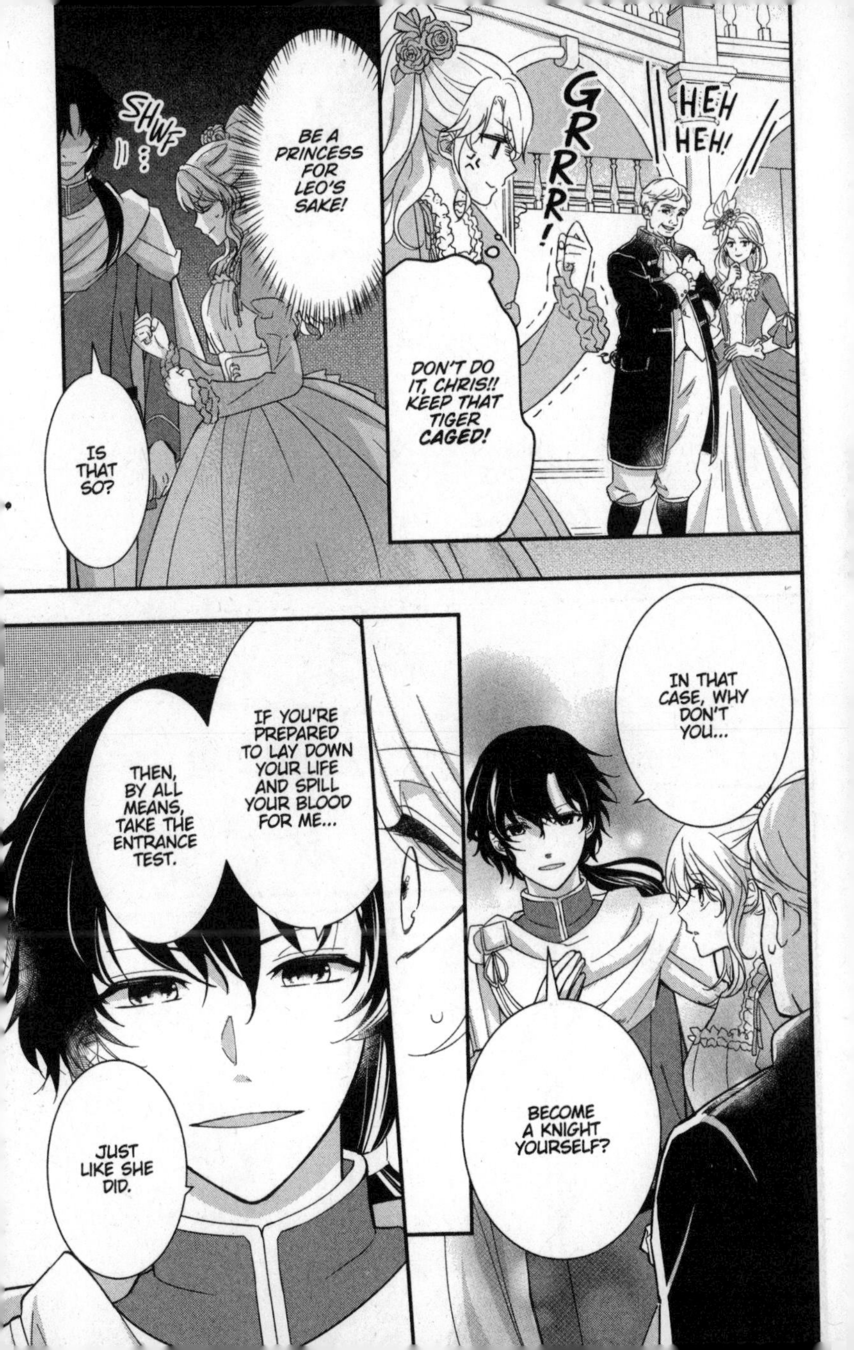
HEH HEH!
GRRR!
DON'T DO IT, CHRIS!! KEEP THAT TIGER CAGED!
BE A PRINCESS FOR LEO'S SAKE!
SHWF
IS THAT SO?
IN THAT CASE, WHY DON'T YOU...
BECOME A KNIGHT YOURSELF?
IF YOU'RE PREPARED TO LAY DOWN YOUR LIFE AND SPILL YOUR BLOOD FOR ME...
THEN, BY ALL MEANS, TAKE THE ENTRANCE TEST.
JUST LIKE SHE DID.

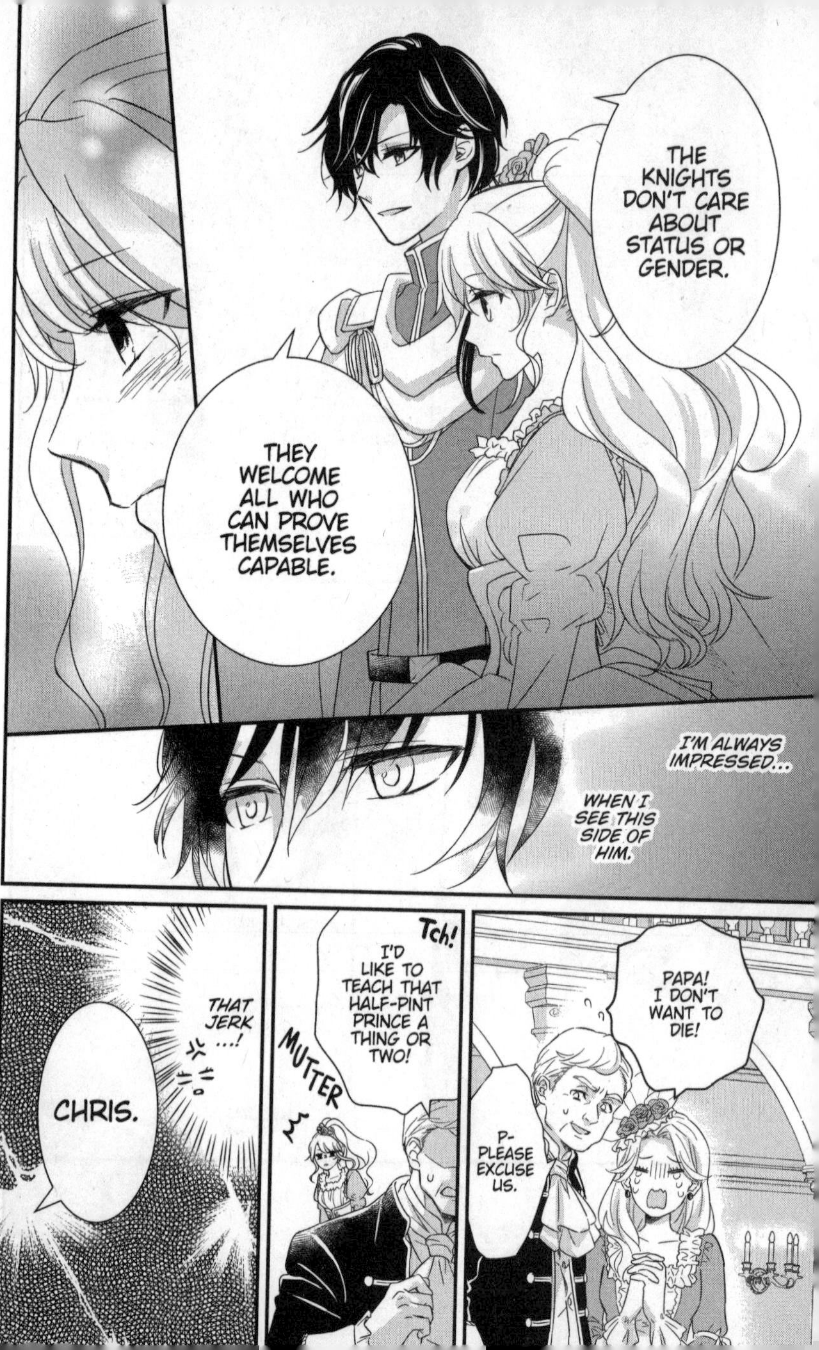
THE KNIGHTS DON'T CARE ABOUT STATUS OR GENDER.
THEY WELCOME ALL WHO CAN PROVE THEMSELVES CAPABLE.
I'M ALWAYS IMPRESSED...
WHEN I SEE THIS SIDE OF HIM.
PAPA! I DON'T WANT TO DIE!
P-PLEASE EXCUSE US.
Tch!
I'D LIKE TO TEACH THAT HALF-PINT PRINCE A THING OR TWO!
MUTTER
THAT JERK ...!
CHRIS.

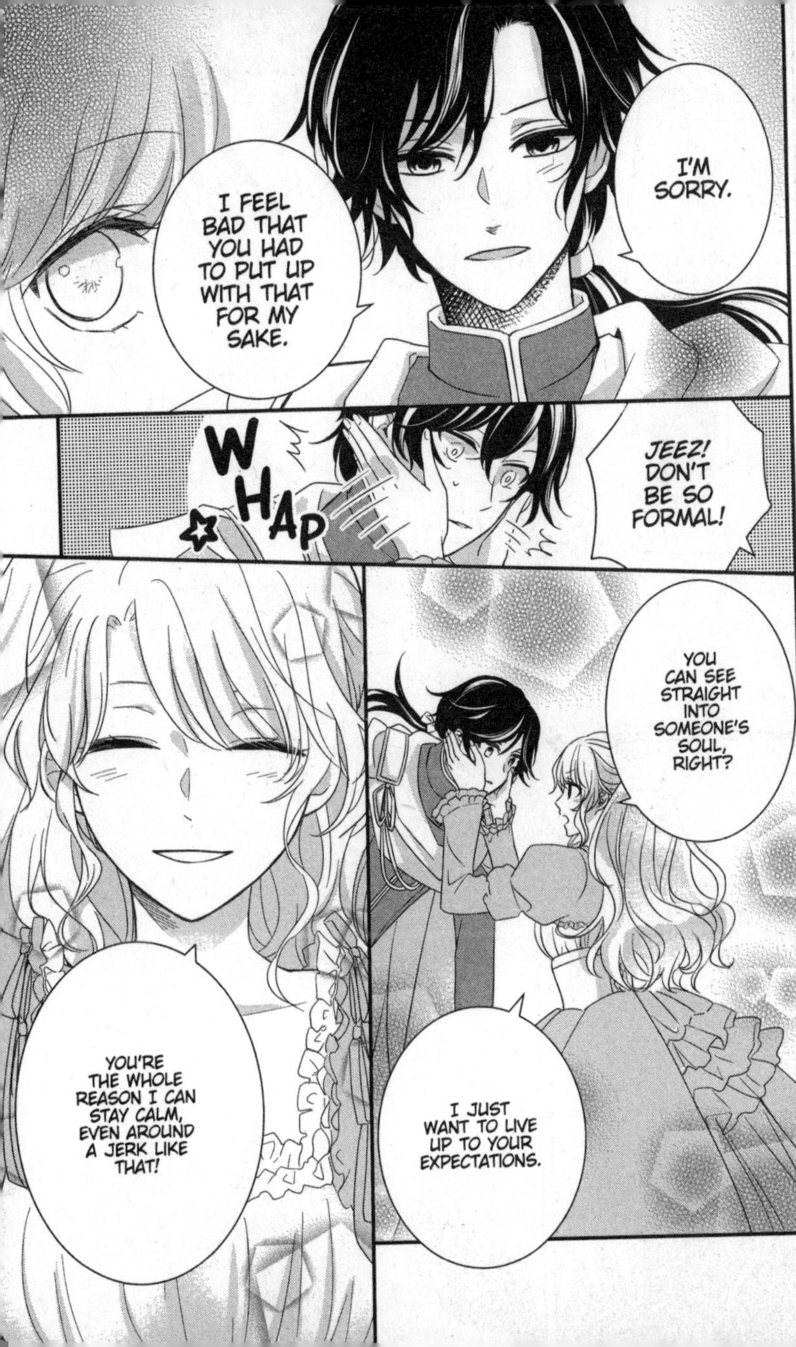
I'M SORRY.
I FEEL BAD THAT YOU HAD TO PUT UP WITH THAT FOR MY SAKE.
JEEZ! DON'T BE SO FORMAL!
WHAP
YOU CAN SEE STRAIGHT INTO SOMEONE'S SOUL, RIGHT?
I JUST WANT TO LIVE UP TO YOUR EXPECTATIONS.
YOU'RE THE WHOLE REASON I CAN STAY CALM, EVEN AROUND A JERK LIKE THAT!

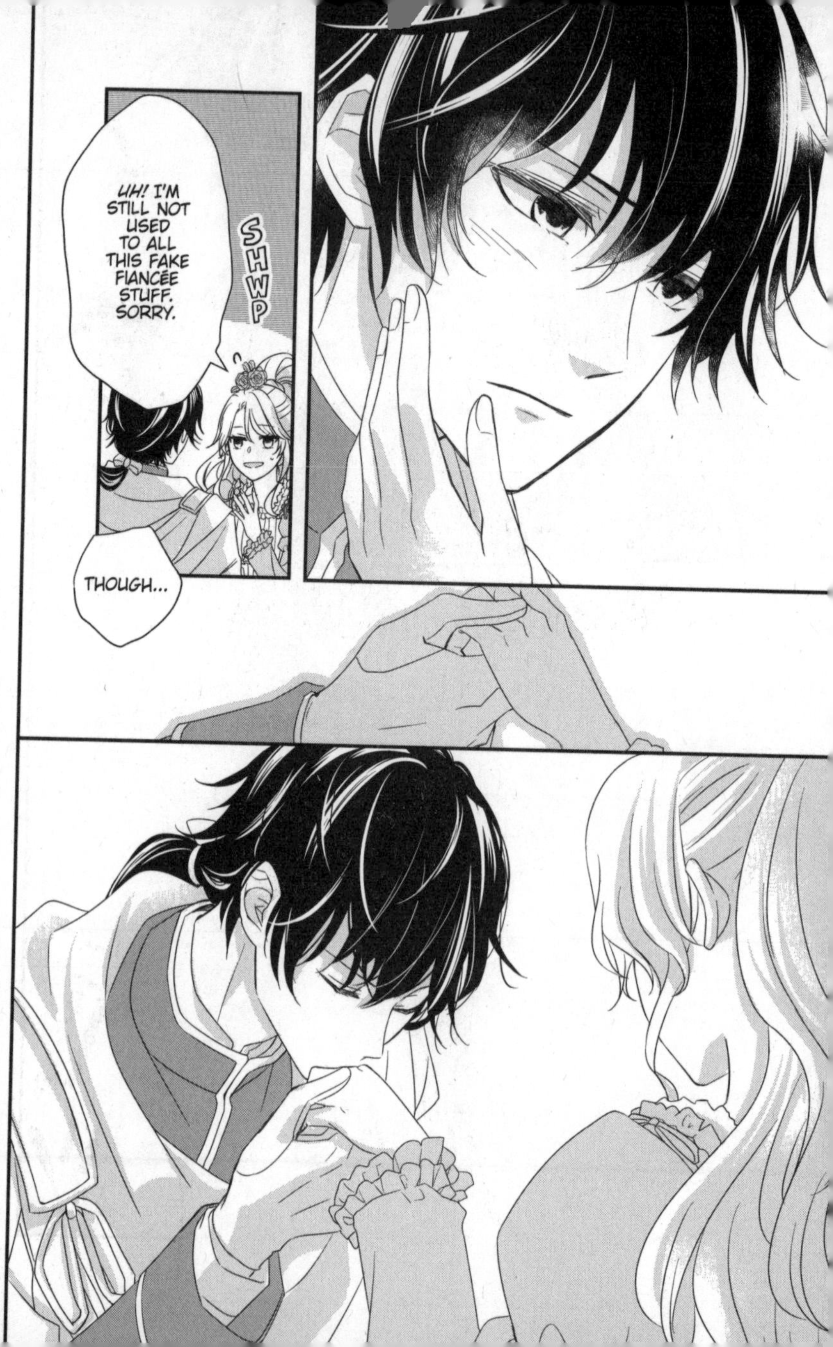
UH! I'M STILL NOT USED TO ALL THIS FAKE FIANCÉE STUFF. SORRY.
SHWP
THOUGH...

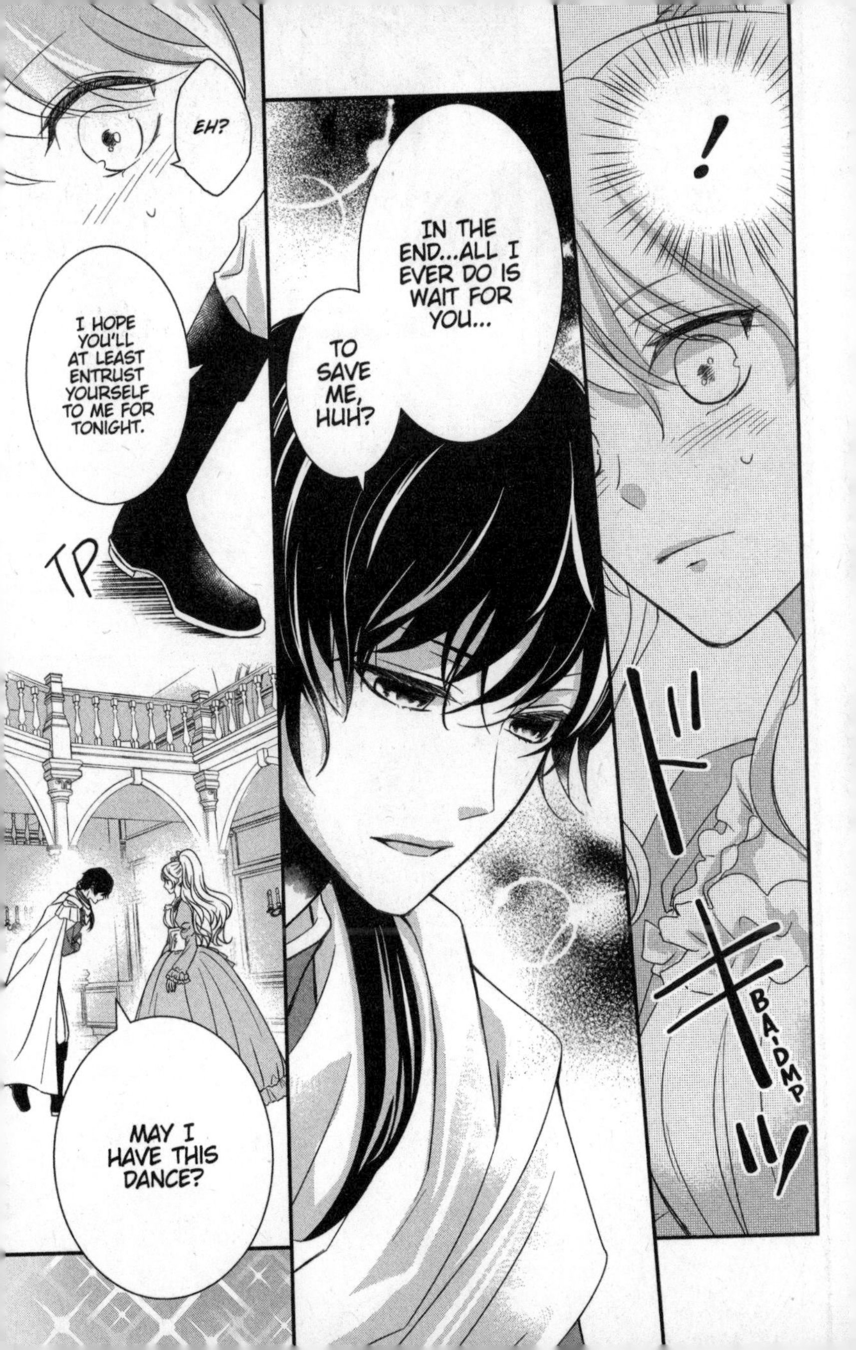
!
BA-DMP
IN THE END...ALL I EVER DO IS WAIT FOR YOU...
TO SAVE ME, HUH?
EH?
I HOPE YOU'LL AT LEAST ENTRUST YOURSELF TO ME FOR TONIGHT.
TP
MAY I HAVE THIS DANCE?

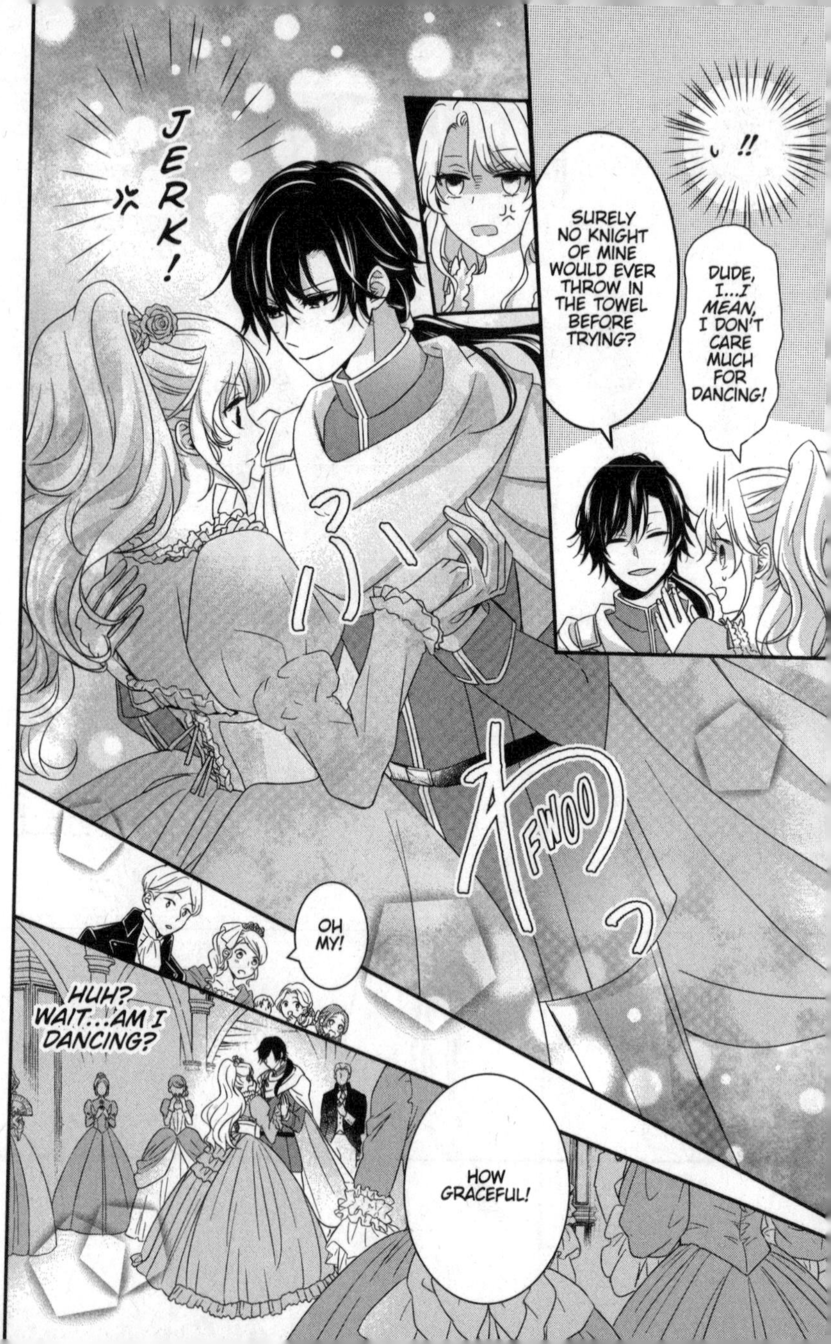
!!
DUDE, I...I MEAN, I DON'T CARE MUCH FOR DANCING!
SURELY NO KNIGHT OF MINE WOULD EVER THROW IN THE TOWEL BEFORE TRYING?
JERK!
FWOO
OH MY!
HOW GRACEFUL!
HUH? WAIT...AM I DANCING?

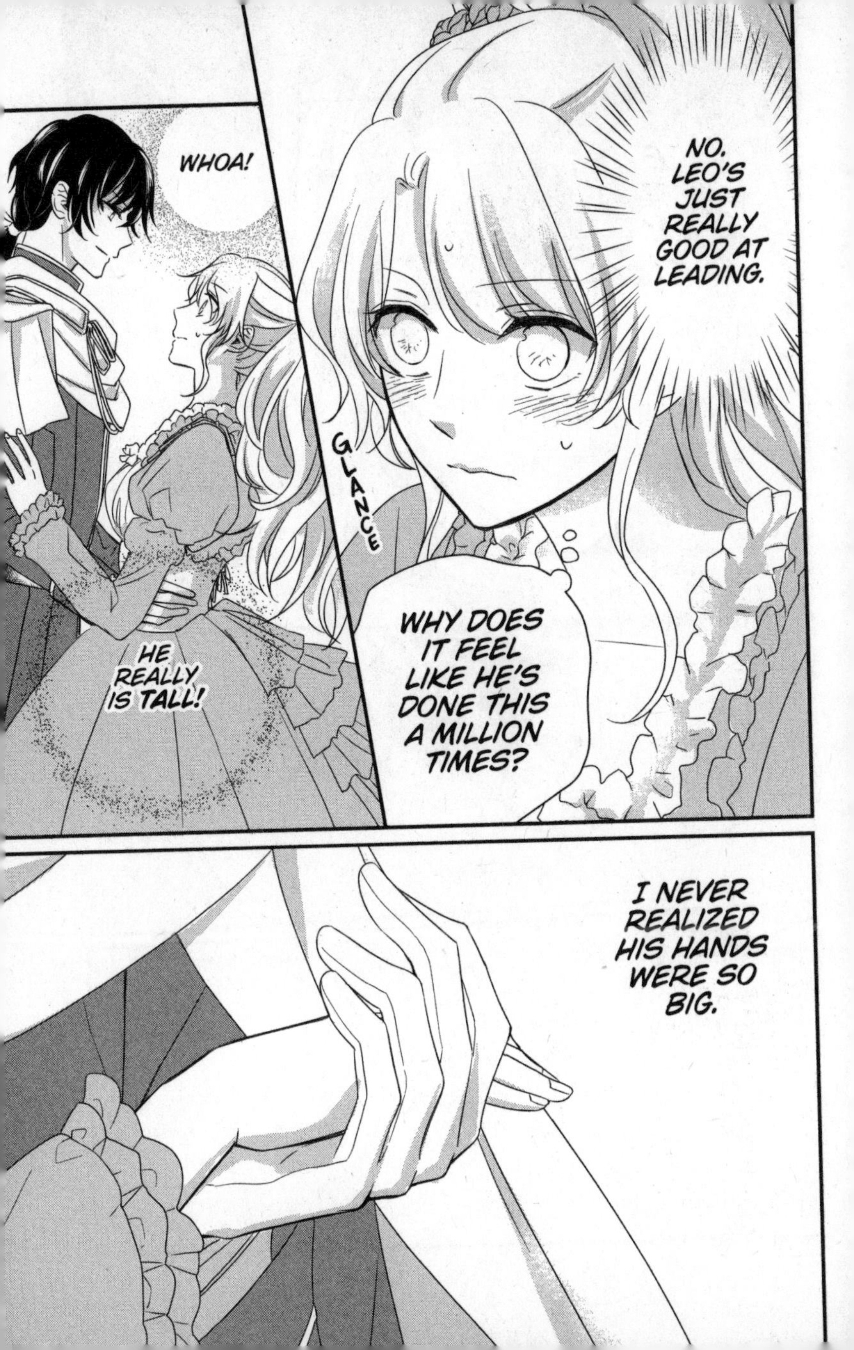
NO. LEO'S JUST REALLY GOOD AT LEADING.
GLANCE
WHY DOES IT FEEL LIKE HE'S DONE THIS A MILLION TIMES?
WHOA!
HE REALLY IS TALL!
I NEVER REALIZED HIS HANDS WERE SO BIG.

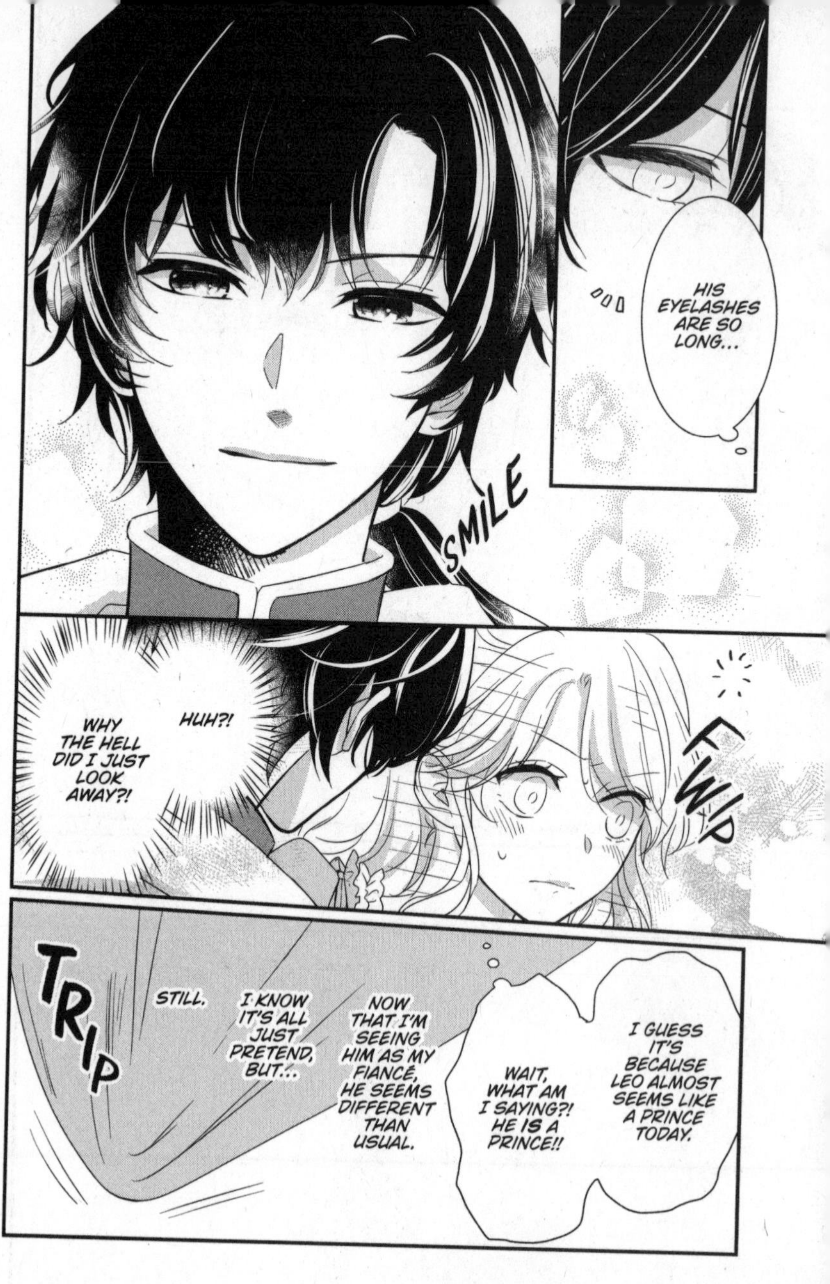
HIS EYELASHES ARE SO LONG...
SMILE
FWIP
HUH?!
WHY THE HELL DID I JUST LOOK AWAY?!
I GUESS IT'S BECAUSE LEO ALMOST SEEMS LIKE A PRINCE TODAY.
WAIT, WHAT AM I SAYING?! HE IS A PRINCE!!
NOW THAT I'M SEEING HIM AS MY FIANCÉ, HE SEEMS DIFFERENT THAN USUAL.
I KNOW IT'S ALL JUST PRETEND, BUT...
STILL.
TRIP

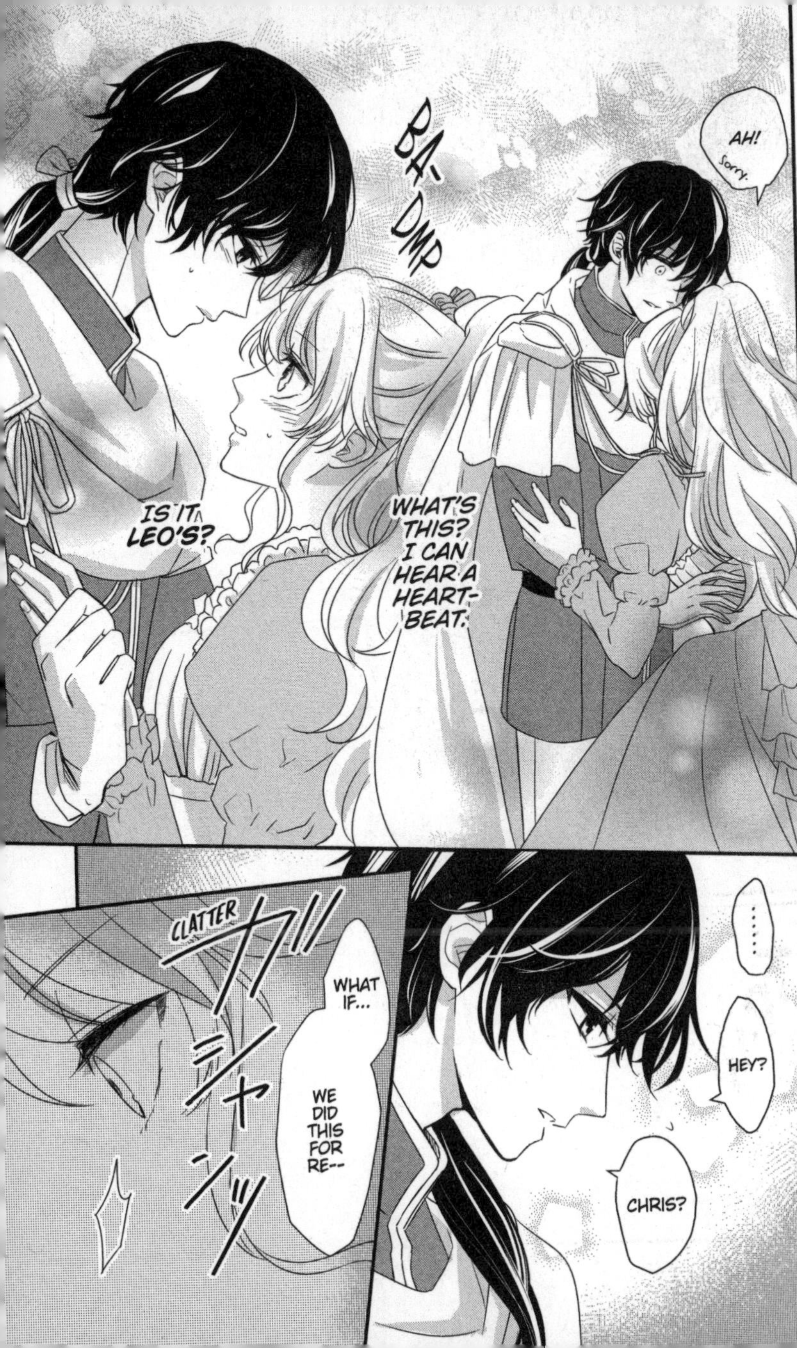
AH!
Sorry.
BA-DUMP
WHAT'S THIS? I CAN HEAR A HEARTBEAT.
IS IT LEO'S?
......
HEY?
CHRIS?
WHAT IF...
WE DID THIS FOR RE--
CLATTER
ガシャンッ

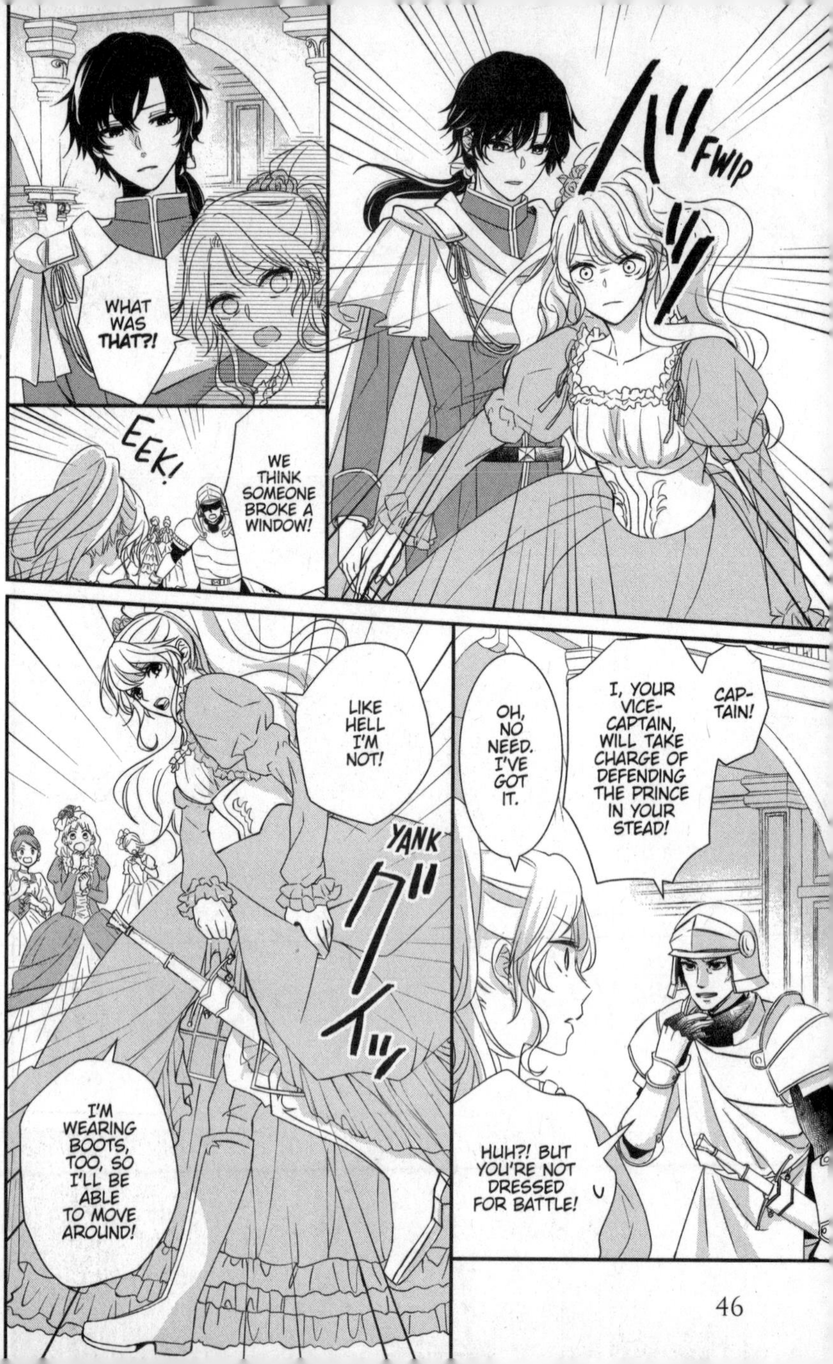
FWIP
WHAT WAS THAT?!
EEK!
WE THINK SOMEONE BROKE A WINDOW!
CAPTAIN!
I, YOUR VICE-CAPTAIN, WILL TAKE CHARGE OF DEFENDING THE PRINCE IN YOUR STEAD!
OH, NO NEED. I'VE GOT IT.
HUH?! BUT YOU'RE NOT DRESSED FOR BATTLE!
LIKE HELL I'M NOT!
YANK
I'M WEARING BOOTS, TOO, SO I'LL BE ABLE TO MOVE AROUND!

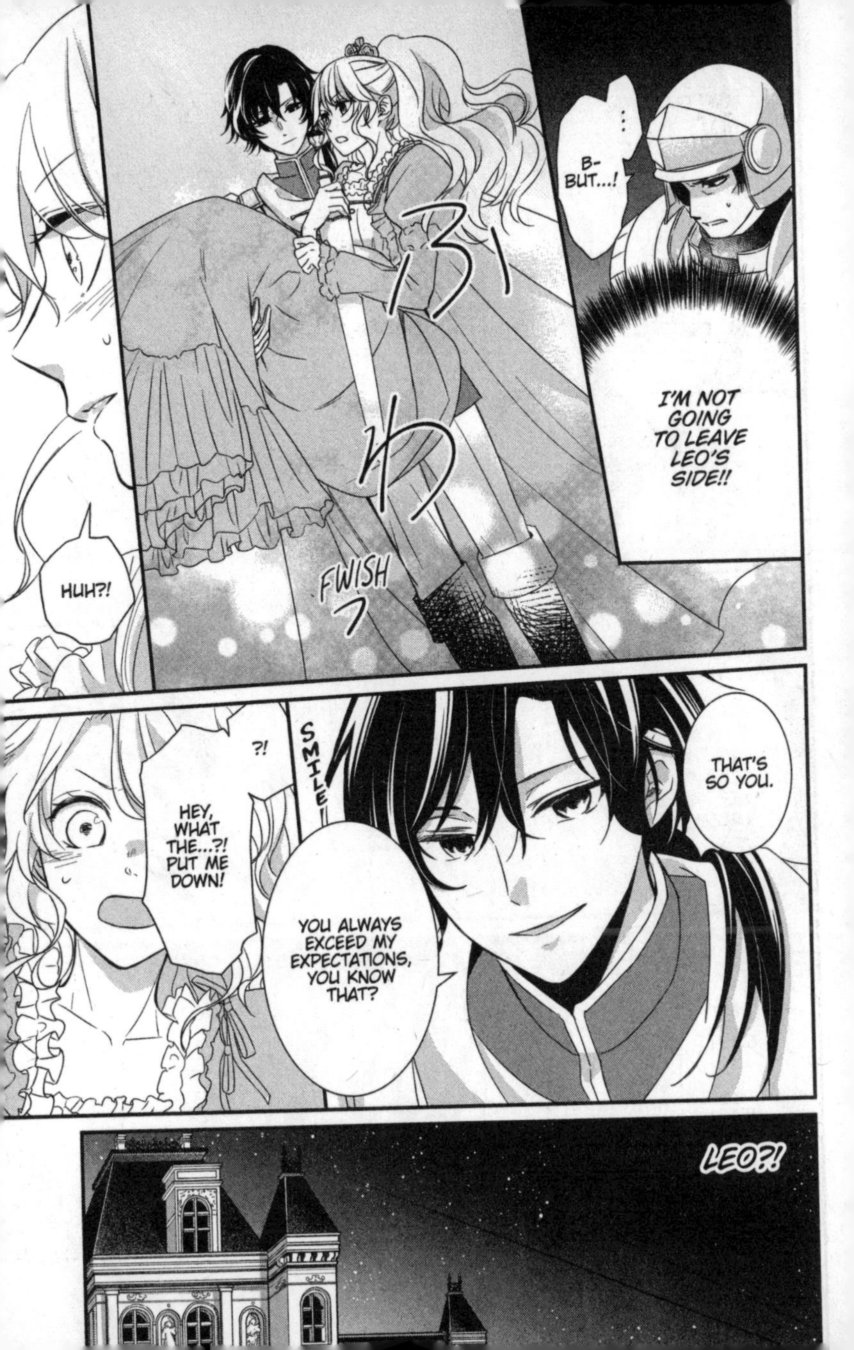
...
B-BUT...!
I'M NOT GOING TO LEAVE LEO'S SIDE!!
ふわ
FWISH
HUH?!
THAT'S SO YOU.
SMILE
YOU ALWAYS EXCEED MY EXPECTATIONS, YOU KNOW THAT?
?!
HEY, WHAT THE...?! PUT ME DOWN!
LEO?!

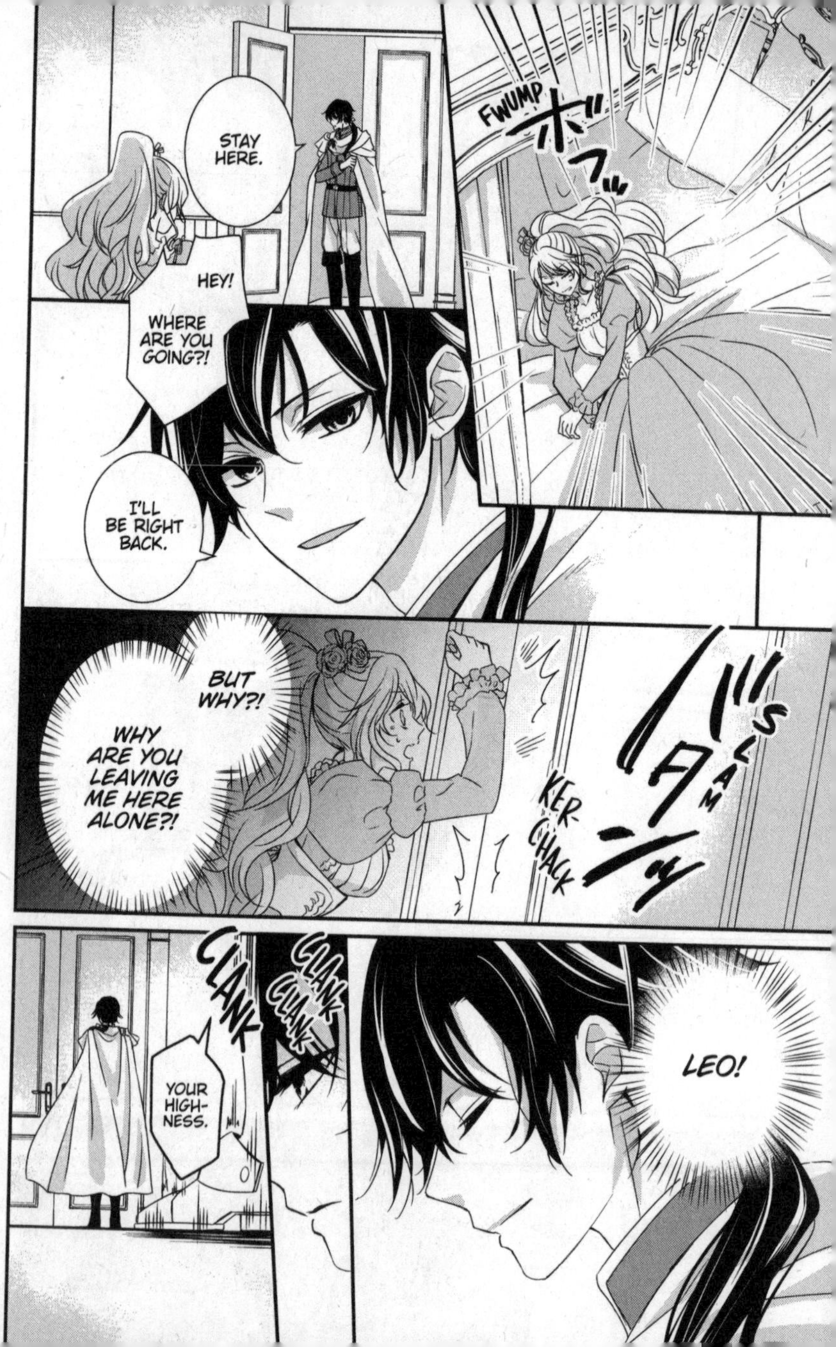
FWUMP
STAY HERE.
HEY!
WHERE ARE YOU GOING?!
I'LL BE RIGHT BACK.
SLAM
KER-CHACK
BUT WHY?!
WHY ARE YOU LEAVING ME HERE ALONE?!
LEO!
CLANK CLANK
CLANK
YOUR HIGHNESS.

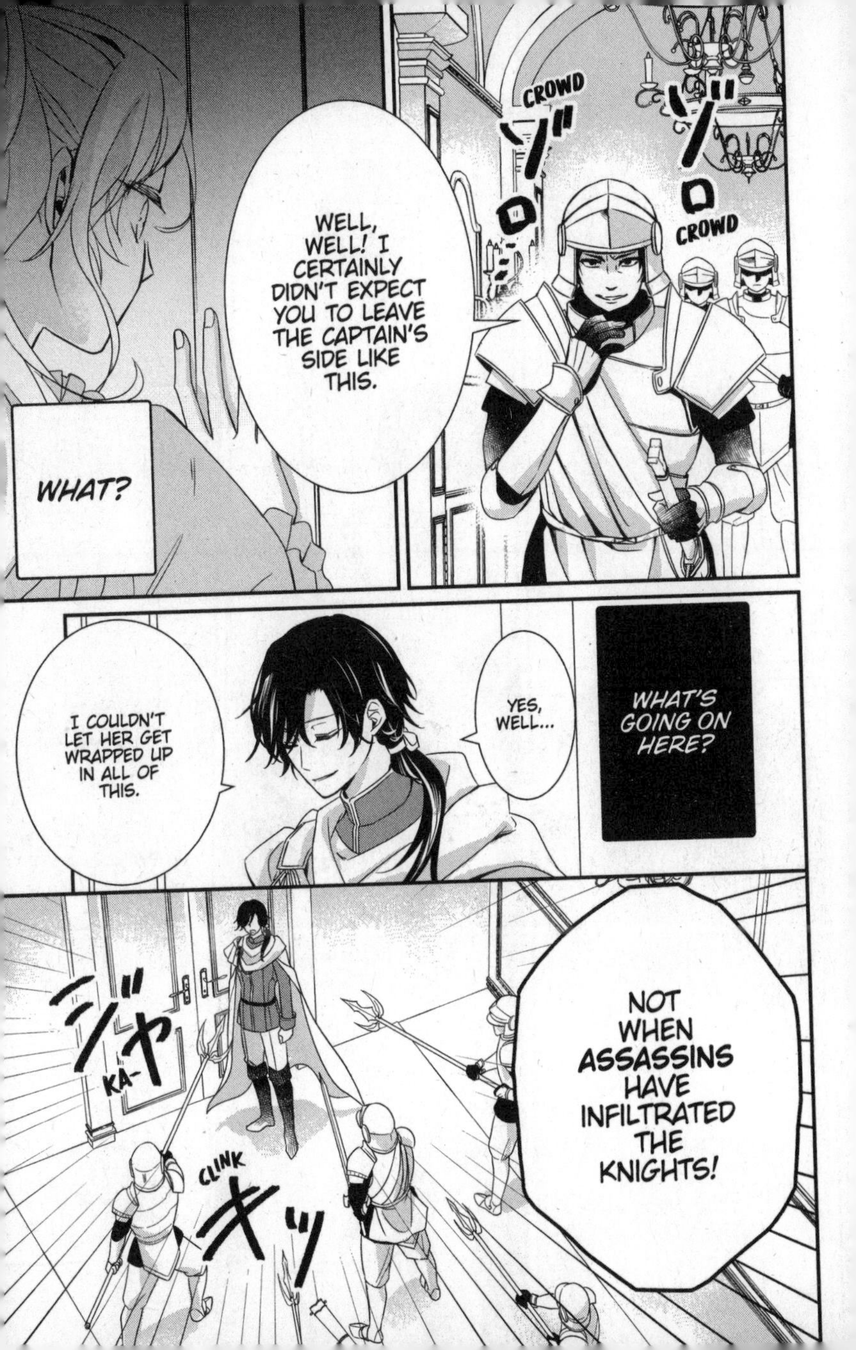
CROWD
CROWD
WELL, WELL! I CERTAINLY DIDN'T EXPECT YOU TO LEAVE THE CAPTAIN'S SIDE LIKE THIS.
WHAT?
WHAT'S GOING ON HERE?
YES, WELL...
I COULDN'T LET HER GET WRAPPED UP IN ALL OF THIS.
NOT WHEN ASSASSINS HAVE INFILTRATED THE KNIGHTS!
KA-
CLINK

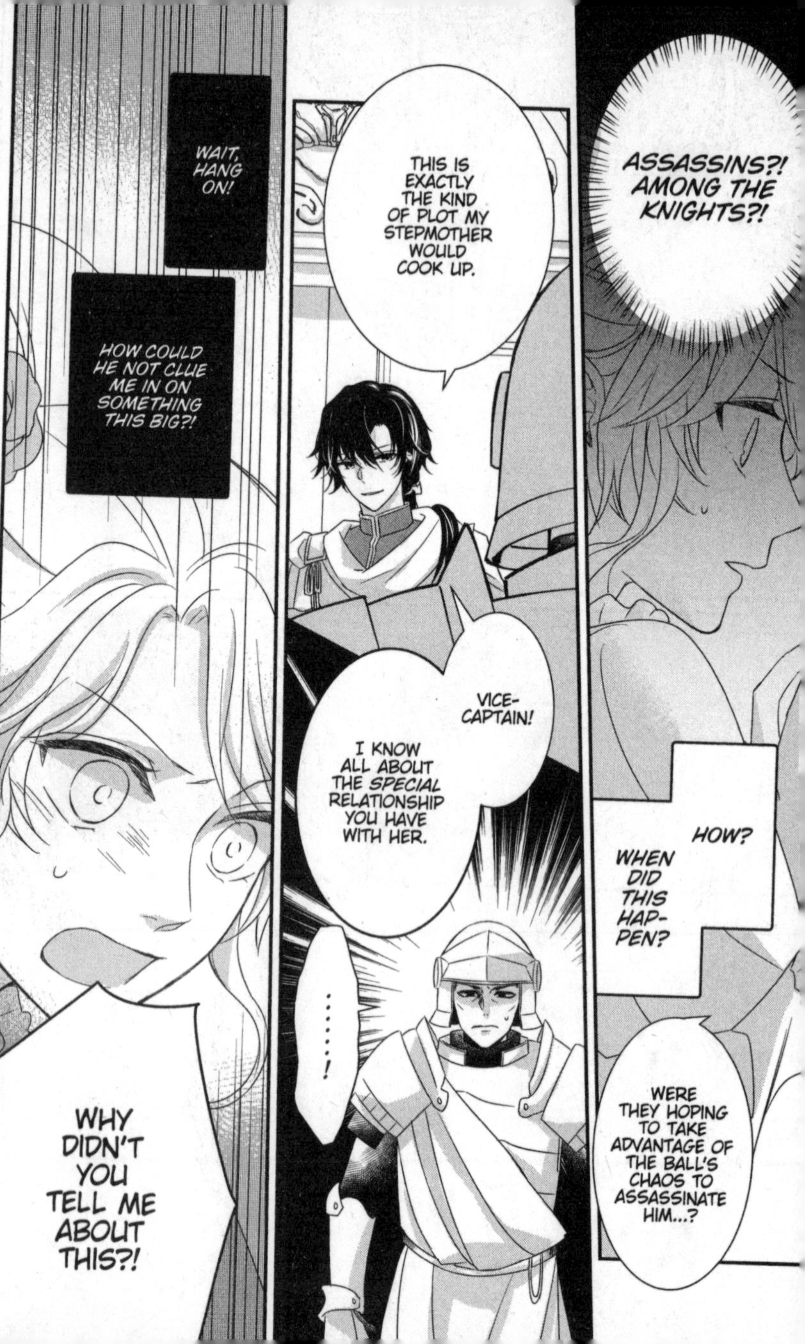
ASSASSINS?! AMONG THE KNIGHTS?!
HOW?
WHEN DID THIS HAP-PEN?
WERE THEY HOPING TO TAKE ADVANTAGE OF THE BALL'S CHAOS TO ASSASSINATE HIM...?
THIS IS EXACTLY THE KIND OF PLOT MY STEPMOTHER WOULD COOK UP.
VICE-CAPTAIN!
I KNOW ALL ABOUT THE *SPECIAL* RELATIONSHIP YOU HAVE WITH HER.
......!
WAIT, HANG ON!
HOW COULD HE NOT CLUE ME IN ON SOMETHING THIS BIG?!
WHY DIDN'T YOU TELL ME ABOUT THIS?!

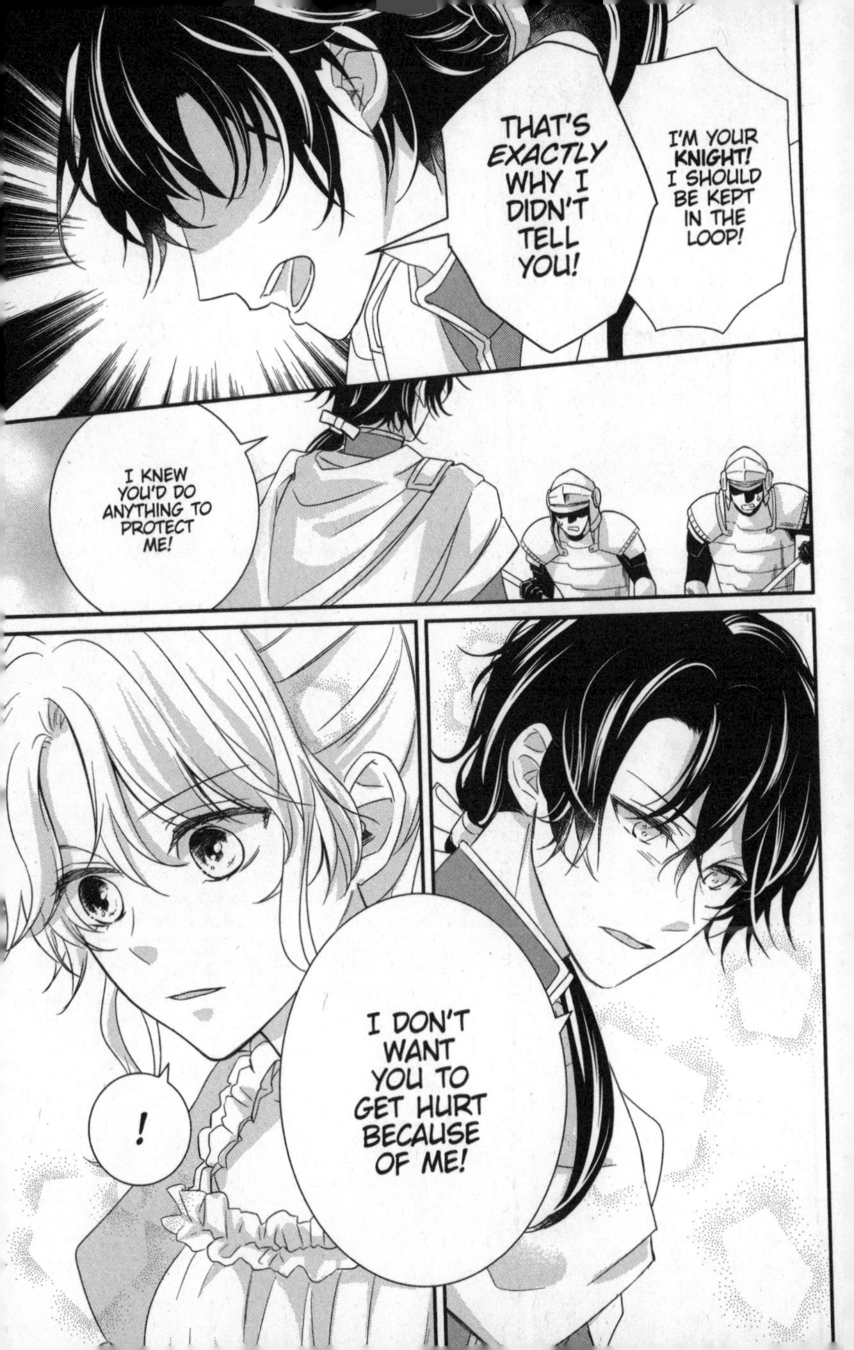
I'M YOUR KNIGHT! I SHOULD BE KEPT IN THE LOOP!
THAT'S EXACTLY WHY I DIDN'T TELL YOU!
I KNEW YOU'D DO ANYTHING TO PROTECT ME!
I DON'T WANT YOU TO GET HURT BECAUSE OF ME!
!

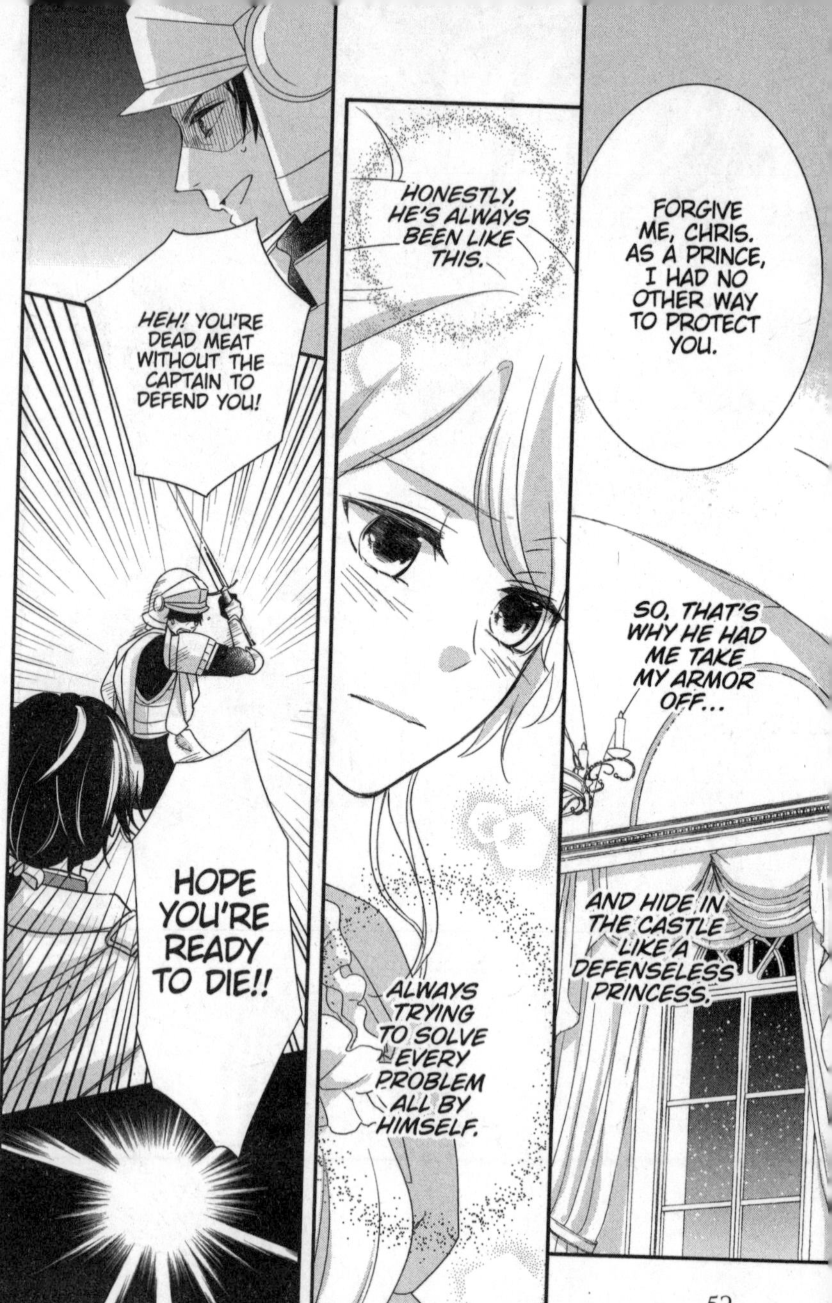
FORGIVE ME, CHRIS. AS A PRINCE, I HAD NO OTHER WAY TO PROTECT YOU.
SO, THAT'S WHY HE HAD ME TAKE MY ARMOR OFF...
AND HIDE IN THE CASTLE LIKE A DEFENSELESS PRINCESS.
HONESTLY, HE'S ALWAYS BEEN LIKE THIS.
ALWAYS TRYING TO SOLVE EVERY PROBLEM ALL BY HIMSELF.
HEH! YOU'RE DEAD MEAT WITHOUT THE CAPTAIN TO DEFEND YOU!
HOPE YOU'RE READY TO DIE!!

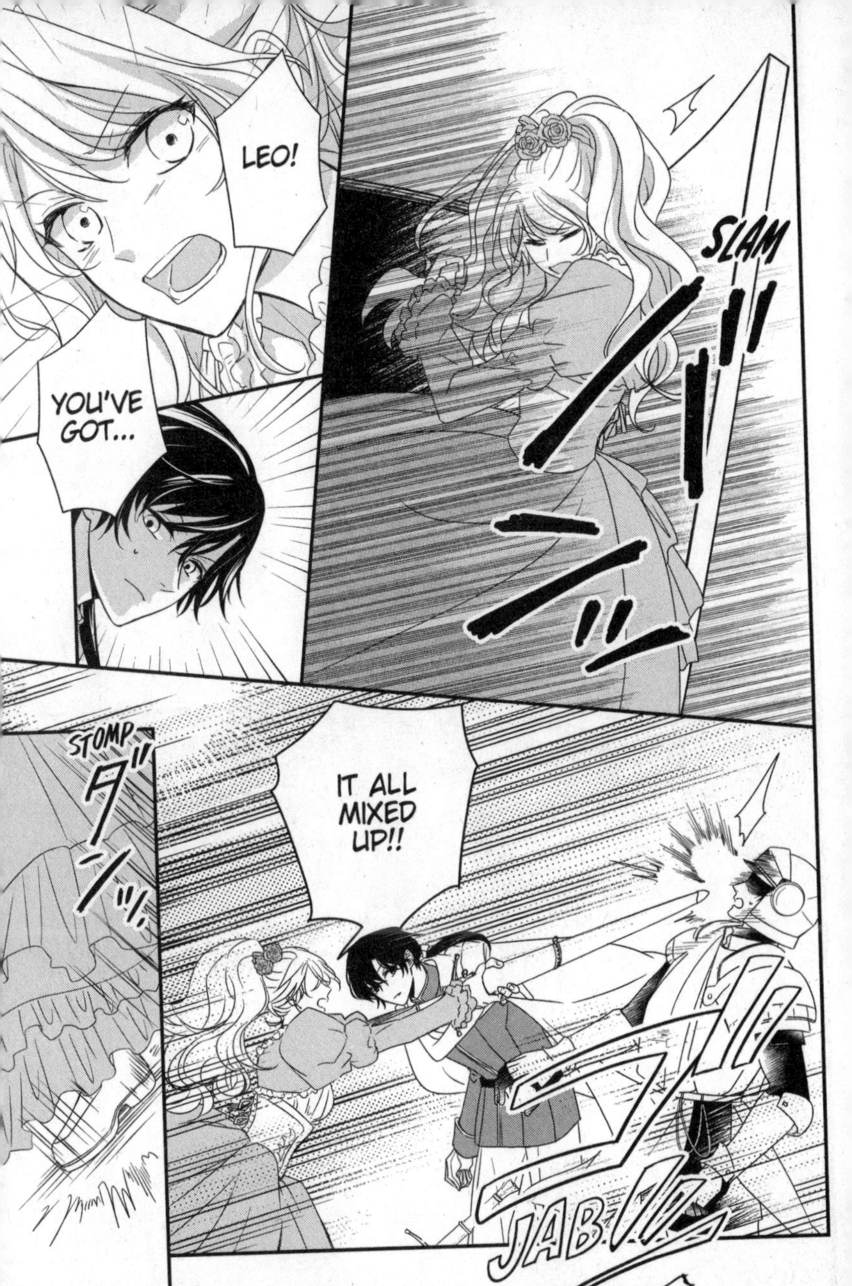
SLAM
LEO!
YOU'VE GOT...
IT ALL MIXED UP!!
JAB
STOMP

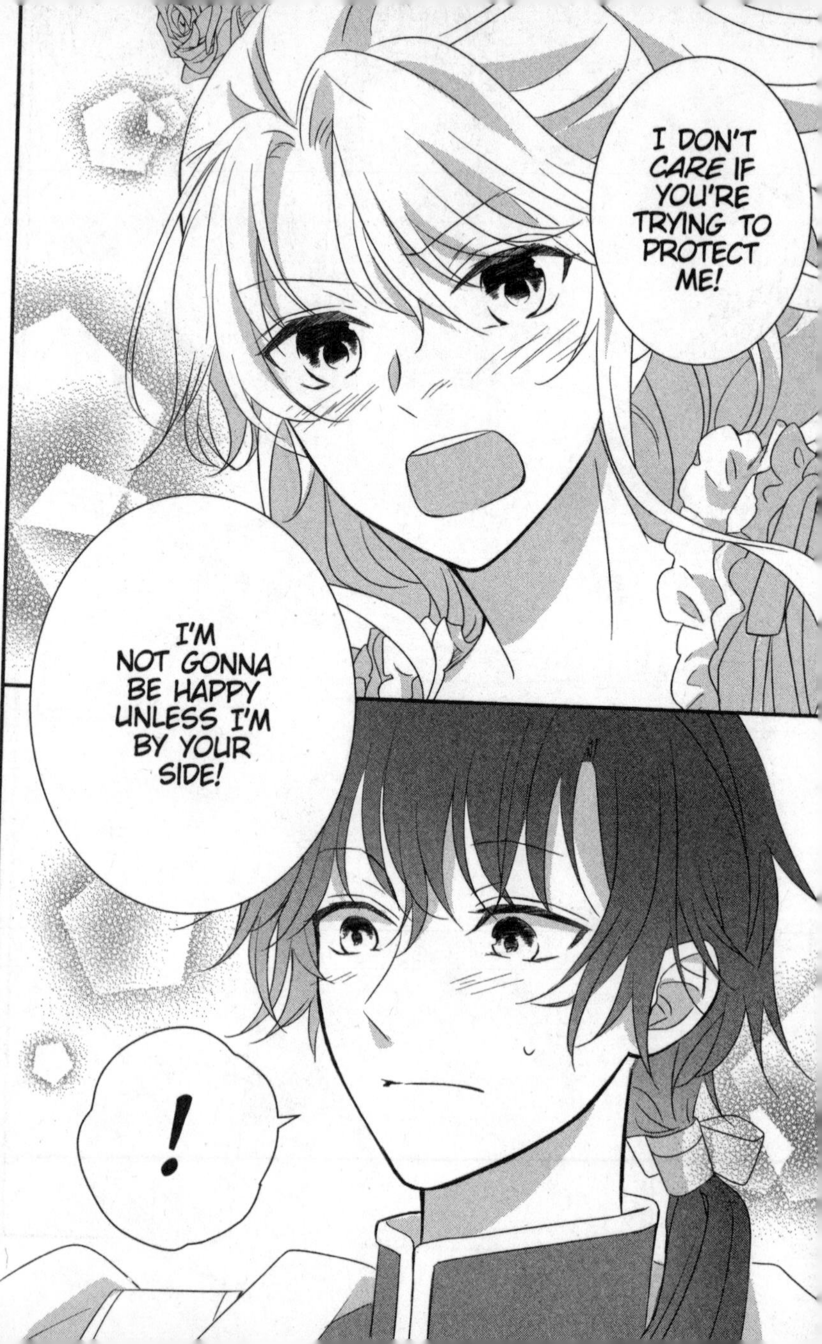
I DON'T CARE IF YOU'RE TRYING TO PROTECT ME!
I'M NOT GONNA BE HAPPY UNLESS I'M BY YOUR SIDE!
!

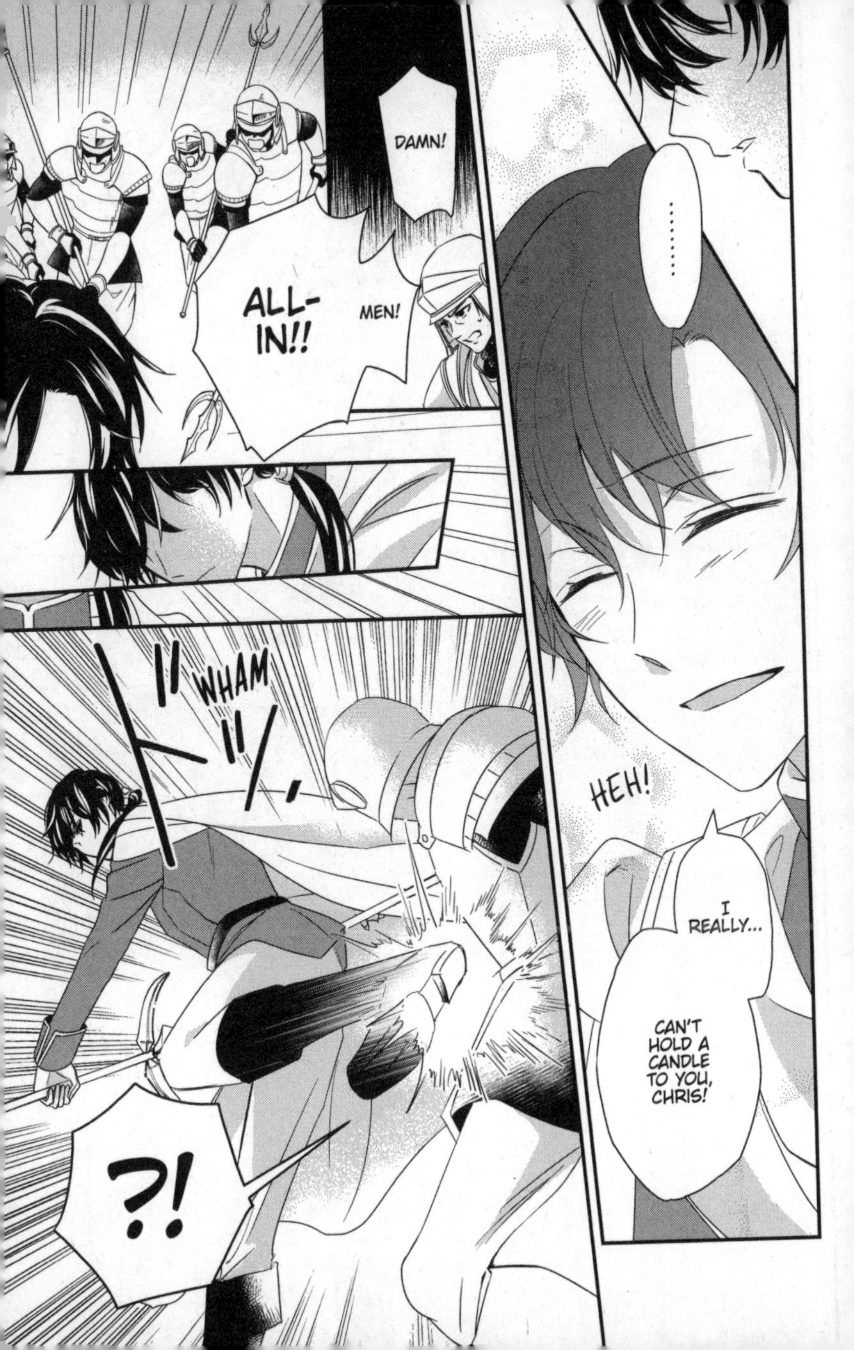
......
HEH!
I REALLY...
CAN'T HOLD A CANDLE TO YOU, CHRIS!
DAMN!
MEN!
ALL-IN!!
WHAM
?!

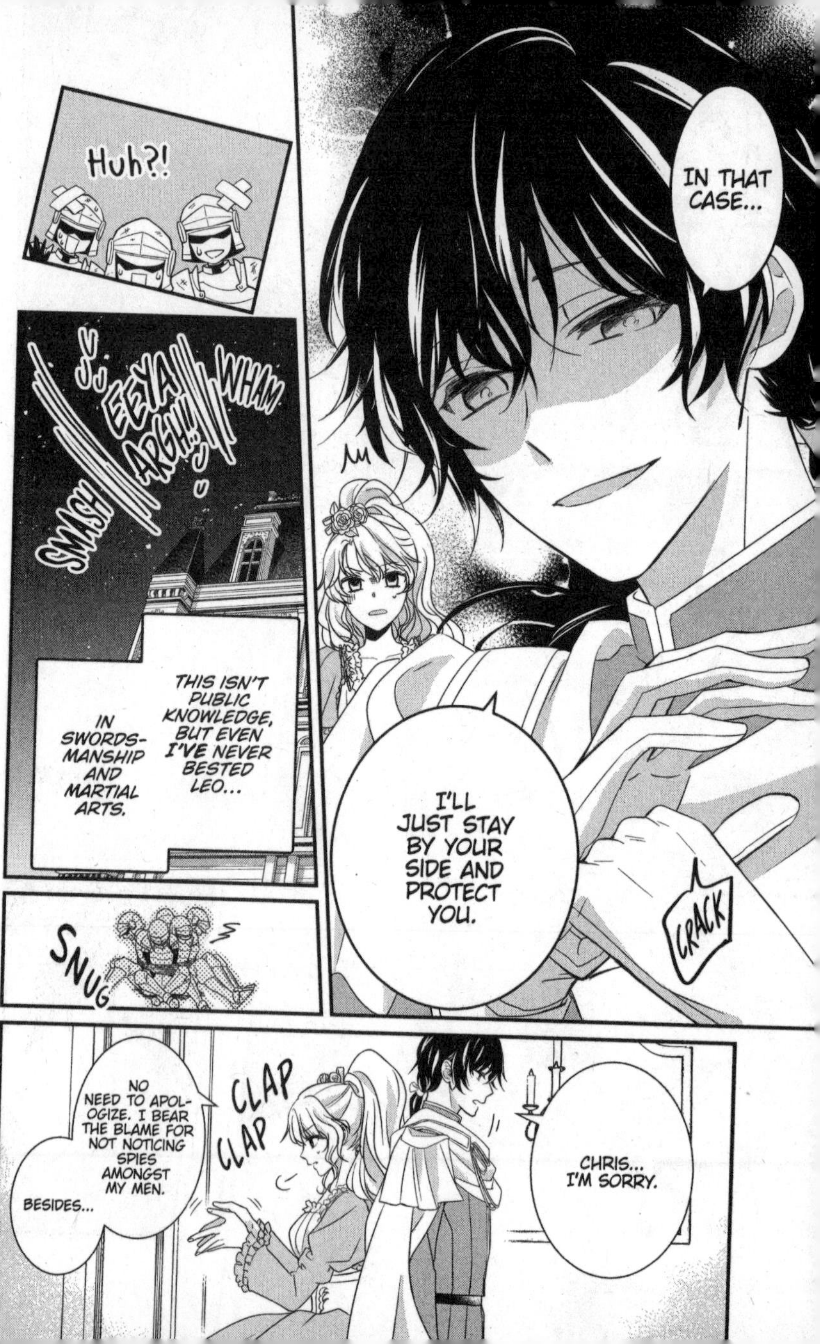
IN THAT CASE...
I'LL JUST STAY BY YOUR SIDE AND PROTECT YOU.
CRACK
Huh?!
WHAM
EEYA
ARGH!!
SMASH
THIS ISN'T PUBLIC KNOWLEDGE, BUT EVEN I'VE NEVER BESTED LEO...
IN SWORDS-MANSHIP AND MARTIAL ARTS.
SNUG
CHRIS... I'M SORRY.
CLAP CLAP
NO NEED TO APOL-OGIZE. I BEAR THE BLAME FOR NOT NOTICING SPIES AMONGST MY MEN.
BESIDES...

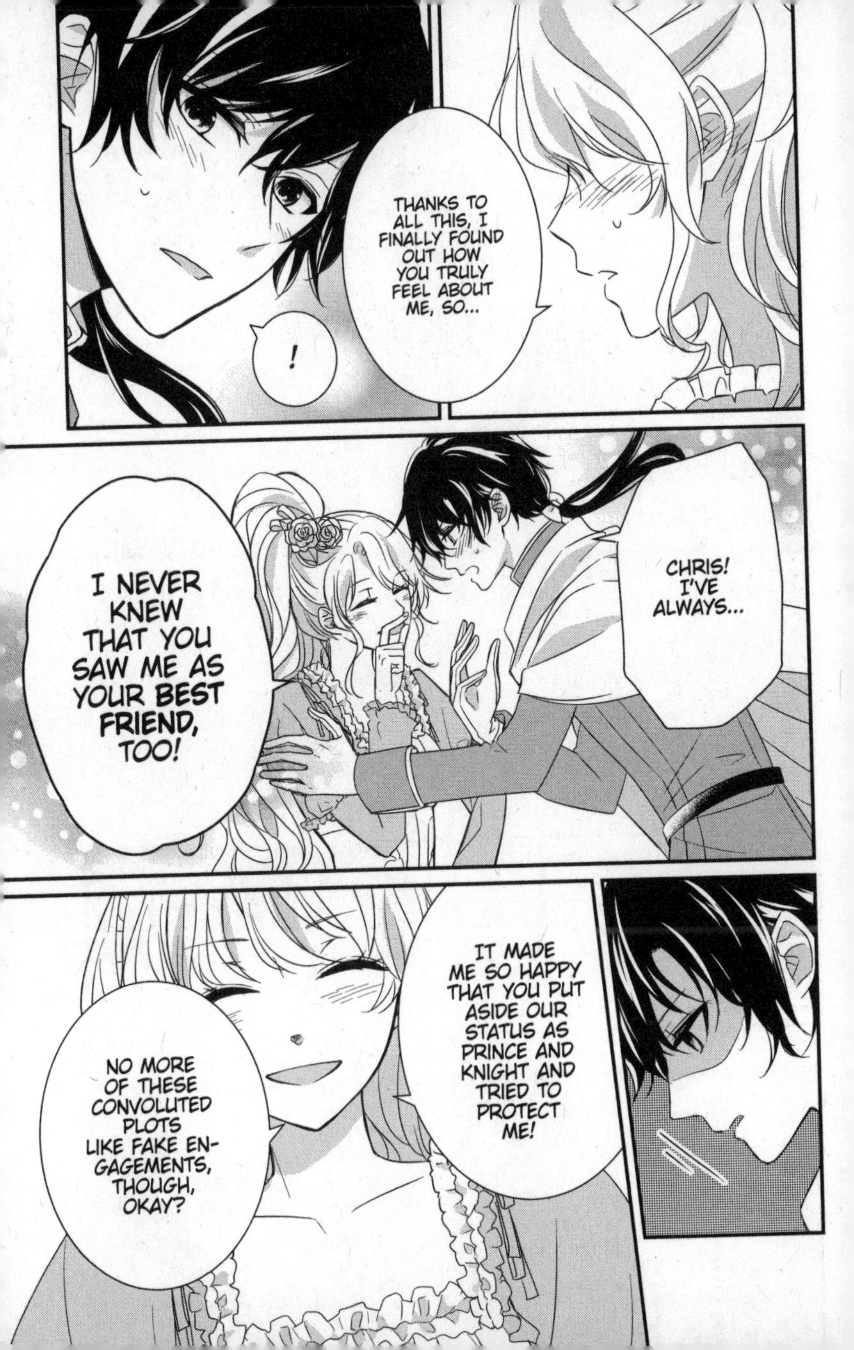
THANKS TO ALL THIS, I FINALLY FOUND OUT HOW YOU TRULY FEEL ABOUT ME, SO...
!
CHRIS! I'VE ALWAYS...
I NEVER KNEW THAT YOU SAW ME AS YOUR BEST FRIEND, TOO!
IT MADE ME SO HAPPY THAT YOU PUT ASIDE OUR STATUS AS PRINCE AND KNIGHT AND TRIED TO PROTECT ME!
NO MORE OF THESE CONVOLUTED PLOTS LIKE FAKE EN- GAGEMENTS, THOUGH, OKAY?

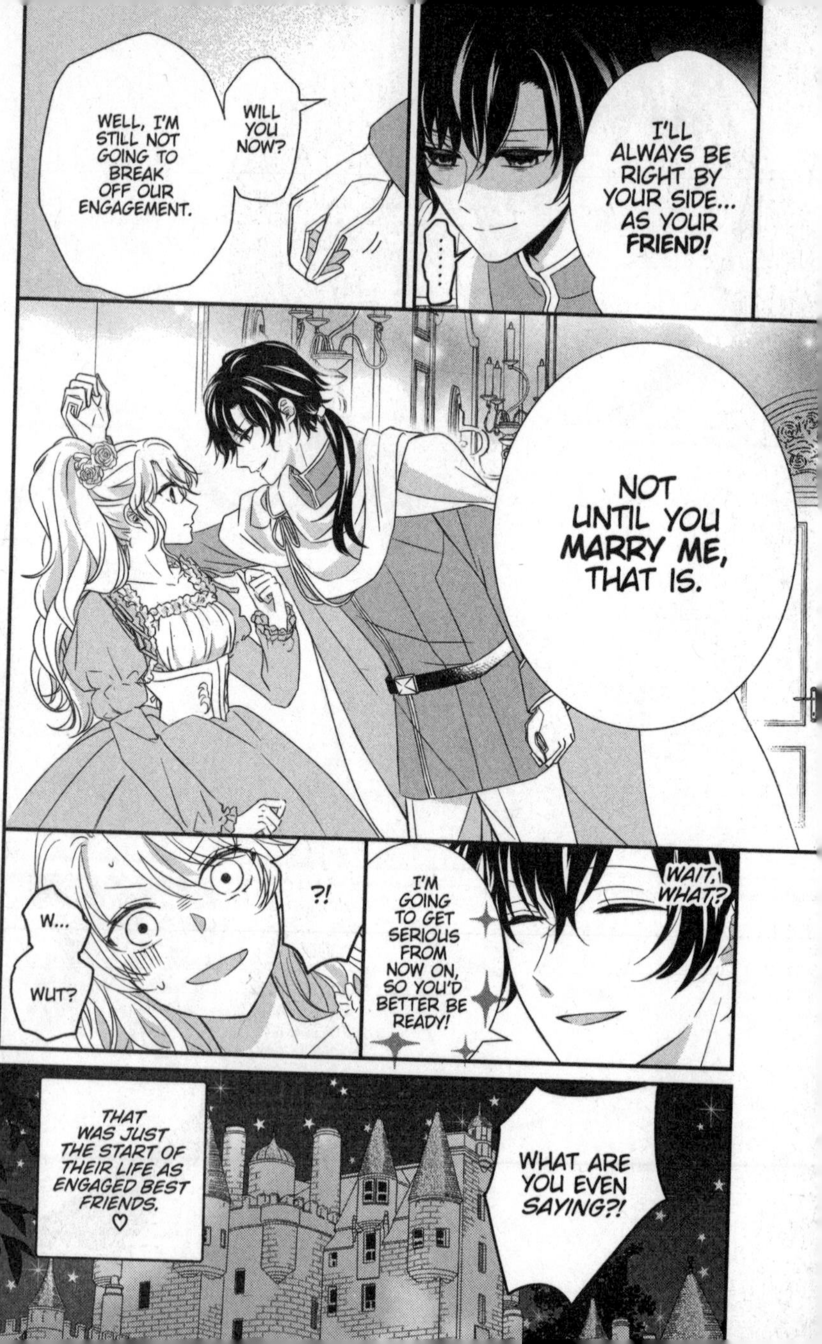
I'LL ALWAYS BE RIGHT BY YOUR SIDE... AS YOUR FRIEND!
......
WILL YOU NOW?
WELL, I'M STILL NOT GOING TO BREAK OFF OUR ENGAGEMENT.
NOT UNTIL YOU MARRY ME, THAT IS.
WAIT, WHAT?
I'M GOING TO GET SERIOUS FROM NOW ON, SO YOU'D BETTER BE READY!
?!
W...
WUT?
WHAT ARE YOU EVEN SAYING?!
THAT WAS JUST THE START OF THEIR LIFE AS ENGAGED BEST FRIENDS. ♡

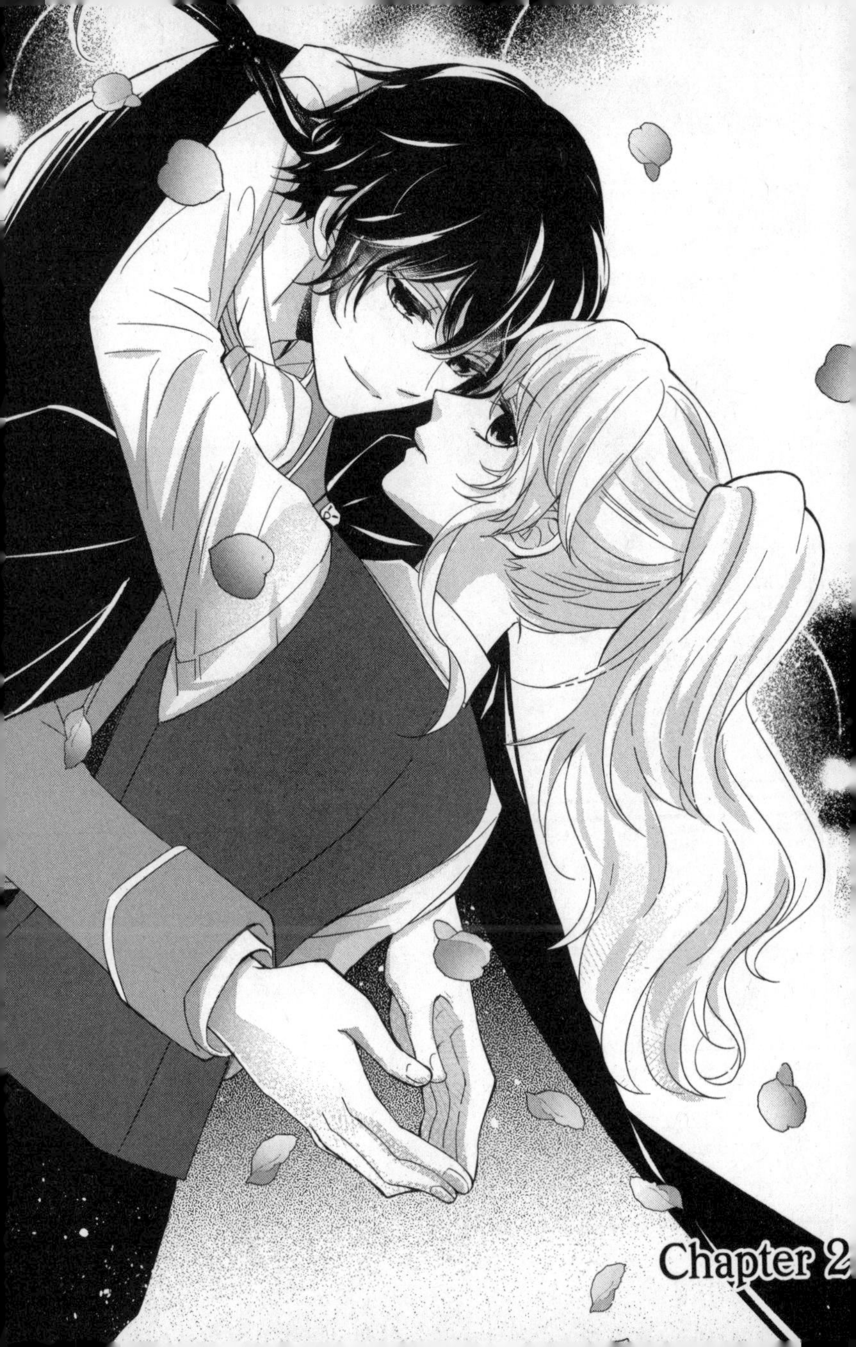
Chapter 2

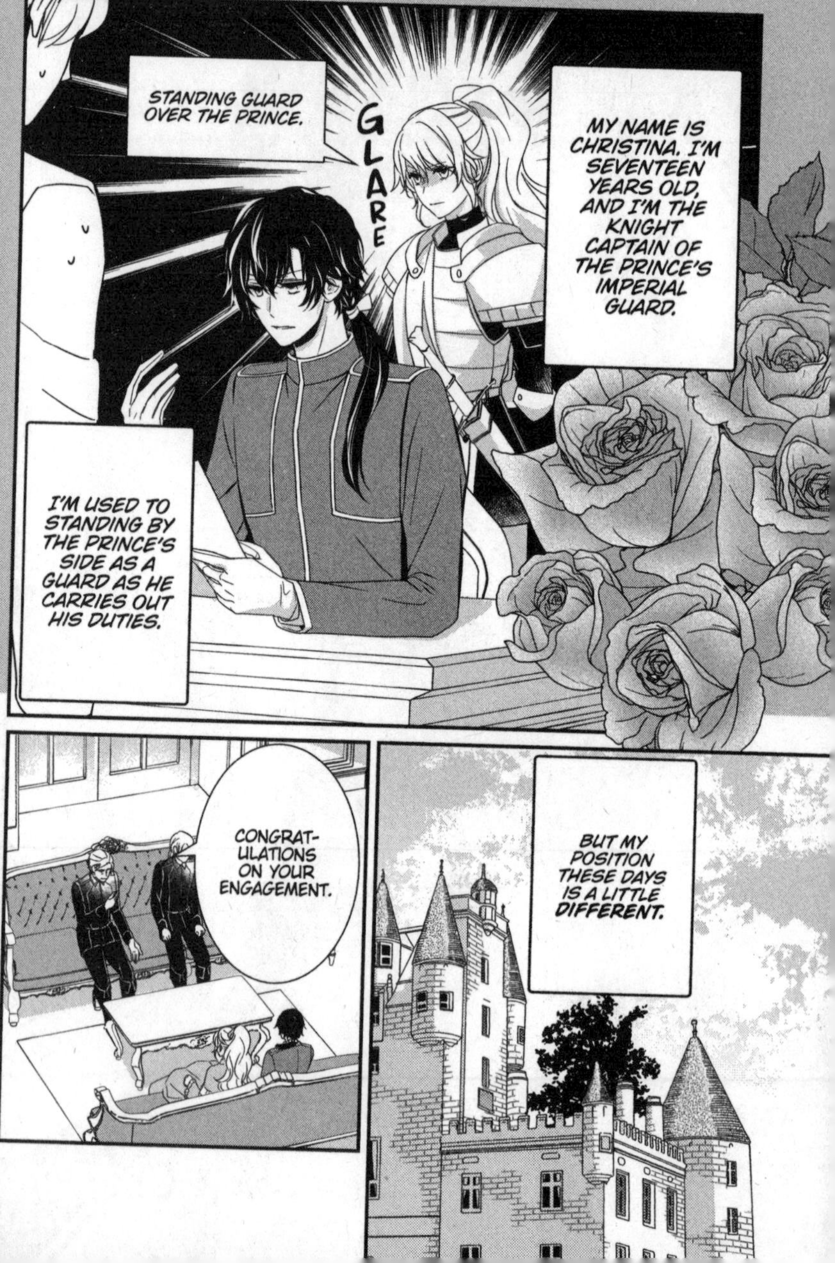
MY NAME IS CHRISTINA. I'M SEVENTEEN YEARS OLD, AND I'M THE KNIGHT CAPTAIN OF THE PRINCE'S IMPERIAL GUARD.
GLARE
STANDING GUARD OVER THE PRINCE.
I'M USED TO STANDING BY THE PRINCE'S SIDE AS A GUARD AS HE CARRIES OUT HIS DUTIES.
BUT MY POSITION THESE DAYS IS A LITTLE DIFFERENT.
CONGRAT-ULATIONS ON YOUR ENGAGEMENT.

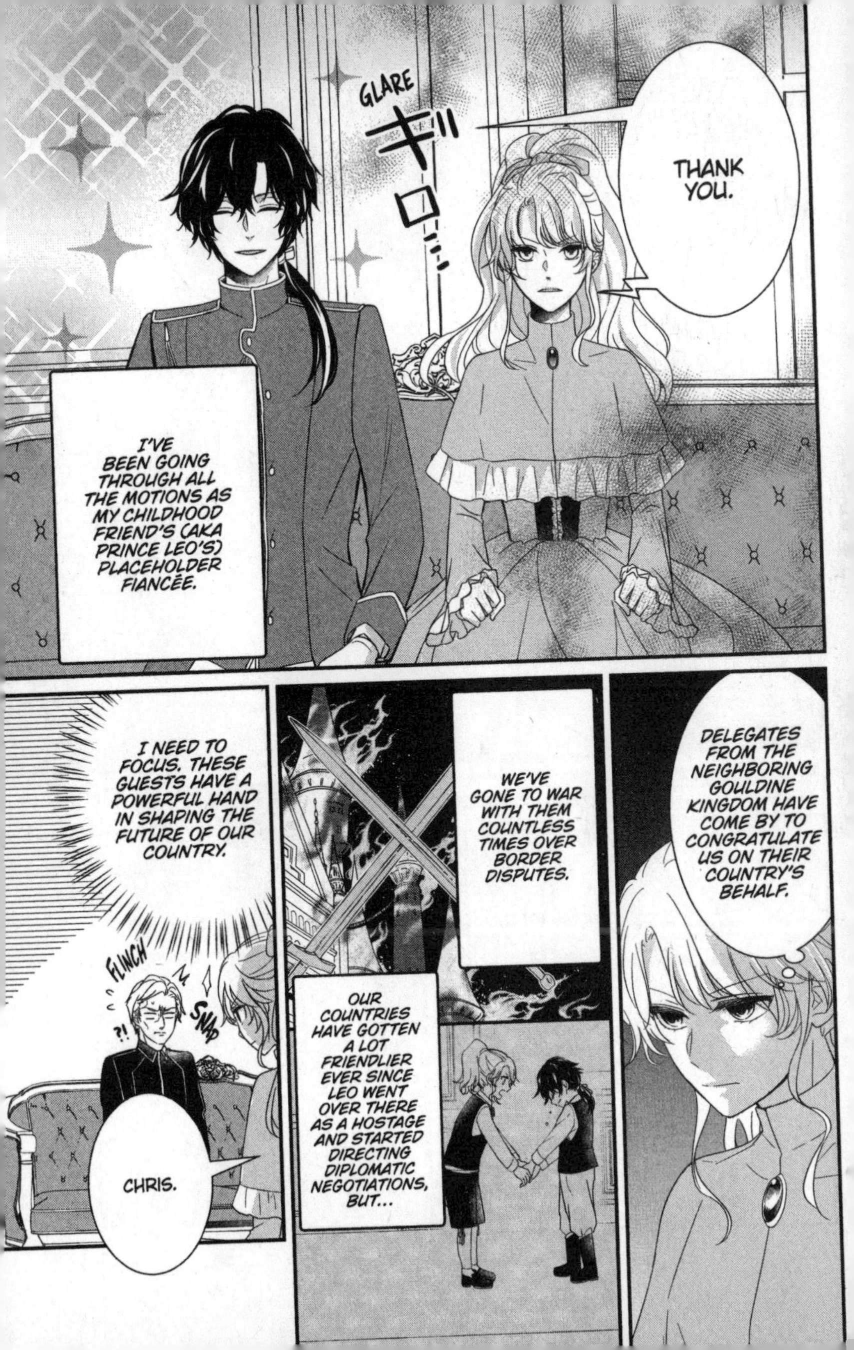
THANK YOU.
GLARE
ギロ
I'VE BEEN GOING THROUGH ALL THE MOTIONS AS MY CHILDHOOD FRIEND'S (AKA PRINCE LEO'S) PLACEHOLDER FIANCÉE.
DELEGATES FROM THE NEIGHBORING GOULDINE KINGDOM HAVE COME BY TO CONGRATULATE US ON THEIR COUNTRY'S BEHALF.
WE'VE GONE TO WAR WITH THEM COUNTLESS TIMES OVER BORDER DISPUTES.
OUR COUNTRIES HAVE GOTTEN A LOT FRIENDLIER EVER SINCE LEO WENT OVER THERE AS A HOSTAGE AND STARTED DIRECTING DIPLOMATIC NEGOTIATIONS, BUT...
I NEED TO FOCUS. THESE GUESTS HAVE A POWERFUL HAND IN SHAPING THE FUTURE OF OUR COUNTRY.
SNAP
FLINCH
?!
CHRIS.

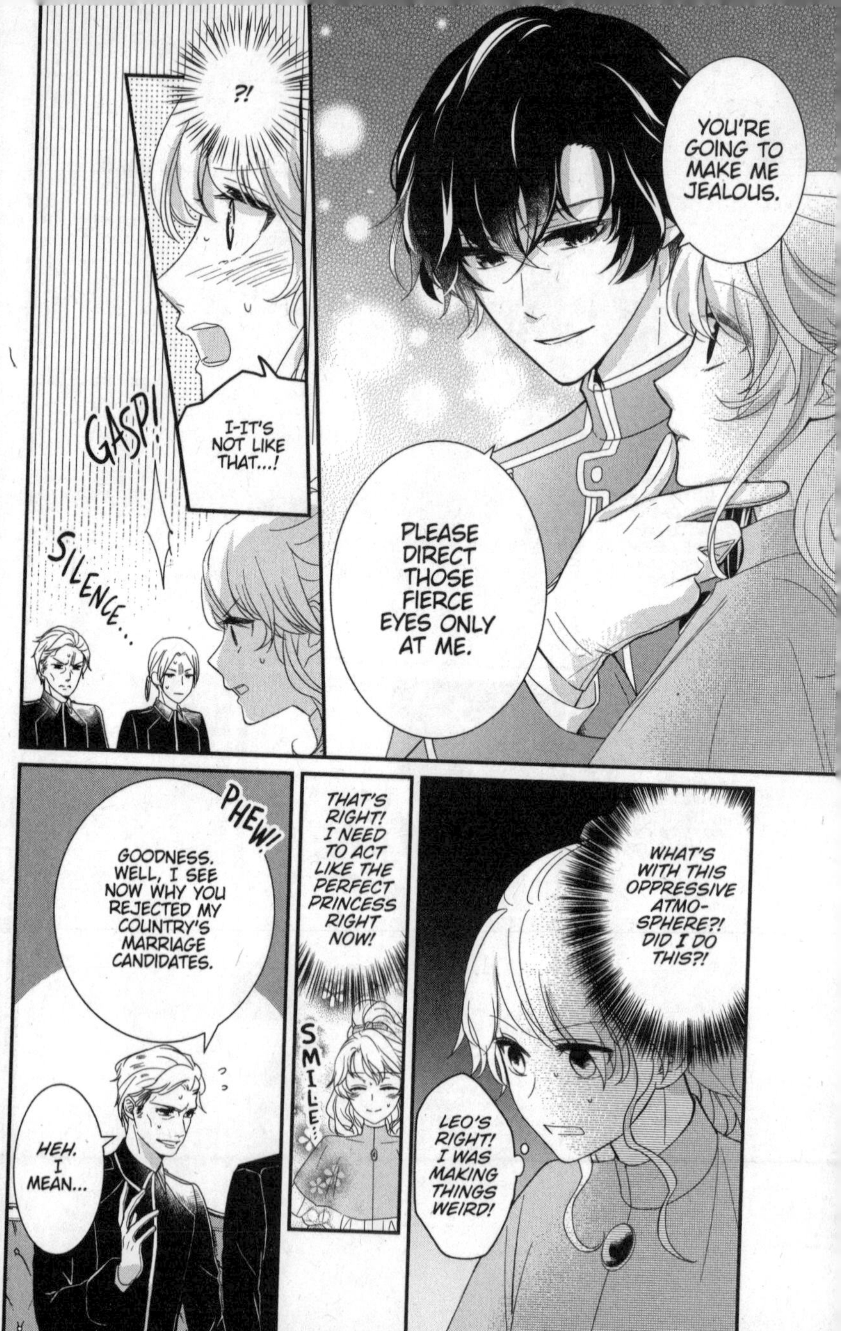
YOU'RE GOING TO MAKE ME JEALOUS.
PLEASE DIRECT THOSE FIERCE EYES ONLY AT ME.
?!
GASP!
I-IT'S NOT LIKE THAT...!
SILENCE...
WHAT'S WITH THIS OPPRESSIVE ATMO-SPHERE?! DID I DO THIS?!
LEO'S RIGHT! I WAS MAKING THINGS WEIRD!
THAT'S RIGHT! I NEED TO ACT LIKE THE PERFECT PRINCESS RIGHT NOW!
SMILE...
PHEW!
GOODNESS. WELL, I SEE NOW WHY YOU REJECTED MY COUNTRY'S MARRIAGE CANDIDATES.
HEH. I MEAN...

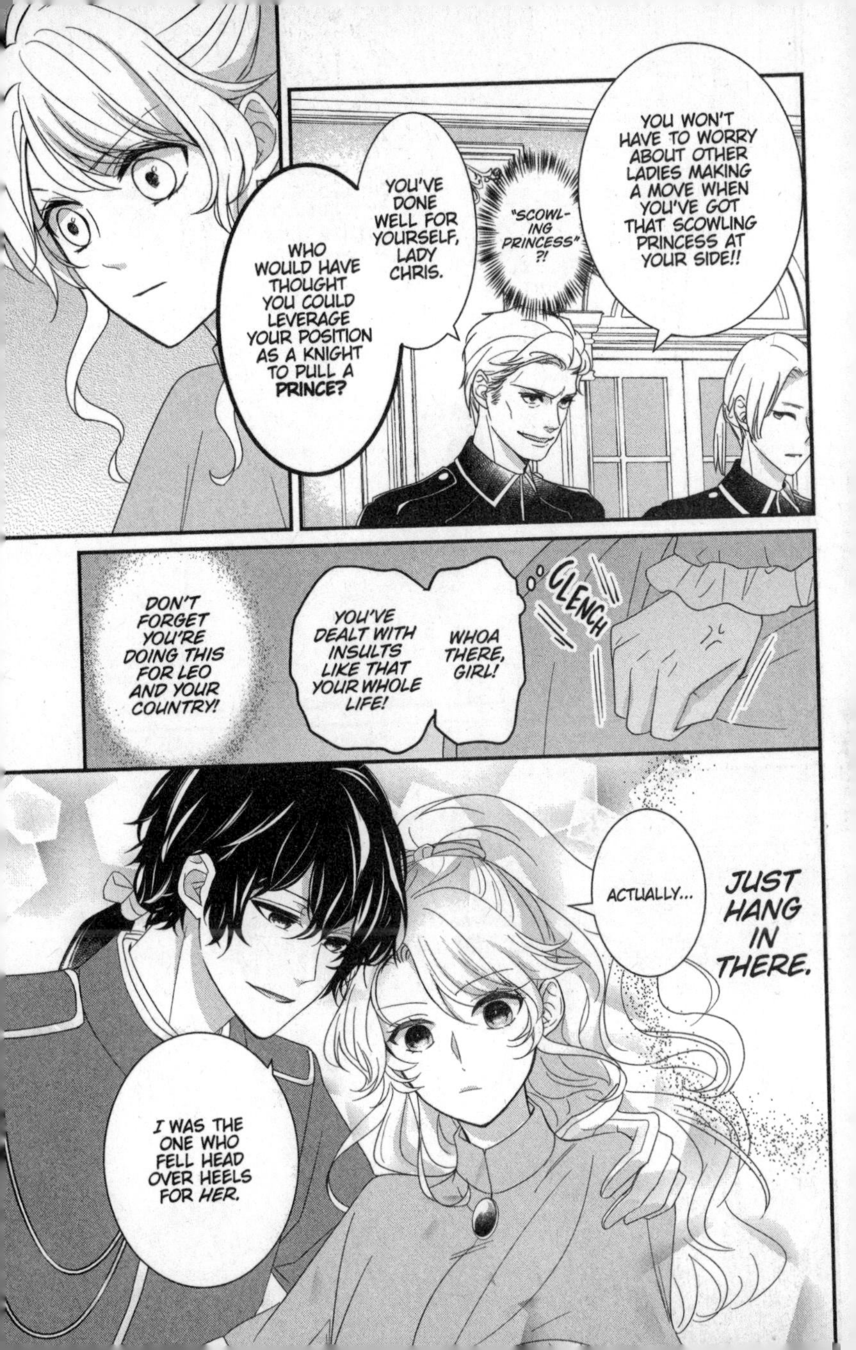
YOU WON'T HAVE TO WORRY ABOUT OTHER LADIES MAKING A MOVE WHEN YOU'VE GOT THAT SCOWLING PRINCESS AT YOUR SIDE!!
"SCOWLING PRINCESS"?!
YOU'VE DONE WELL FOR YOURSELF, LADY CHRIS.
WHO WOULD HAVE THOUGHT YOU COULD LEVERAGE YOUR POSITION AS A KNIGHT TO PULL A **PRINCE**?
CLENCH
WHOA THERE, GIRL!
YOU'VE DEALT WITH INSULTS LIKE THAT YOUR WHOLE LIFE!
DON'T FORGET YOU'RE DOING THIS FOR LEO AND YOUR COUNTRY!
JUST HANG IN THERE.
ACTUALLY...
I WAS THE ONE WHO FELL HEAD OVER HEELS FOR *HER*.

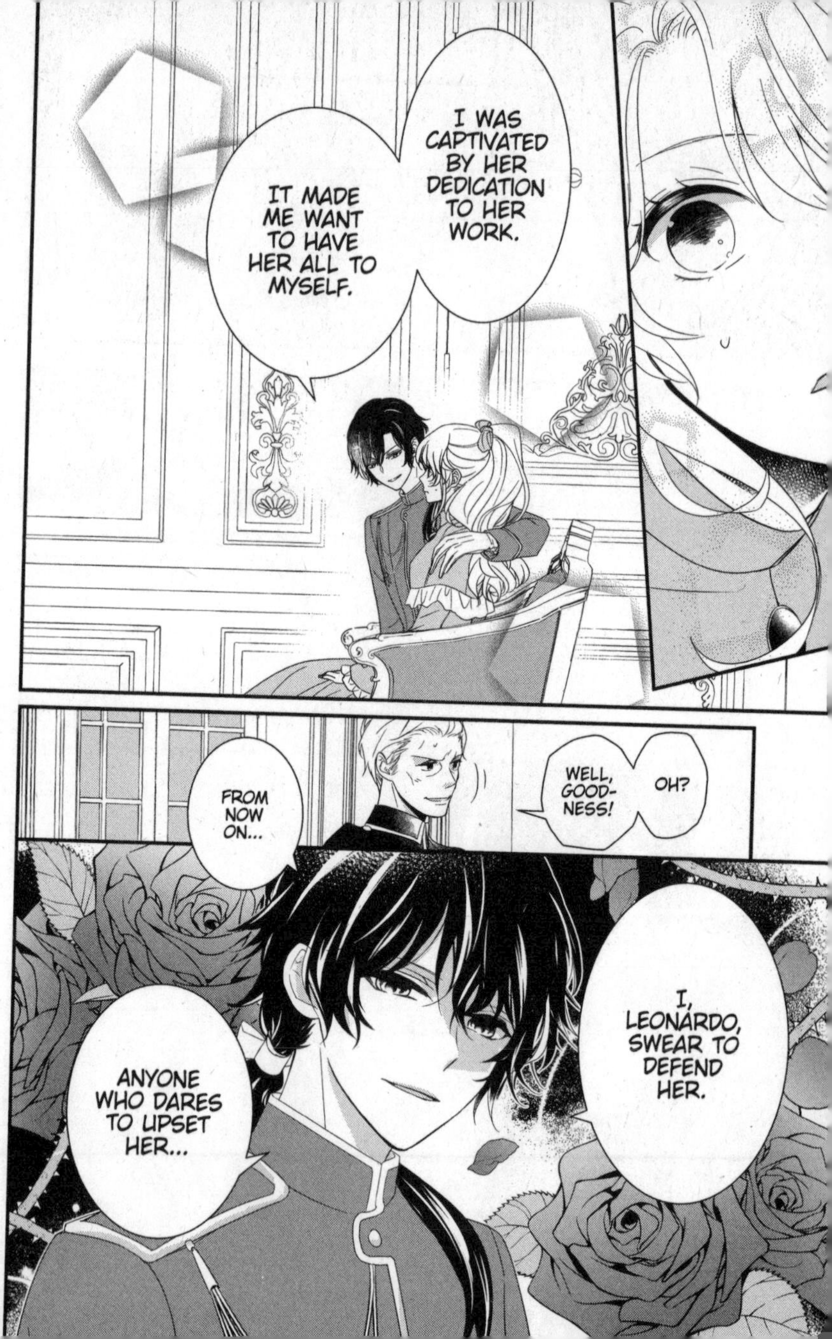
I WAS CAPTIVATED BY HER DEDICATION TO HER WORK.
IT MADE ME WANT TO HAVE HER ALL TO MYSELF.
OH?
WELL, GOODNESS!
FROM NOW ON...
I, LEONARDO, SWEAR TO DEFEND HER.
ANYONE WHO DARES TO UPSET HER...

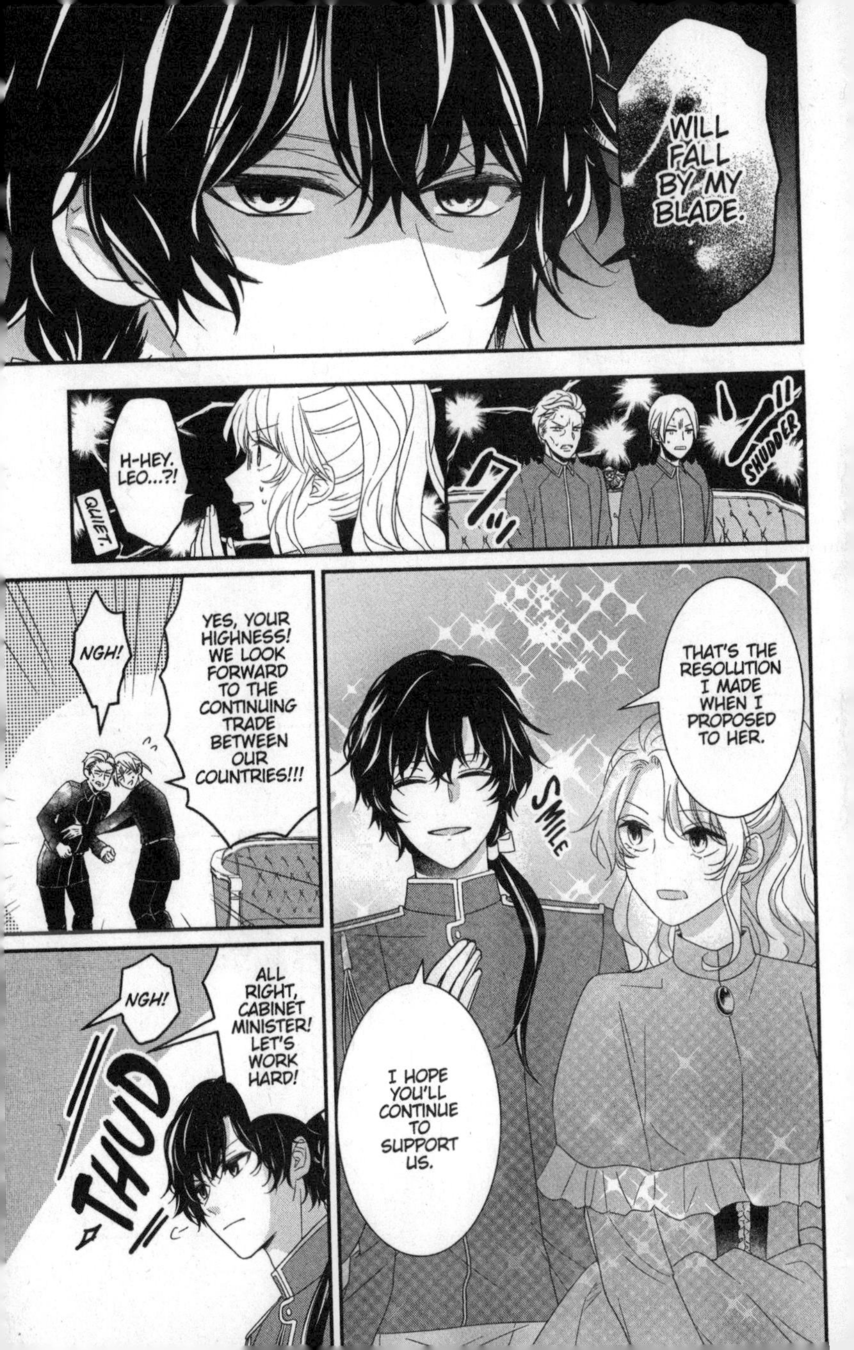
WILL FALL BY MY BLADE.
SHUDDER
H-HEY. LEO...?!
QUIET.
THAT'S THE RESOLUTION I MADE WHEN I PROPOSED TO HER.
SMILE
I HOPE YOU'LL CONTINUE TO SUPPORT US.
YES, YOUR HIGHNESS! WE LOOK FORWARD TO THE CONTINUING TRADE BETWEEN OUR COUNTRIES!!!
NGH!
ALL RIGHT, CABINET MINISTER! LET'S WORK HARD!
NGH!
THUD

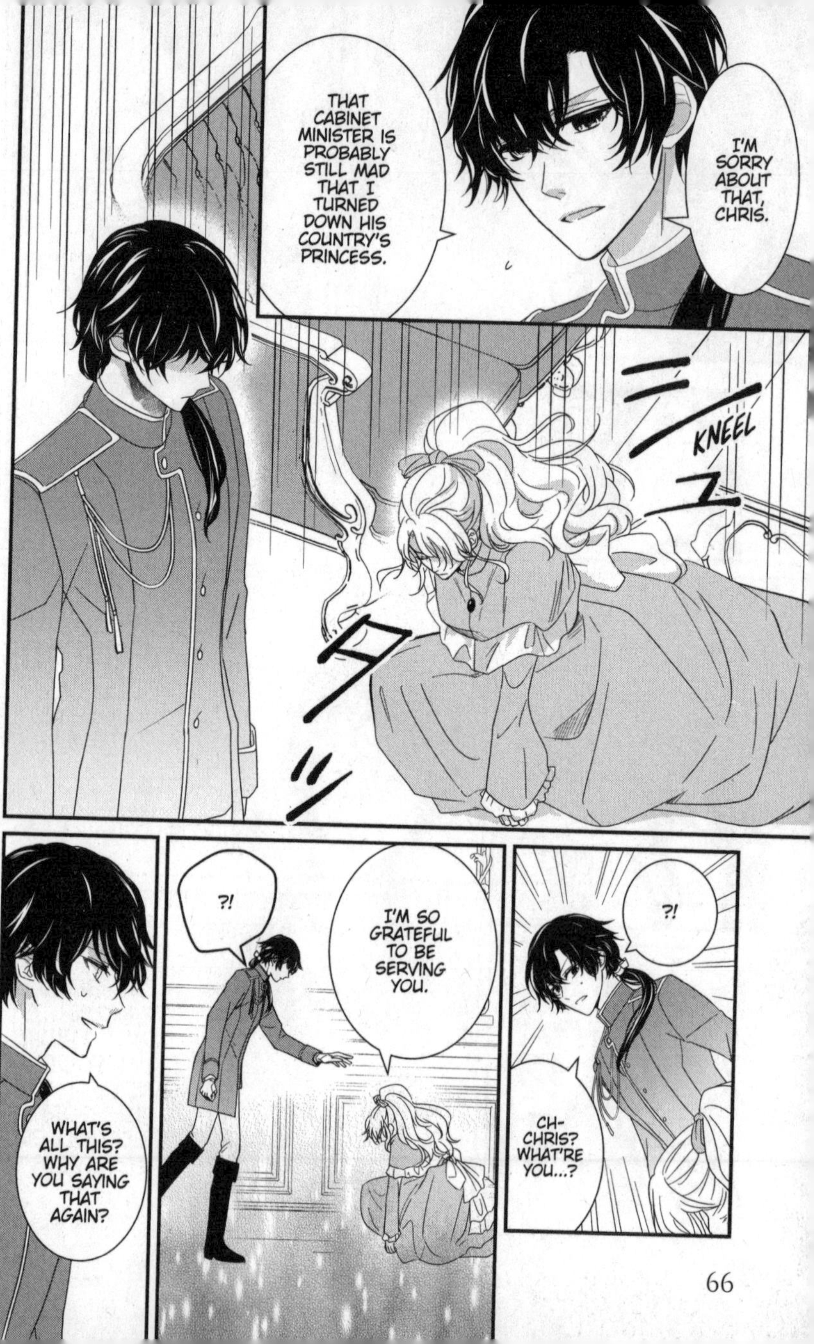
I'M SORRY ABOUT THAT, CHRIS.
THAT CABINET MINISTER IS PROBABLY STILL MAD THAT I TURNED DOWN HIS COUNTRY'S PRINCESS.
KNEEL
?!
CH-CHRIS? WHAT'RE YOU...?
I'M SO GRATEFUL TO BE SERVING YOU.
?!
WHAT'S ALL THIS? WHY ARE YOU SAYING THAT AGAIN?

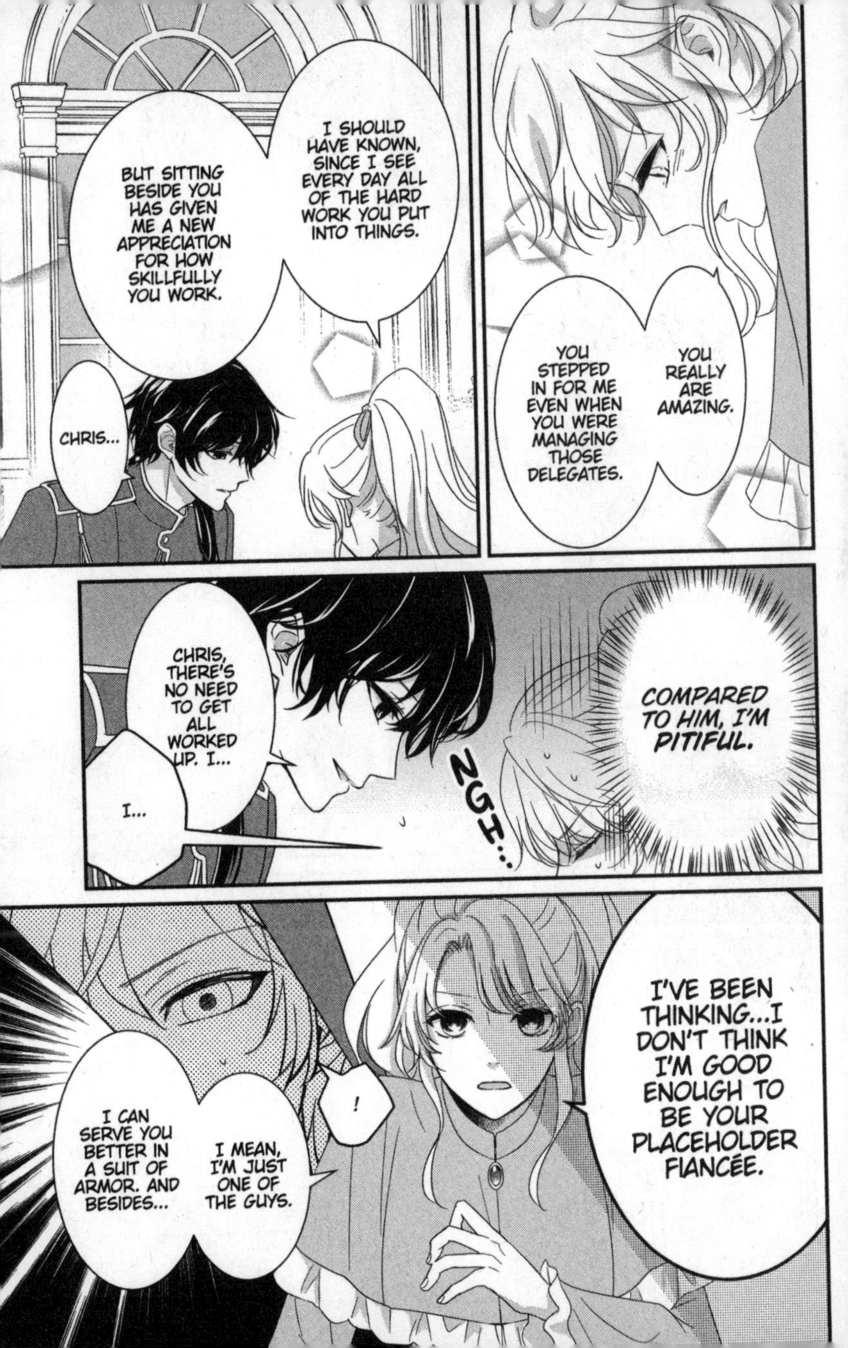
YOU REALLY ARE AMAZING.
YOU STEPPED IN FOR ME EVEN WHEN YOU WERE MANAGING THOSE DELEGATES.
I SHOULD HAVE KNOWN, SINCE I SEE EVERY DAY ALL OF THE HARD WORK YOU PUT INTO THINGS.
BUT SITTING BESIDE YOU HAS GIVEN ME A NEW APPRECIATION FOR HOW SKILLFULLY YOU WORK.
CHRIS...
COMPARED TO HIM, I'M PITIFUL.
NGH...
CHRIS, THERE'S NO NEED TO GET ALL WORKED UP. I...
I...
I'VE BEEN THINKING...I DON'T THINK I'M GOOD ENOUGH TO BE YOUR PLACEHOLDER FIANCÉE.
!
I MEAN, I'M JUST ONE OF THE GUYS.
I CAN SERVE YOU BETTER IN A SUIT OF ARMOR. AND BESIDES...

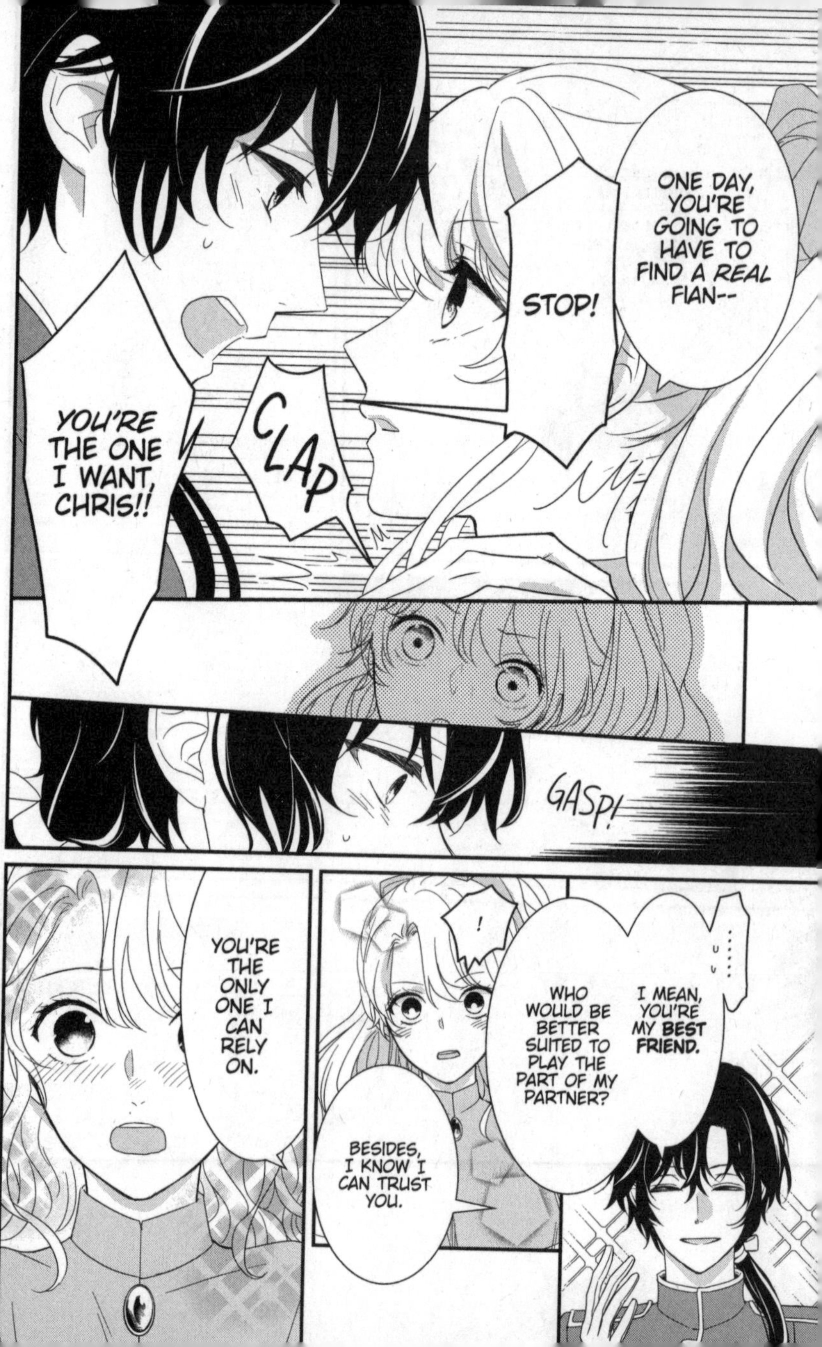
ONE DAY, YOU'RE GOING TO HAVE TO FIND A *REAL* FIAN--
STOP!
CLAP
YOU'RE THE ONE I WANT, CHRIS!!
GASP!
......
I MEAN, YOU'RE MY **BEST FRIEND.**
WHO WOULD BE BETTER SUITED TO PLAY THE PART OF MY PARTNER?
!
BESIDES, I KNOW I CAN TRUST YOU.
YOU'RE THE ONLY ONE I CAN RELY ON.

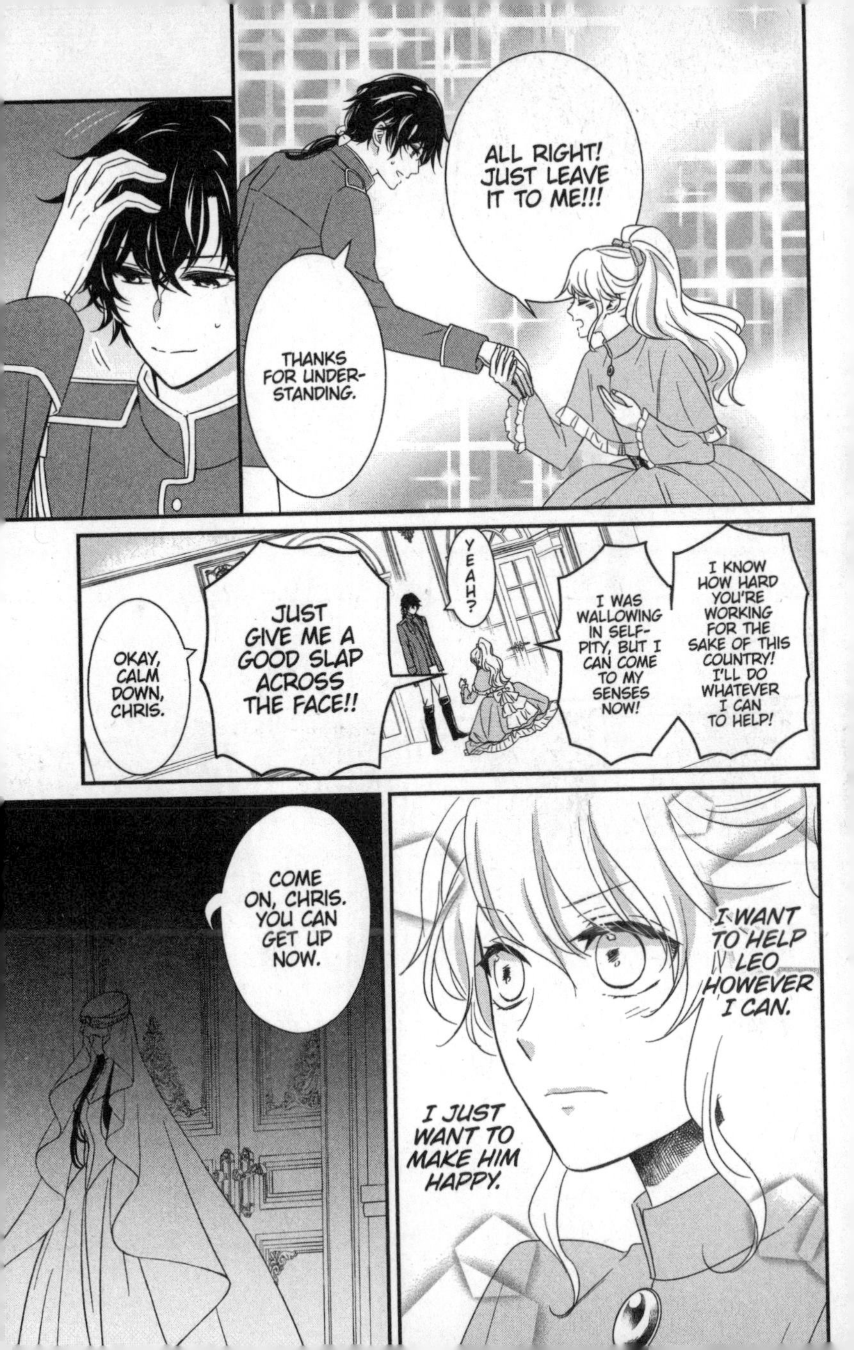
ALL RIGHT! JUST LEAVE IT TO ME!!!
THANKS FOR UNDER-STANDING.
I KNOW HOW HARD YOU'RE WORKING FOR THE SAKE OF THIS COUNTRY! I'LL DO WHATEVER I CAN TO HELP!
I WAS WALLOWING IN SELF-PITY, BUT I CAN COME TO MY SENSES NOW!
YEAH?
JUST GIVE ME A GOOD SLAP ACROSS THE FACE!!
OKAY, CALM DOWN, CHRIS.
I WANT TO HELP LEO HOWEVER I CAN.
I JUST WANT TO MAKE HIM HAPPY.
COME ON, CHRIS. YOU CAN GET UP NOW.

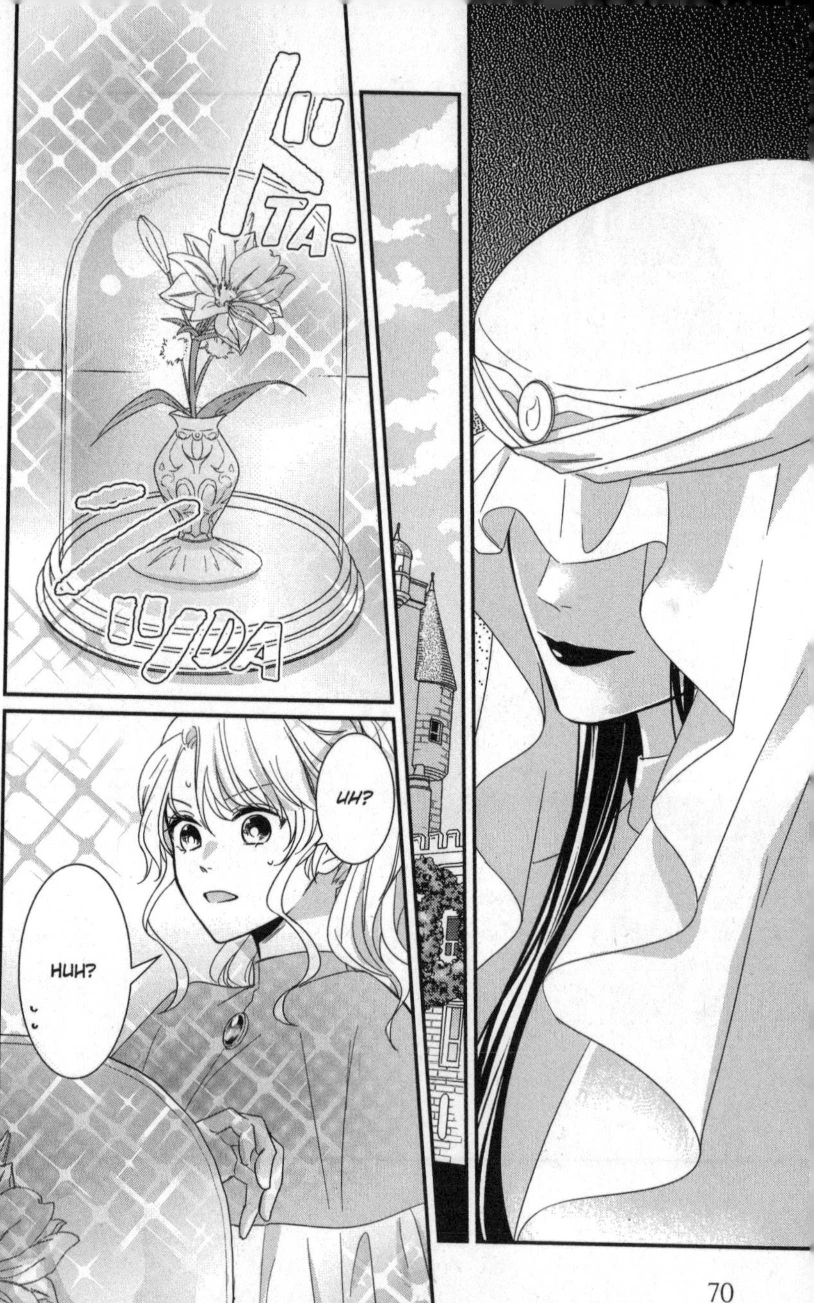
TA-
DA
UH?
HUH?

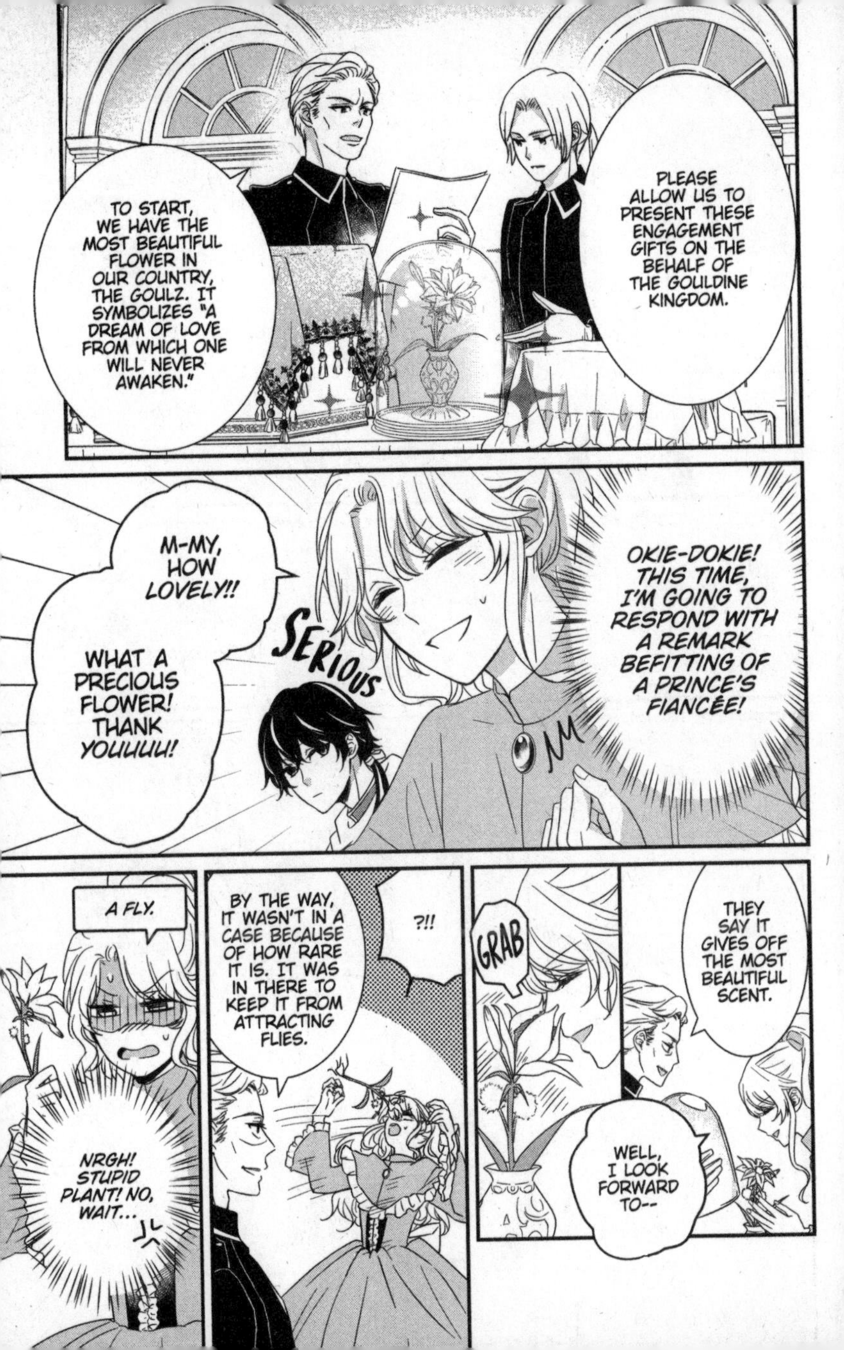
PLEASE ALLOW US TO PRESENT THESE ENGAGEMENT GIFTS ON THE BEHALF OF THE GOULDINE KINGDOM.
TO START, WE HAVE THE MOST BEAUTIFUL FLOWER IN OUR COUNTRY, THE GOULZ. IT SYMBOLIZES "A DREAM OF LOVE FROM WHICH ONE WILL NEVER AWAKEN."
OKIE-DOKIE! THIS TIME, I'M GOING TO RESPOND WITH A REMARK BEFITTING OF A PRINCE'S FIANCÉE!
M-MY, HOW LOVELY!!
SERIOUS
WHAT A PRECIOUS FLOWER! THANK YOUUUU!
THEY SAY IT GIVES OFF THE MOST BEAUTIFUL SCENT.
GRAB
WELL, I LOOK FORWARD TO--
?!!
BY THE WAY, IT WASN'T IN A CASE BECAUSE OF HOW RARE IT IS. IT WAS IN THERE TO KEEP IT FROM ATTRACTING FLIES.
A FLY.
NRGH! STUPID PLANT! NO, WAIT...

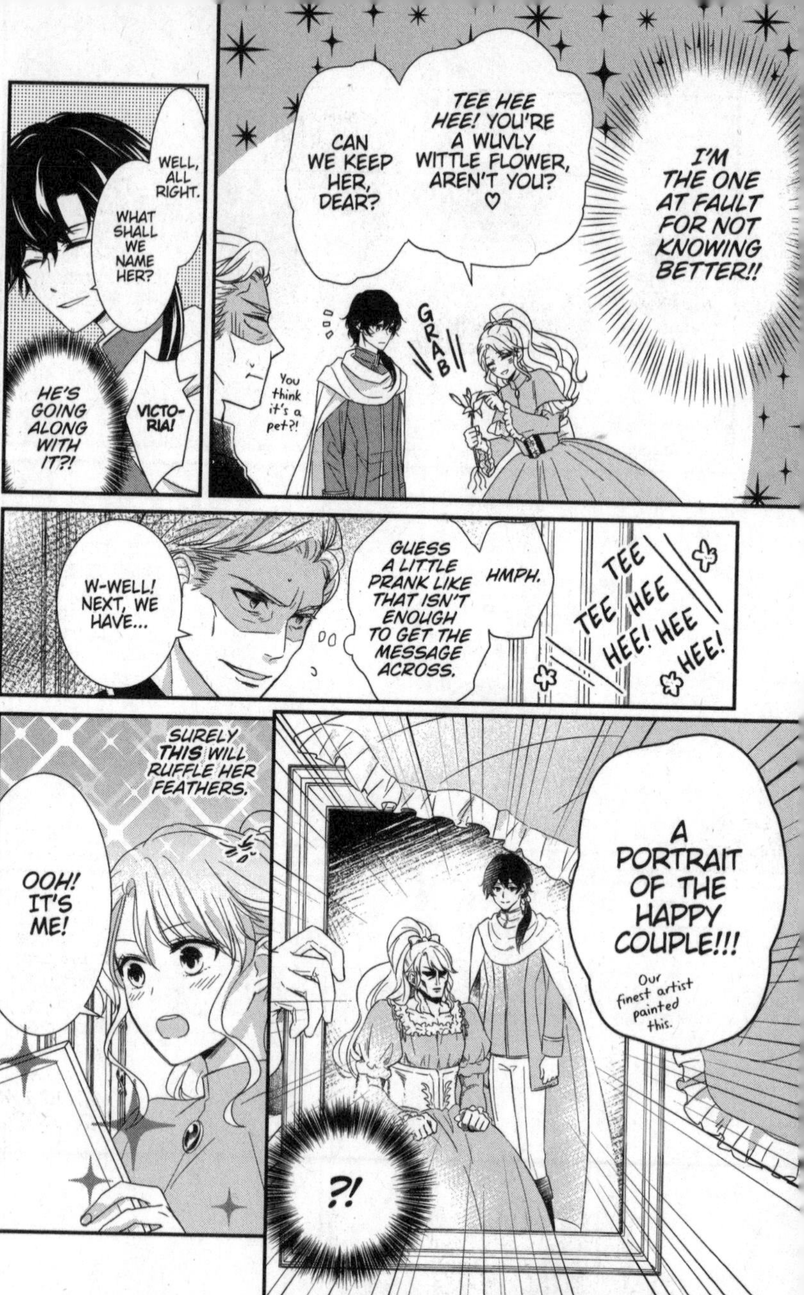
I'M THE ONE AT FAULT FOR NOT KNOWING BETTER!!
TEE HEE HEE! YOU'RE A WUVLY WITTLE FLOWER, AREN'T YOU? ♡
CAN WE KEEP HER, DEAR?
GRAB
You think it's a pet?!
WELL, ALL RIGHT.
WHAT SHALL WE NAME HER?
VICTORIA!
HE'S GOING ALONG WITH IT?!
TEE HEE HEE! TEE HEE HEE!
HMPH.
GUESS A LITTLE PRANK LIKE THAT ISN'T ENOUGH TO GET THE MESSAGE ACROSS.
W-WELL! NEXT, WE HAVE...
A PORTRAIT OF THE HAPPY COUPLE!!!
Our finest artist painted this.
?!
SURELY THIS WILL RUFFLE HER FEATHERS.
OOH! IT'S ME!

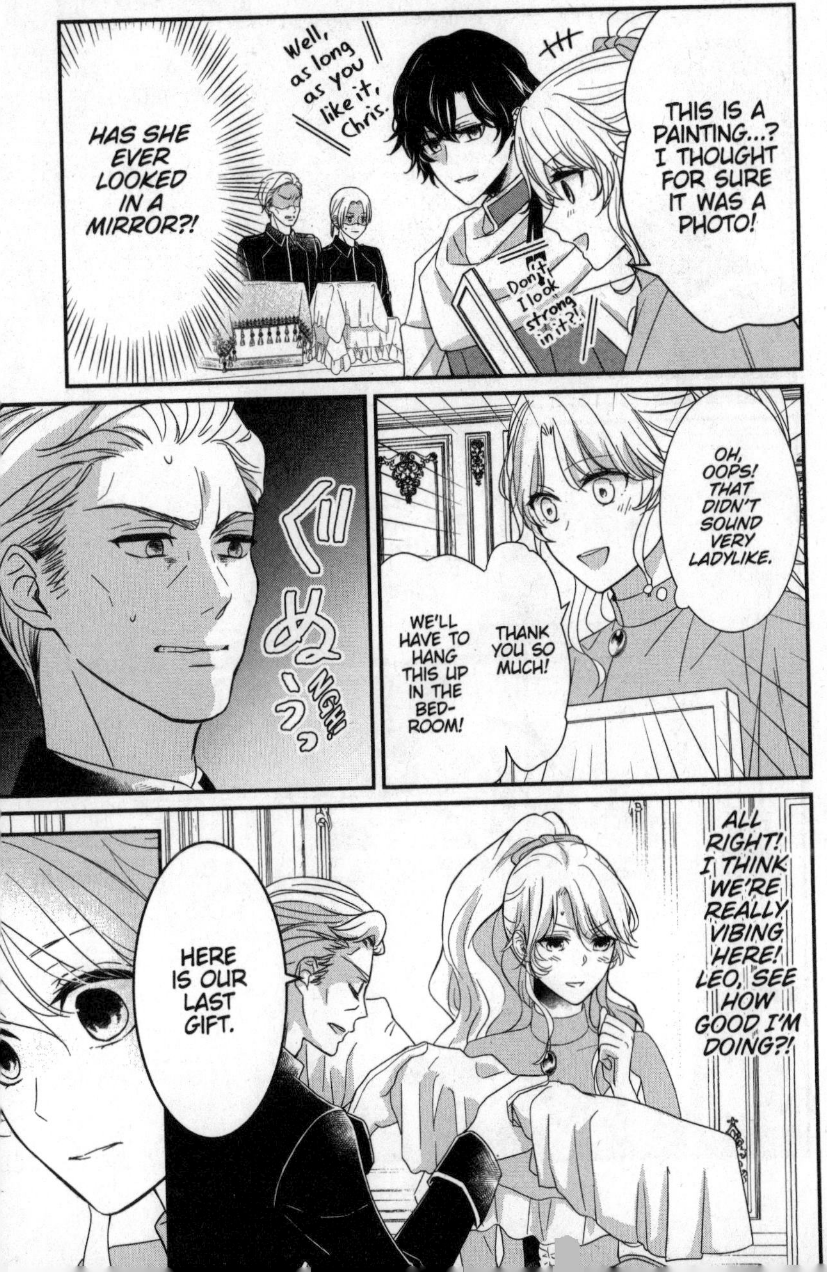
THIS IS A PAINTING...? I THOUGHT FOR SURE IT WAS A PHOTO!
Don't I look strong in it?!
Well, as long as you like it, Chris.
HAS SHE EVER LOOKED IN A MIRROR?!
OH, OOPS! THAT DIDN'T SOUND VERY LADYLIKE.
THANK YOU SO MUCH!
WE'LL HAVE TO HANG THIS UP IN THE BED-ROOM!
ぐぬっ
NGH!
ALL RIGHT! I THINK WE'RE REALLY VIBING HERE! LEO, SEE HOW GOOD I'M DOING?!
HERE IS OUR LAST GIFT.

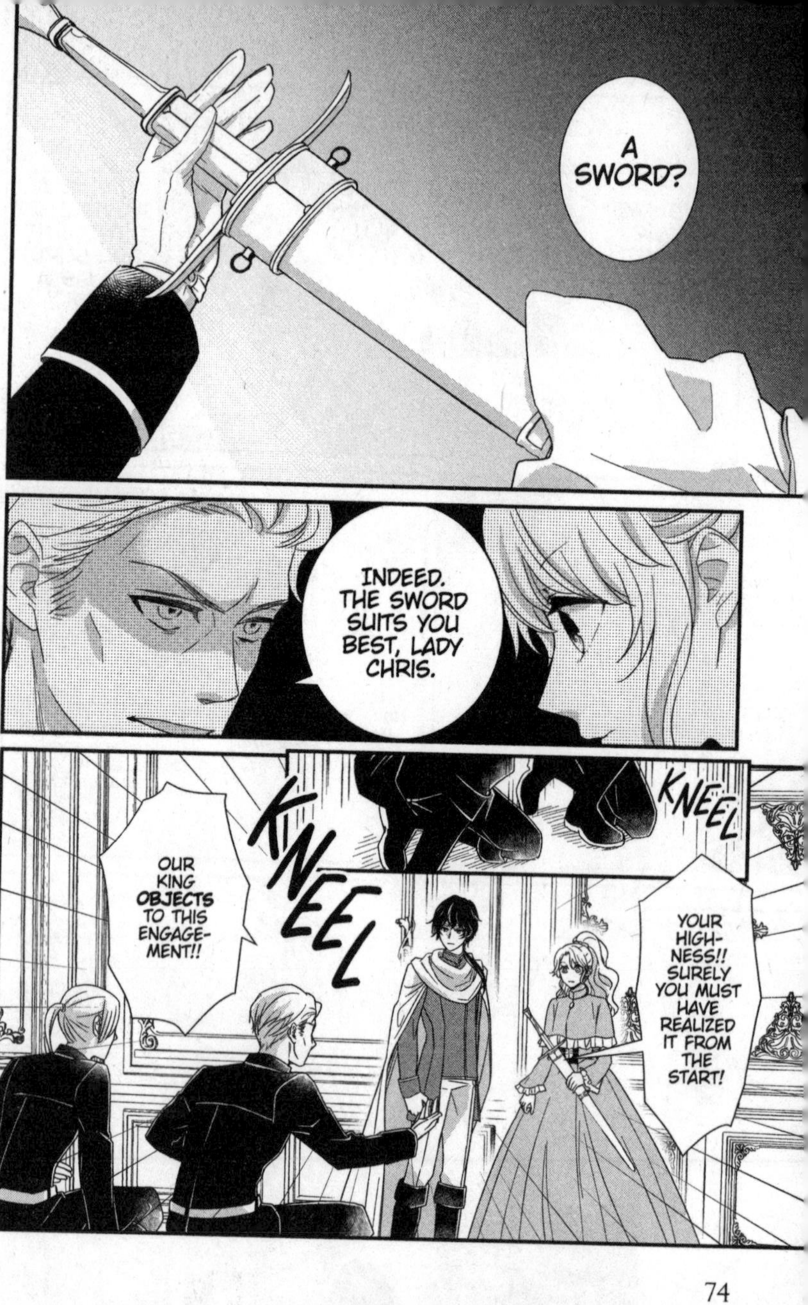
A SWORD?
INDEED. THE SWORD SUITS YOU BEST, LADY CHRIS.
KNEEL
KNEEL
YOUR HIGHNESS!! SURELY YOU MUST HAVE REALIZED IT FROM THE START!
OUR KING OBJECTS TO THIS ENGAGEMENT!!

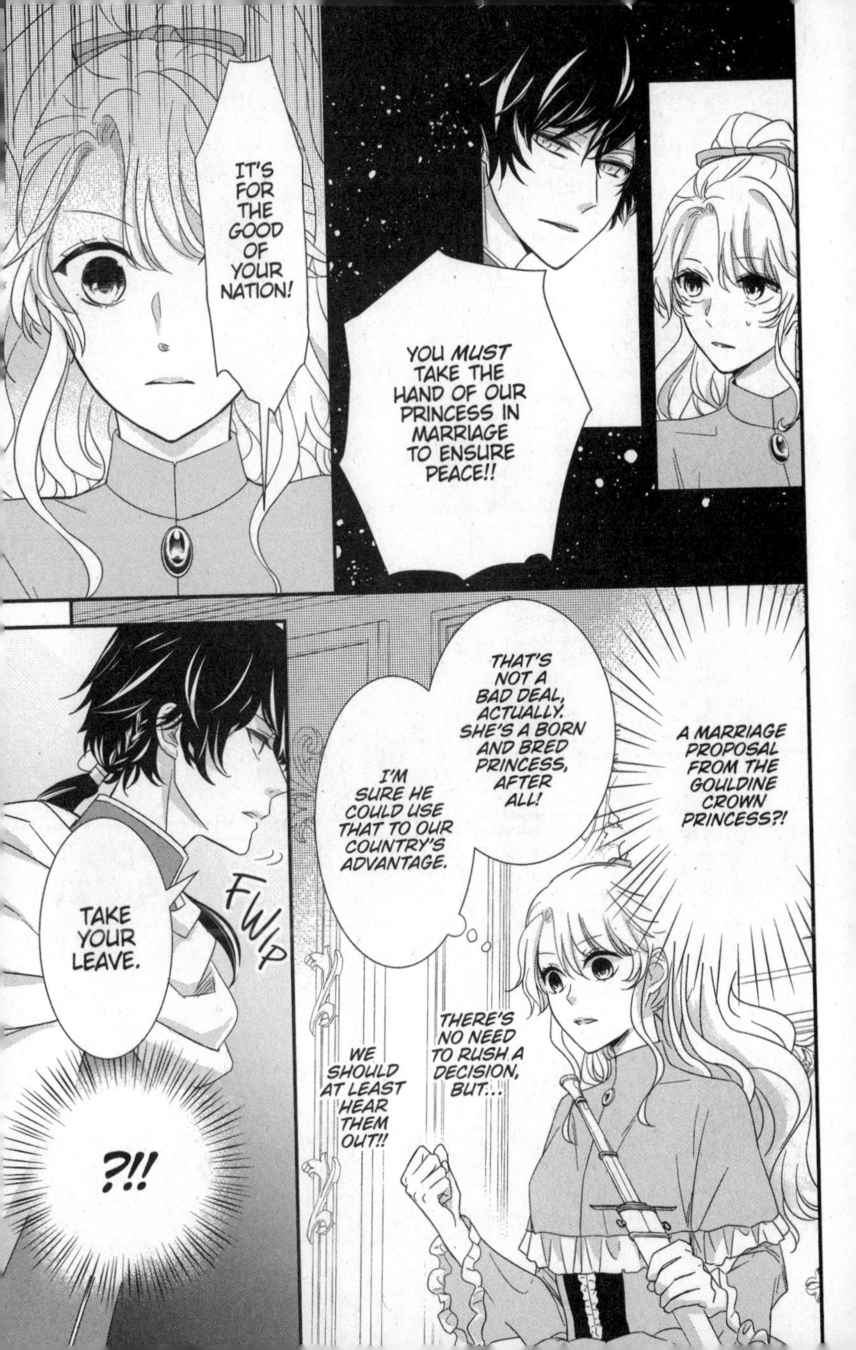
YOU MUST TAKE THE HAND OF OUR PRINCESS IN MARRIAGE TO ENSURE PEACE!!
IT'S FOR THE GOOD OF YOUR NATION!
A MARRIAGE PROPOSAL FROM THE GOULDINE CROWN PRINCESS?!
THAT'S NOT A BAD DEAL, ACTUALLY. SHE'S A BORN AND BRED PRINCESS, AFTER ALL!
I'M SURE HE COULD USE THAT TO OUR COUNTRY'S ADVANTAGE.
THERE'S NO NEED TO RUSH A DECISION, BUT...
WE SHOULD AT LEAST HEAR THEM OUT!!
TAKE YOUR LEAVE.
FWIP
?!!

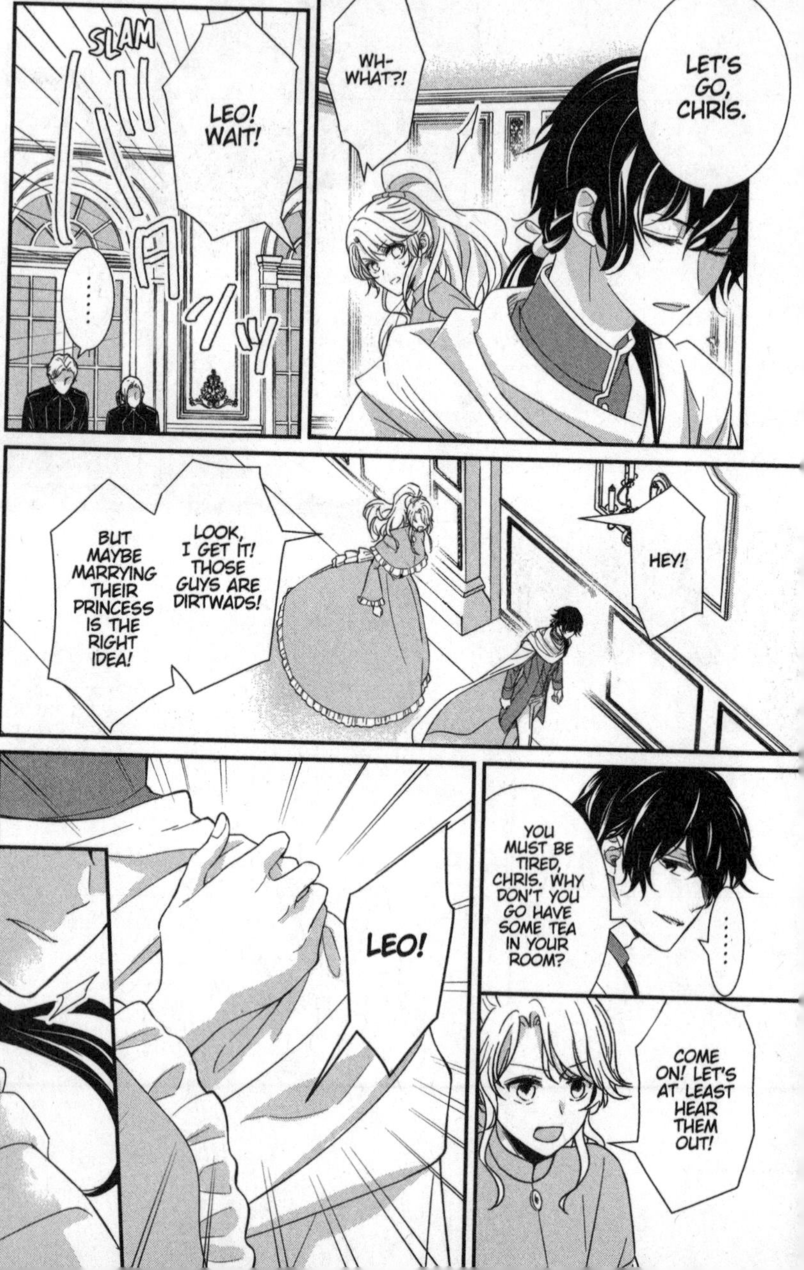
LET'S GO, CHRIS.
WH- WHAT?!
LEO! WAIT!
SLAM
......
HEY!
LOOK, I GET IT! THOSE GUYS ARE DIRTWADS!
BUT MAYBE MARRYING THEIR PRINCESS IS THE RIGHT IDEA!
YOU MUST BE TIRED, CHRIS. WHY DON'T YOU GO HAVE SOME TEA IN YOUR ROOM?
......
COME ON! LET'S AT LEAST HEAR THEM OUT!
LEO!

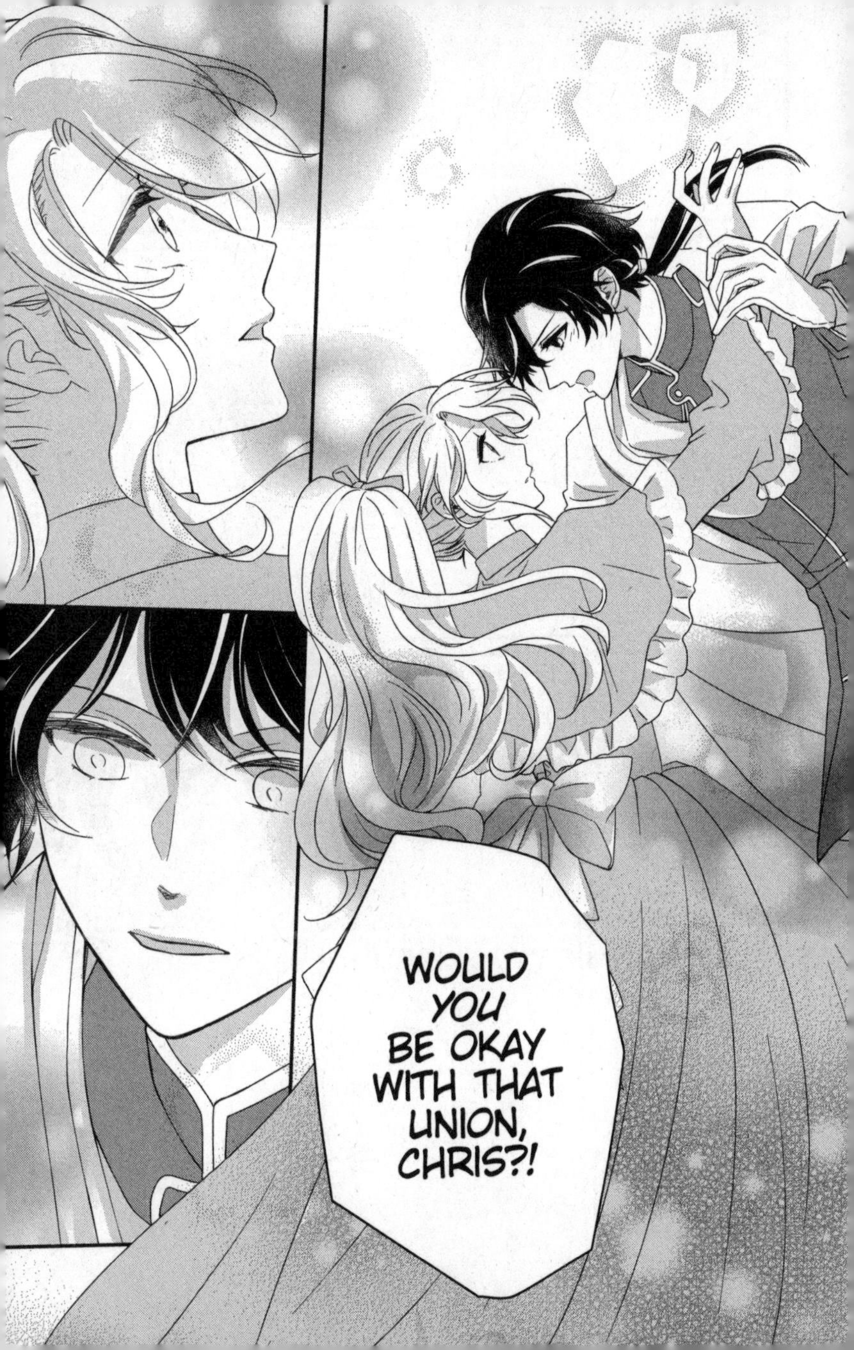
WOULD YOU BE OKAY WITH THAT UNION, CHRIS?!

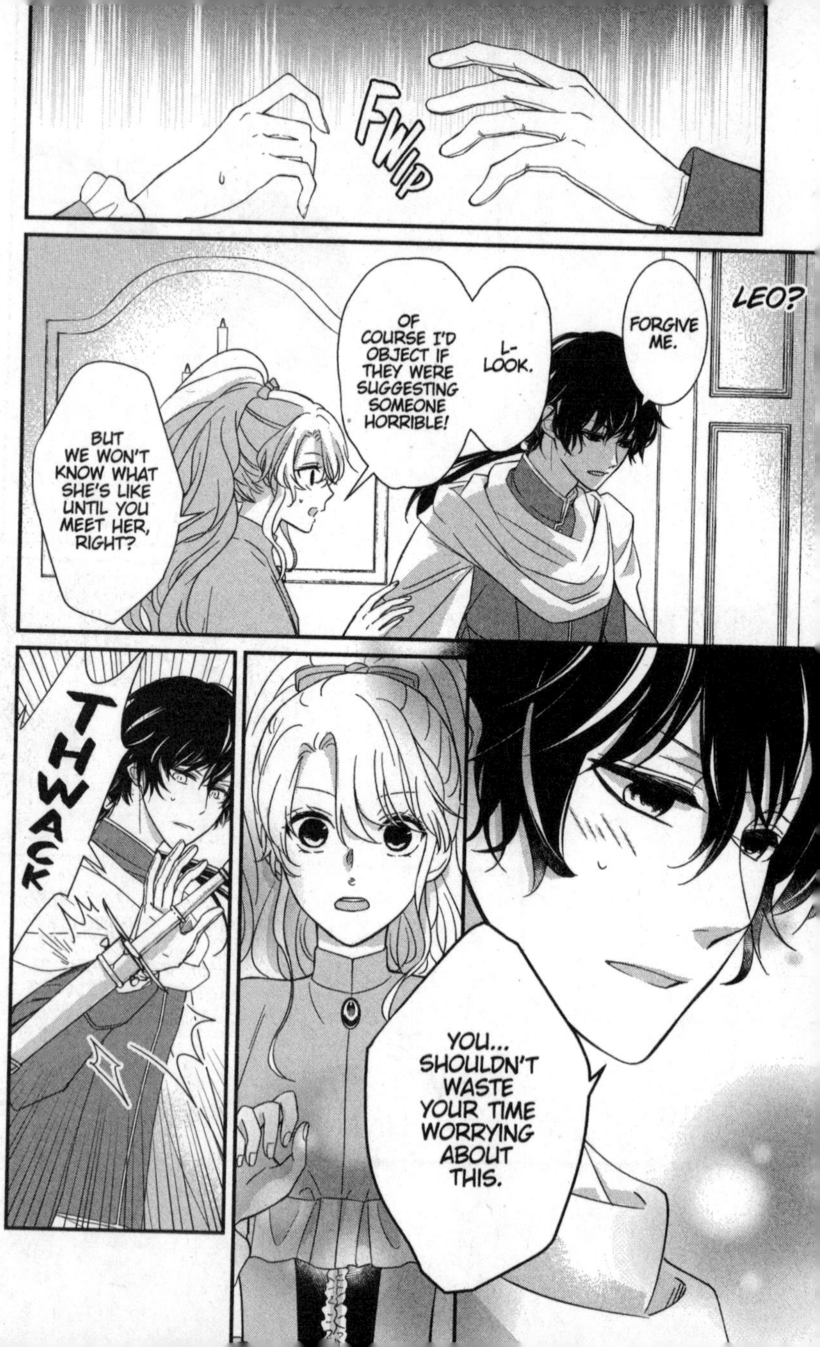
FWIP
LEO?
FORGIVE ME.
L-LOOK.
OF COURSE I'D OBJECT IF THEY WERE SUGGESTING SOMEONE HORRIBLE!
BUT WE WON'T KNOW WHAT SHE'S LIKE UNTIL YOU MEET HER, RIGHT?
YOU... SHOULDN'T WASTE YOUR TIME WORRYING ABOUT THIS.
THWACK

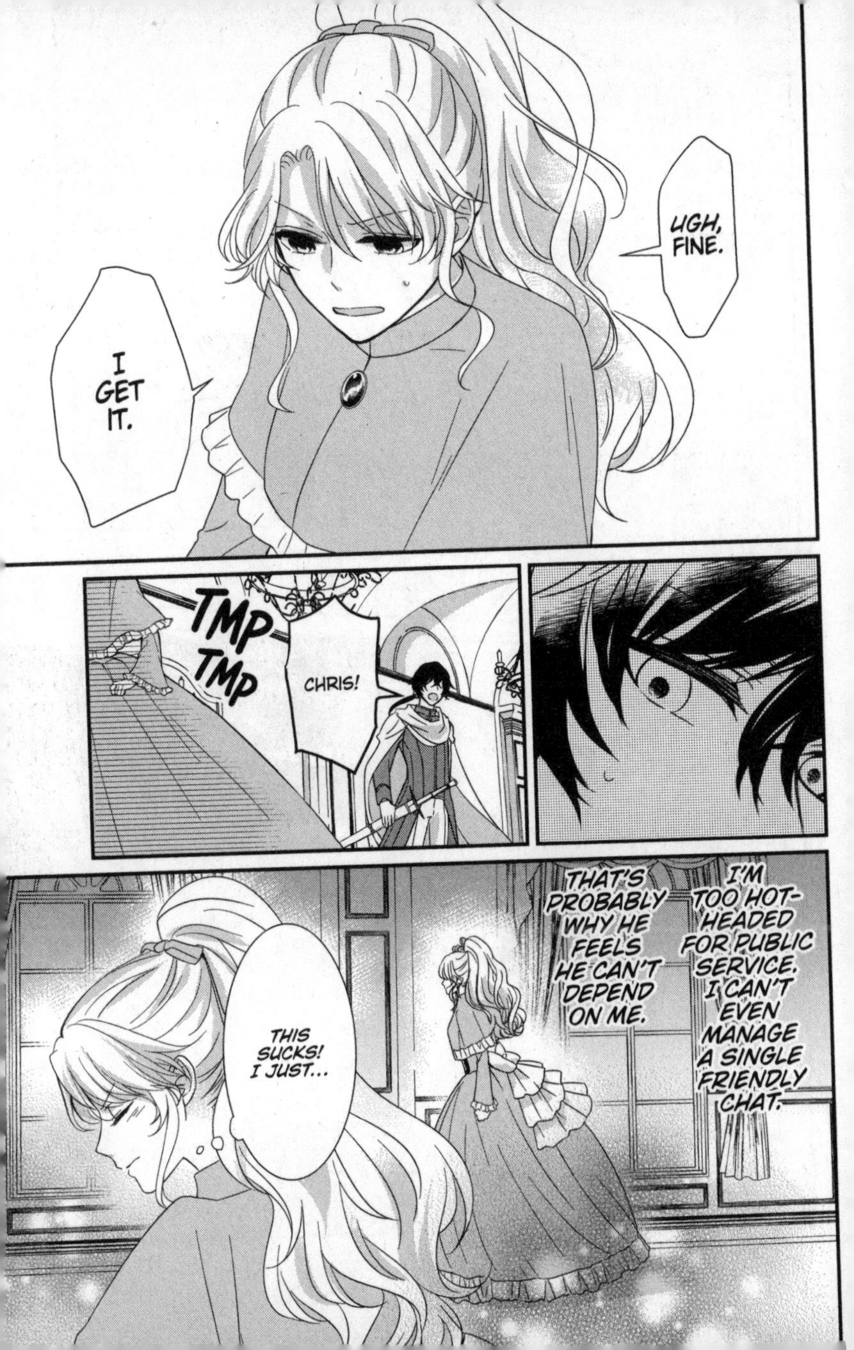
UGH, FINE.
I GET IT.
TMP TMP
CHRIS!
I'M TOO HOT-HEADED FOR PUBLIC SERVICE. I CAN'T EVEN MANAGE A SINGLE FRIENDLY CHAT.
THAT'S PROBABLY WHY HE FEELS HE CAN'T DEPEND ON ME.
THIS SUCKS! I JUST...

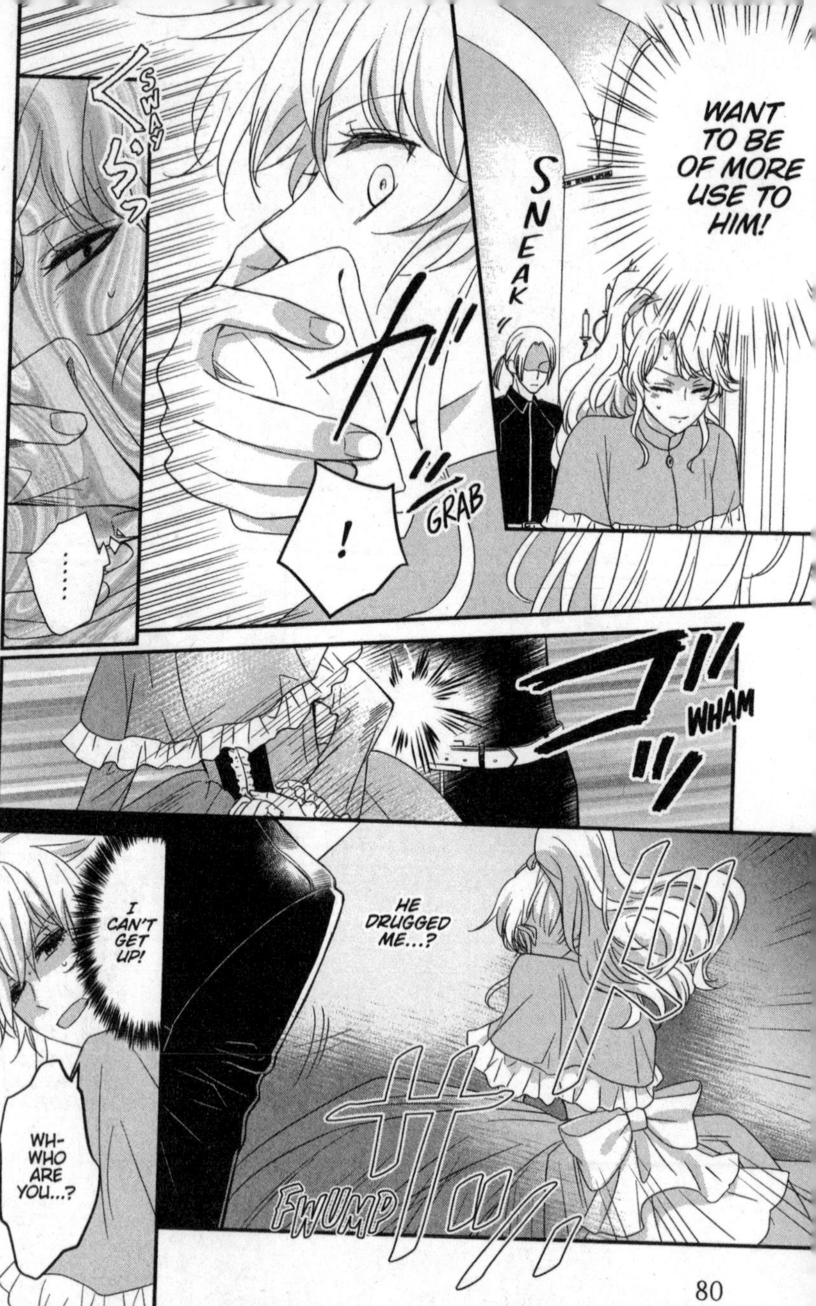
WANT TO BE OF MORE USE TO HIM!
SNEAK
GRAB
!
SWAY
......
WHAM
HE DRUGGED ME...?
FWUMP
I CAN'T GET UP!
WH-WHO ARE YOU...?

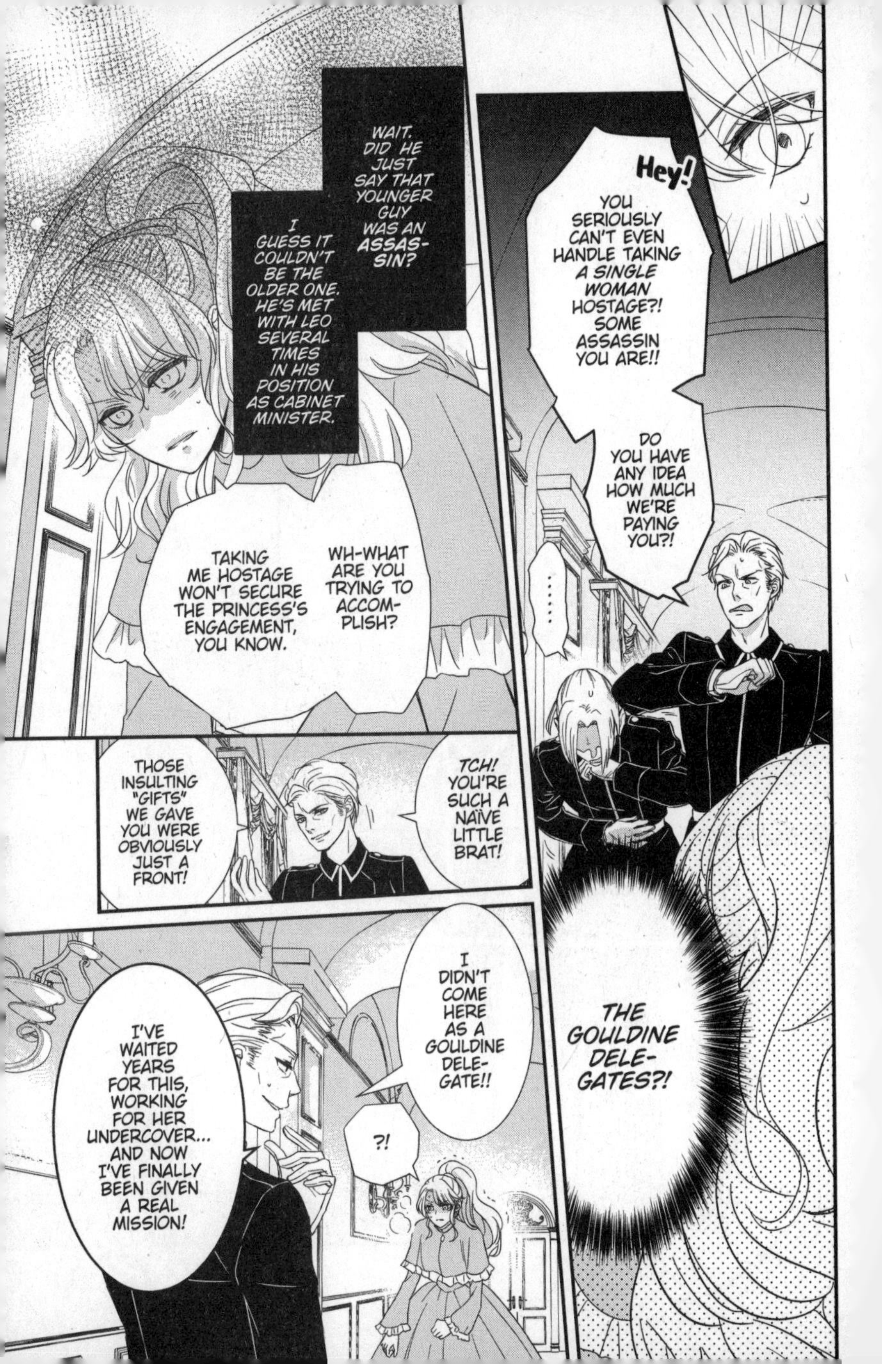
Hey!
YOU SERIOUSLY CAN'T EVEN HANDLE TAKING A SINGLE WOMAN HOSTAGE?! SOME ASSASSIN YOU ARE!!
DO YOU HAVE ANY IDEA HOW MUCH WE'RE PAYING YOU?!
......
THE GOULDINE DELE-GATES?!
WAIT. DID HE JUST SAY THAT YOUNGER GUY WAS AN ASSAS-SIN?
I GUESS IT COULDN'T BE THE OLDER ONE. HE'S MET WITH LEO SEVERAL TIMES IN HIS POSITION AS CABINET MINISTER.
WH-WHAT ARE YOU TRYING TO ACCOM-PLISH?
TAKING ME HOSTAGE WON'T SECURE THE PRINCESS'S ENGAGEMENT, YOU KNOW.
TCH! YOU'RE SUCH A NAÏVE LITTLE BRAT!
THOSE INSULTING "GIFTS" WE GAVE YOU WERE OBVIOUSLY JUST A FRONT!
I DIDN'T COME HERE AS A GOULDINE DELE-GATE!!
?!
I'VE WAITED YEARS FOR THIS, WORKING FOR HER UNDERCOVER... AND NOW I'VE FINALLY BEEN GIVEN A REAL MISSION!

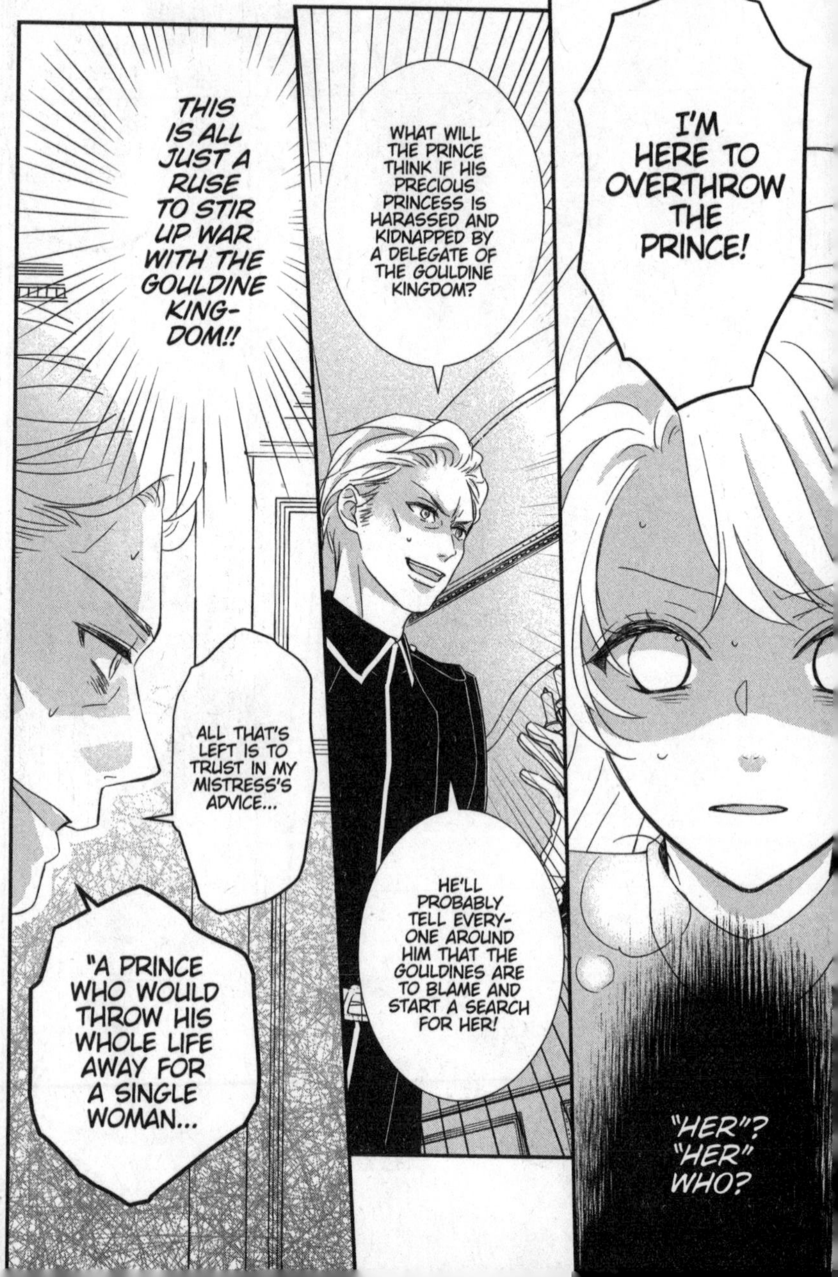
I'M HERE TO OVERTHROW THE PRINCE!
"HER"? "HER" WHO?
WHAT WILL THE PRINCE THINK IF HIS PRECIOUS PRINCESS IS HARASSED AND KIDNAPPED BY A DELEGATE OF THE GOULDINE KINGDOM?
HE'LL PROBABLY TELL EVERYONE AROUND HIM THAT THE GOULDINES ARE TO BLAME AND START A SEARCH FOR HER!
THIS IS ALL JUST A RUSE TO STIR UP WAR WITH THE GOULDINE KINGDOM!!
ALL THAT'S LEFT IS TO TRUST IN MY MISTRESS'S ADVICE...
"A PRINCE WHO WOULD THROW HIS WHOLE LIFE AWAY FOR A SINGLE WOMAN...

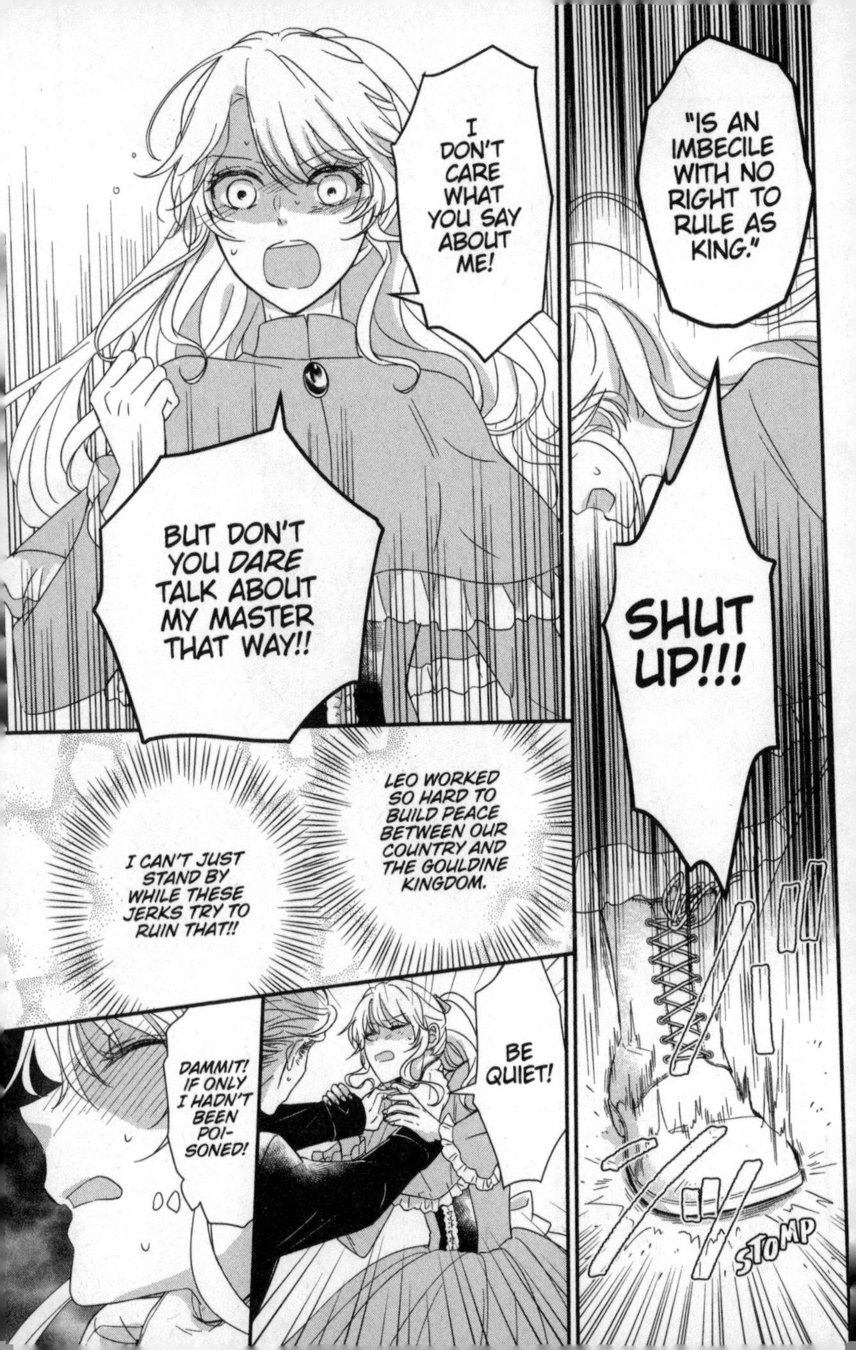
"IS AN IMBECILE WITH NO RIGHT TO RULE AS KING."
SHUT UP!!!
STOMP
I DON'T CARE WHAT YOU SAY ABOUT ME!
BUT DON'T YOU *DARE* TALK ABOUT MY MASTER THAT WAY!!
LEO WORKED SO HARD TO BUILD PEACE BETWEEN OUR COUNTRY AND THE GOULDINE KINGDOM.
I CAN'T JUST STAND BY WHILE THESE JERKS TRY TO RUIN THAT!!
BE QUIET!
DAMMIT! IF ONLY I HADN'T BEEN POI-SONED!

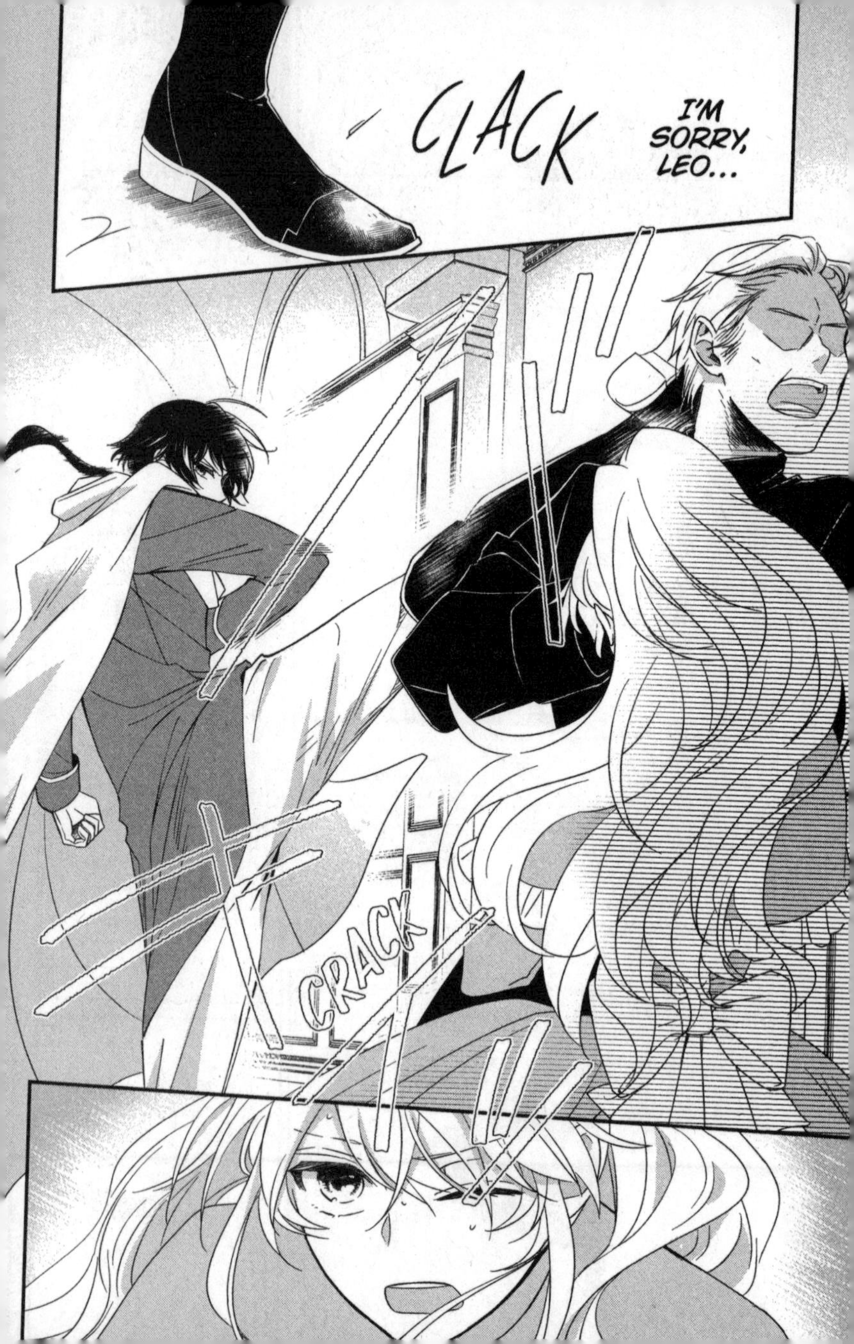
I'M SORRY, LEO...
CLACK
CRACK

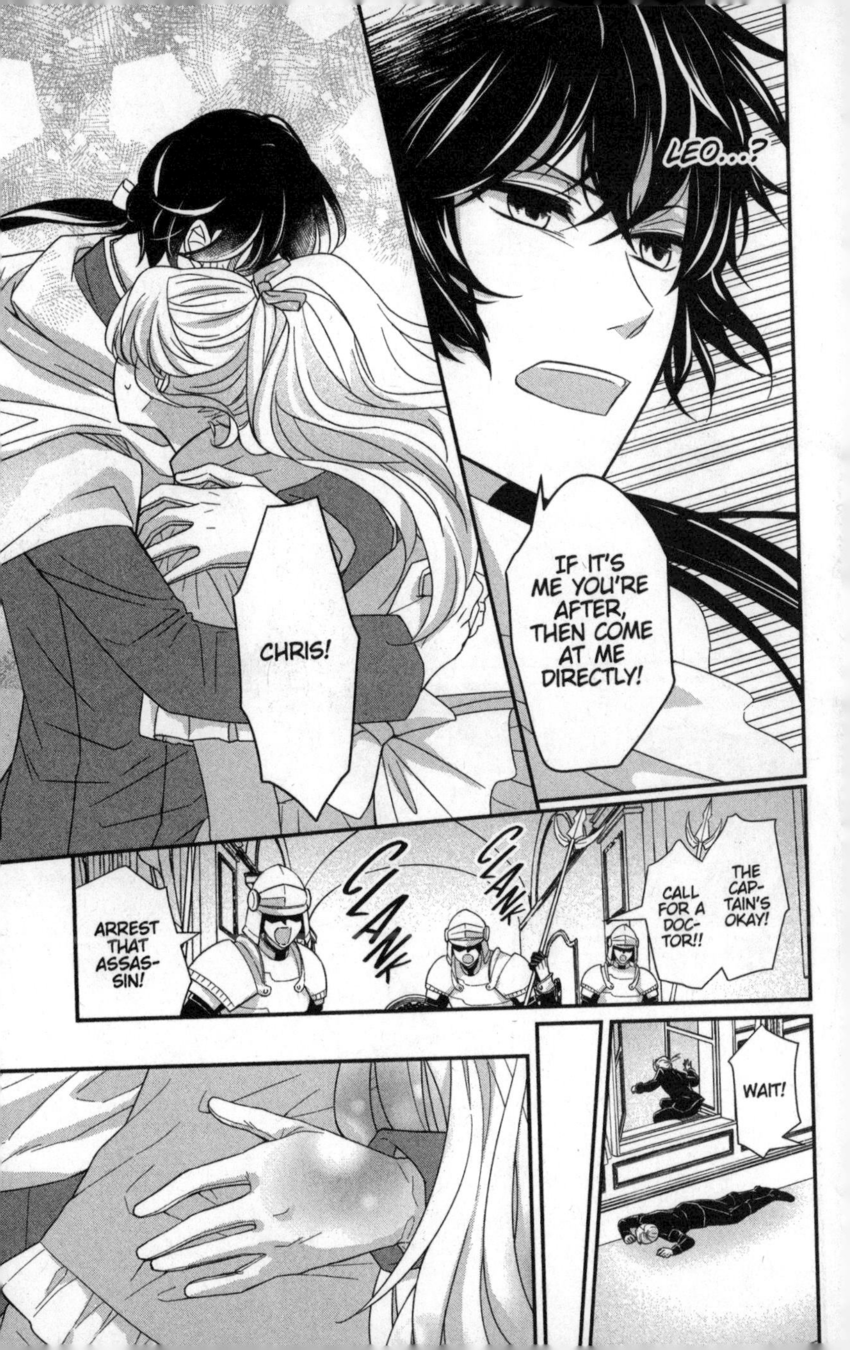
LEO...?
IF IT'S ME YOU'RE AFTER, THEN COME AT ME DIRECTLY!
CHRIS!
THE CAP-TAIN'S OKAY!
CALL FOR A DOC-TOR!!
CLANK
CLANK
ARREST THAT ASSAS-SIN!
WAIT!

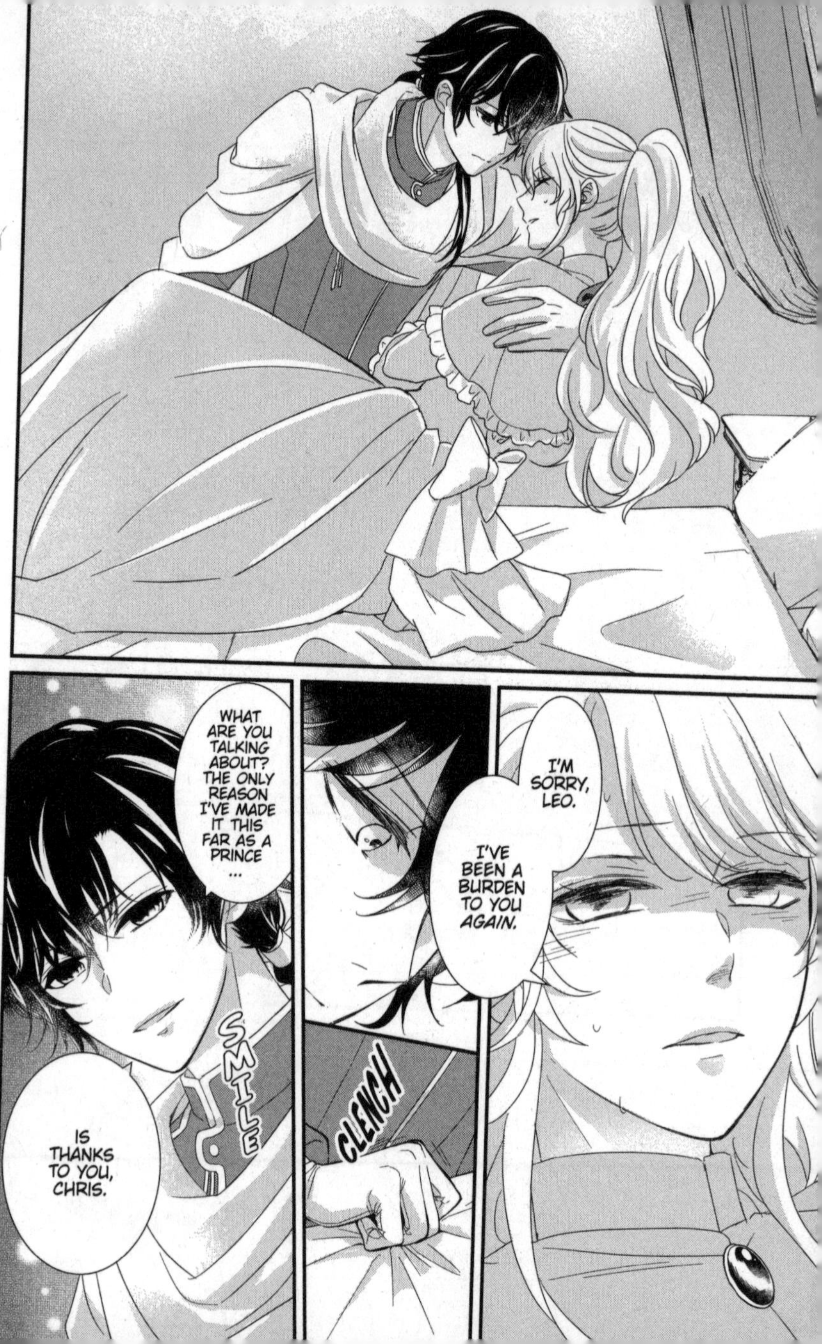
I'M SORRY, LEO.
I'VE BEEN A BURDEN TO YOU AGAIN.
CLENCH
WHAT ARE YOU TALKING ABOUT? THE ONLY REASON I'VE MADE IT THIS FAR AS A PRINCE ...
SMILE
IS THANKS TO YOU, CHRIS.

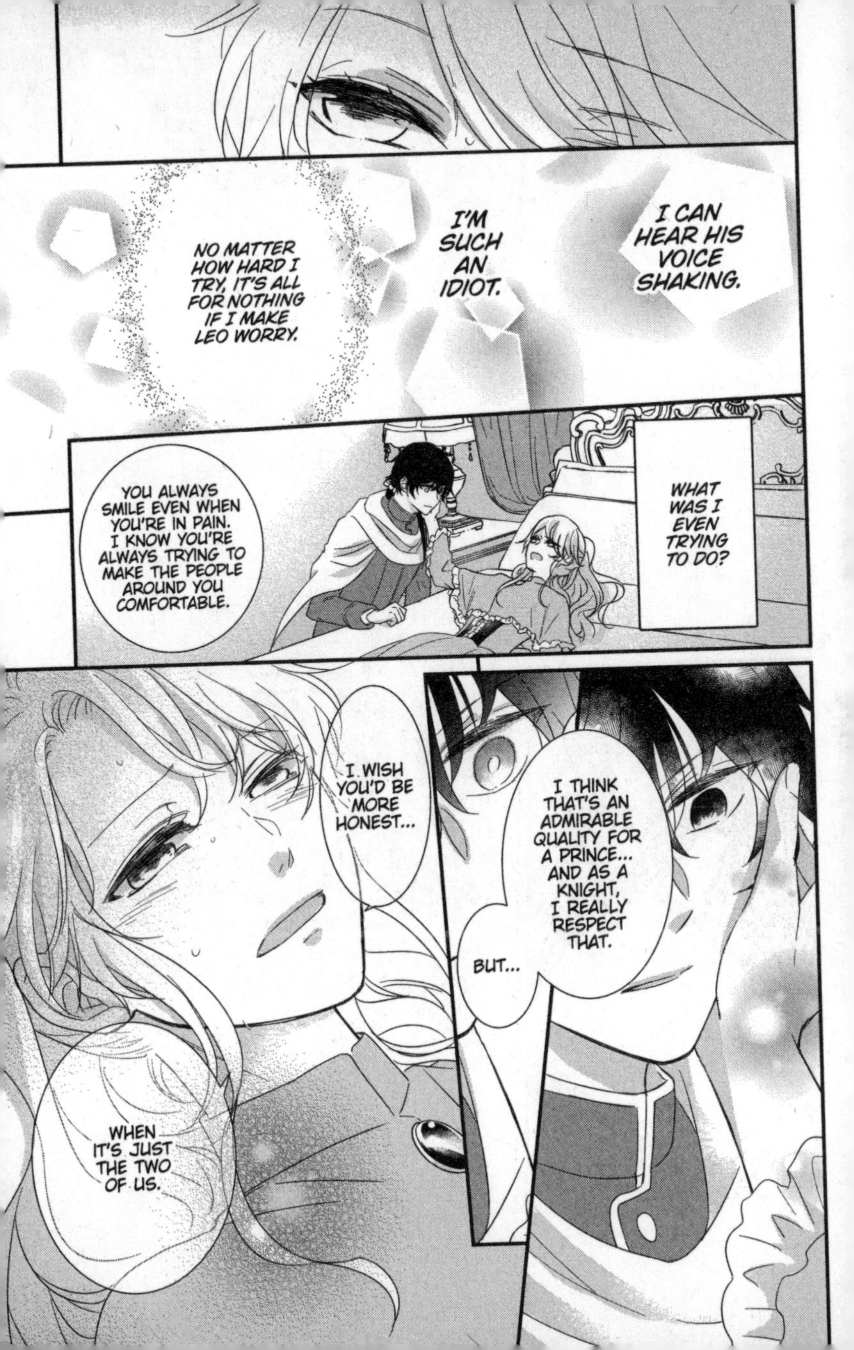
I CAN HEAR HIS VOICE SHAKING.
I'M SUCH AN IDIOT.
NO MATTER HOW HARD I TRY, IT'S ALL FOR NOTHING IF I MAKE LEO WORRY.
WHAT WAS I EVEN TRYING TO DO?
YOU ALWAYS SMILE EVEN WHEN YOU'RE IN PAIN. I KNOW YOU'RE ALWAYS TRYING TO MAKE THE PEOPLE AROUND YOU COMFORTABLE.
I THINK THAT'S AN ADMIRABLE QUALITY FOR A PRINCE... AND AS A KNIGHT, I REALLY RESPECT THAT.
BUT...
I WISH YOU'D BE MORE HONEST...
WHEN IT'S JUST THE TWO OF US.

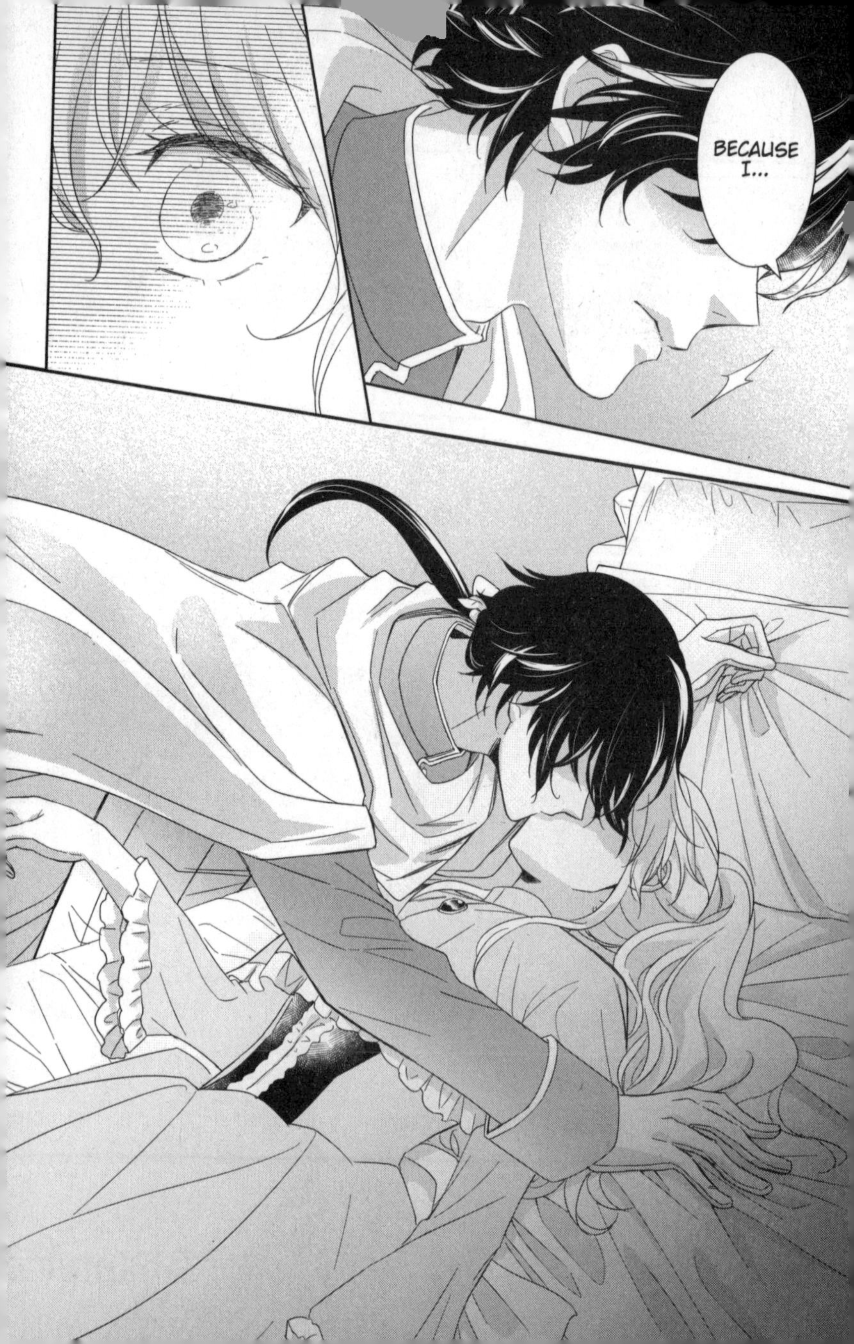
BECAUSE I...

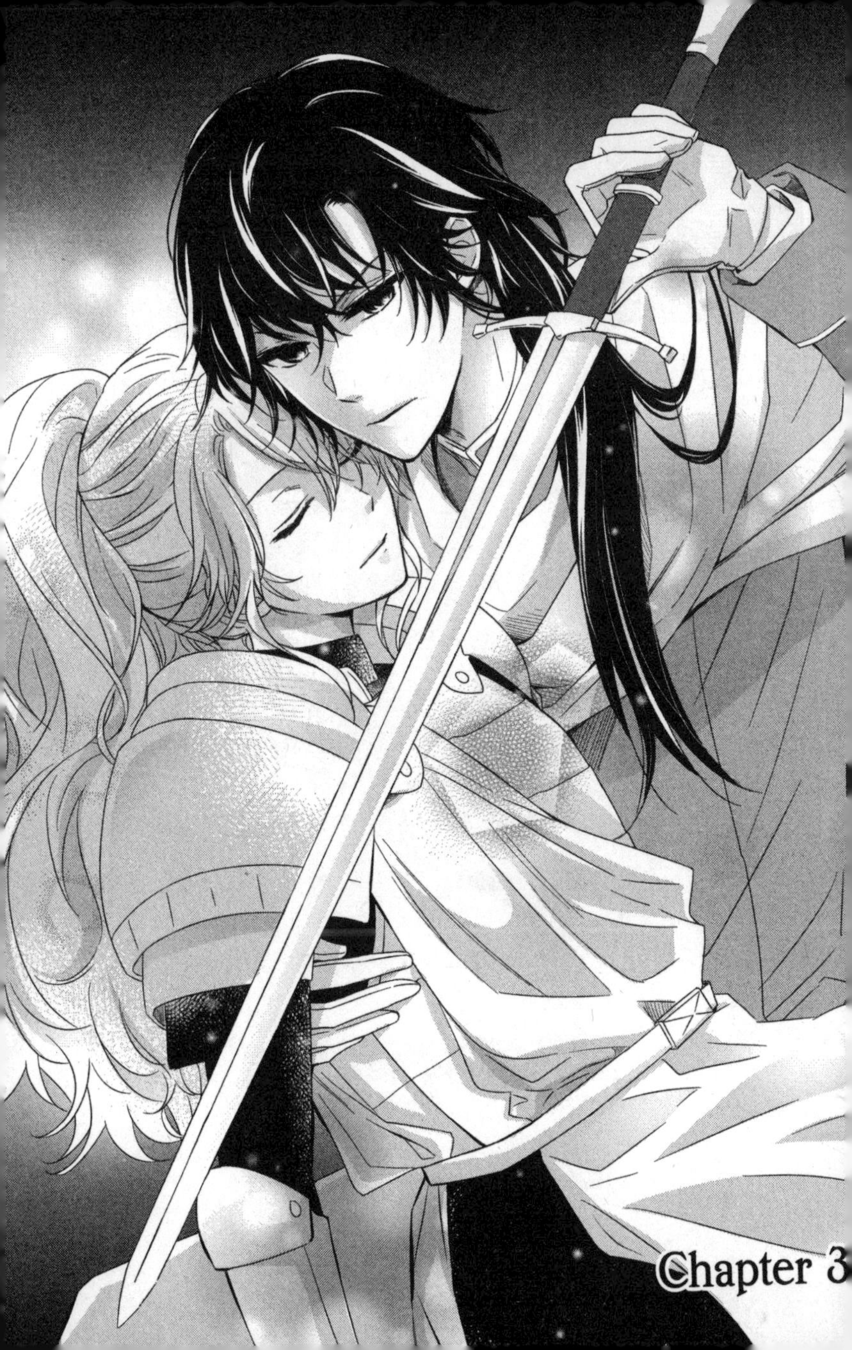
Chapter 3

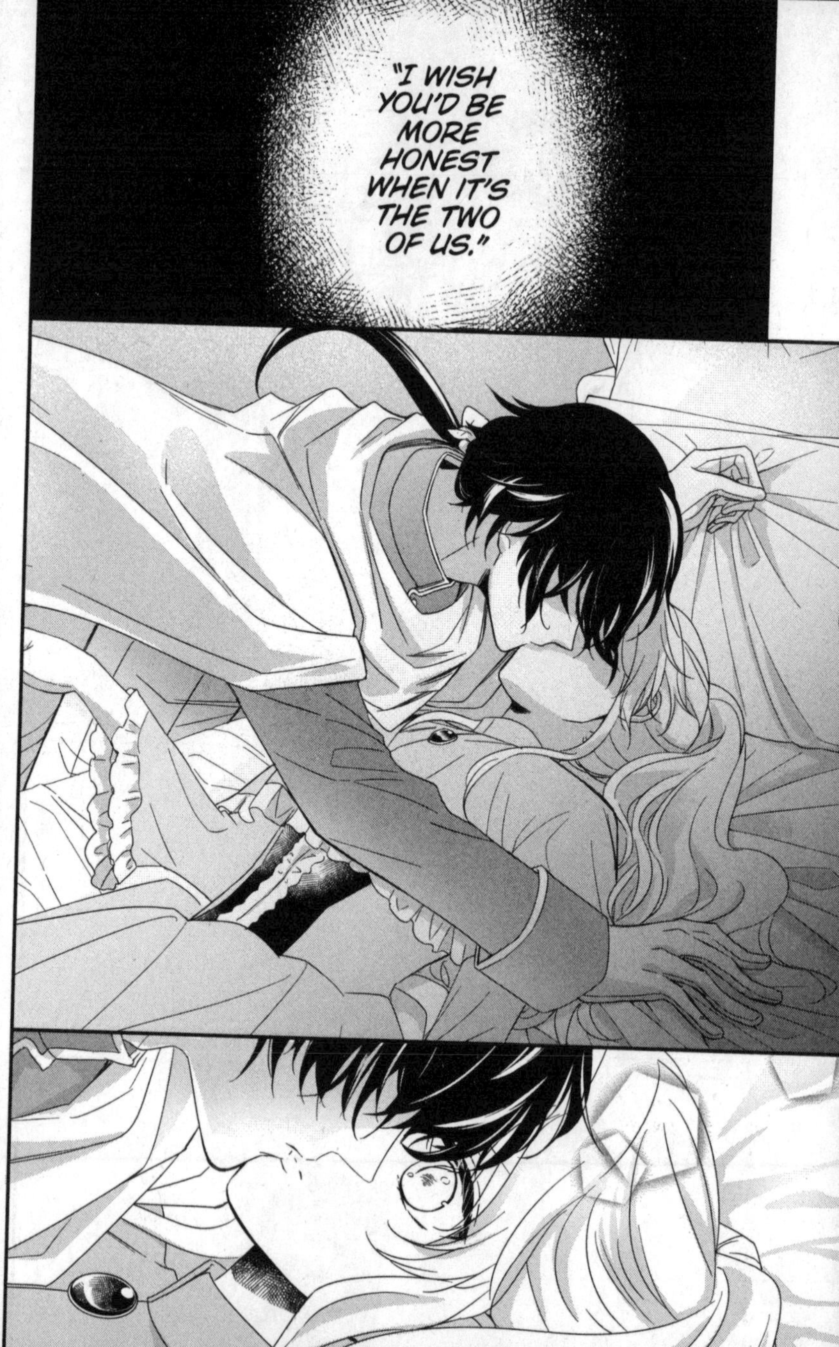
"I WISH YOU'D BE MORE HONEST WHEN IT'S THE TWO OF US."

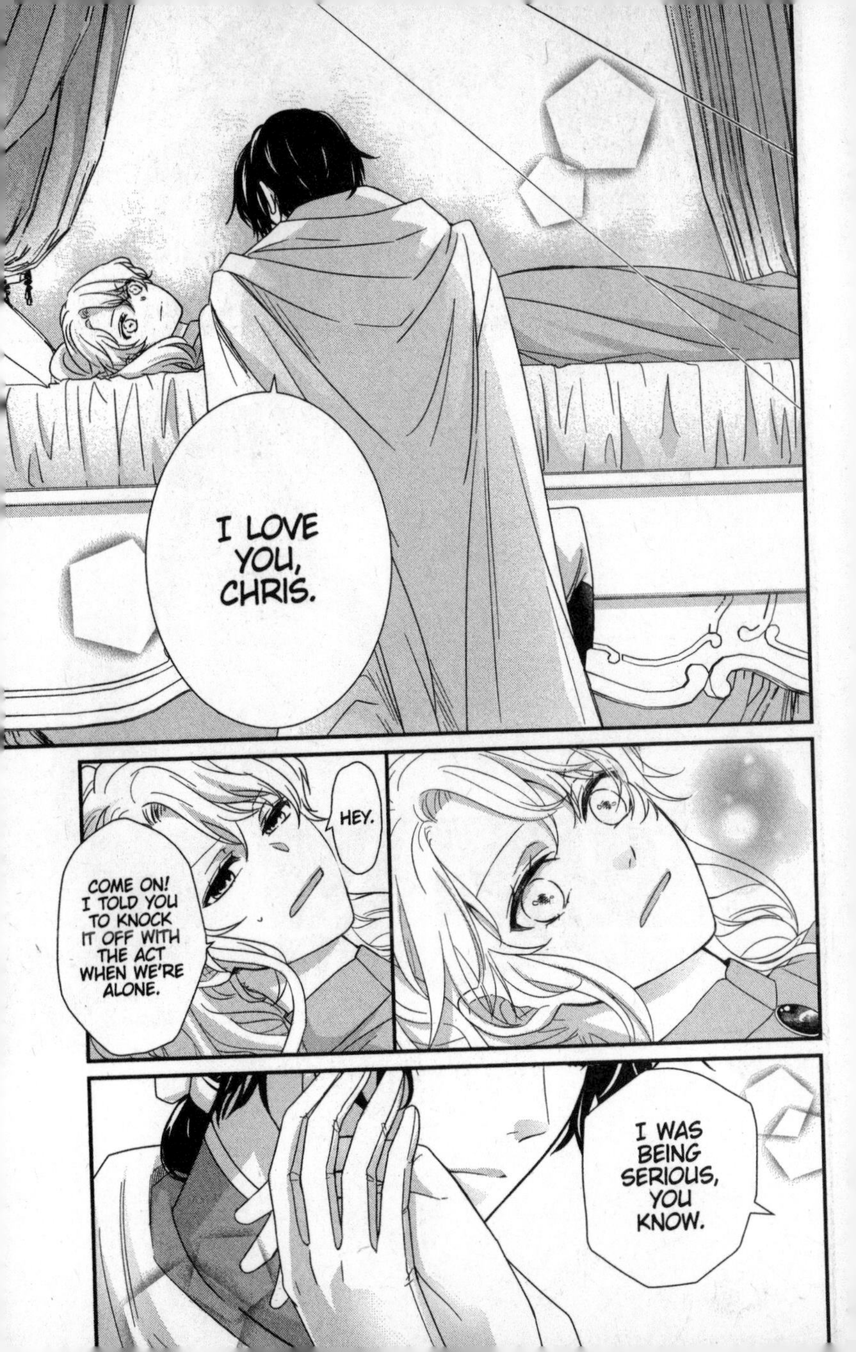
I LOVE YOU, CHRIS.
HEY.
COME ON! I TOLD YOU TO KNOCK IT OFF WITH THE ACT WHEN WE'RE ALONE.
I WAS BEING SERIOUS, YOU KNOW.

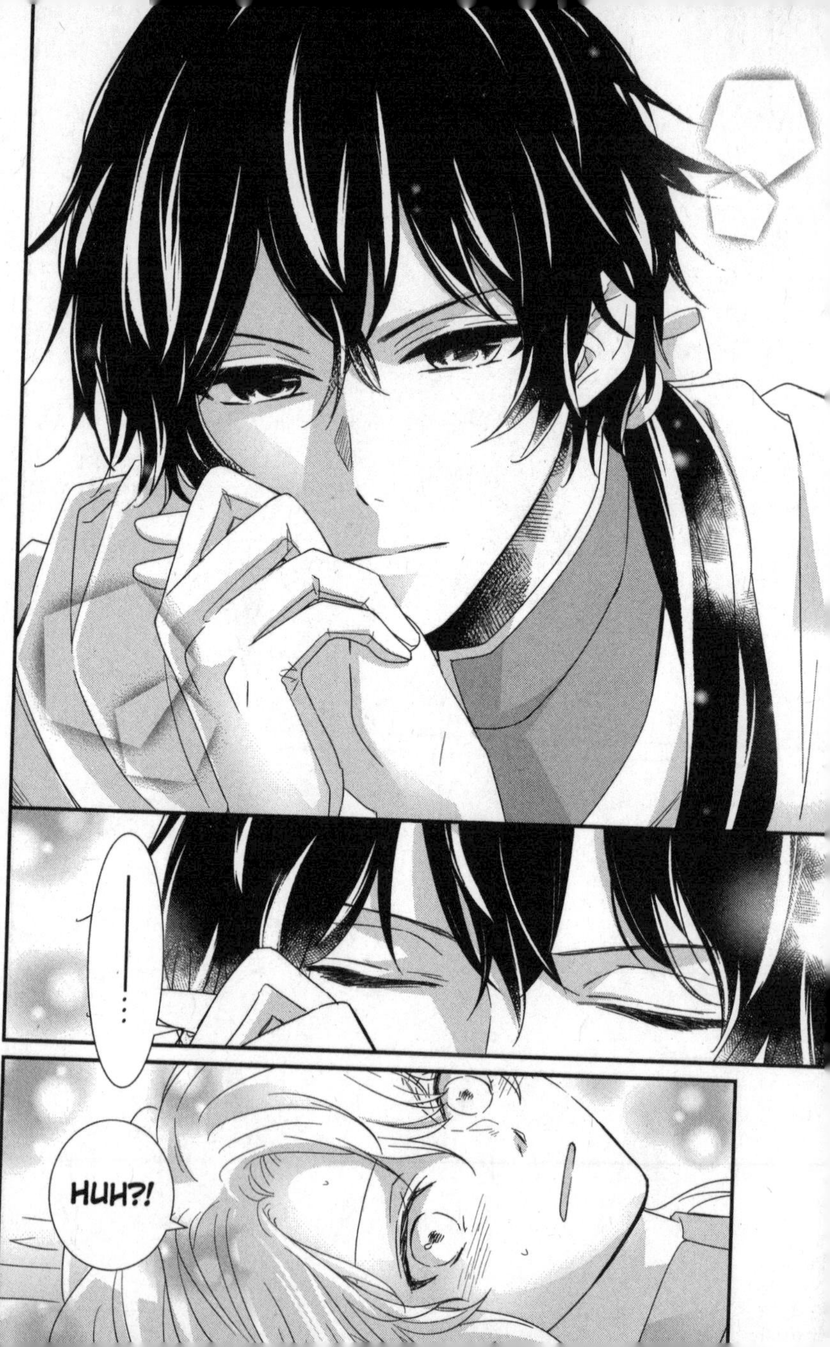

!
......
HUH?!

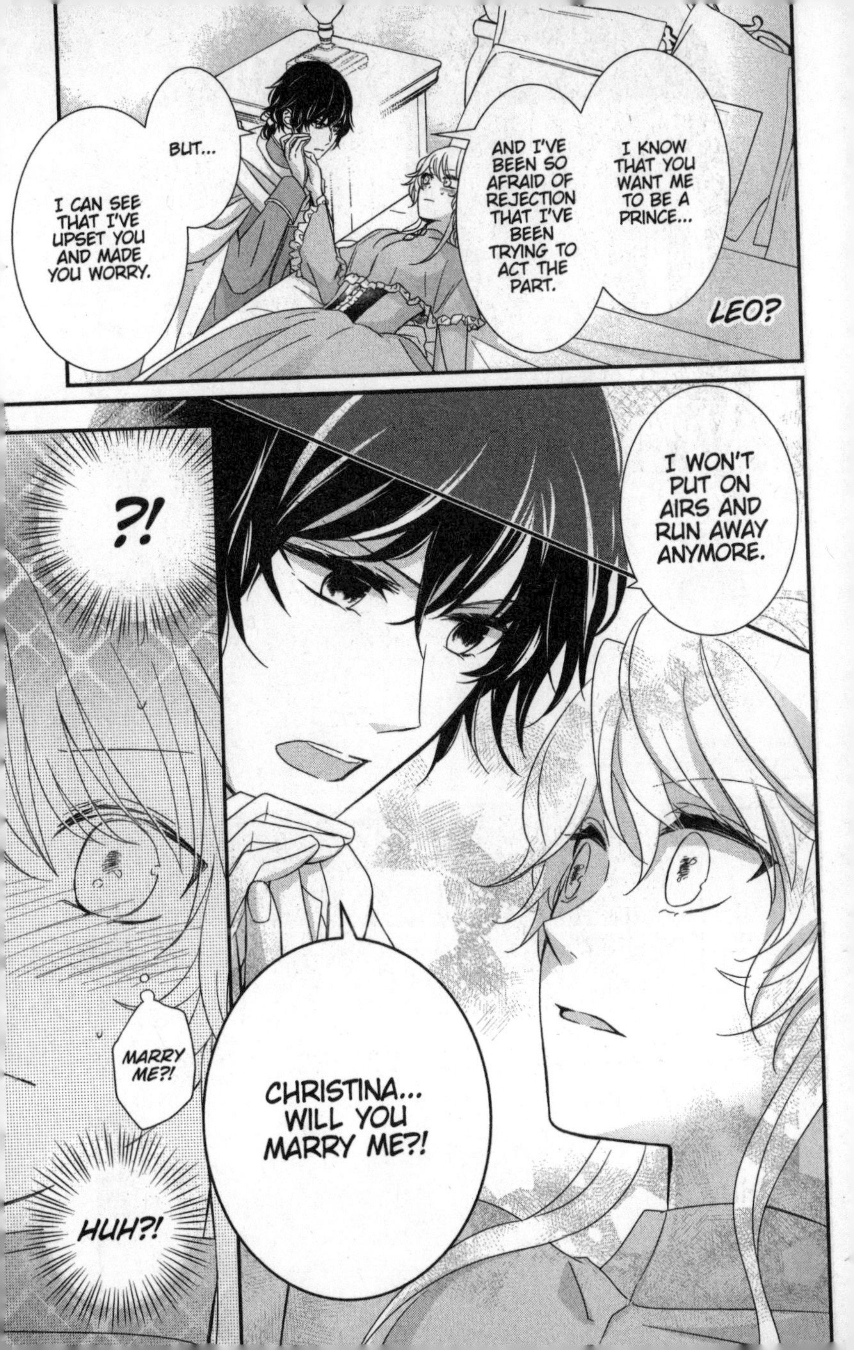
LEO?
I KNOW THAT YOU WANT ME TO BE A PRINCE...
AND I'VE BEEN SO AFRAID OF REJECTION THAT I'VE BEEN TRYING TO ACT THE PART.
BUT...
I CAN SEE THAT I'VE UPSET YOU AND MADE YOU WORRY.
I WON'T PUT ON AIRS AND RUN AWAY ANYMORE.
CHRISTINA... WILL YOU MARRY ME?!
?!
MARRY ME?!
HUH?!

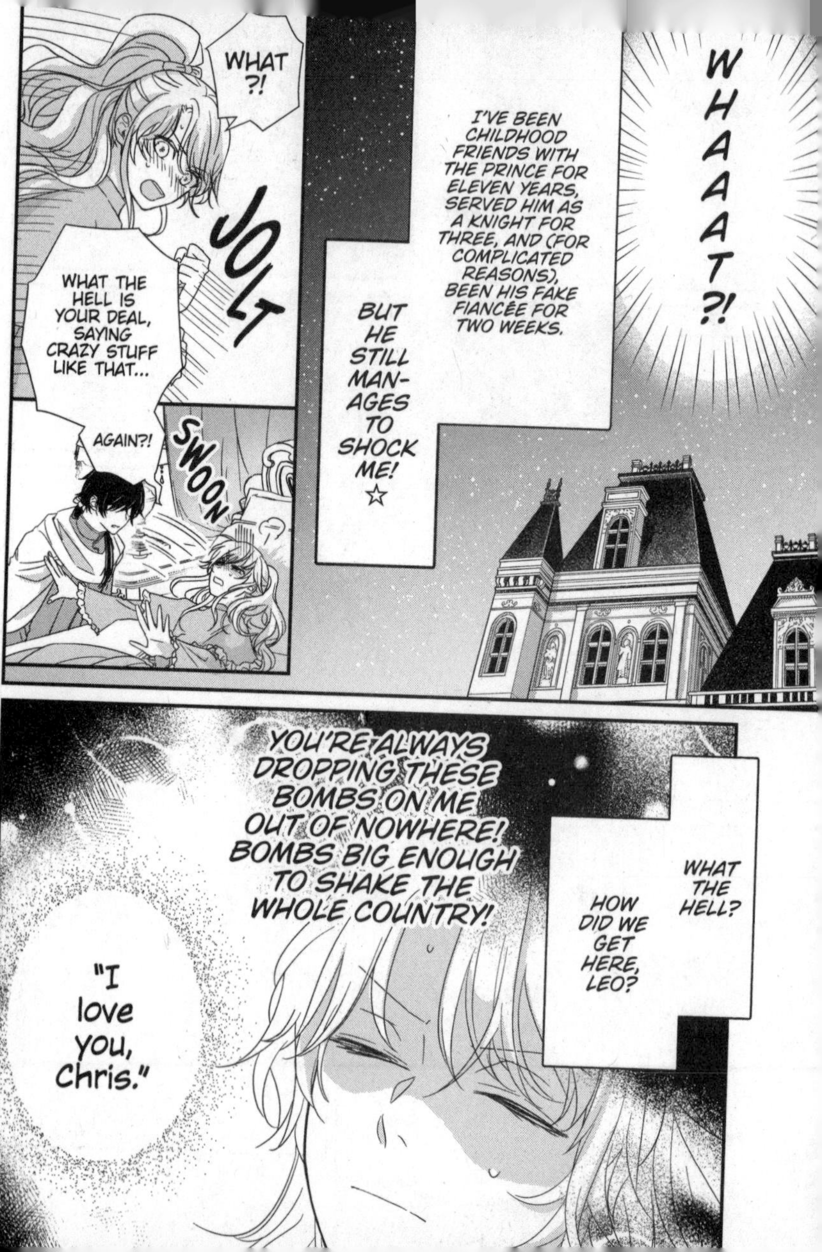
WHAAAT?!
I'VE BEEN CHILDHOOD FRIENDS WITH THE PRINCE FOR ELEVEN YEARS, SERVED HIM AS A KNIGHT FOR THREE, AND (FOR COMPLICATED REASONS), BEEN HIS FAKE FIANCÉE FOR TWO WEEKS.
BUT HE STILL MAN-AGES TO SHOCK ME! ☆
WHAT?!
JOLT
WHAT THE HELL IS YOUR DEAL, SAYING CRAZY STUFF LIKE THAT...
SWOON
AGAIN?!
WHAT THE HELL?
HOW DID WE GET HERE, LEO?
YOU'RE ALWAYS DROPPING THESE BOMBS ON ME OUT OF NOWHERE! BOMBS BIG ENOUGH TO SHAKE THE WHOLE COUNTRY!
"I love you, Chris."

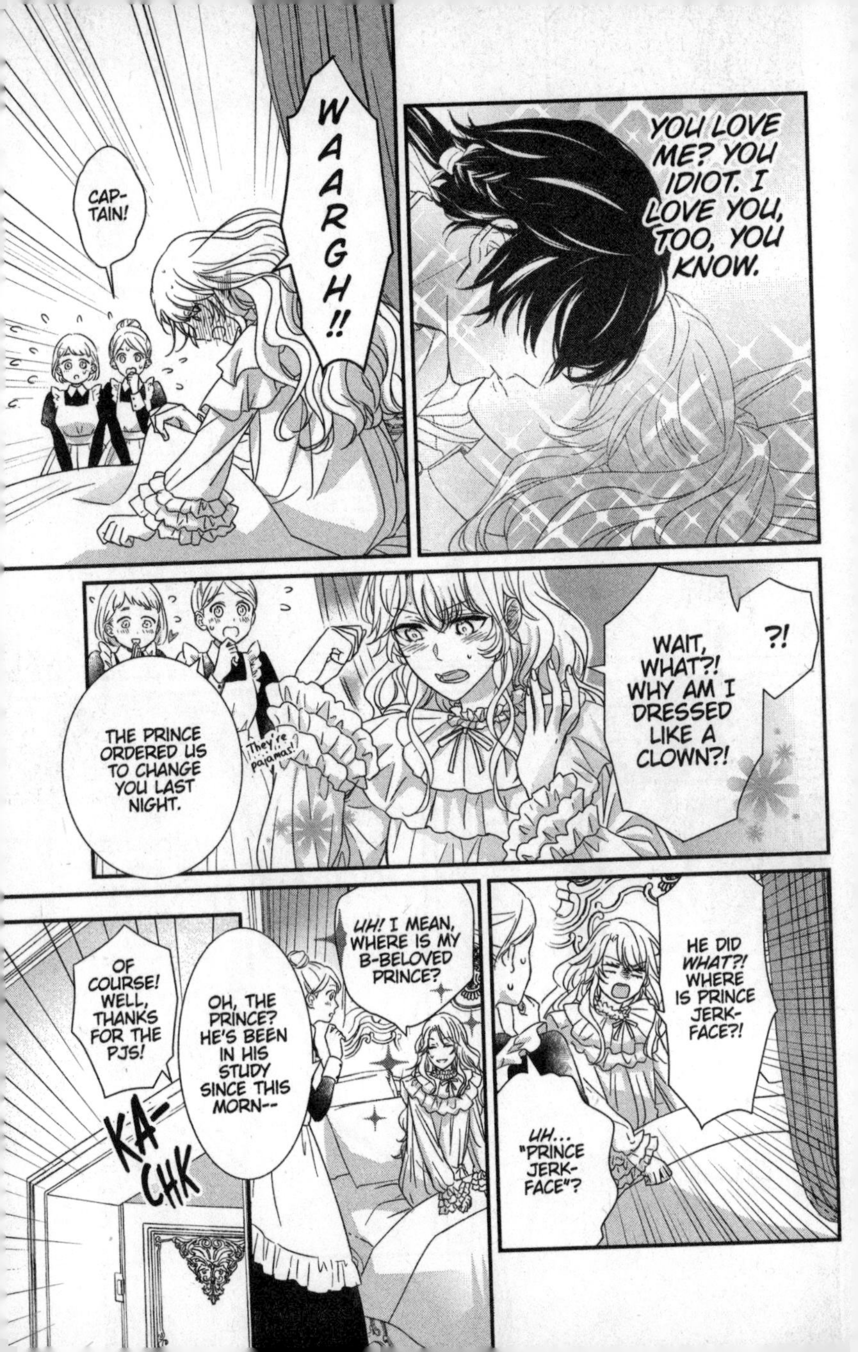
YOU LOVE ME? YOU IDIOT. I LOVE YOU, TOO, YOU KNOW.
WAAARGH!!
CAP-TAIN!
?!
WAIT, WHAT?! WHY AM I DRESSED LIKE A CLOWN?!
They're pajamas!
THE PRINCE ORDERED US TO CHANGE YOU LAST NIGHT.
HE DID WHAT?! WHERE IS PRINCE JERK-FACE?!
UH... "PRINCE JERK-FACE"?
UH! I MEAN, WHERE IS MY B-BELOVED PRINCE?
OH, THE PRINCE? HE'S BEEN IN HIS STUDY SINCE THIS MORN--
OF COURSE! WELL, THANKS FOR THE PJS!
KA-CHK

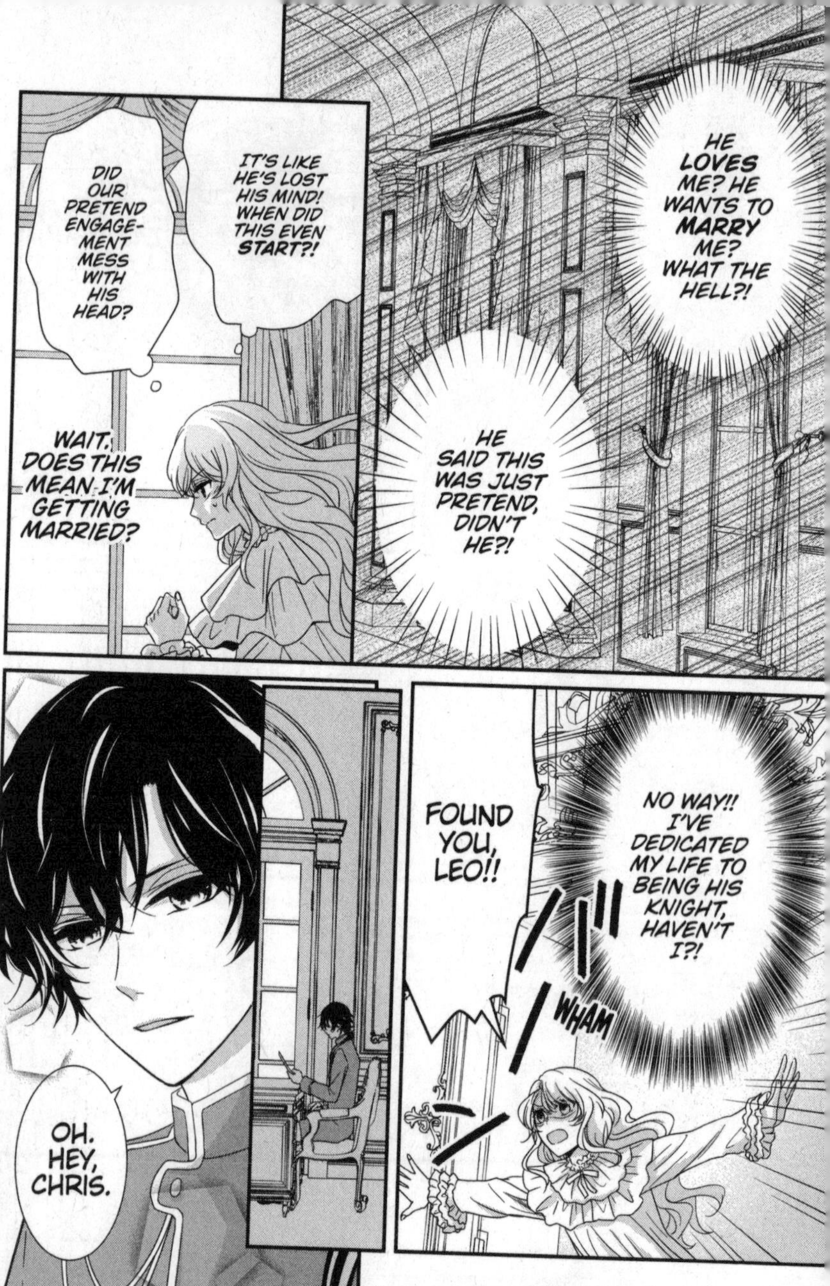
HE LOVES ME? HE WANTS TO MARRY ME? WHAT THE HELL?!
HE SAID THIS WAS JUST PRETEND, DIDN'T HE?!
IT'S LIKE HE'S LOST HIS MIND! WHEN DID THIS EVEN START?!
DID OUR PRETEND ENGAGEMENT MESS WITH HIS HEAD?
WAIT. DOES THIS MEAN I'M GETTING MARRIED?
NO WAY!! I'VE DEDICATED MY LIFE TO BEING HIS KNIGHT, HAVEN'T I?!
WHAM
FOUND YOU, LEO!!
OH. HEY, CHRIS.

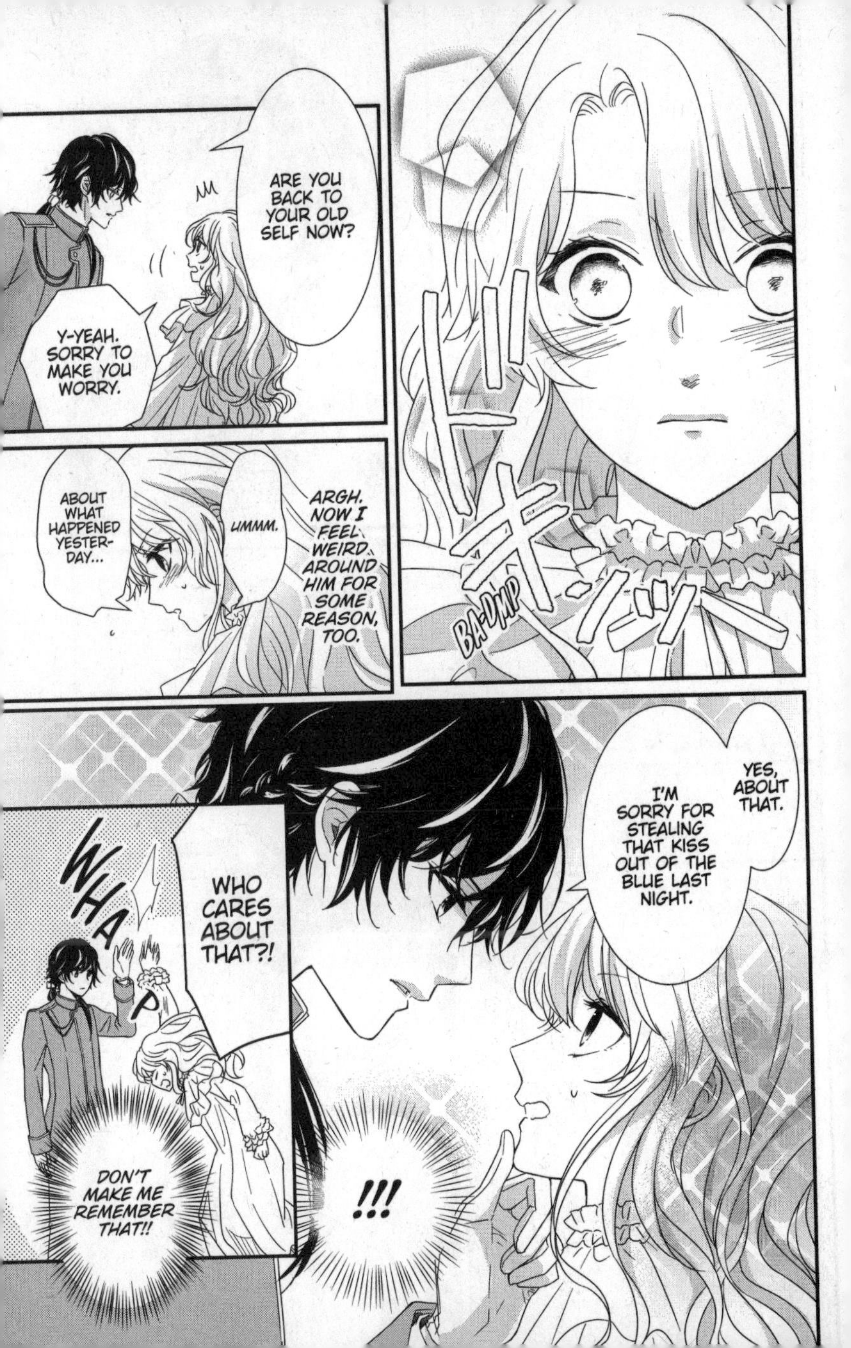
BA-DMP
ARE YOU BACK TO YOUR OLD SELF NOW?
Y-YEAH. SORRY TO MAKE YOU WORRY.
ARGH. NOW I FEEL WEIRD AROUND HIM FOR SOME REASON, TOO.
UMMM.
ABOUT WHAT HAPPENED YESTER-DAY...
YES, ABOUT THAT.
I'M SORRY FOR STEALING THAT KISS OUT OF THE BLUE LAST NIGHT.
WHO CARES ABOUT THAT?!
!!!
WHAP
DON'T MAKE ME REMEMBER THAT!!

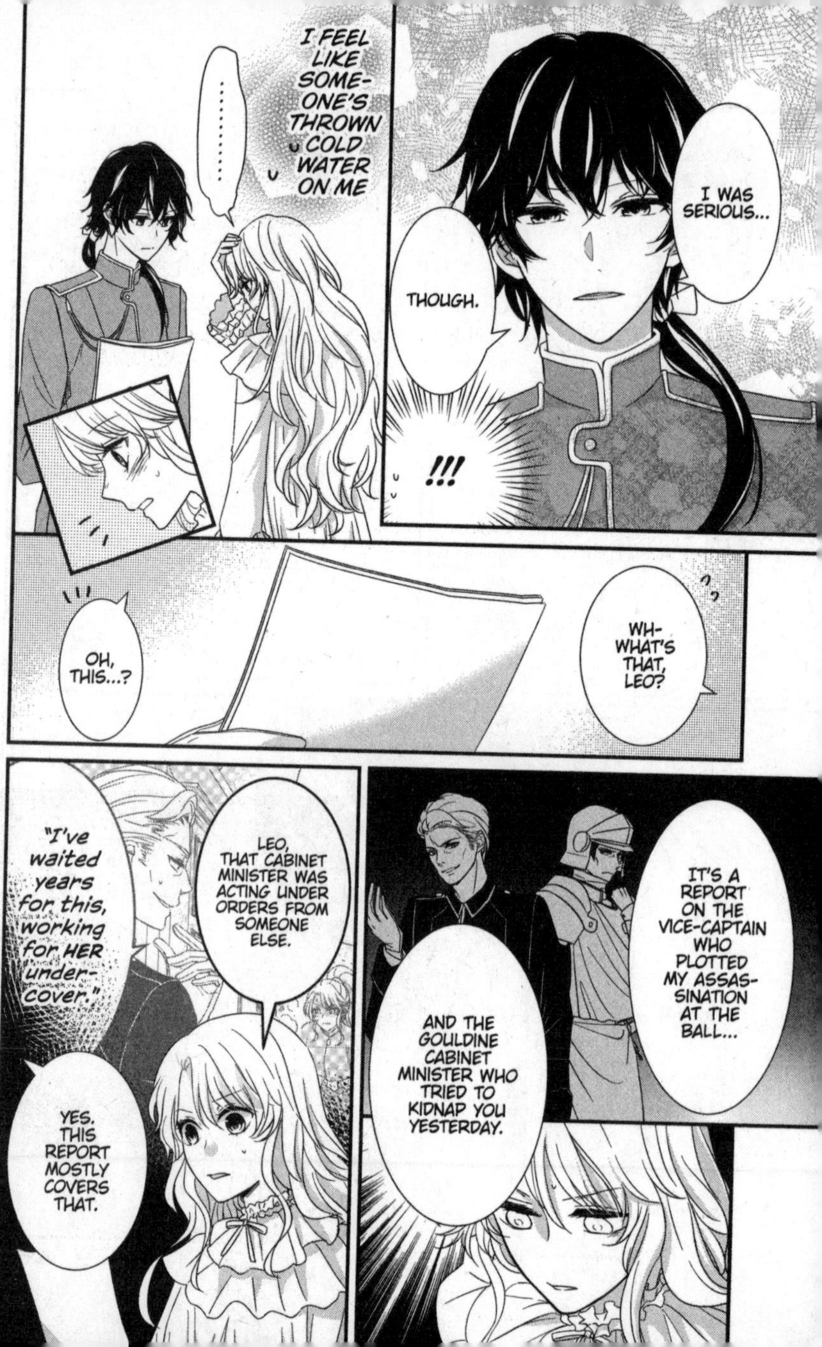
I WAS SERIOUS...
THOUGH.
!!!
I FEEL LIKE SOME-ONE'S THROWN COLD WATER ON ME
......
WH-WHAT'S THAT, LEO?
OH, THIS...?
IT'S A REPORT ON THE VICE-CAPTAIN WHO PLOTTED MY ASSAS-SINATION AT THE BALL...
AND THE GOULDINE CABINET MINISTER WHO TRIED TO KIDNAP YOU YESTERDAY.
LEO, THAT CABINET MINISTER WAS ACTING UNDER ORDERS FROM SOMEONE ELSE.
"I've waited years for this, working for HER under-cover."
YES. THIS REPORT MOSTLY COVERS THAT.

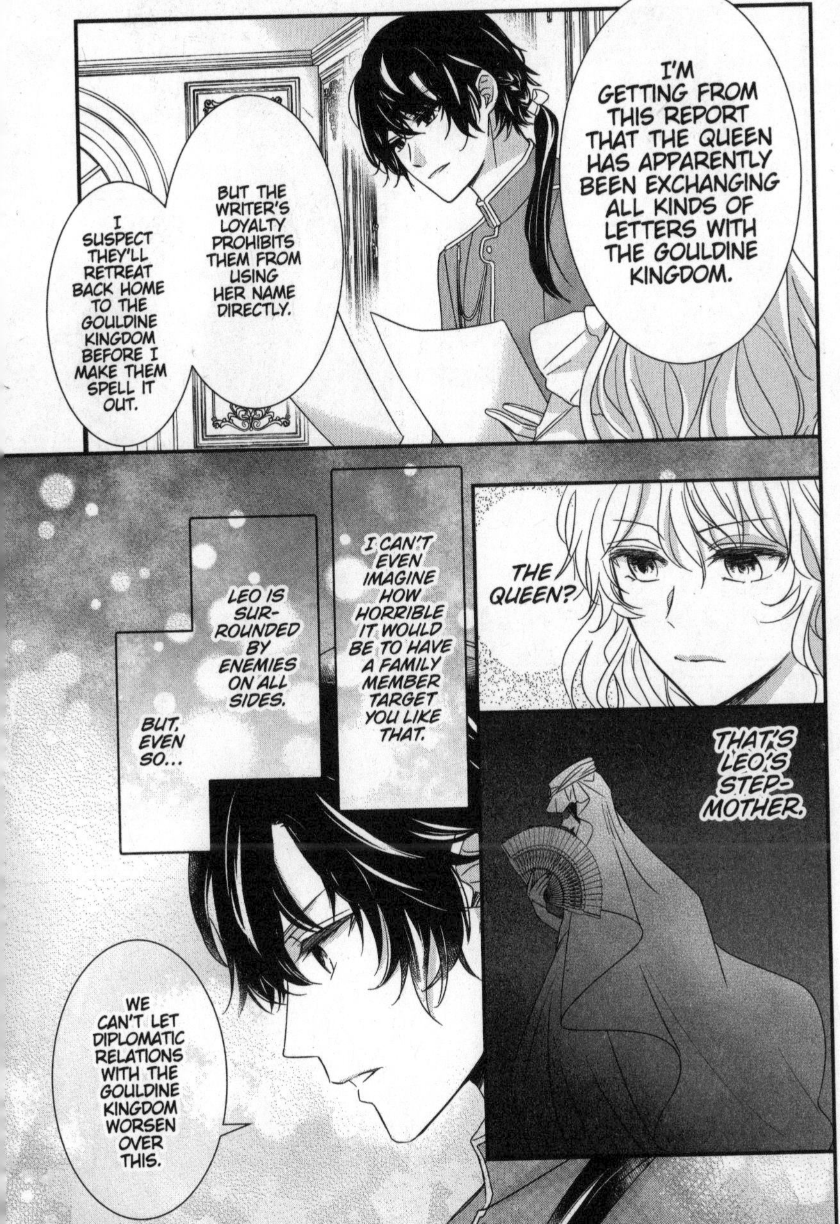
I'M GETTING FROM THIS REPORT THAT THE QUEEN HAS APPARENTLY BEEN EXCHANGING ALL KINDS OF LETTERS WITH THE GOULDINE KINGDOM.
BUT THE WRITER'S LOYALTY PROHIBITS THEM FROM USING HER NAME DIRECTLY.
I SUSPECT THEY'LL RETREAT BACK HOME TO THE GOULDINE KINGDOM BEFORE I MAKE THEM SPELL IT OUT.
THE QUEEN?
THAT'S LEO'S STEP-MOTHER.
I CAN'T EVEN IMAGINE HOW HORRIBLE IT WOULD BE TO HAVE A FAMILY MEMBER TARGET YOU LIKE THAT.
LEO IS SUR-ROUNDED BY ENEMIES ON ALL SIDES.
BUT, EVEN SO...
WE CAN'T LET DIPLOMATIC RELATIONS WITH THE GOULDINE KINGDOM WORSEN OVER THIS.

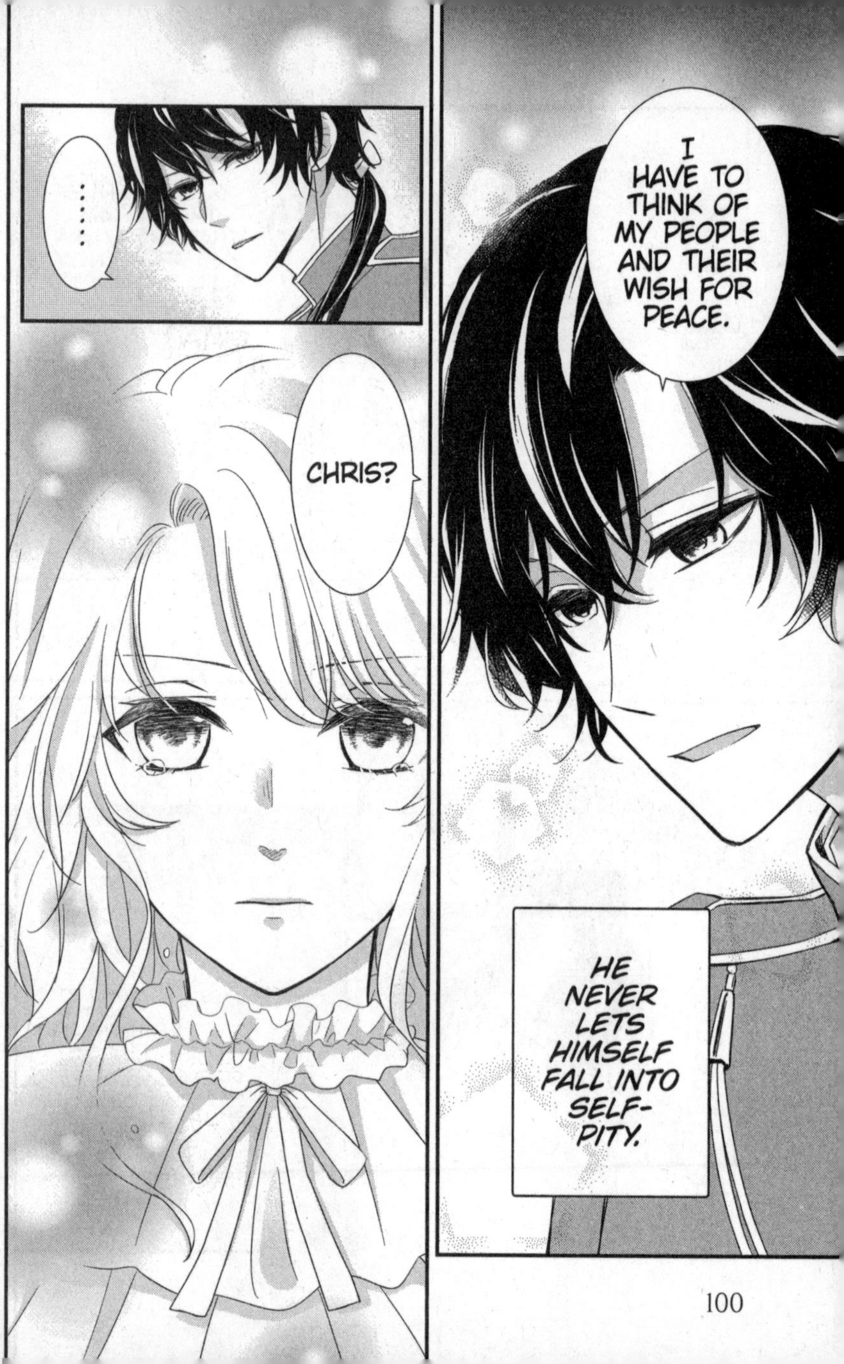
I HAVE TO THINK OF MY PEOPLE AND THEIR WISH FOR PEACE.
HE NEVER LETS HIMSELF FALL INTO SELF-PITY.
......
CHRIS?

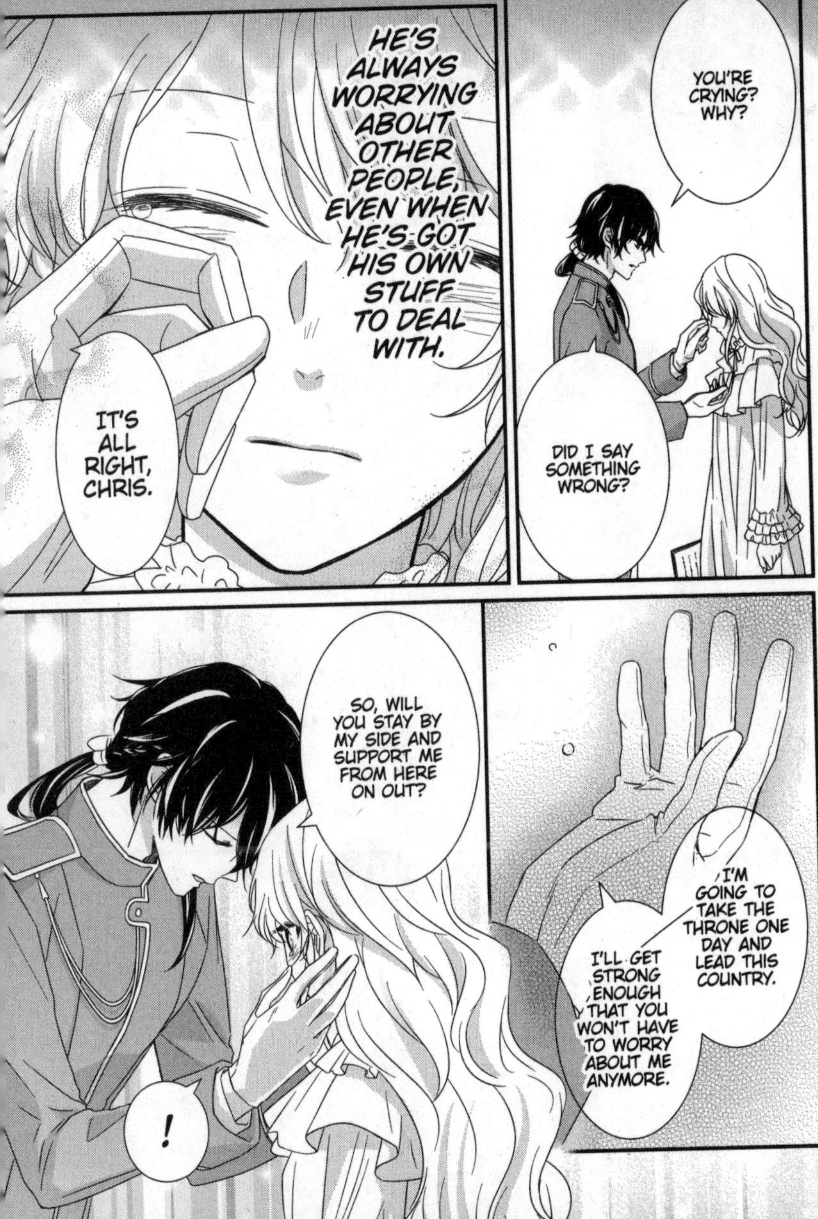
YOU'RE CRYING? WHY?
DID I SAY SOMETHING WRONG?
HE'S ALWAYS WORRYING ABOUT OTHER PEOPLE, EVEN WHEN HE'S GOT HIS OWN STUFF TO DEAL WITH.
IT'S ALL RIGHT, CHRIS.
I'M GOING TO TAKE THE THRONE ONE DAY AND LEAD THIS COUNTRY.
I'LL GET STRONG ENOUGH THAT YOU WON'T HAVE TO WORRY ABOUT ME ANYMORE.
SO, WILL YOU STAY BY MY SIDE AND SUPPORT ME FROM HERE ON OUT?
!

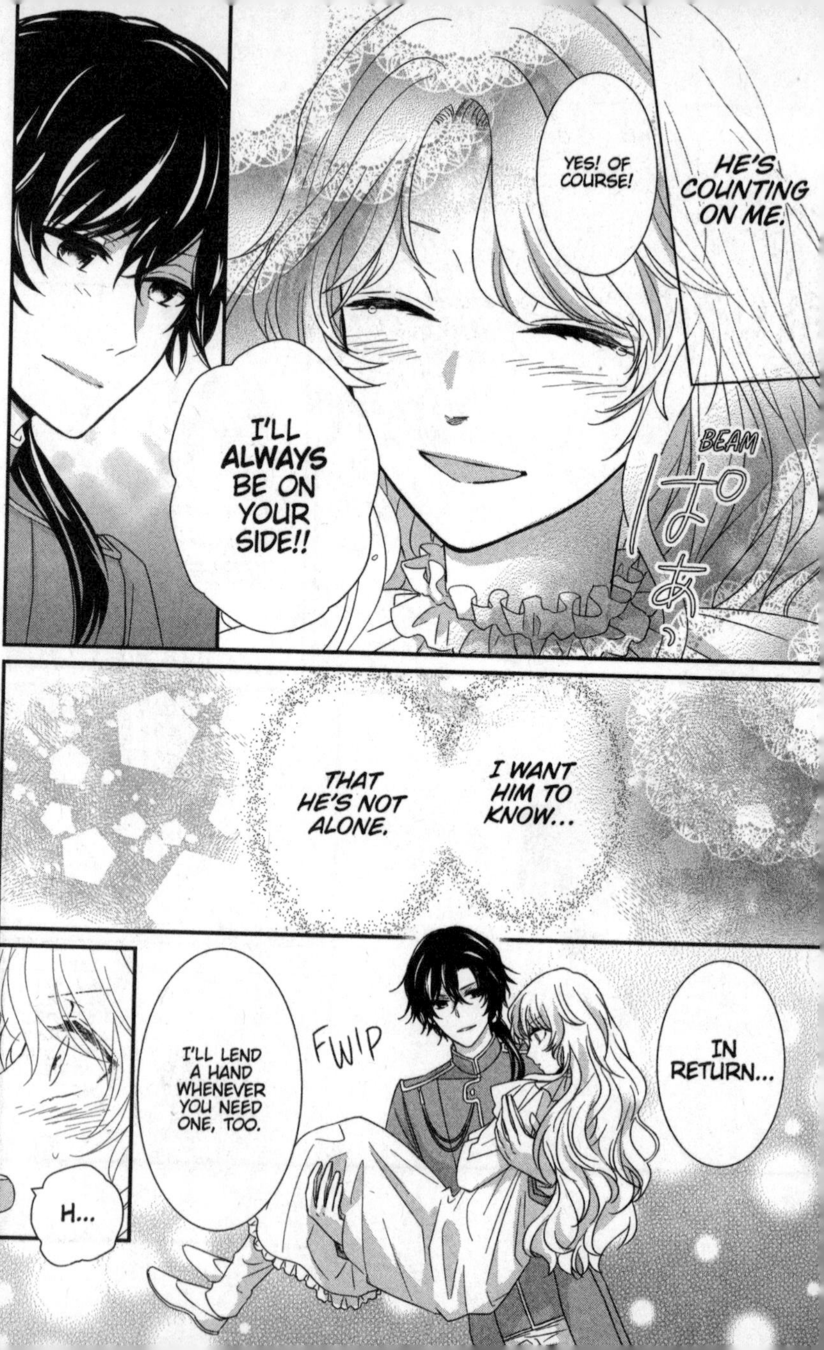
HE'S COUNTING ON ME.
YES! OF COURSE!
BEAM
ぱあっ
I'LL ALWAYS BE ON YOUR SIDE!!
I WANT HIM TO KNOW...
THAT HE'S NOT ALONE.
IN RETURN...
FWIP
I'LL LEND A HAND WHENEVER YOU NEED ONE, TOO.
H...

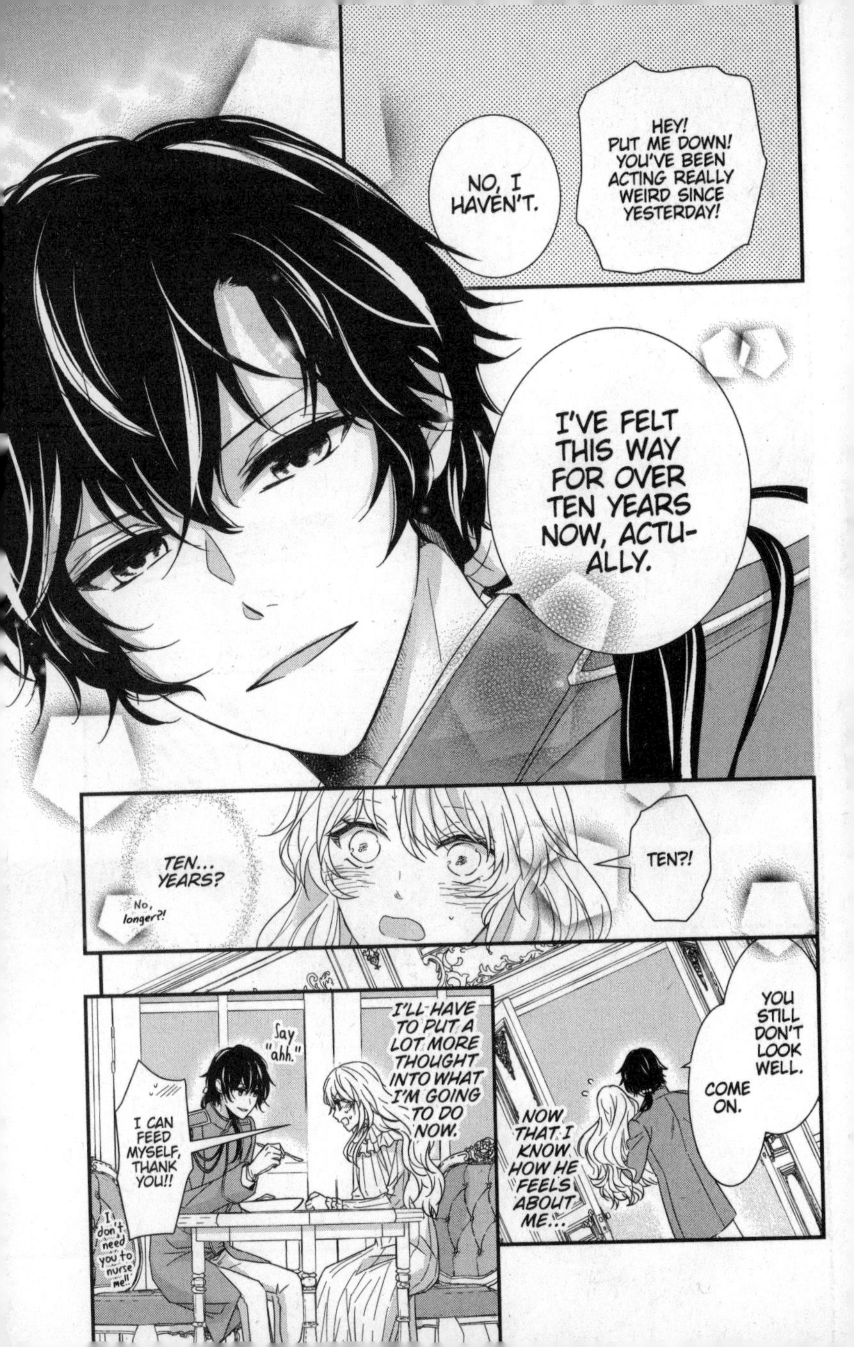
HEY! PUT ME DOWN! YOU'VE BEEN ACTING REALLY WEIRD SINCE YESTERDAY!
NO, I HAVEN'T.
I'VE FELT THIS WAY FOR OVER TEN YEARS NOW, ACTU-ALLY.
TEN?!
TEN... YEARS?
No, longer?!
YOU STILL DON'T LOOK WELL.
COME ON.
NOW THAT I KNOW HOW HE FEELS ABOUT ME...
I'LL HAVE TO PUT A LOT MORE THOUGHT INTO WHAT I'M GOING TO DO NOW.
Say "ahh."
I CAN FEED MYSELF, THANK YOU!!
I don't need you to nurse me!!

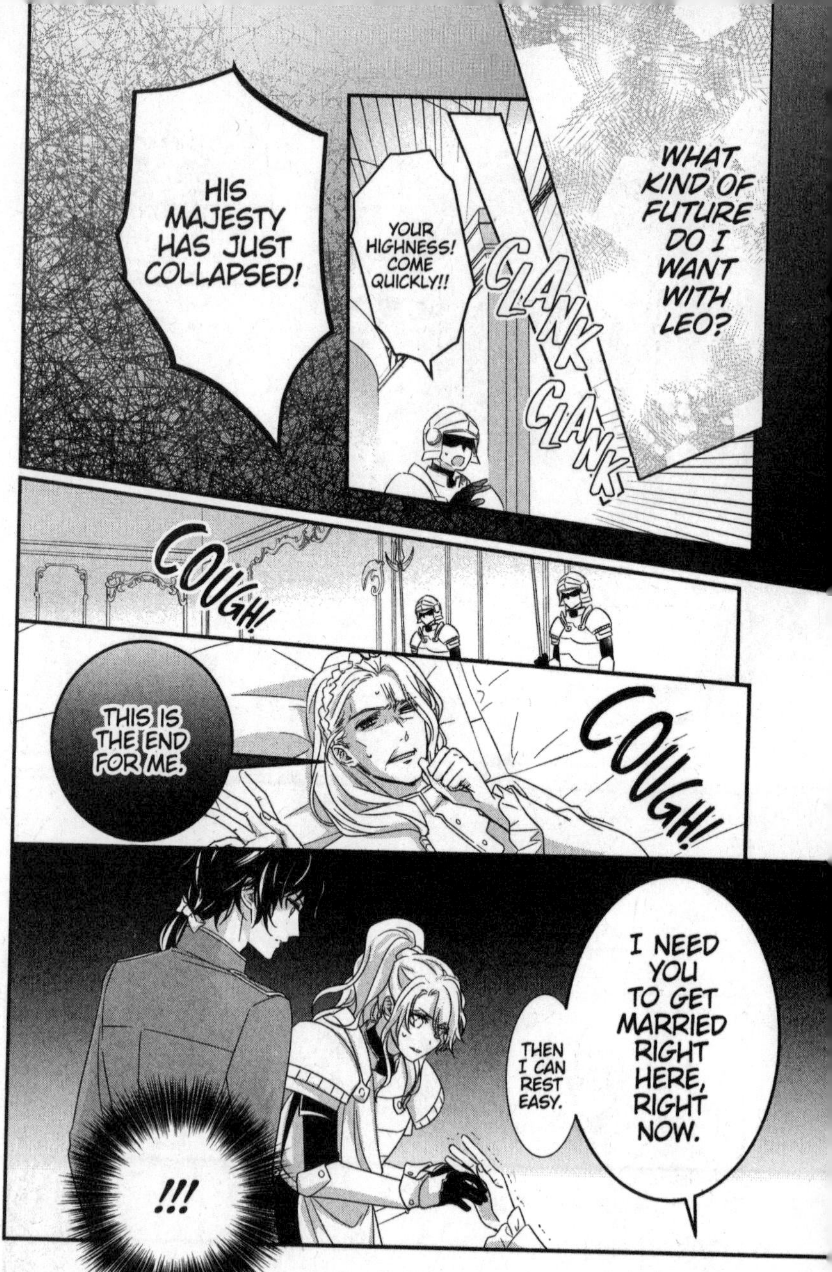
WHAT KIND OF FUTURE DO I WANT WITH LEO?
CLANK
CLANK
YOUR HIGHNESS! COME QUICKLY!!
HIS MAJESTY HAS JUST COLLAPSED!
COUGH!
COUGH!
THIS IS THE END FOR ME.
I NEED YOU TO GET MARRIED RIGHT HERE, RIGHT NOW.
THEN I CAN REST EASY.
!!!

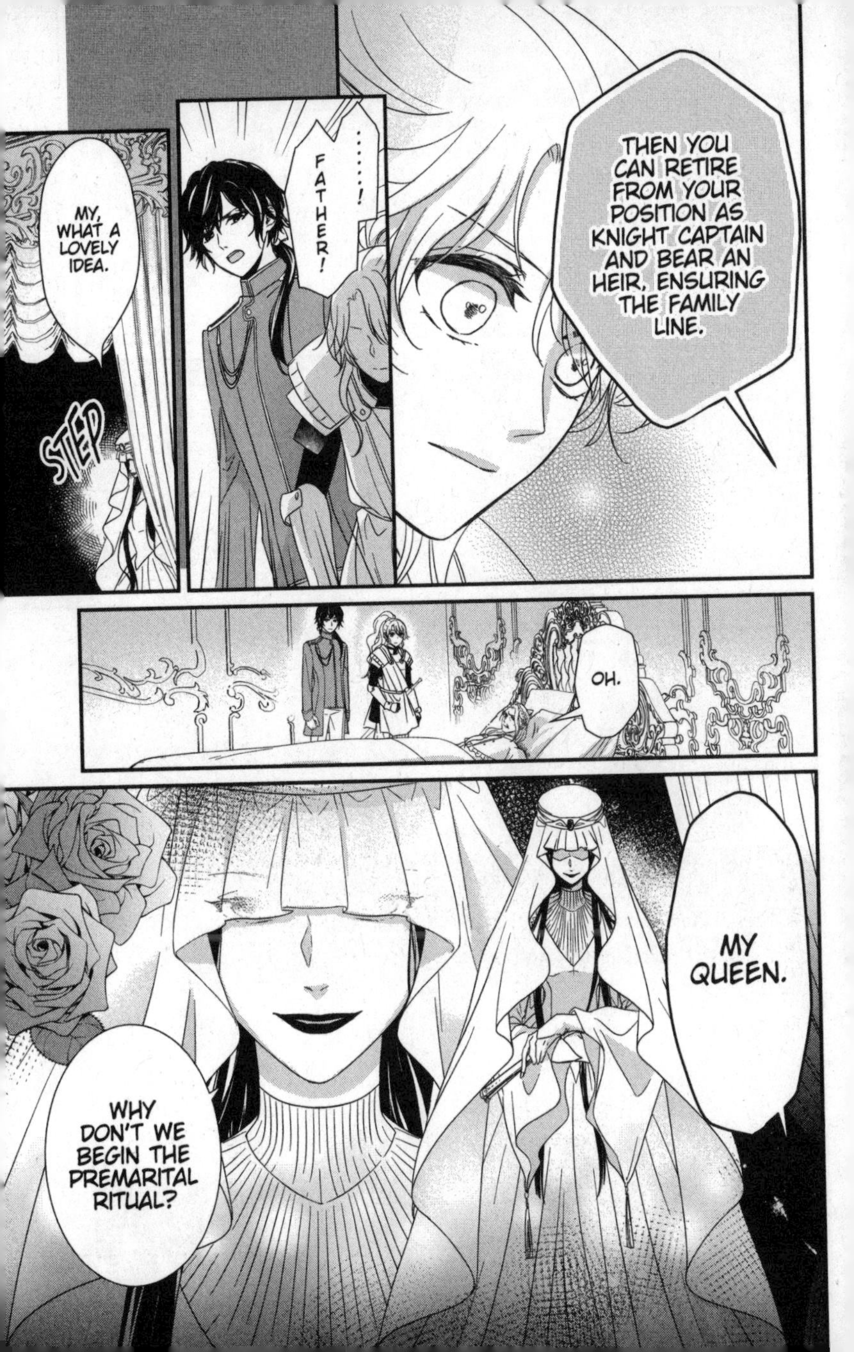
THEN YOU CAN RETIRE FROM YOUR POSITION AS KNIGHT CAPTAIN AND BEAR AN HEIR, ENSURING THE FAMILY LINE.
......!
FATHER!
MY, WHAT A LOVELY IDEA.
STEP
OH.
MY QUEEN.
WHY DON'T WE BEGIN THE PREMARITAL RITUAL?

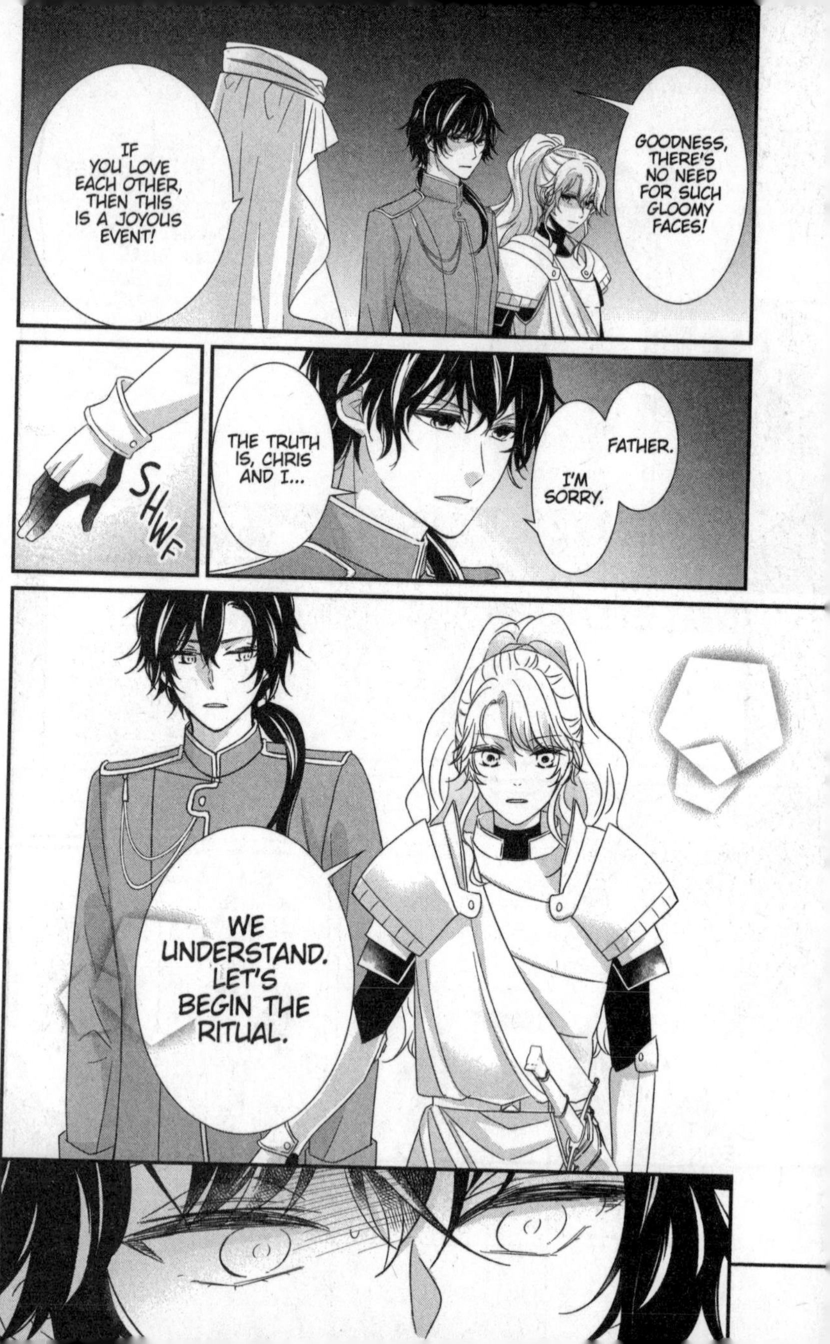
GOODNESS, THERE'S NO NEED FOR SUCH GLOOMY FACES!
IF YOU LOVE EACH OTHER, THEN THIS IS A JOYOUS EVENT!
FATHER. I'M SORRY.
THE TRUTH IS, CHRIS AND I...
SHWF
WE UNDERSTAND. LET'S BEGIN THE RITUAL.

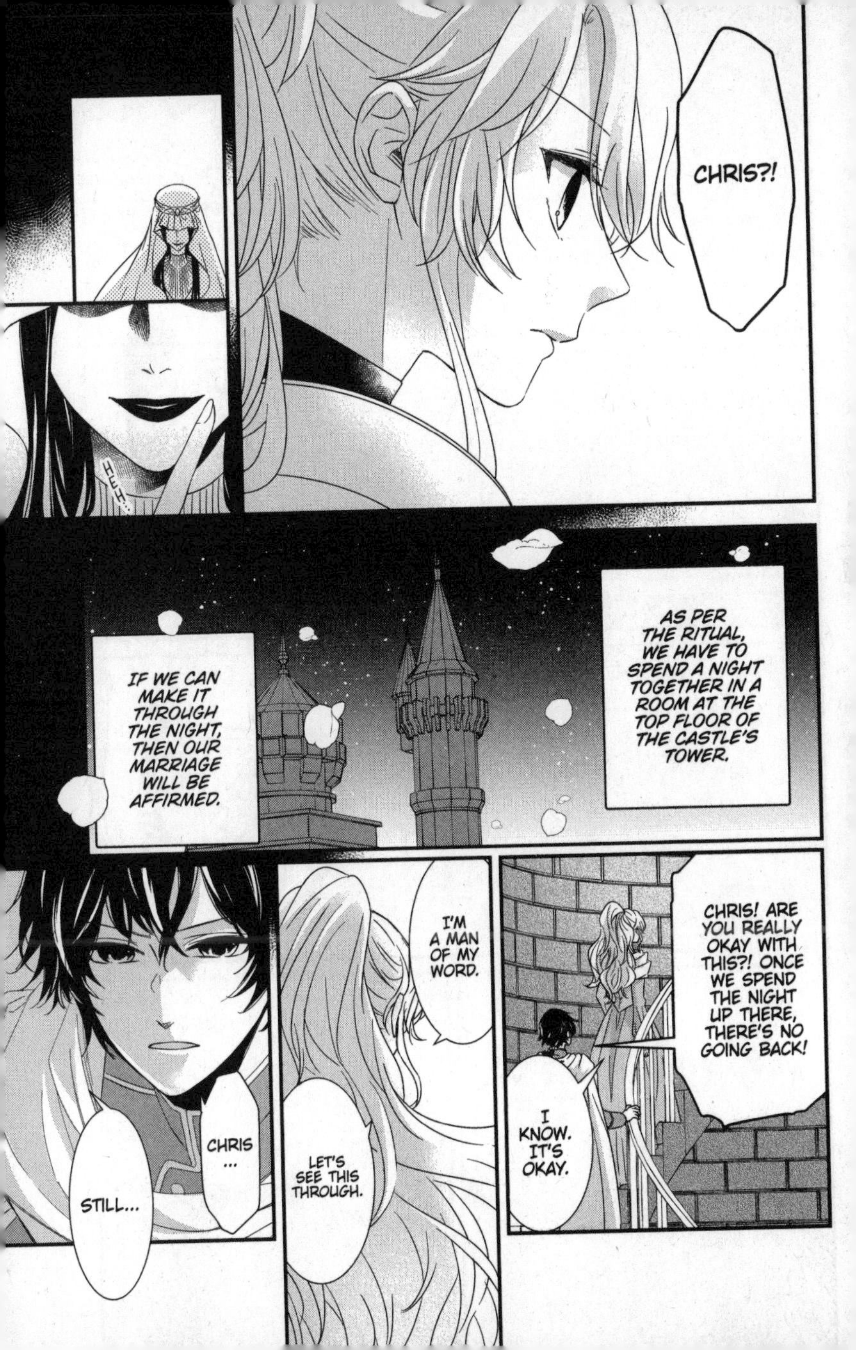
CHRIS?!
HEH...
AS PER THE RITUAL, WE HAVE TO SPEND A NIGHT TOGETHER IN A ROOM AT THE TOP FLOOR OF THE CASTLE'S TOWER.
IF WE CAN MAKE IT THROUGH THE NIGHT, THEN OUR MARRIAGE WILL BE AFFIRMED.
CHRIS! ARE YOU REALLY OKAY WITH THIS?! ONCE WE SPEND THE NIGHT UP THERE, THERE'S NO GOING BACK!
I KNOW. IT'S OKAY.
I'M A MAN OF MY WORD.
LET'S SEE THIS THROUGH.
CHRIS ...
STILL...

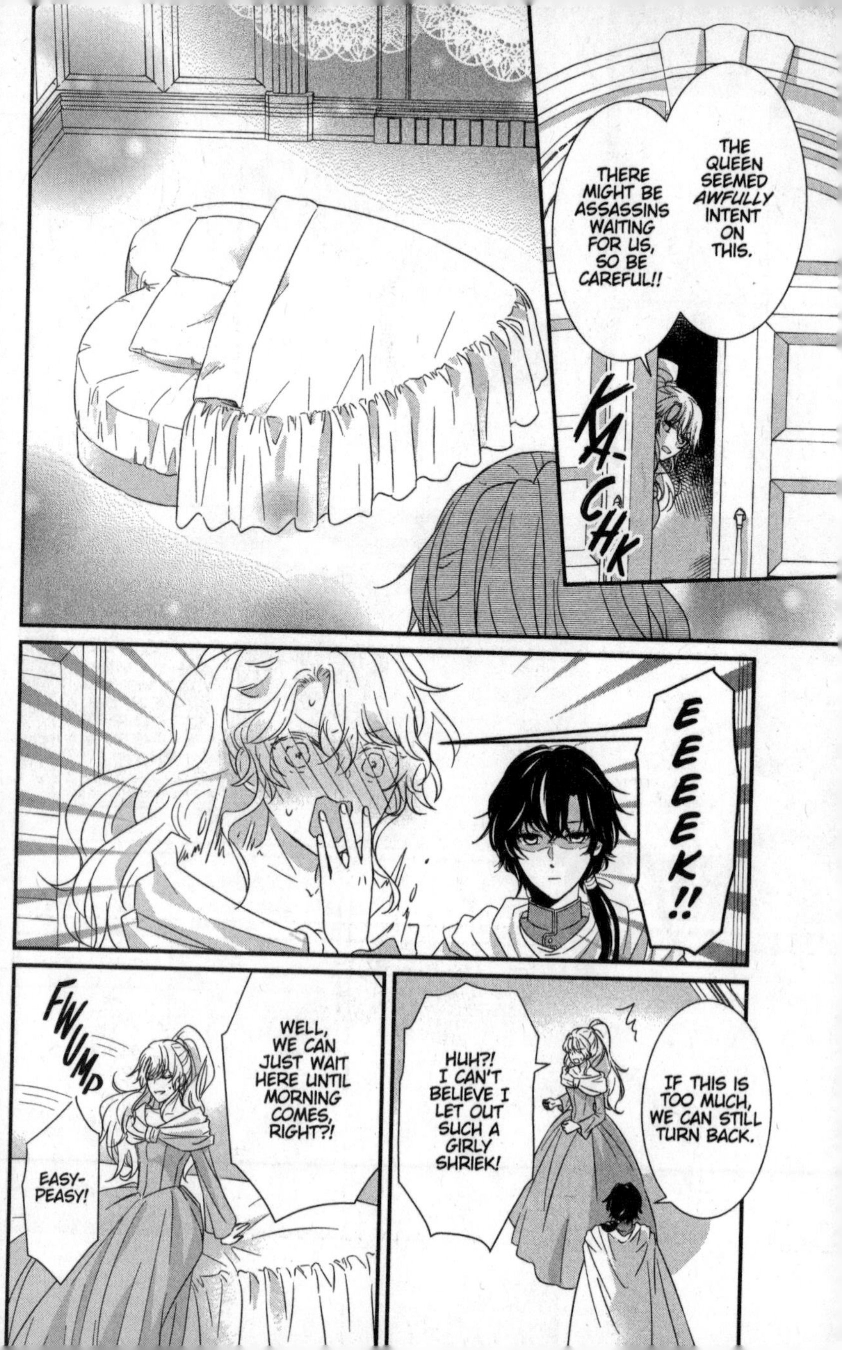
THE QUEEN SEEMED AWFULLY INTENT ON THIS.
THERE MIGHT BE ASSASSINS WAITING FOR US, SO BE CAREFUL!!
KA-CHK
EEEEEK!!
IF THIS IS TOO MUCH, WE CAN STILL TURN BACK.
HUH?! I CAN'T BELIEVE I LET OUT SUCH A GIRLY SHRIEK!
WELL, WE CAN JUST WAIT HERE UNTIL MORNING COMES, RIGHT?!
FWUMP
EASY-PEASY!

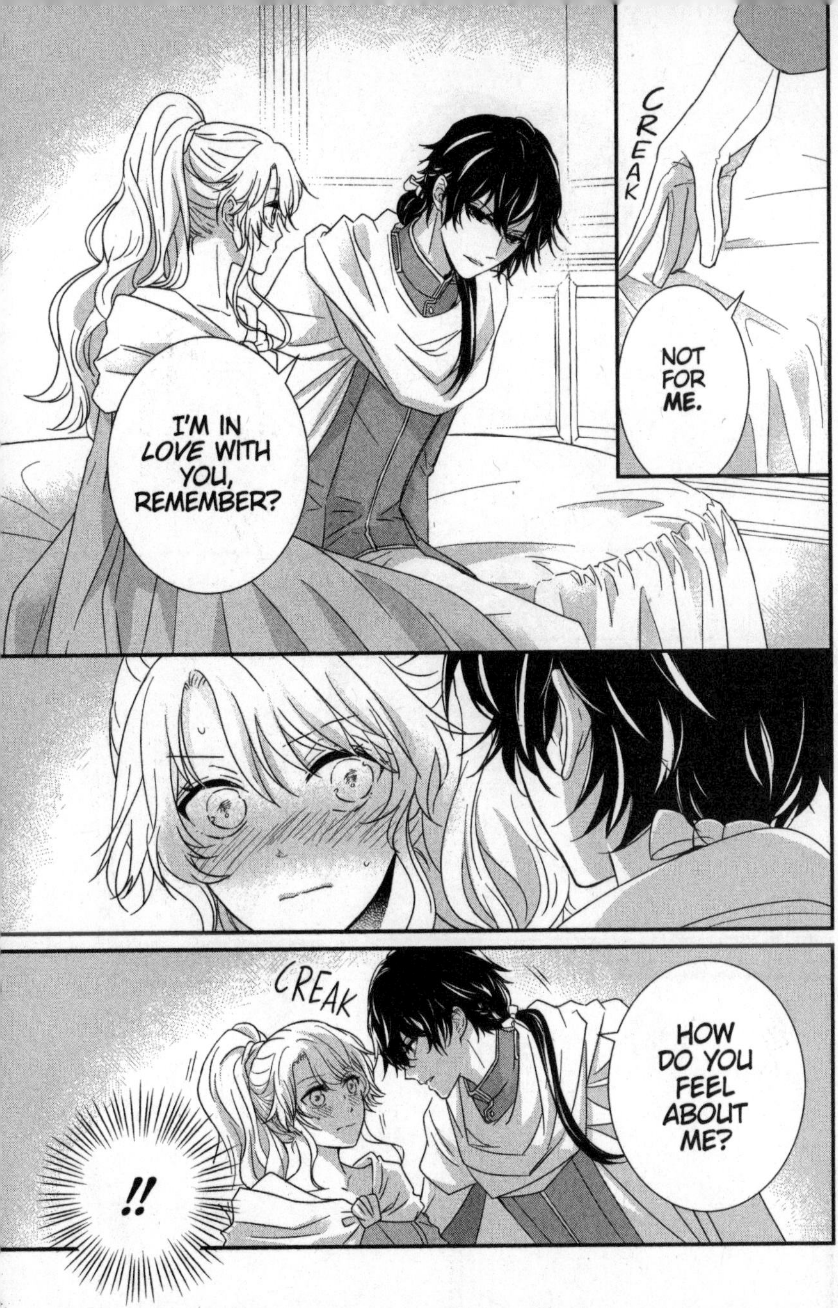
CREAK
NOT FOR ME.
I'M IN *LOVE* WITH YOU, REMEMBER?
CREAK
HOW DO YOU FEEL ABOUT ME?
!!

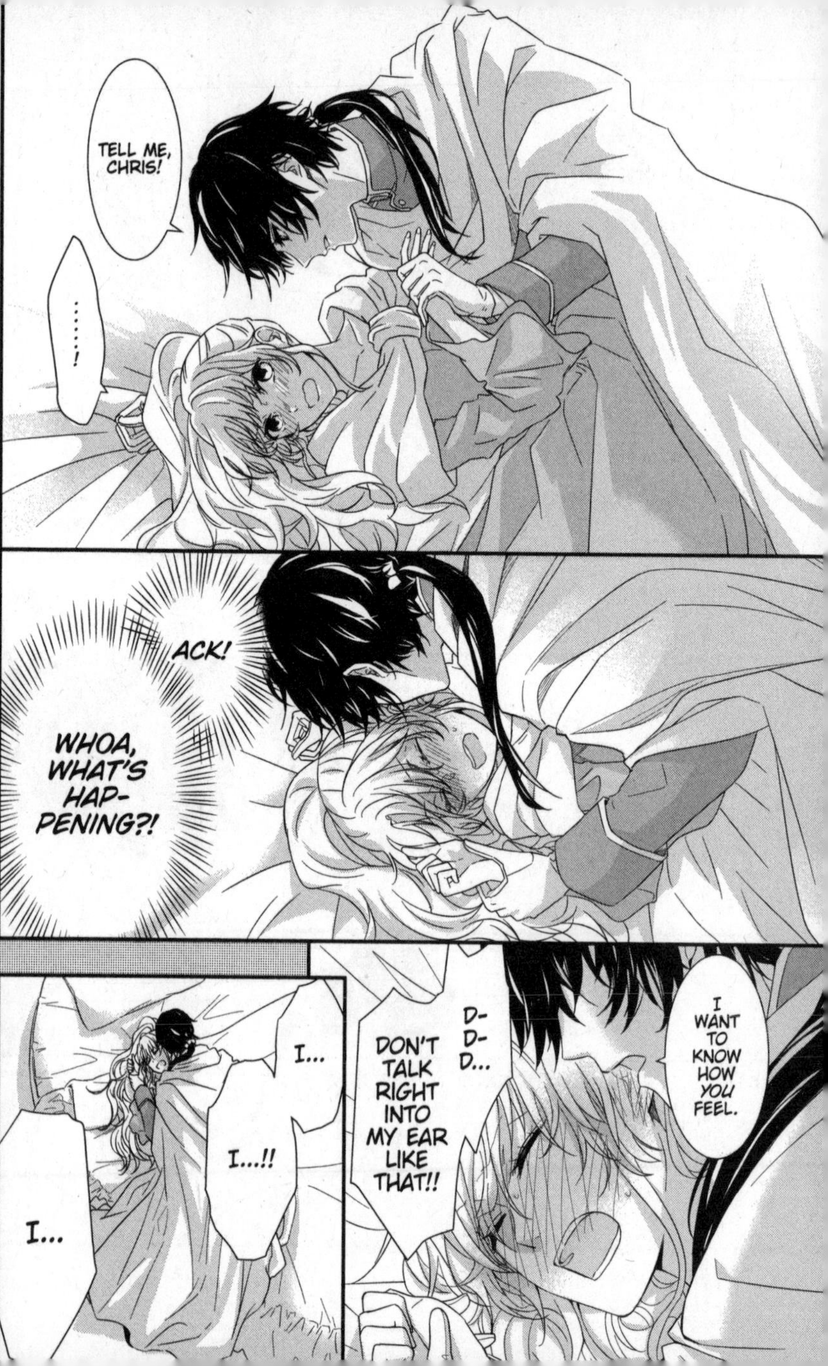
TELL ME, CHRIS!
......!
ACK!
WHOA, WHAT'S HAP-PENING?!
I WANT TO KNOW HOW YOU FEEL.
D-D-D...
DON'T TALK RIGHT INTO MY EAR LIKE THAT!!
I...
I...!!
I...

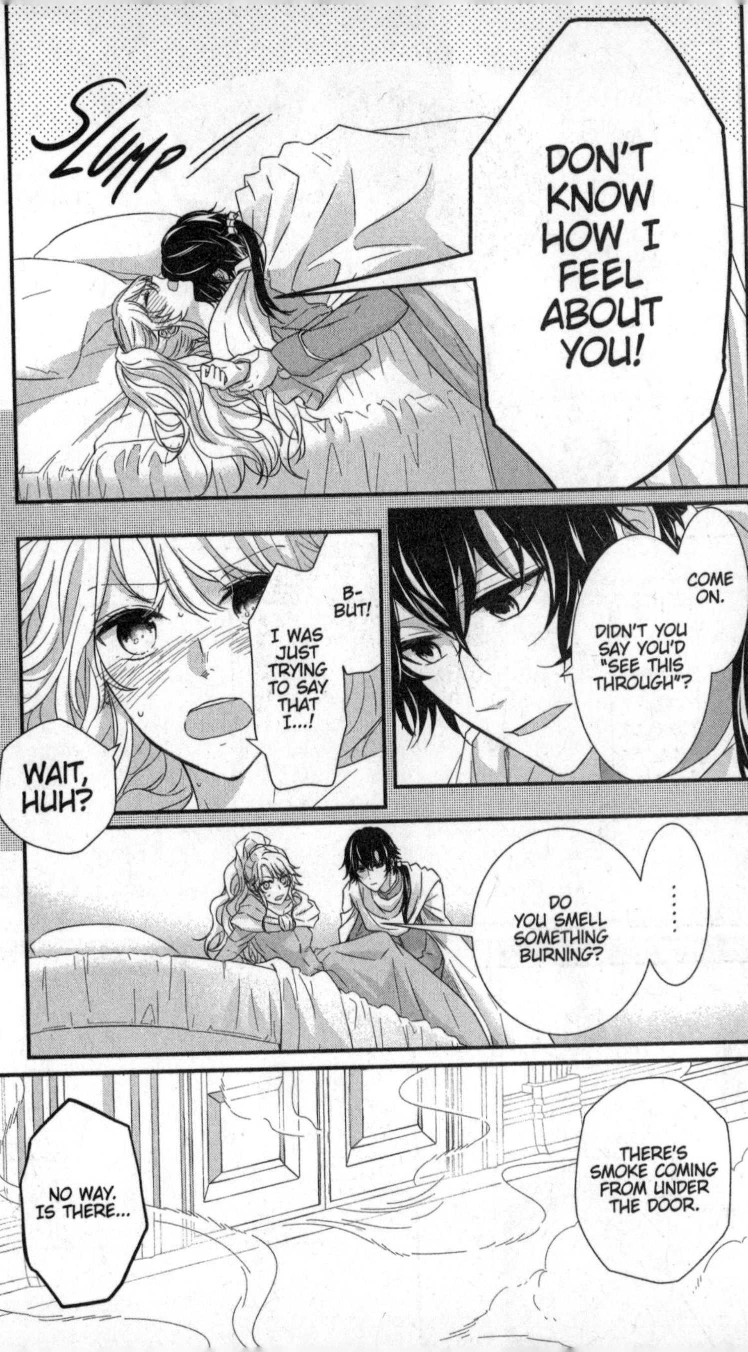
DON'T KNOW HOW I FEEL ABOUT YOU!
SLUMP
COME ON.
DIDN'T YOU SAY YOU'D "SEE THIS THROUGH"?
B-BUT!
I WAS JUST TRYING TO SAY THAT I...!
WAIT, HUH?
......
DO YOU SMELL SOMETHING BURNING?
THERE'S SMOKE COMING FROM UNDER THE DOOR.
NO WAY. IS THERE...

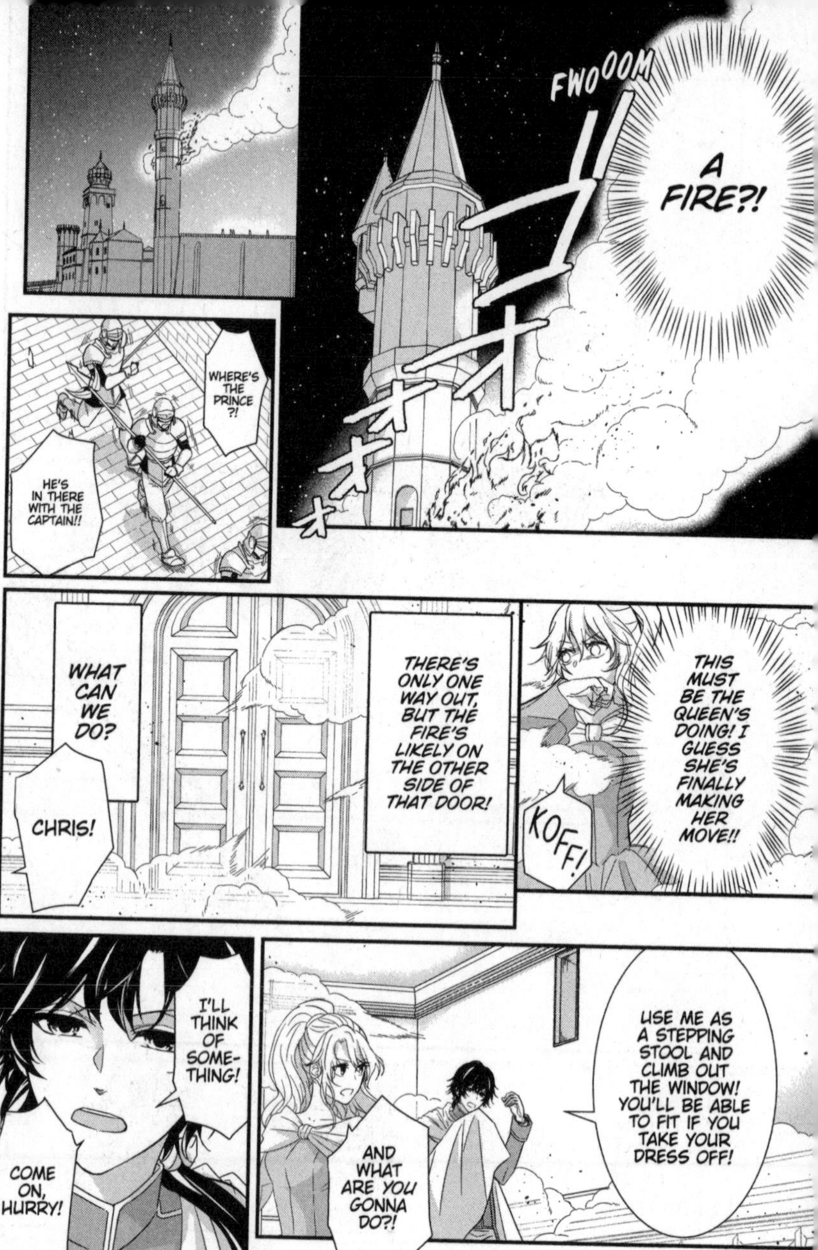
FWOOOM
A FIRE?!
WHERE'S THE PRINCE?!
HE'S IN THERE WITH THE CAPTAIN!!
THIS MUST BE THE QUEEN'S DOING! I GUESS SHE'S FINALLY MAKING HER MOVE!!
KOFF!
THERE'S ONLY ONE WAY OUT, BUT THE FIRE'S LIKELY ON THE OTHER SIDE OF THAT DOOR!
WHAT CAN WE DO?
CHRIS!
USE ME AS A STEPPING STOOL AND CLIMB OUT THE WINDOW! YOU'LL BE ABLE TO FIT IF YOU TAKE YOUR DRESS OFF!
AND WHAT ARE YOU GONNA DO?!
I'LL THINK OF SOMETHING!
COME ON, HURRY!

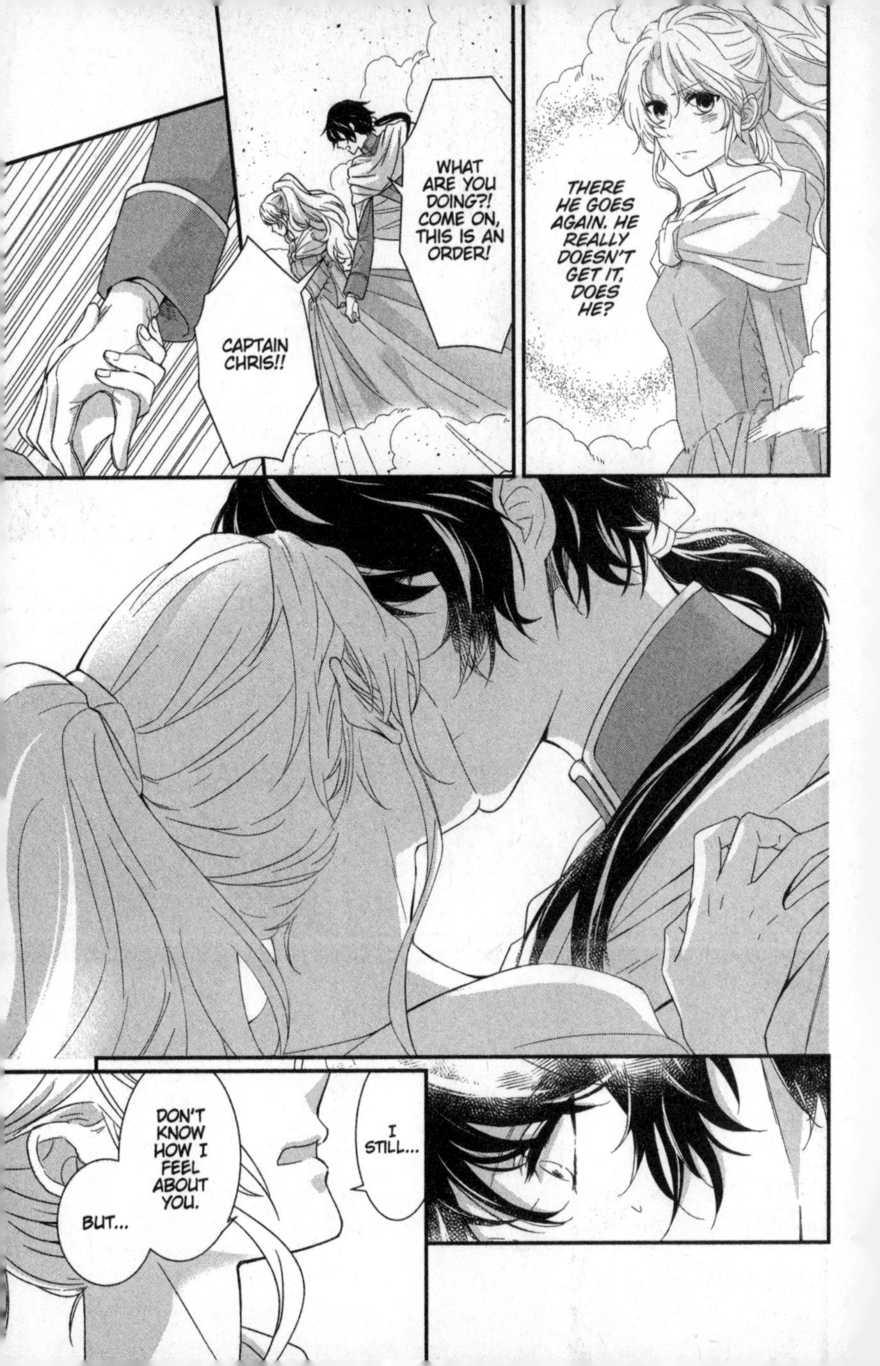
THERE HE GOES AGAIN. HE REALLY DOESN'T GET IT, DOES HE?
WHAT ARE YOU DOING?! COME ON, THIS IS AN ORDER!
CAPTAIN CHRIS!!
I STILL...
DON'T KNOW HOW I FEEL ABOUT YOU.
BUT...

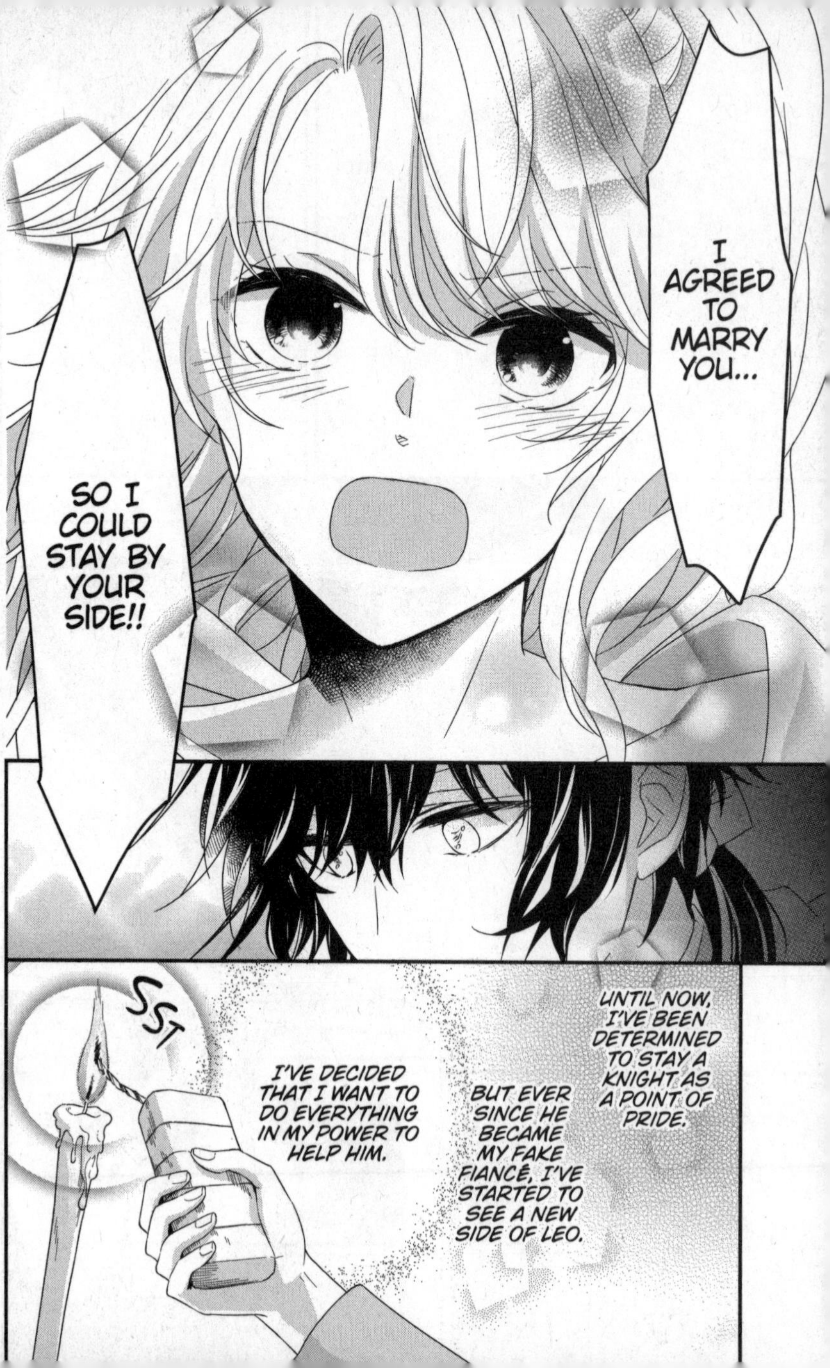
I AGREED TO MARRY YOU...
SO I COULD STAY BY YOUR SIDE!!
UNTIL NOW, I'VE BEEN DETERMINED TO STAY A KNIGHT AS A POINT OF PRIDE.
BUT EVER SINCE HE BECAME MY FAKE FIANCÉ, I'VE STARTED TO SEE A NEW SIDE OF LEO.
I'VE DECIDED THAT I WANT TO DO EVERYTHING IN MY POWER TO HELP HIM.
SST

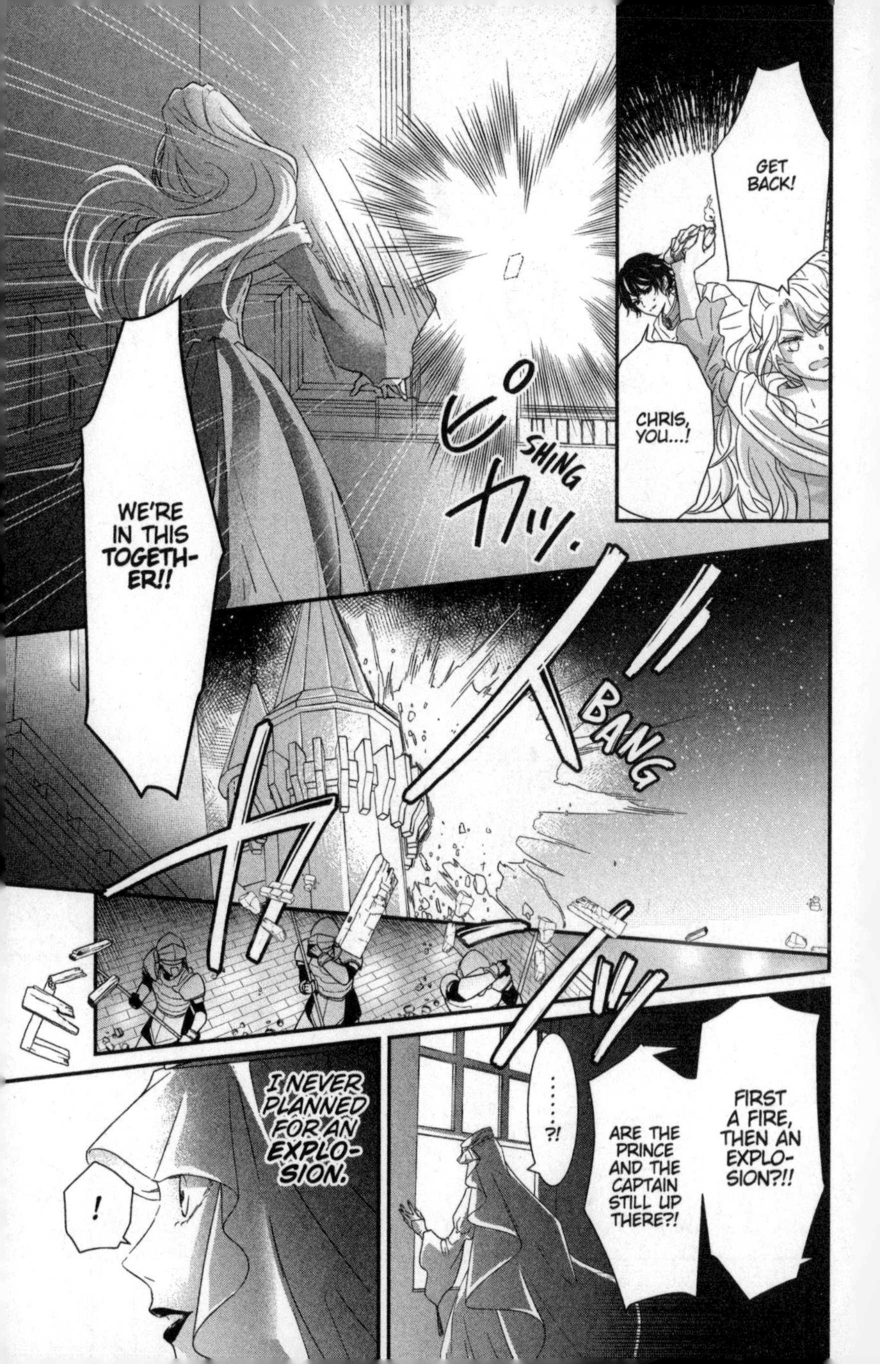
GET BACK!
CHRIS, YOU...!
WE'RE IN THIS TOGETHER!!
ピカッ
SHING
ドン
BANG
FIRST A FIRE, THEN AN EXPLOSION?!!
ARE THE PRINCE AND THE CAPTAIN STILL UP THERE?!
......?!
I NEVER PLANNED FOR AN EXPLOSION.
!

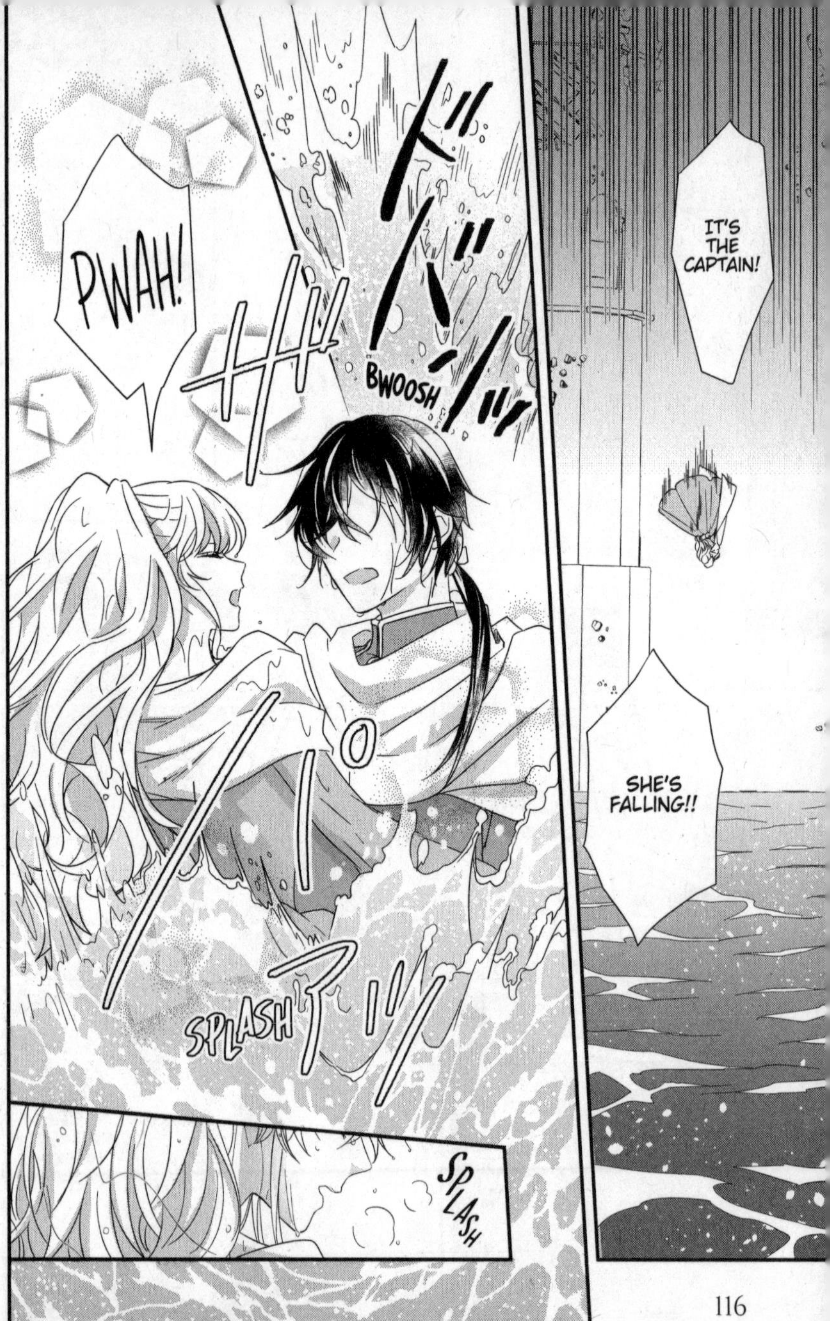
IT'S THE CAPTAIN!
SHE'S FALLING!!
BWOOSH
PWAH!
SPLASH
SPLASH

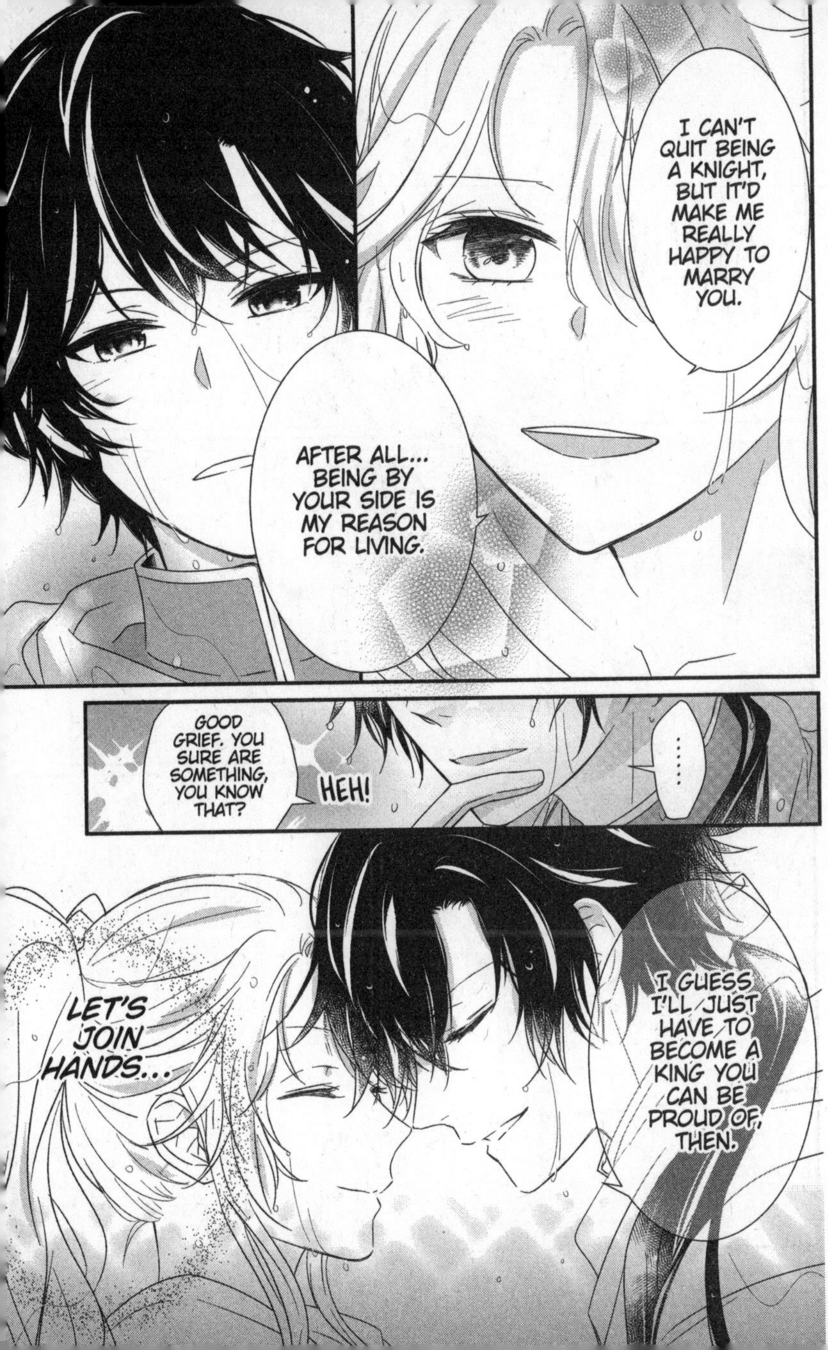
I CAN'T QUIT BEING A KNIGHT, BUT IT'D MAKE ME REALLY HAPPY TO MARRY YOU.
AFTER ALL... BEING BY YOUR SIDE IS MY REASON FOR LIVING.
......
HEH!
GOOD GRIEF. YOU SURE ARE SOMETHING, YOU KNOW THAT?
I GUESS I'LL JUST HAVE TO BECOME A KING YOU CAN BE PROUD OF, THEN.
LET'S JOIN HANDS...

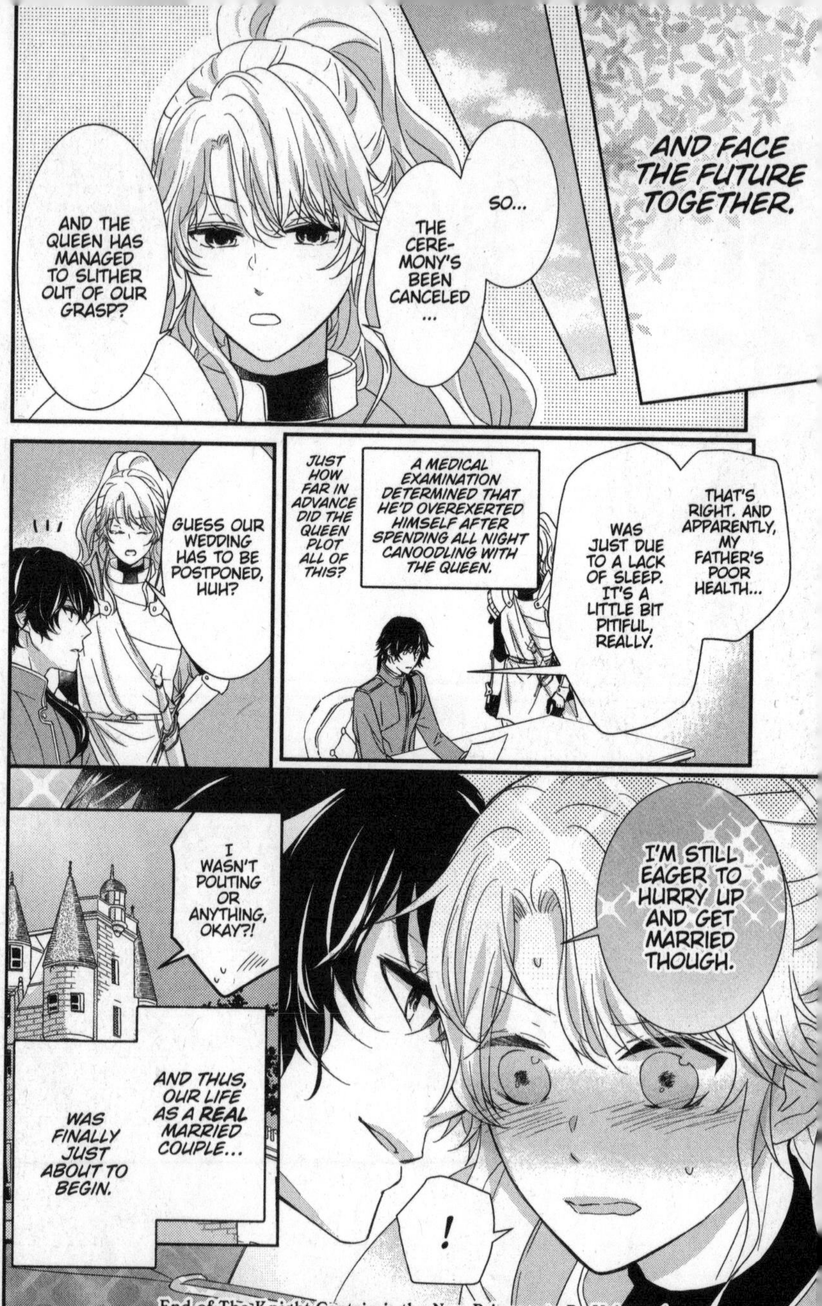
AND FACE THE FUTURE TOGETHER.
SO...
THE CEREMONY'S BEEN CANCELED...
AND THE QUEEN HAS MANAGED TO SLITHER OUT OF OUR GRASP?
THAT'S RIGHT. AND APPARENTLY, MY FATHER'S POOR HEALTH...
WAS JUST DUE TO A LACK OF SLEEP. IT'S A LITTLE BIT PITIFUL, REALLY.
A MEDICAL EXAMINATION DETERMINED THAT HE'D OVEREXERTED HIMSELF AFTER SPENDING ALL NIGHT CANOODLING WITH THE QUEEN.
JUST HOW FAR IN ADVANCE DID THE QUEEN PLOT ALL OF THIS?
GUESS OUR WEDDING HAS TO BE POSTPONED, HUH?
I'M STILL EAGER TO HURRY UP AND GET MARRIED THOUGH.
!
I WASN'T POUTING OR ANYTHING, OKAY?!
AND THUS, OUR LIFE AS A REAL MARRIED COUPLE...
WAS FINALLY JUST ABOUT TO BEGIN.

End of The Knight Captain is the New Princess-to-Be Volume 1

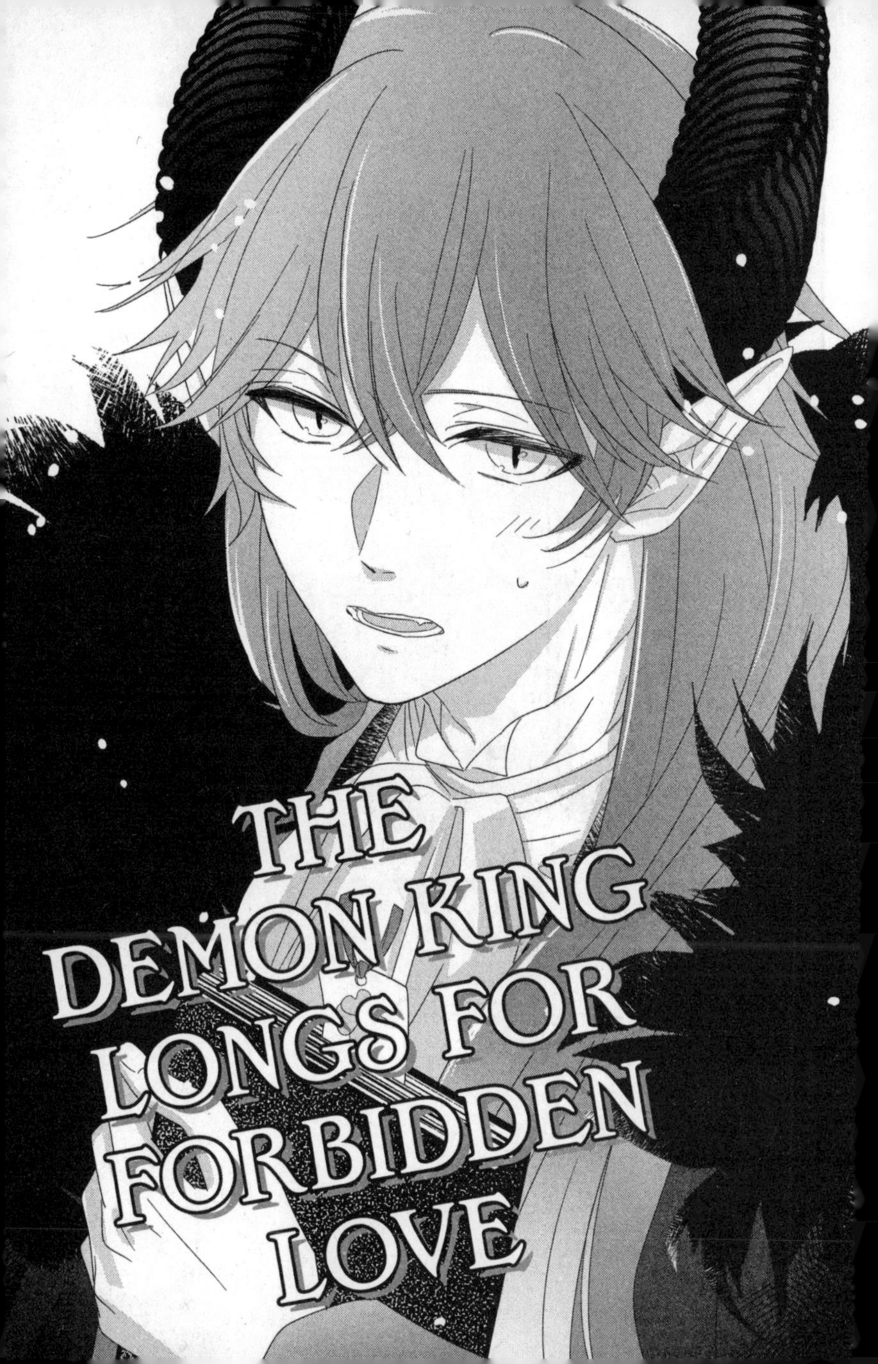
THE
DEMON KING
LONGS FOR
FORBIDDEN
LOVE

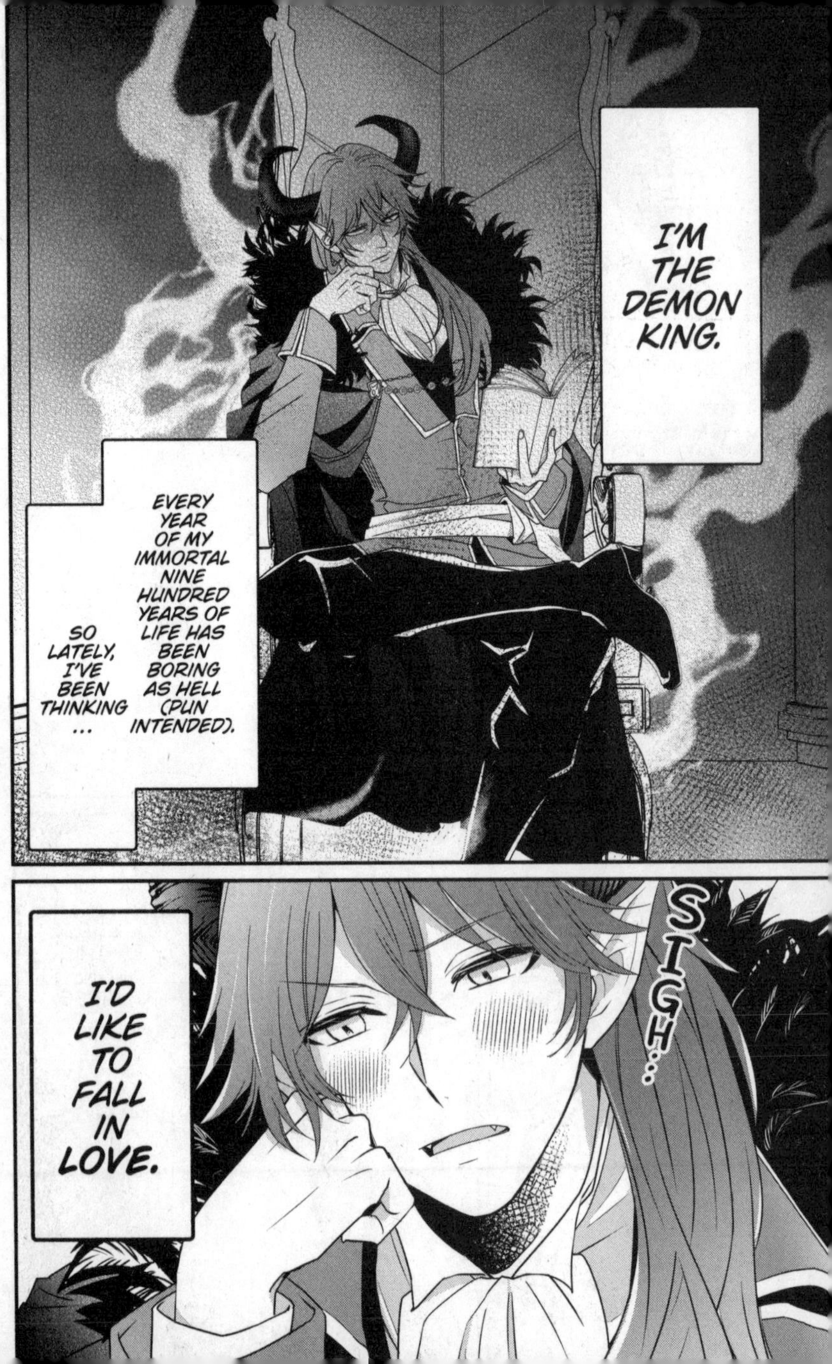
I'M THE DEMON KING.
EVERY YEAR OF MY IMMORTAL NINE HUNDRED YEARS OF LIFE HAS BEEN BORING AS HELL (PUN INTENDED).
SO LATELY, I'VE BEEN THINKING...
SIGH...
I'D LIKE TO FALL IN LOVE.

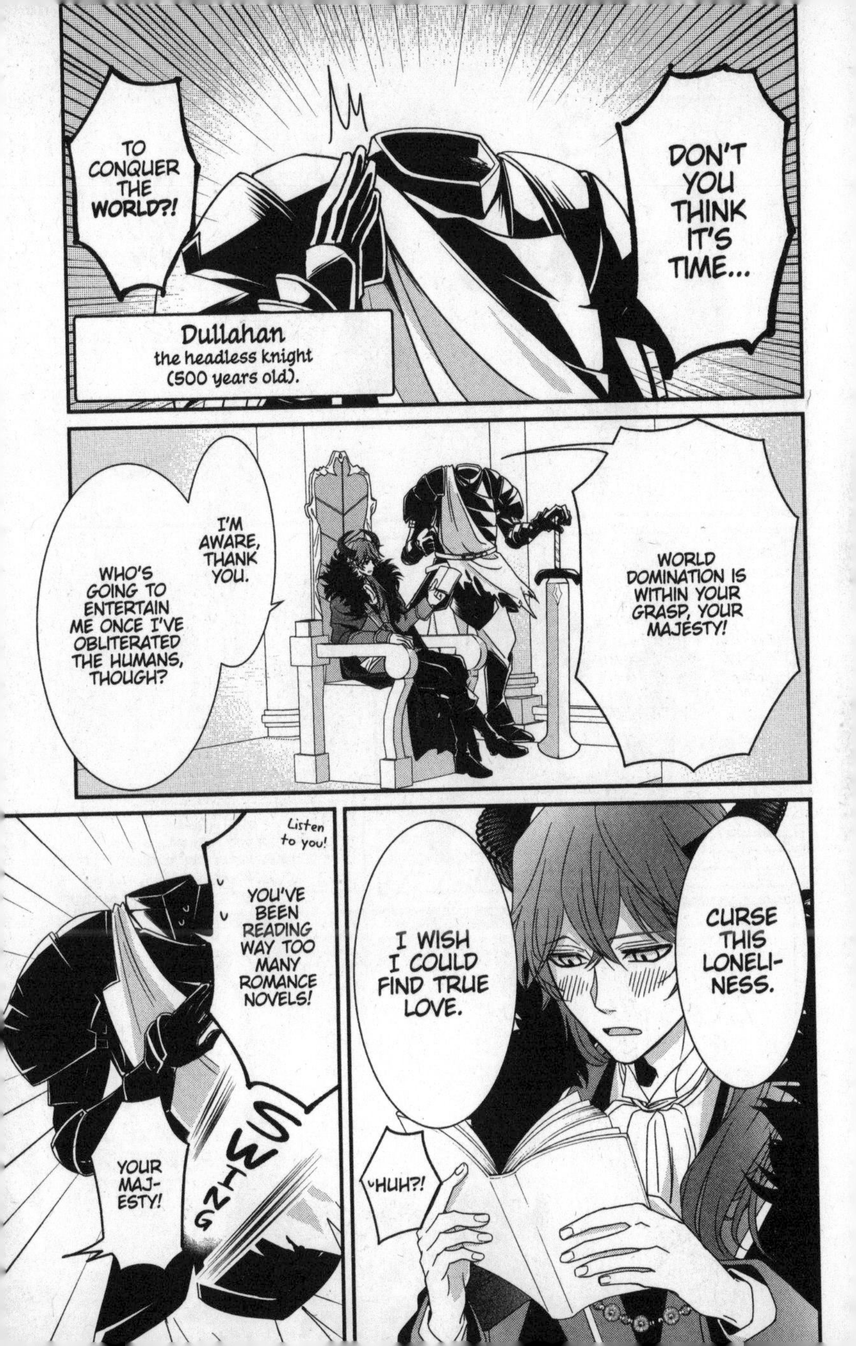
DON'T YOU THINK IT'S TIME...
TO CONQUER THE WORLD?!
Dullahan the headless knight (500 years old).
WORLD DOMINATION IS WITHIN YOUR GRASP, YOUR MAJESTY!
I'M AWARE, THANK YOU.
WHO'S GOING TO ENTERTAIN ME ONCE I'VE OBLITERATED THE HUMANS, THOUGH?
CURSE THIS LONELI-NESS.
I WISH I COULD FIND TRUE LOVE.
HUH?!
Listen to you!
YOU'VE BEEN READING WAY TOO MANY ROMANCE NOVELS!
SWING
YOUR MAJ-ESTY!

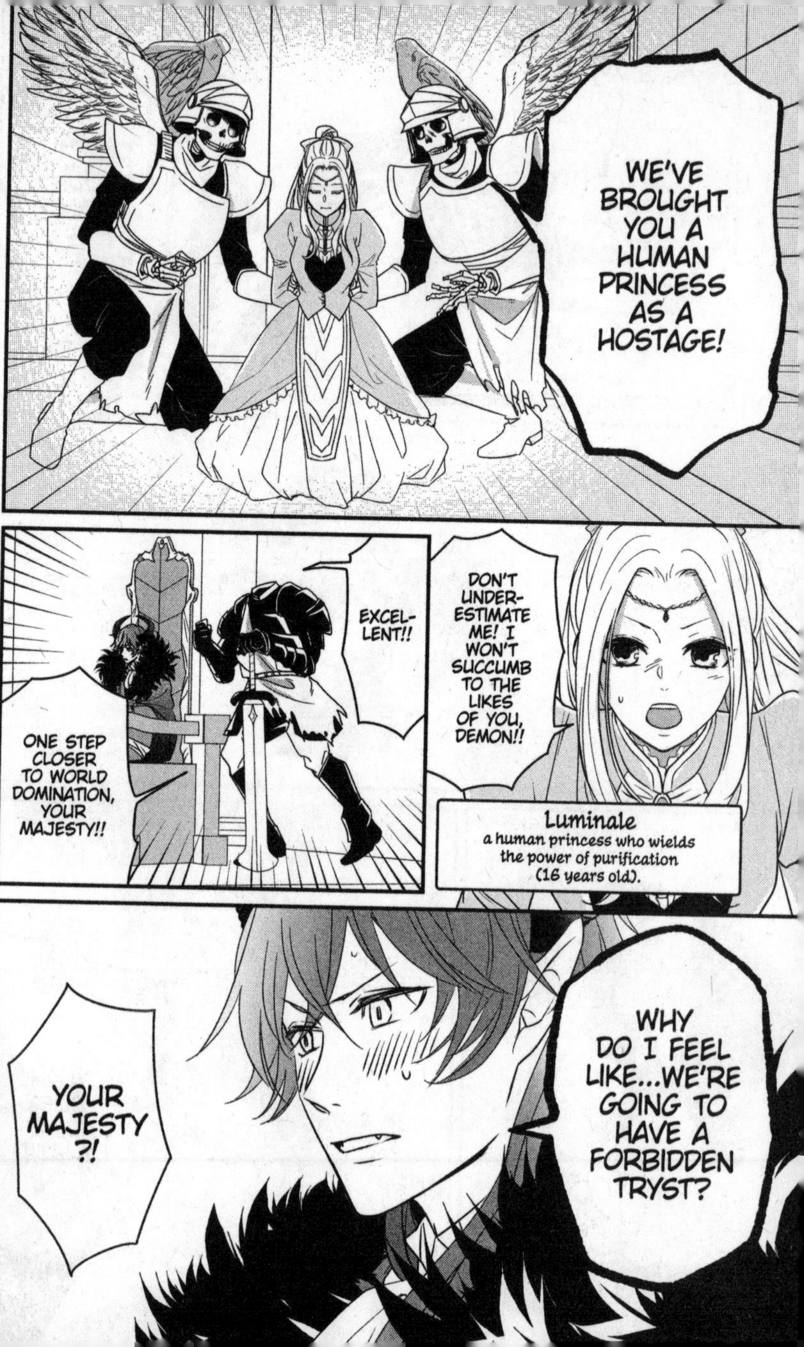
WE'VE BROUGHT YOU A HUMAN PRINCESS AS A HOSTAGE!
DON'T UNDER-ESTIMATE ME! I WON'T SUCCUMB TO THE LIKES OF YOU, DEMON!!
Luminale
a human princess who wields the power of purification (16 years old).
EXCEL-LENT!!
ONE STEP CLOSER TO WORLD DOMINATION, YOUR MAJESTY!!
WHY DO I FEEL LIKE...WE'RE GOING TO HAVE A FORBIDDEN TRYST?
YOUR MAJESTY?!

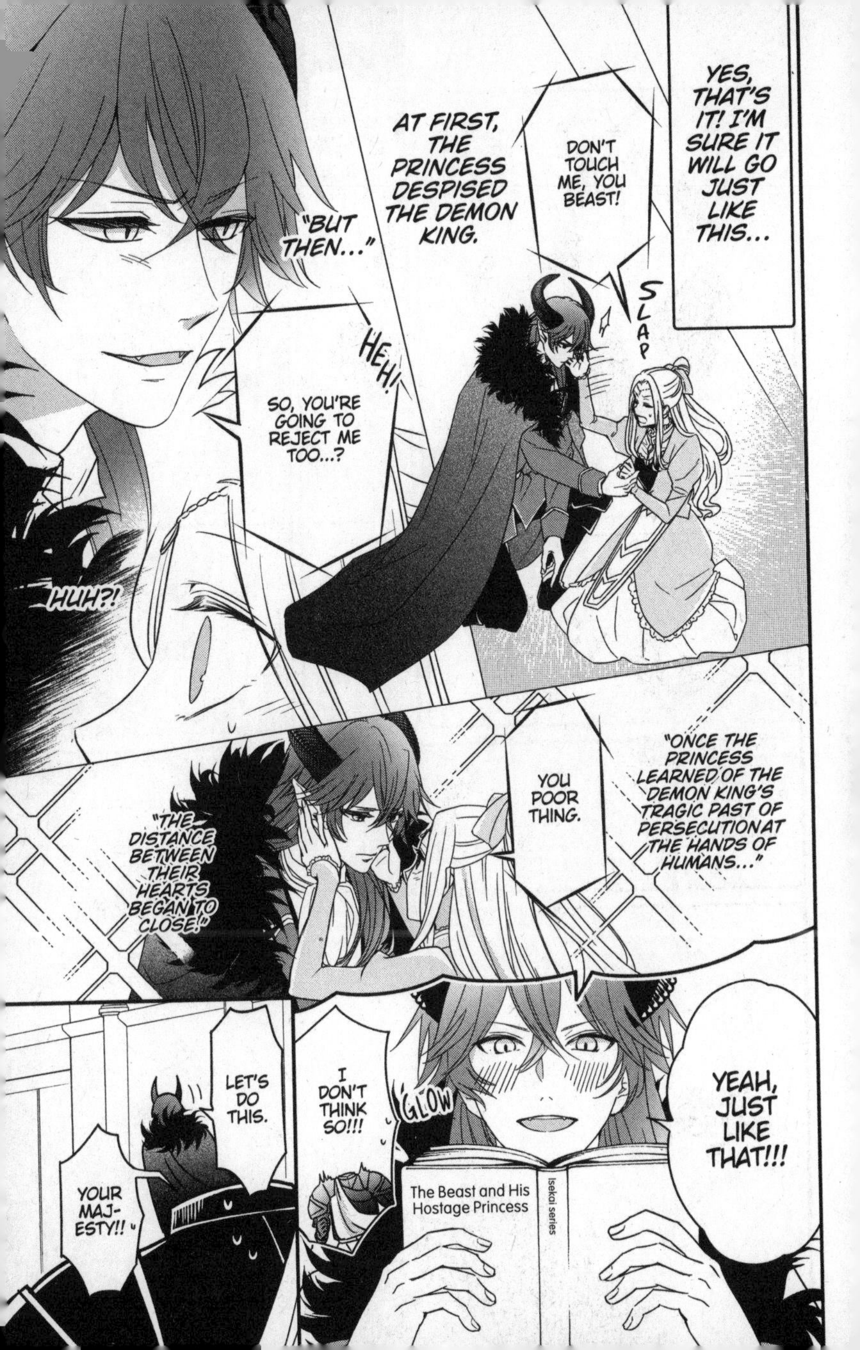
YES, THAT'S IT! I'M SURE IT WILL GO JUST LIKE THIS...
AT FIRST, THE PRINCESS DESPISED THE DEMON KING.
DON'T TOUCH ME, YOU BEAST!
SLAP
"BUT THEN..."
HEH!
SO, YOU'RE GOING TO REJECT ME TOO...?
HUH?!
"ONCE THE PRINCESS LEARNED OF THE DEMON KING'S TRAGIC PAST OF PERSECUTION AT THE HANDS OF HUMANS..."
YOU POOR THING.
"THE DISTANCE BETWEEN THEIR HEARTS BEGAN TO CLOSE."
YEAH, JUST LIKE THAT!!!
GLOW
The Beast and His Hostage Princess
Isekai series
I DON'T THINK SO!!!
LET'S DO THIS.
YOUR MAJ-ESTY!!

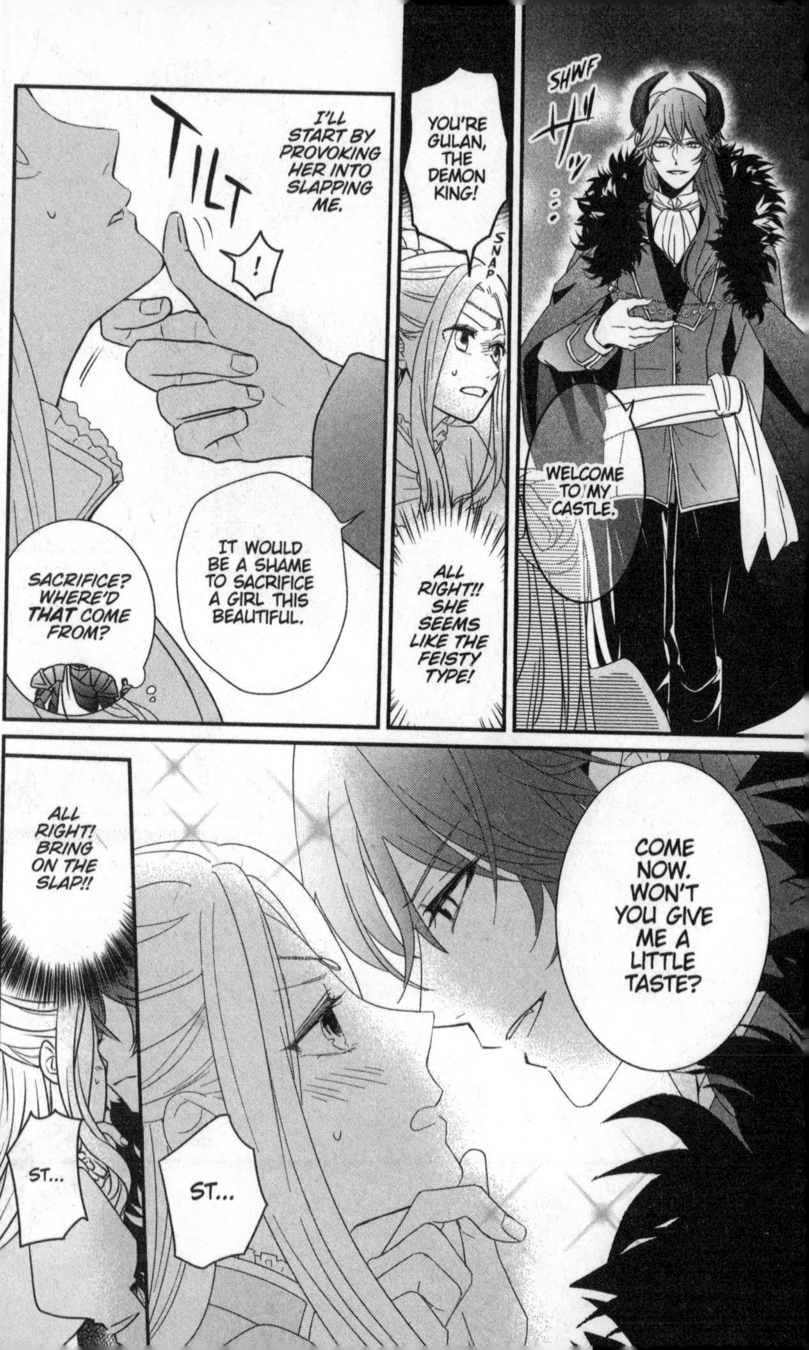
SHWF
WELCOME TO MY CASTLE.
YOU'RE GULAN, THE DEMON KING!
SNAP
ALL RIGHT!! SHE SEEMS LIKE THE FEISTY TYPE!
I'LL START BY PROVOKING HER INTO SLAPPING ME.
TILT
!
IT WOULD BE A SHAME TO SACRIFICE A GIRL THIS BEAUTIFUL.
SACRIFICE? WHERE'D THAT COME FROM?
COME NOW. WON'T YOU GIVE ME A LITTLE TASTE?
ALL RIGHT! BRING ON THE SLAP!!
ST...
ST...

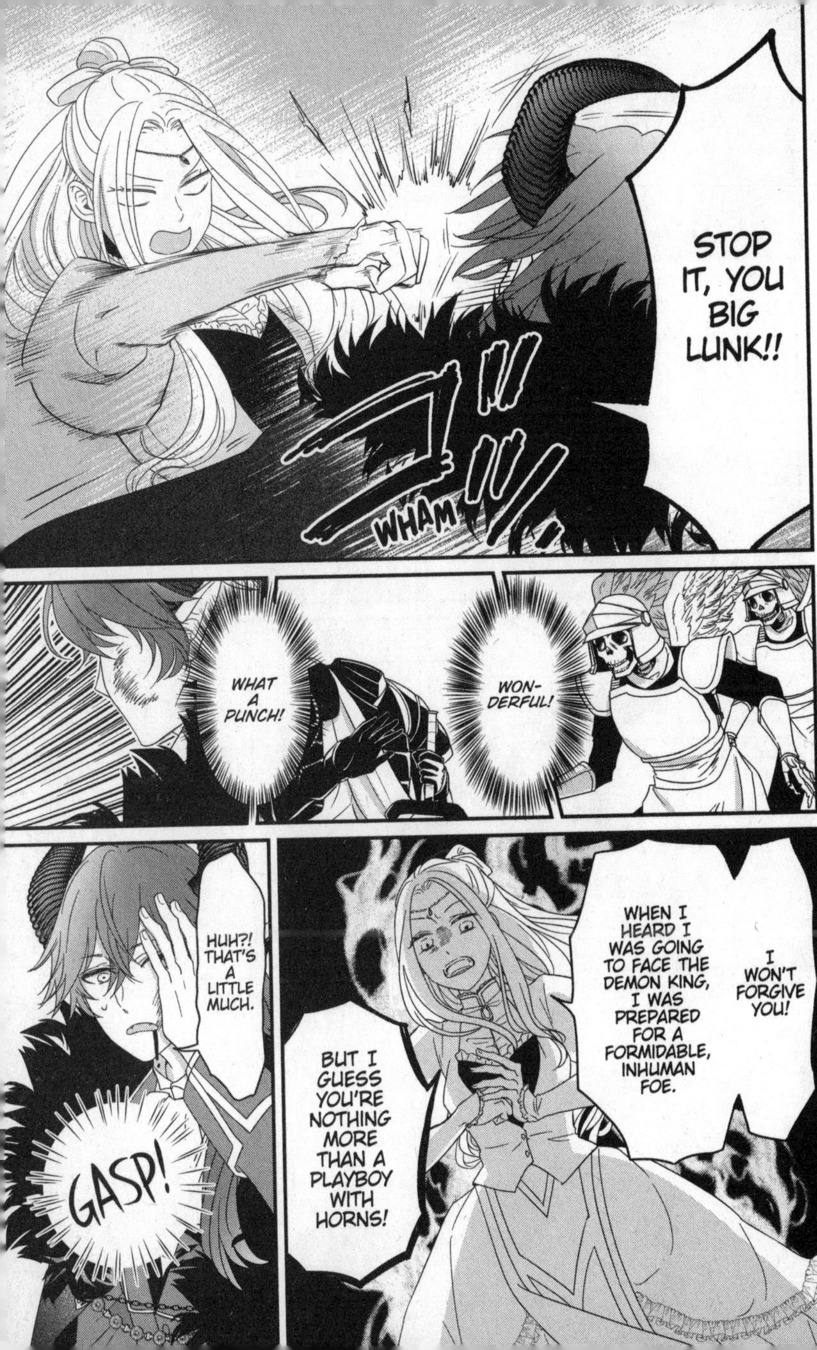

STOP IT, YOU BIG LUNK!!
WHAM
WON-DERFUL!
WHAT A PUNCH!
I WON'T FORGIVE YOU!
WHEN I HEARD I WAS GOING TO FACE THE DEMON KING, I WAS PREPARED FOR A FORMIDABLE, INHUMAN FOE.
BUT I GUESS YOU'RE NOTHING MORE THAN A PLAYBOY WITH HORNS!
HUH?! THAT'S A LITTLE MUCH.
GASP!

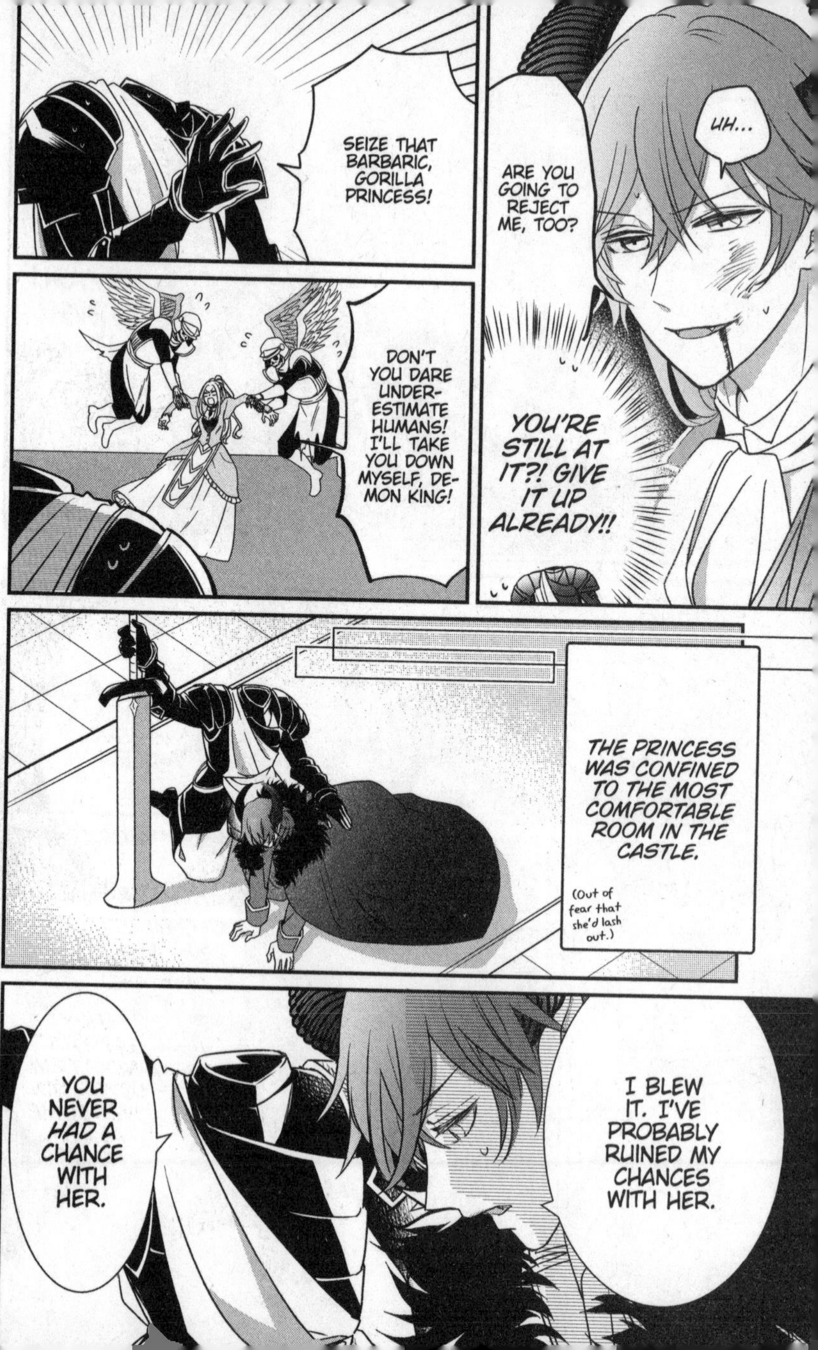
UH...
ARE YOU GOING TO REJECT ME, TOO?
YOU'RE STILL AT IT?! GIVE IT UP ALREADY!!
SEIZE THAT BARBARIC, GORILLA PRINCESS!
DON'T YOU DARE UNDER-ESTIMATE HUMANS! I'LL TAKE YOU DOWN MYSELF, DE-MON KING!
THE PRINCESS WAS CONFINED TO THE MOST COMFORTABLE ROOM IN THE CASTLE.
(Out of fear that she'd lash out.)
I BLEW IT. I'VE PROBABLY RUINED MY CHANCES WITH HER.
YOU NEVER HAD A CHANCE WITH HER.

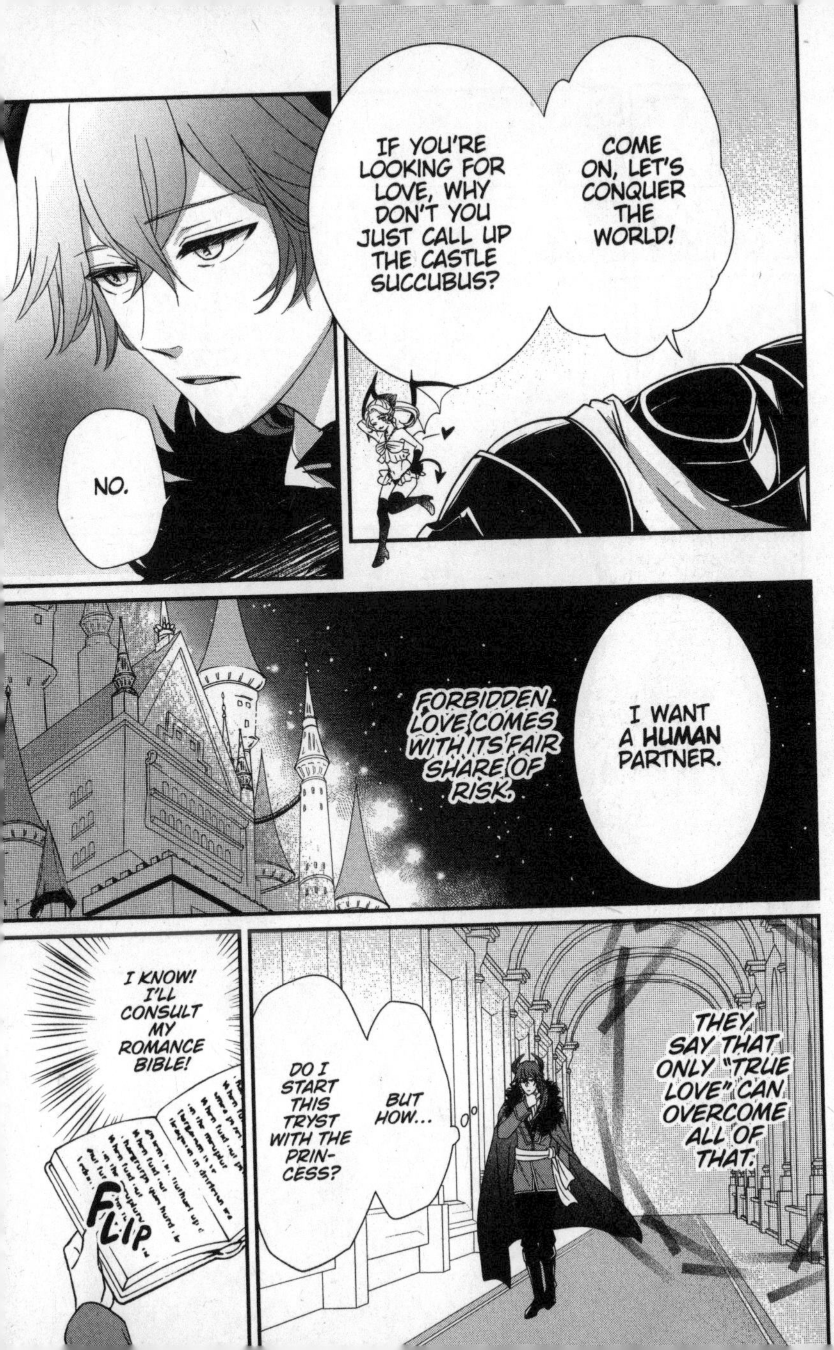
COME ON, LET'S CONQUER THE WORLD!
IF YOU'RE LOOKING FOR LOVE, WHY DON'T YOU JUST CALL UP THE CASTLE SUCCUBUS?
NO.
I WANT A HUMAN PARTNER.
FORBIDDEN LOVE COMES WITH ITS FAIR SHARE OF RISK.
THEY SAY THAT ONLY "TRUE LOVE" CAN OVERCOME ALL OF THAT.
BUT HOW...
DO I START THIS TRYST WITH THE PRINCESS?
I KNOW! I'LL CONSULT MY ROMANCE BIBLE!
FLIP

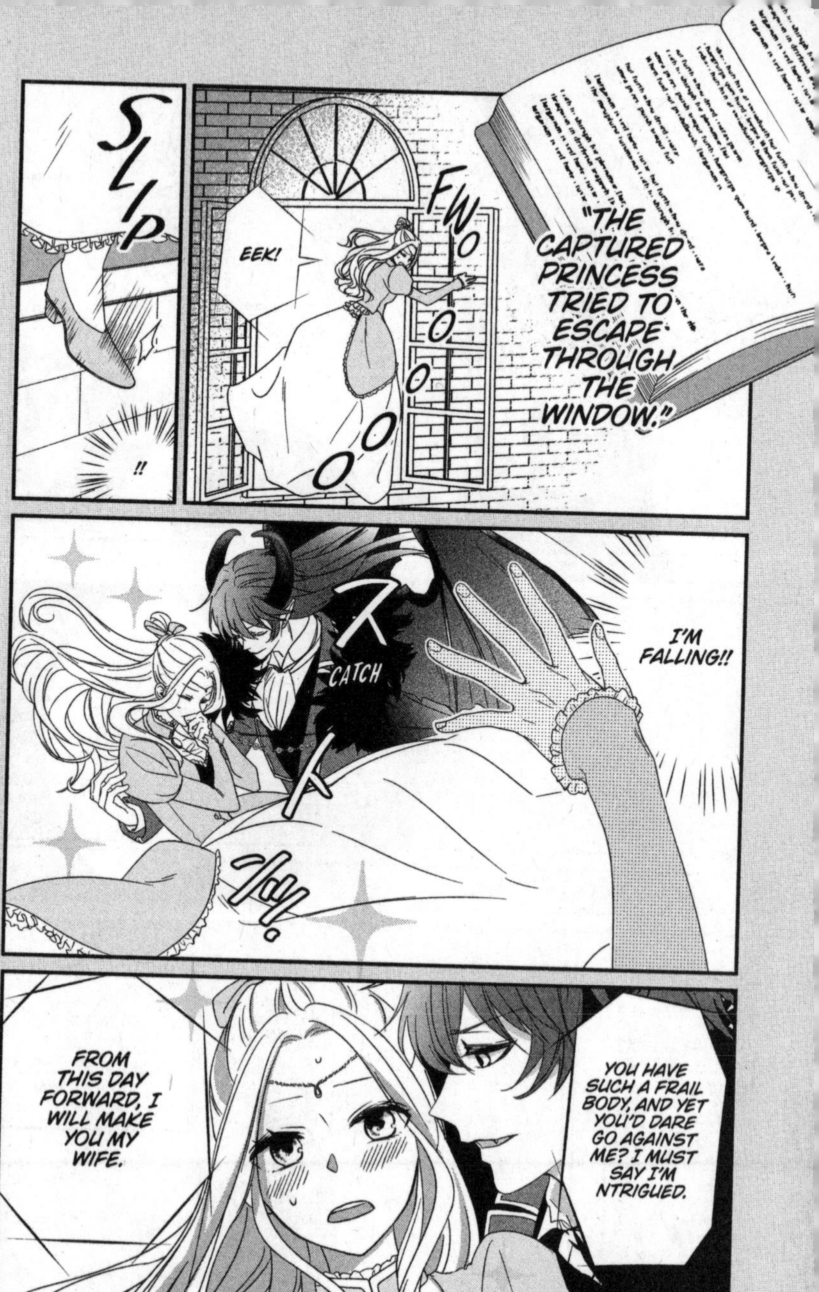
"THE CAPTURED PRINCESS TRIED TO ESCAPE THROUGH THE WINDOW."
FWOOOOOO
EEK!
SLIP
!!
I'M FALLING!!
CATCH
YOU HAVE SUCH A FRAIL BODY, AND YET YOU'D DARE GO AGAINST ME? I MUST SAY I'M NTRIGUED.
FROM THIS DAY FORWARD, I WILL MAKE YOU MY WIFE.

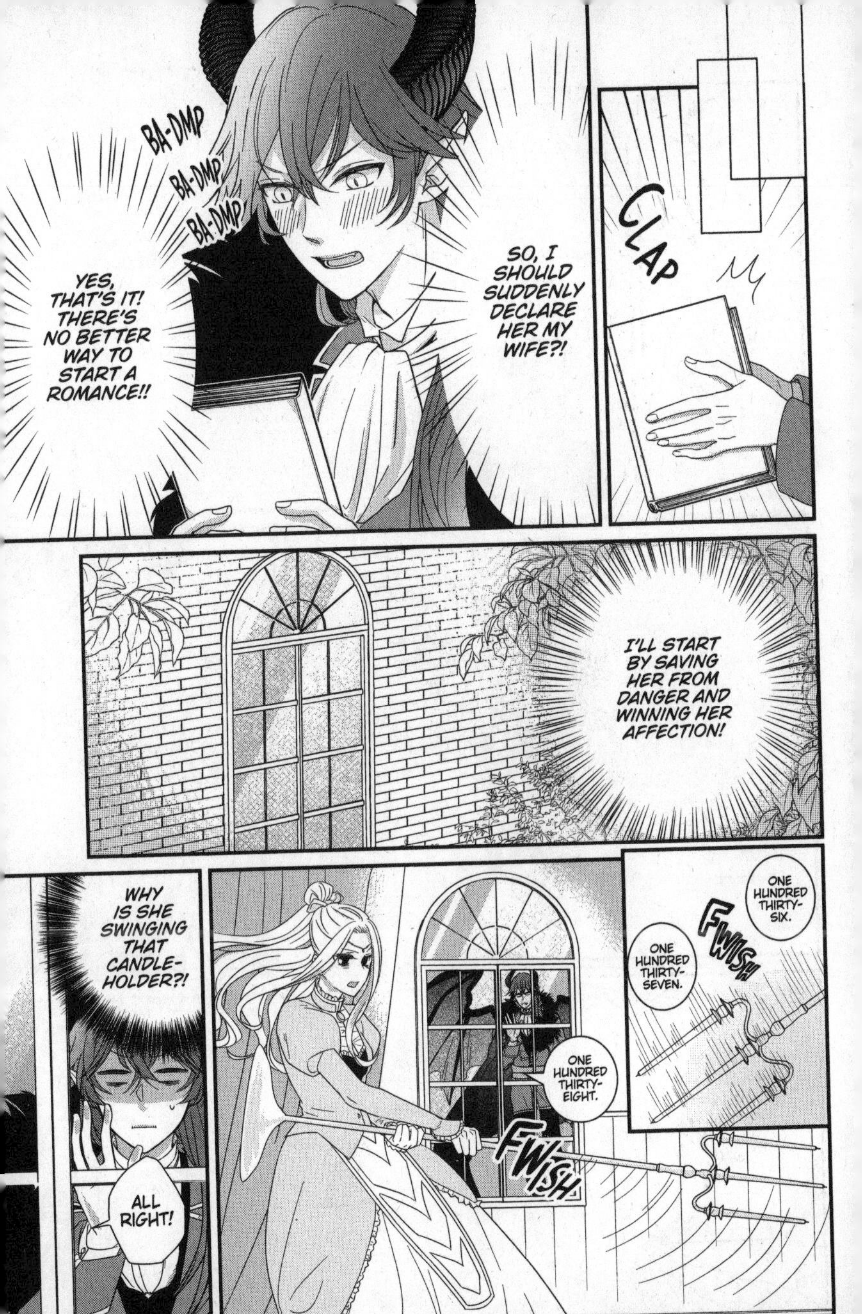
CLAP
SO, I SHOULD SUDDENLY DECLARE HER MY WIFE?!
BA-DMP
BA-DMP
BA-DMP
YES, THAT'S IT! THERE'S NO BETTER WAY TO START A ROMANCE!!
I'LL START BY SAVING HER FROM DANGER AND WINNING HER AFFECTION!
ONE HUNDRED THIRTY-SIX.
FWISH
ONE HUNDRED THIRTY-SEVEN.
ONE HUNDRED THIRTY-EIGHT.
FWISH
WHY IS SHE SWINGING THAT CANDLE-HOLDER?!
ALL RIGHT!

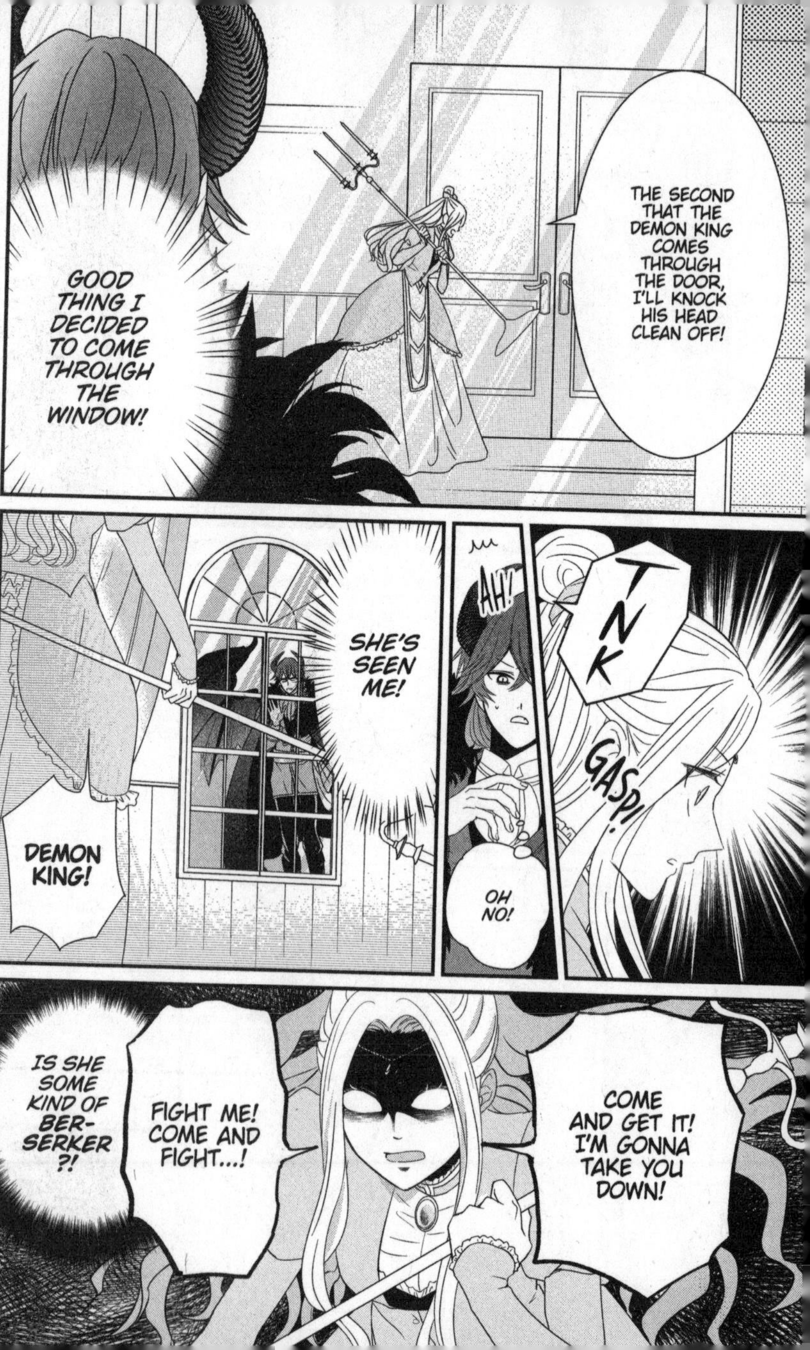
THE SECOND THAT THE DEMON KING COMES THROUGH THE DOOR, I'LL KNOCK HIS HEAD CLEAN OFF!
GOOD THING I DECIDED TO COME THROUGH THE WINDOW!
TNK
GASP!
AH!
OH NO!
SHE'S SEEN ME!
DEMON KING!
COME AND GET IT! I'M GONNA TAKE YOU DOWN!
FIGHT ME! COME AND FIGHT...!
IS SHE SOME KIND OF BER-SERKER?!

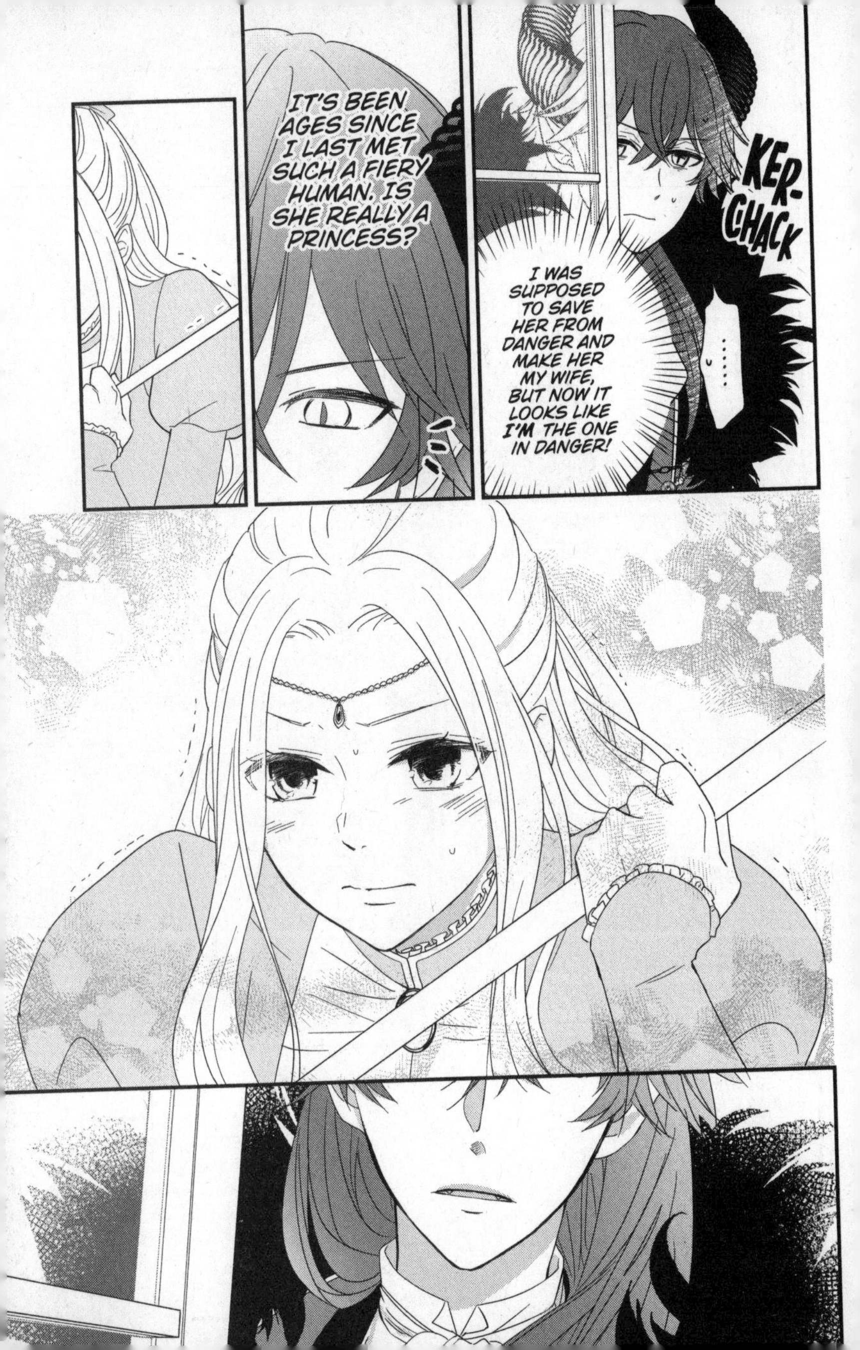
KER-CHACK
I WAS SUPPOSED TO SAVE HER FROM DANGER AND MAKE HER MY WIFE, BUT NOW IT LOOKS LIKE I'M THE ONE IN DANGER!
......
IT'S BEEN AGES SINCE I LAST MET SUCH A FIERY HUMAN. IS SHE REALLY A PRINCESS?

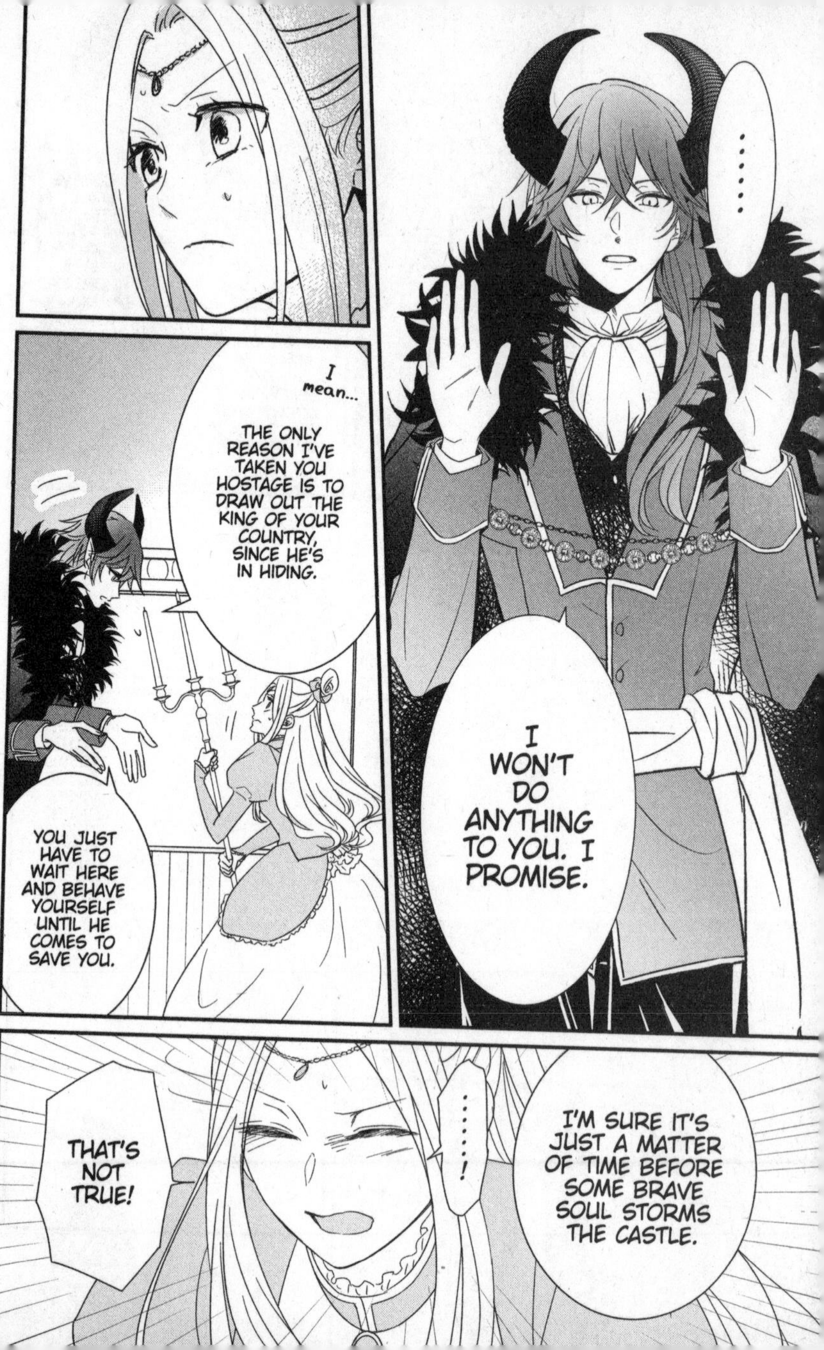
……
I WON'T DO ANYTHING TO YOU. I PROMISE.
I mean...
THE ONLY REASON I'VE TAKEN YOU HOSTAGE IS TO DRAW OUT THE KING OF YOUR COUNTRY, SINCE HE'S IN HIDING.
YOU JUST HAVE TO WAIT HERE AND BEHAVE YOURSELF UNTIL HE COMES TO SAVE YOU.
I'M SURE IT'S JUST A MATTER OF TIME BEFORE SOME BRAVE SOUL STORMS THE CASTLE.
……!
THAT'S NOT TRUE!

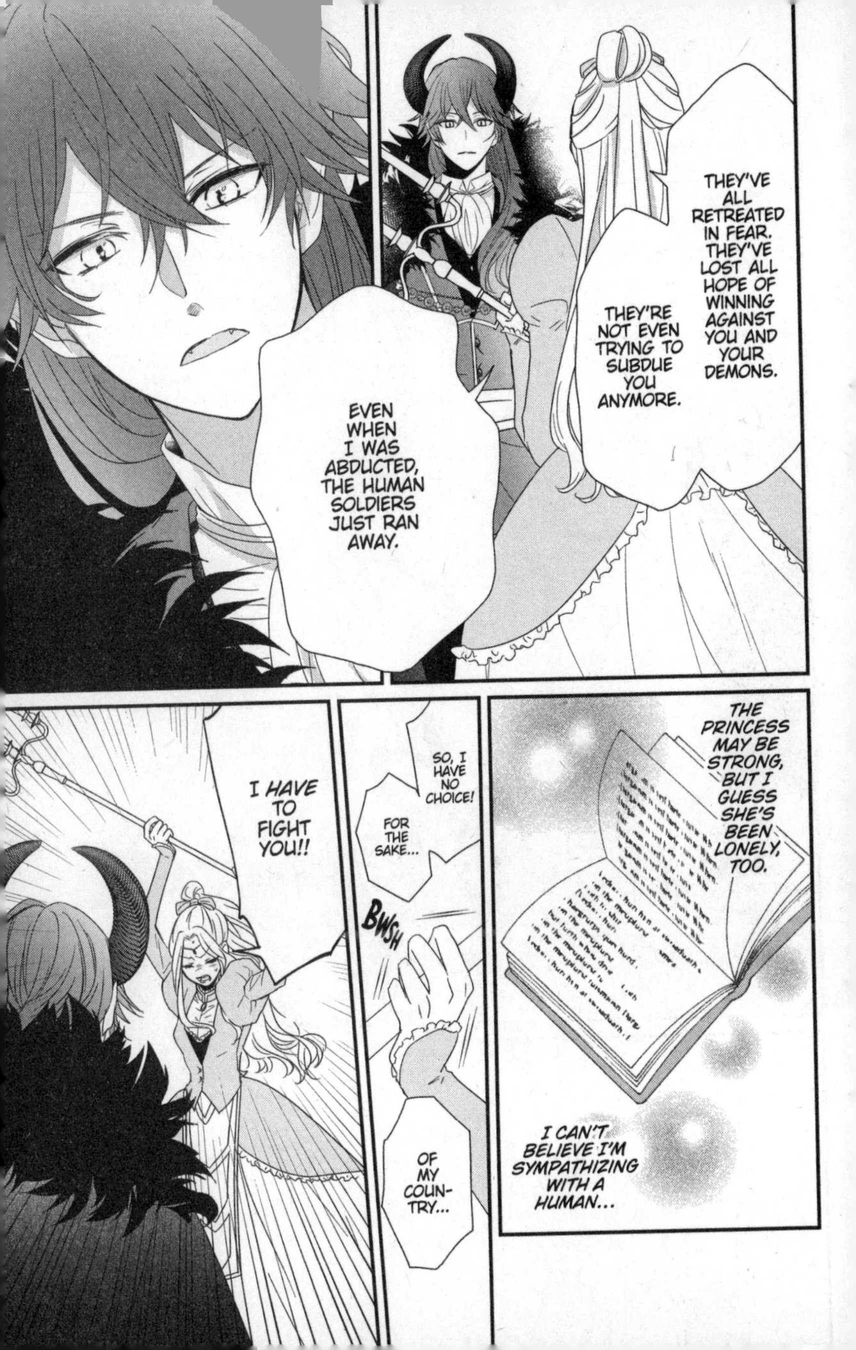
THEY'VE ALL RETREATED IN FEAR. THEY'VE LOST ALL HOPE OF WINNING AGAINST YOU AND YOUR DEMONS.
THEY'RE NOT EVEN TRYING TO SUBDUE YOU ANYMORE.
EVEN WHEN I WAS ABDUCTED, THE HUMAN SOLDIERS JUST RAN AWAY.
THE PRINCESS MAY BE STRONG, BUT I GUESS SHE'S BEEN LONELY, TOO.
I CAN'T BELIEVE I'M SYMPATHIZING WITH A HUMAN...
SO, I HAVE NO CHOICE!
FOR THE SAKE...
BWSH
OF MY COUNTRY...
I HAVE TO FIGHT YOU!!

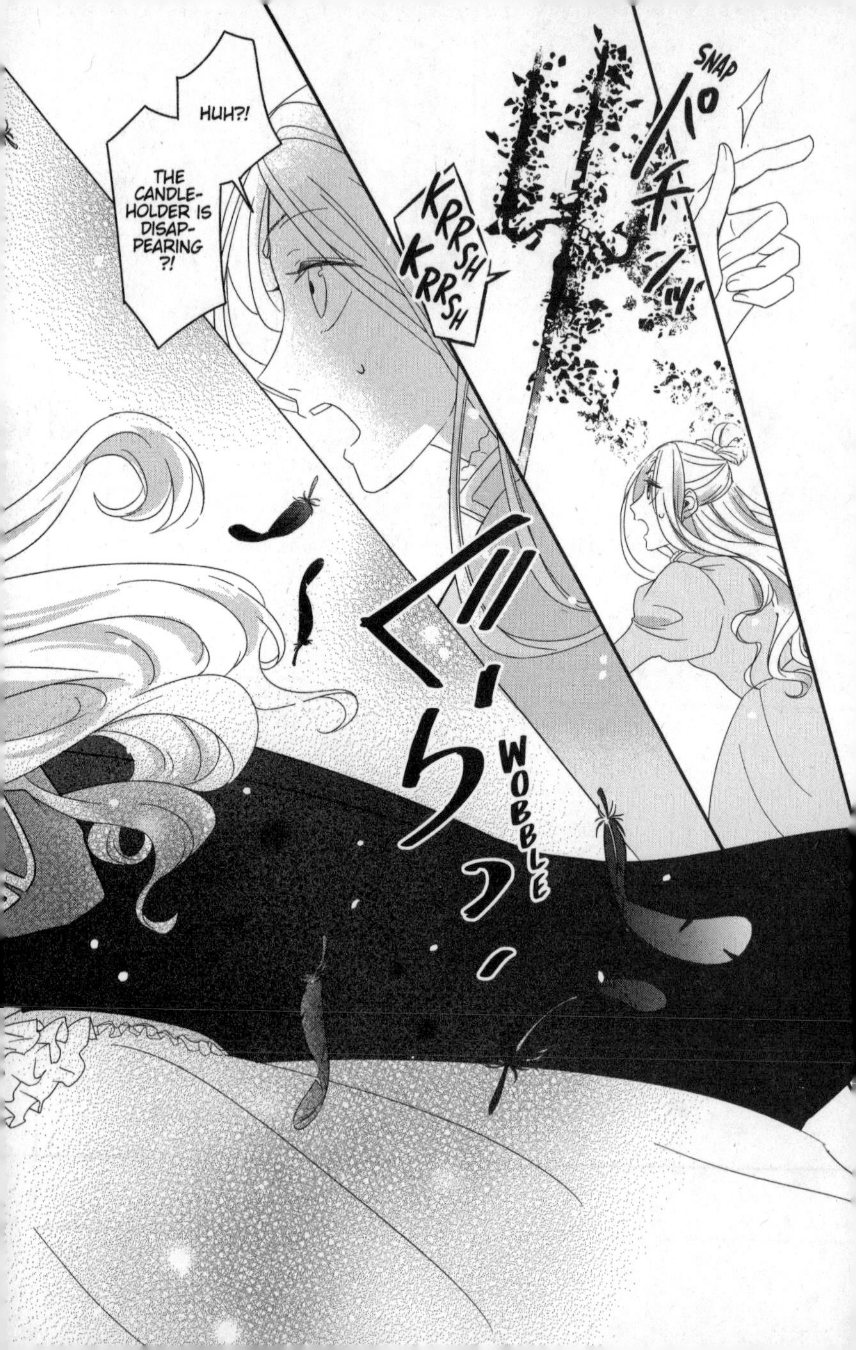
SNAP
KRRSH KRRSH
HUH?!
THE CANDLE-HOLDER IS DISAP-PEARING?!
WOBBLE

Introduction

I'm Yasuko Yamaru.

Nice to meet you!

Thanks for checking

out this manga.

I hope you enjoy

it, and I wish you

a heart-pounding

experience that

brings a smile to

your face! +

Yasuko Yamaru

To my readers,
the LaLa editorial staff,
my editor, my designer,
bookstore staff,
Akari-sama, Yuri-sama,
and my friends and
family...

Thank you!

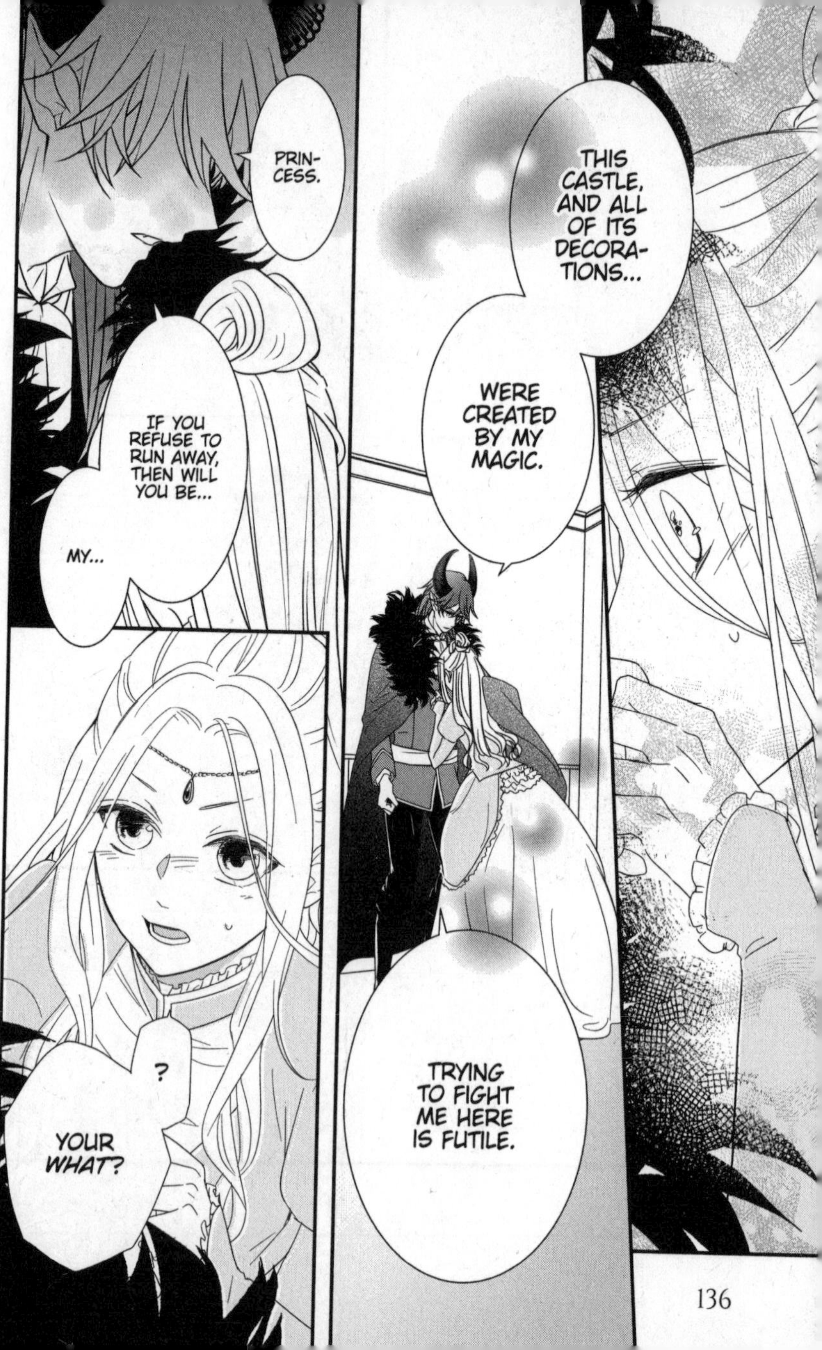
THIS CASTLE, AND ALL OF ITS DECORATIONS...
WERE CREATED BY MY MAGIC.
TRYING TO FIGHT ME HERE IS FUTILE.
PRINCESS.
IF YOU REFUSE TO RUN AWAY, THEN WILL YOU BE...
MY...
?
YOUR WHAT?

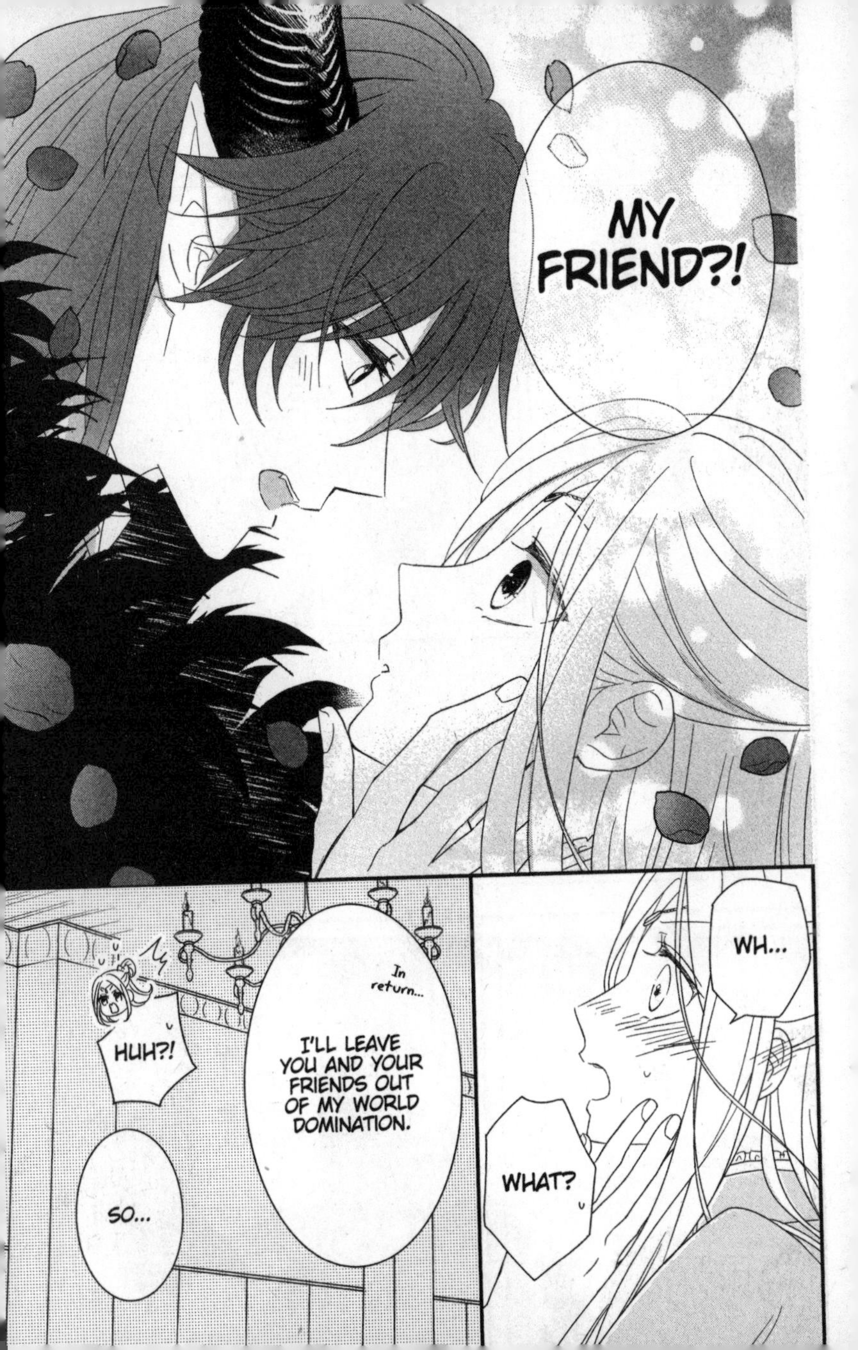
MY FRIEND?!
WH...
WHAT?
In return...
I'LL LEAVE YOU AND YOUR FRIENDS OUT OF MY WORLD DOMINATION.
HUH?!
SO...

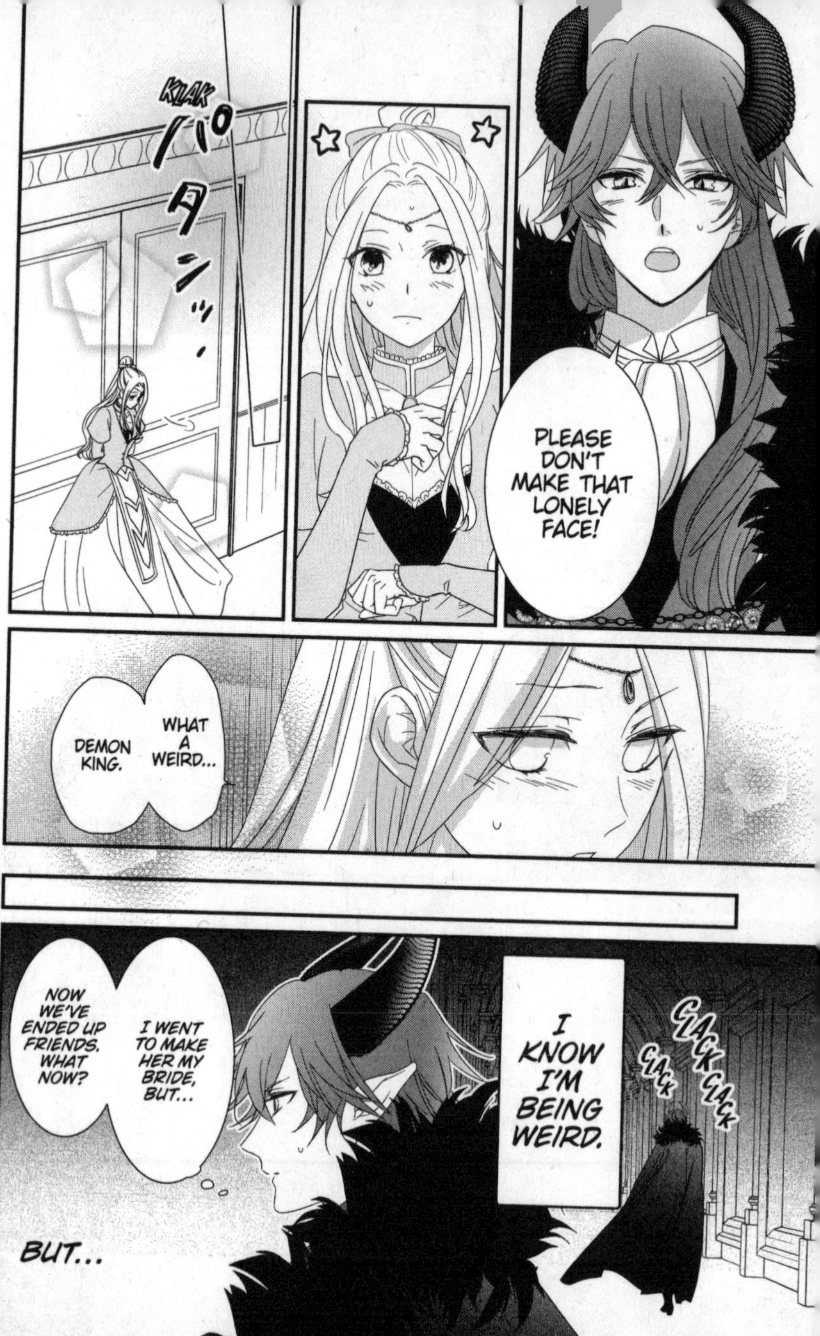
PLEASE DON'T MAKE THAT LONELY FACE!
KLAK
パタンッ
WHAT A WEIRD...
DEMON KING.
I KNOW I'M BEING WEIRD.
CLACK CLACK
CLACK
I WENT TO MAKE HER MY BRIDE, BUT...
NOW WE'VE ENDED UP FRIENDS. WHAT NOW?
BUT...

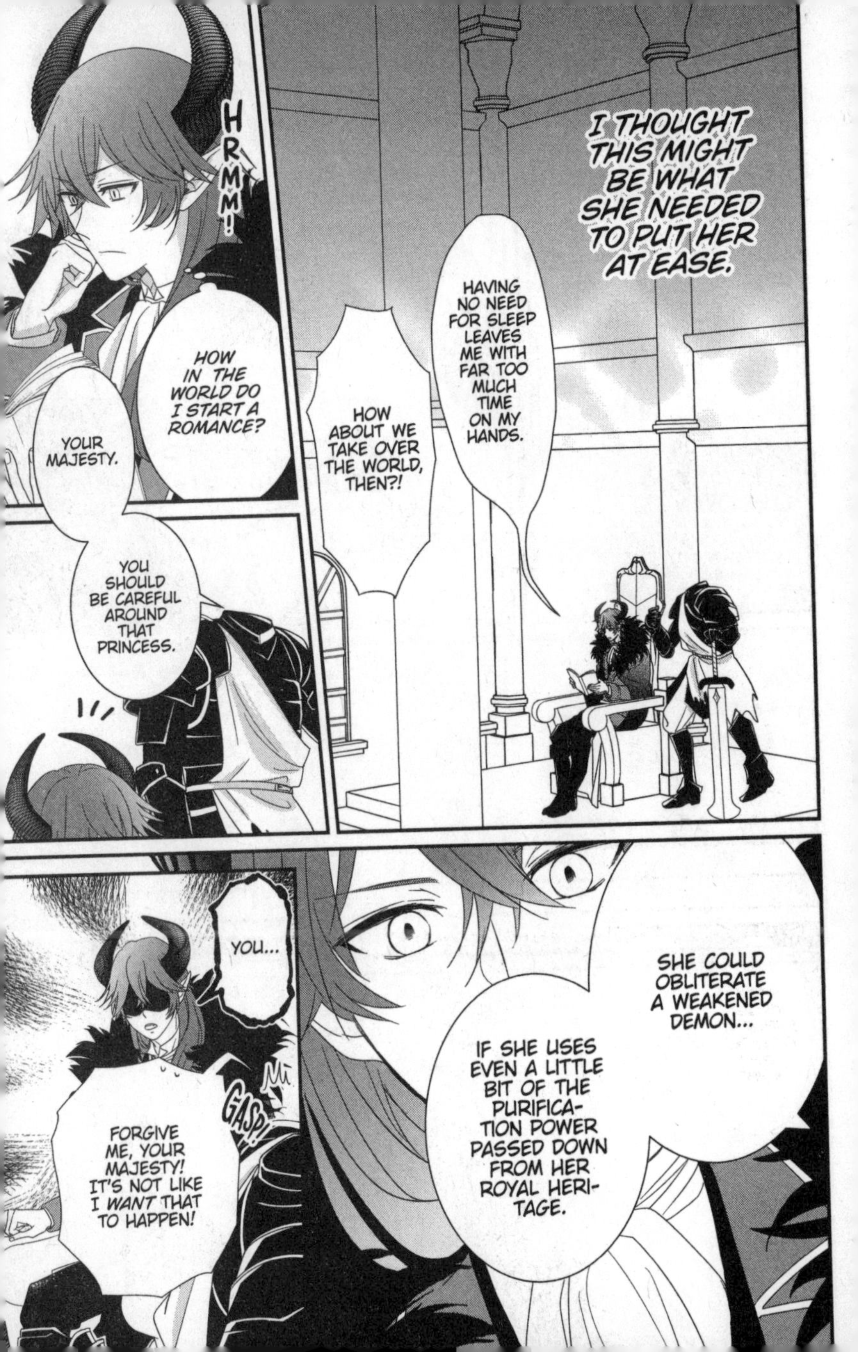
I THOUGHT THIS MIGHT BE WHAT SHE NEEDED TO PUT HER AT EASE.
HAVING NO NEED FOR SLEEP LEAVES ME WITH FAR TOO MUCH TIME ON MY HANDS.
HOW ABOUT WE TAKE OVER THE WORLD, THEN?!
HRMM!
HOW IN THE WORLD DO I START A ROMANCE?
YOUR MAJESTY.
YOU SHOULD BE CAREFUL AROUND THAT PRINCESS.
SHE COULD OBLITERATE A WEAKENED DEMON...
IF SHE USES EVEN A LITTLE BIT OF THE PURIFICA-TION POWER PASSED DOWN FROM HER ROYAL HERI-TAGE.
YOU...
MU
GASP!
FORGIVE ME, YOUR MAJESTY! IT'S NOT LIKE I *WANT* THAT TO HAPPEN!

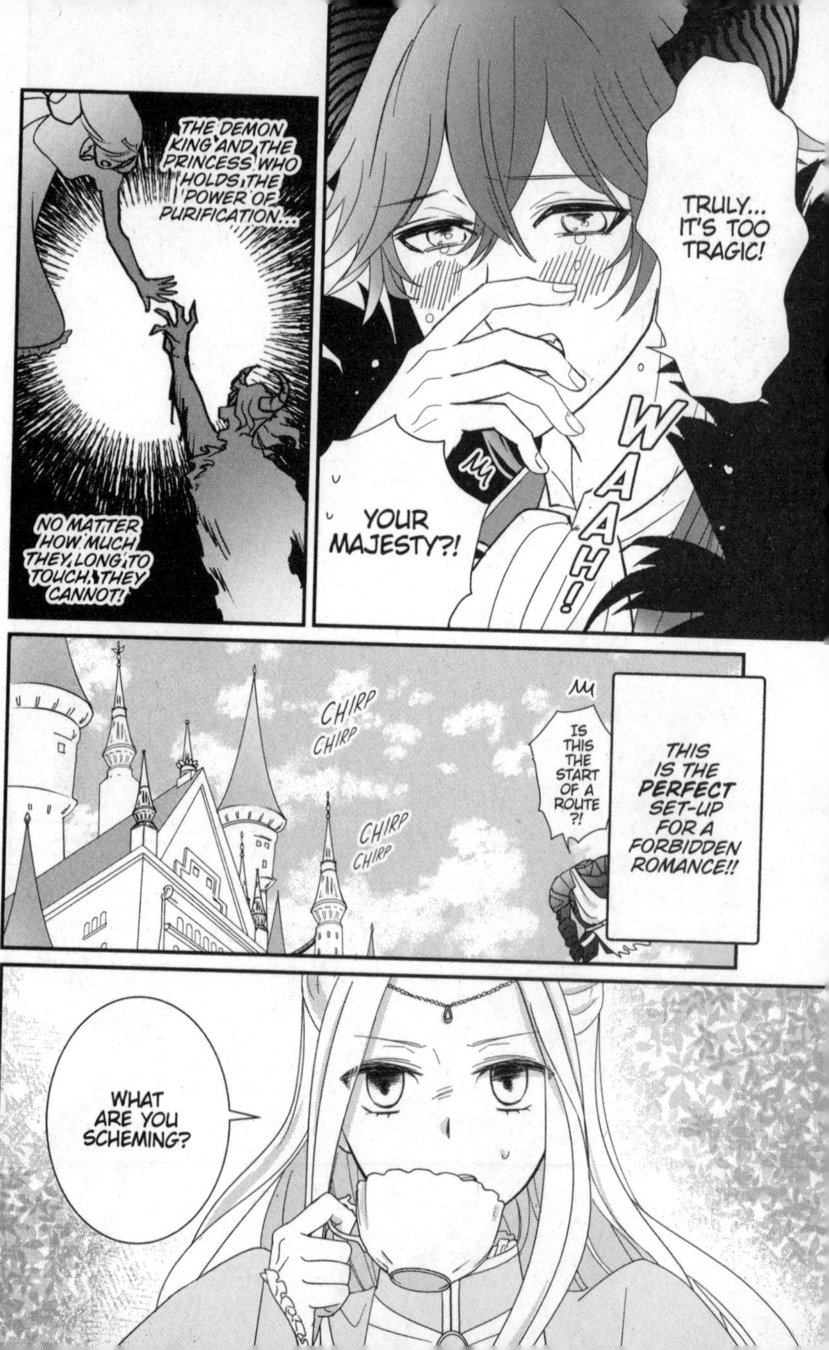
TRULY... IT'S TOO TRAGIC!
WAAAH!
YOUR MAJESTY?!
THE DEMON KING AND THE PRINCESS WHO HOLDS THE POWER OF PURIFICATION...
NO MATTER HOW MUCH THEY LONG TO TOUCH, THEY CANNOT!
THIS IS THE PERFECT SET-UP FOR A FORBIDDEN ROMANCE!!
IS THIS THE START OF A ROUTE ?!
CHIRP CHIRP
CHIRP CHIRP
WHAT ARE YOU SCHEMING?

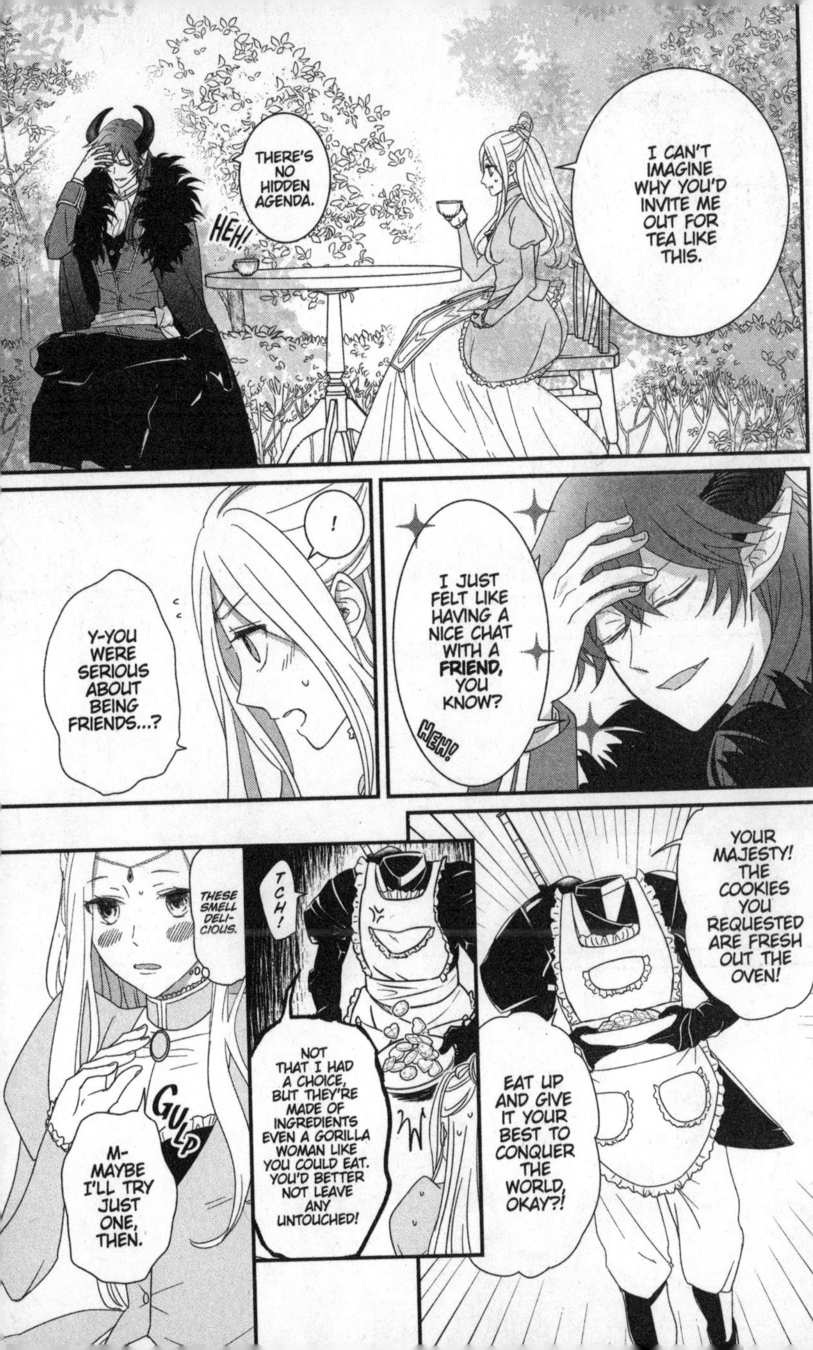
I CAN'T IMAGINE WHY YOU'D INVITE ME OUT FOR TEA LIKE THIS.
THERE'S NO HIDDEN AGENDA.
HEH!
I JUST FELT LIKE HAVING A NICE CHAT WITH A **FRIEND,** YOU KNOW?
HEH!
!
Y-YOU WERE SERIOUS ABOUT BEING FRIENDS...?
YOUR MAJESTY! THE COOKIES YOU REQUESTED ARE FRESH OUT THE OVEN!
EAT UP AND GIVE IT YOUR BEST TO CONQUER THE WORLD, OKAY?!
TCH!
NOT THAT I HAD A CHOICE, BUT THEY'RE MADE OF INGREDIENTS EVEN A GORILLA WOMAN LIKE YOU COULD EAT. YOU'D BETTER NOT LEAVE ANY UNTOUCHED!
THESE SMELL DELI-CIOUS.
GULP
M-MAYBE I'LL TRY JUST ONE, THEN.

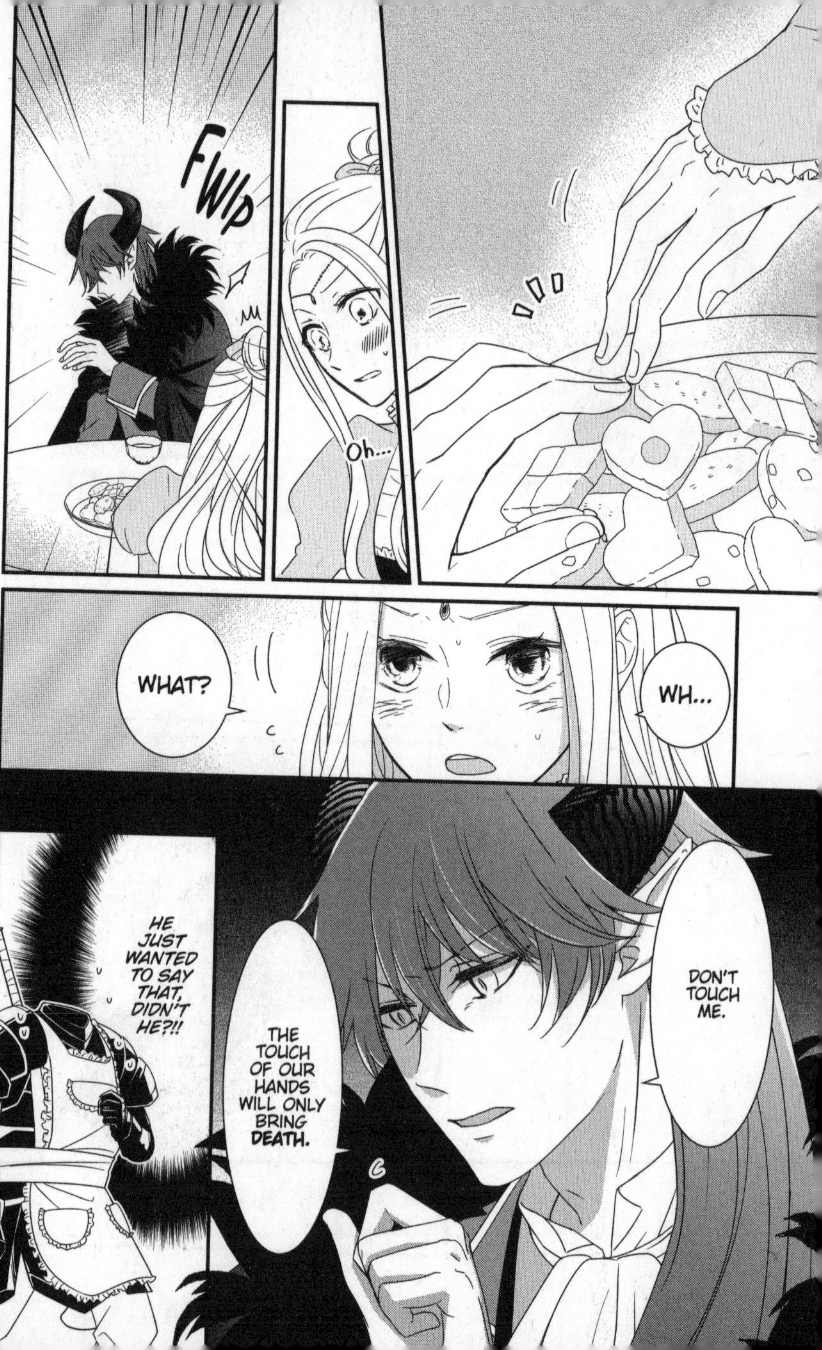
Oh...
FWIP
WH...
WHAT?
DON'T TOUCH ME.
THE TOUCH OF OUR HANDS WILL ONLY BRING DEATH.
HE JUST WANTED TO SAY THAT, DIDN'T HE?!!

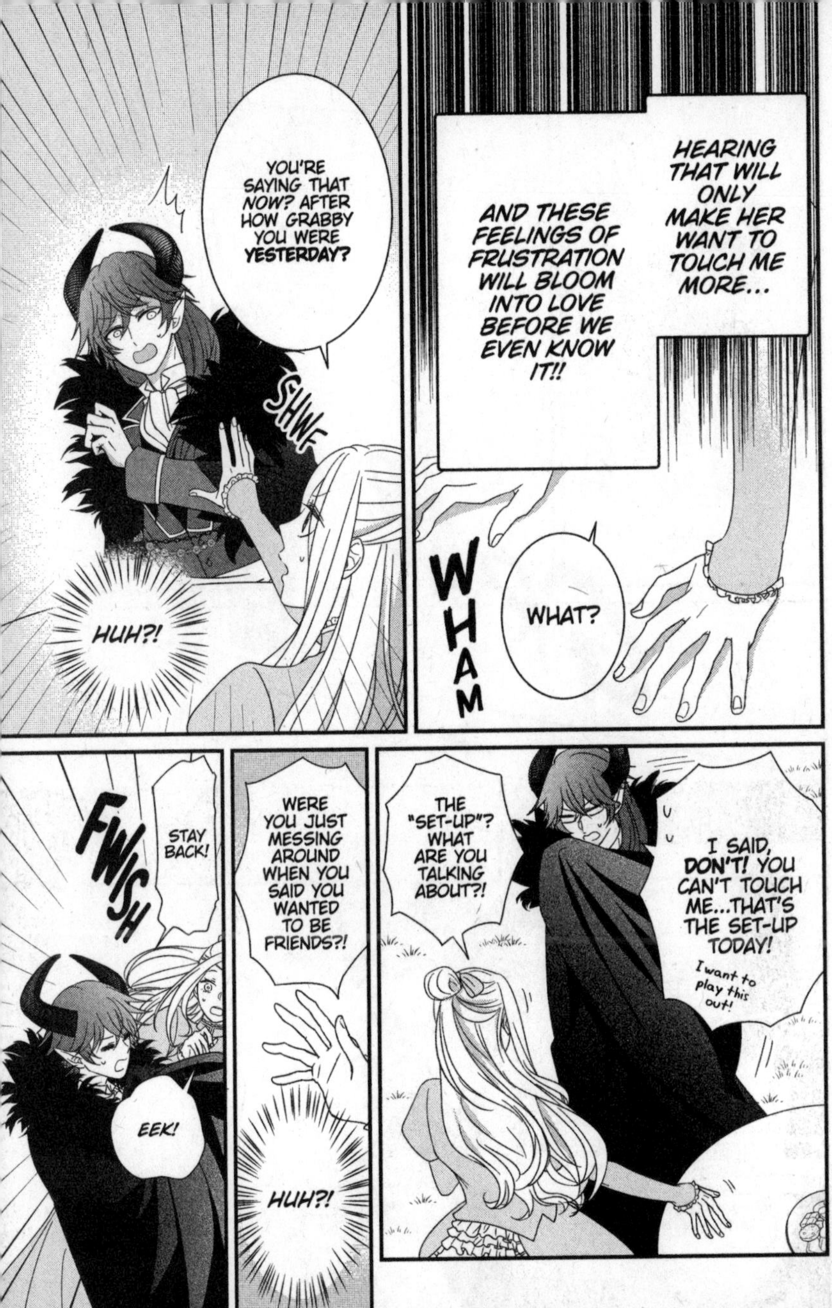
HEARING THAT WILL ONLY MAKE HER WANT TO TOUCH ME MORE...
AND THESE FEELINGS OF FRUSTRATION WILL BLOOM INTO LOVE BEFORE WE EVEN KNOW IT!!
WHAT?
WHAM
SHWF
YOU'RE SAYING THAT NOW? AFTER HOW GRABBY YOU WERE YESTERDAY?
HUH?!
I SAID, DON'T! YOU CAN'T TOUCH ME...THAT'S THE SET-UP TODAY!
I want to play this out!
THE "SET-UP"? WHAT ARE YOU TALKING ABOUT?!
WERE YOU JUST MESSING AROUND WHEN YOU SAID YOU WANTED TO BE FRIENDS?!
HUH?!
STAY BACK!
FWISH
EEK!

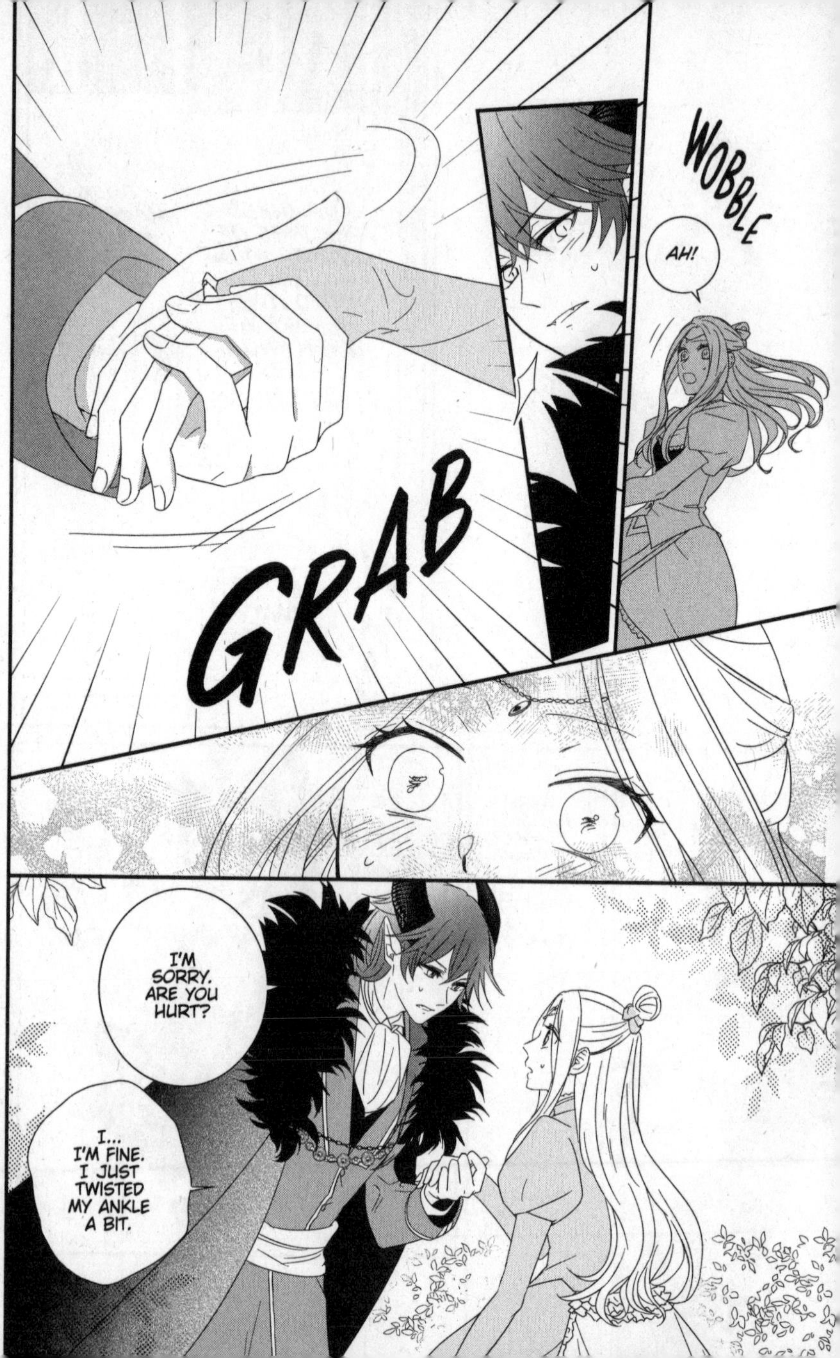
WOBBLE
AH!
GRAB
I'M SORRY. ARE YOU HURT?
I... I'M FINE. I JUST TWISTED MY ANKLE A BIT.

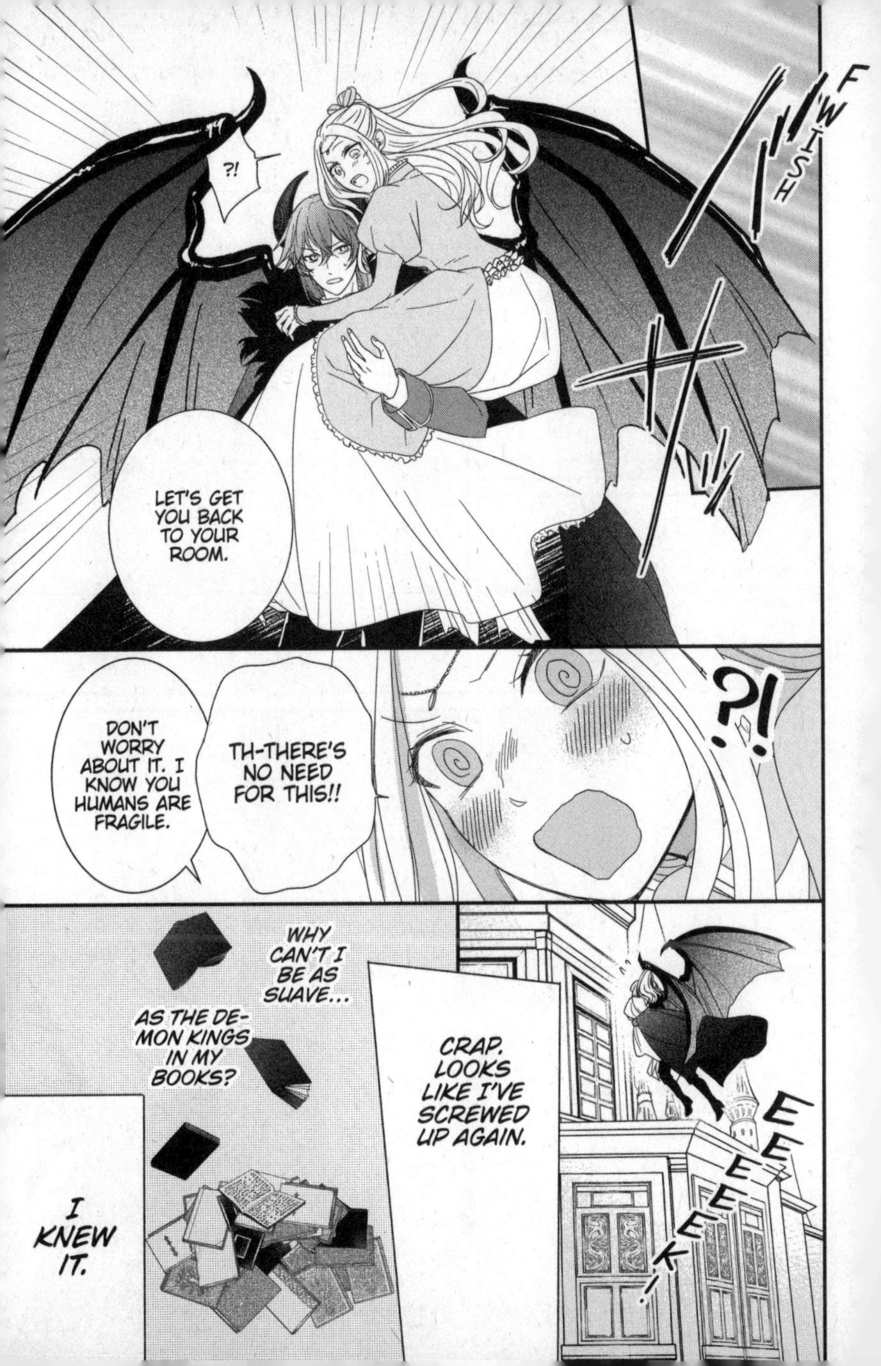
FWISH
?!
LET'S GET YOU BACK TO YOUR ROOM.
?!
TH-THERE'S NO NEED FOR THIS!!
DON'T WORRY ABOUT IT. I KNOW YOU HUMANS ARE FRAGILE.
EEEEEK!
CRAP. LOOKS LIKE I'VE SCREWED UP AGAIN.
WHY CAN'T I BE AS SUAVE...
AS THE DE-MON KINGS IN MY BOOKS?
I KNEW IT.

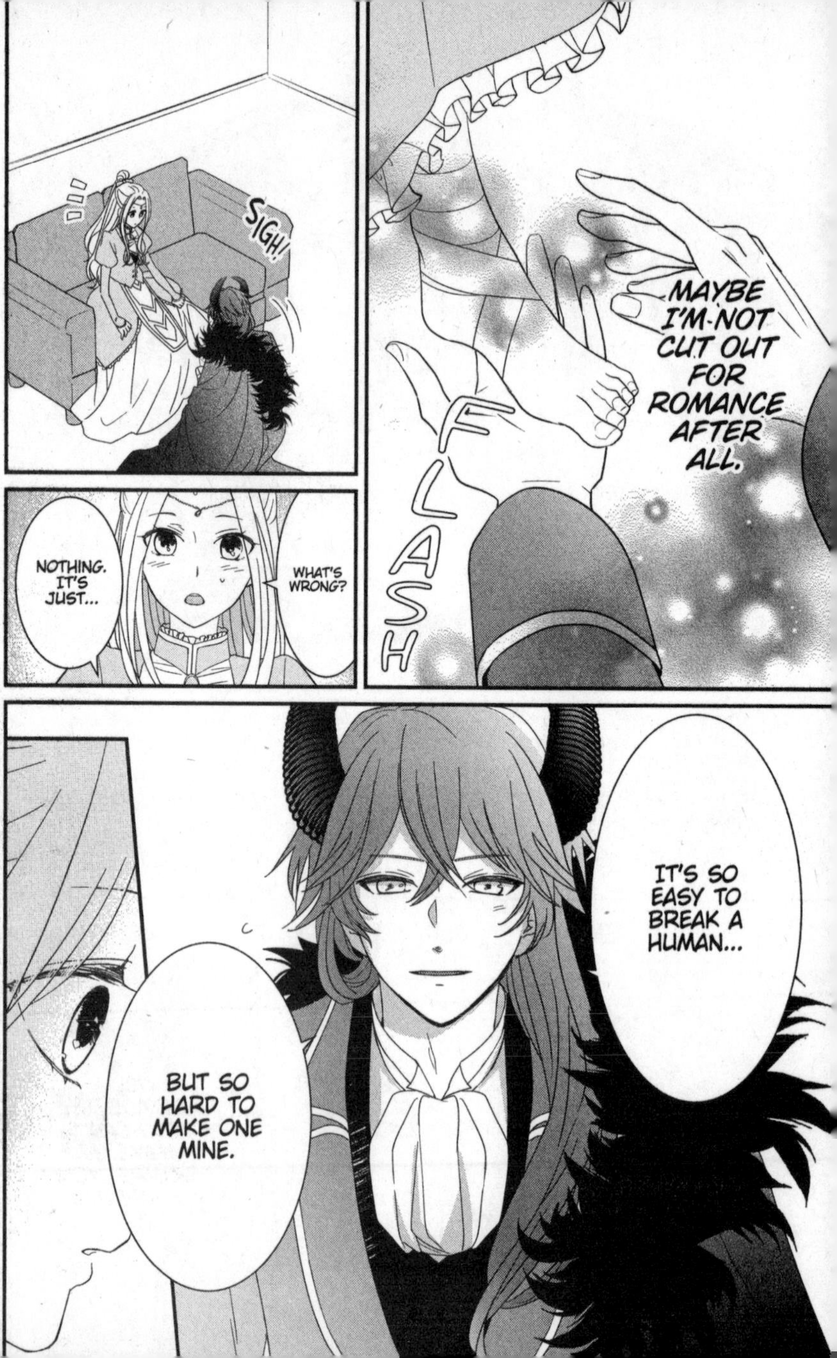
MAYBE I'M NOT CUT OUT FOR ROMANCE AFTER ALL.
FLASH
SIGH!
WHAT'S WRONG?
NOTHING. IT'S JUST...
IT'S SO EASY TO BREAK A HUMAN...
BUT SO HARD TO MAKE ONE MINE.

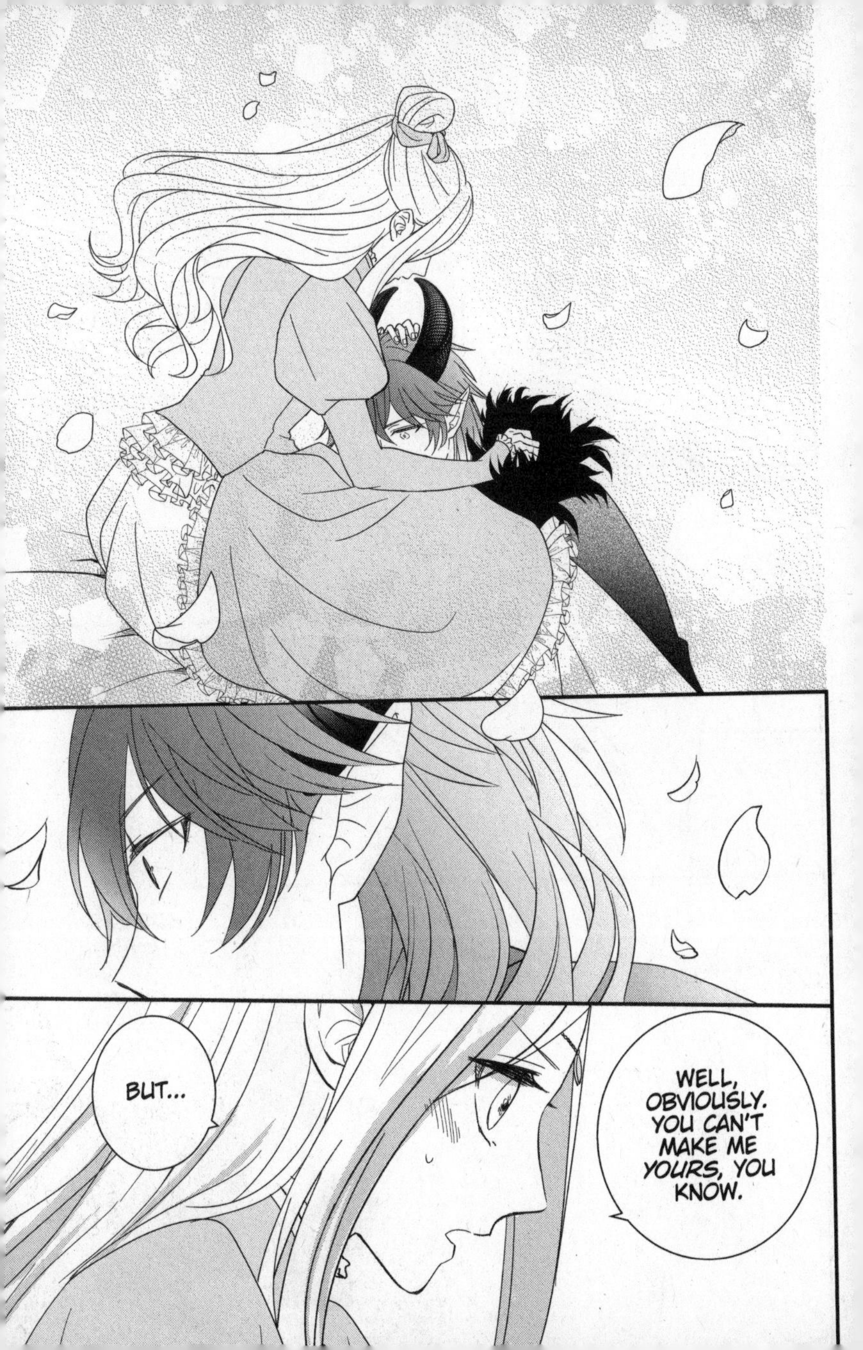
WELL, OBVIOUSLY. YOU CAN'T MAKE ME YOURS, YOU KNOW.
BUT...

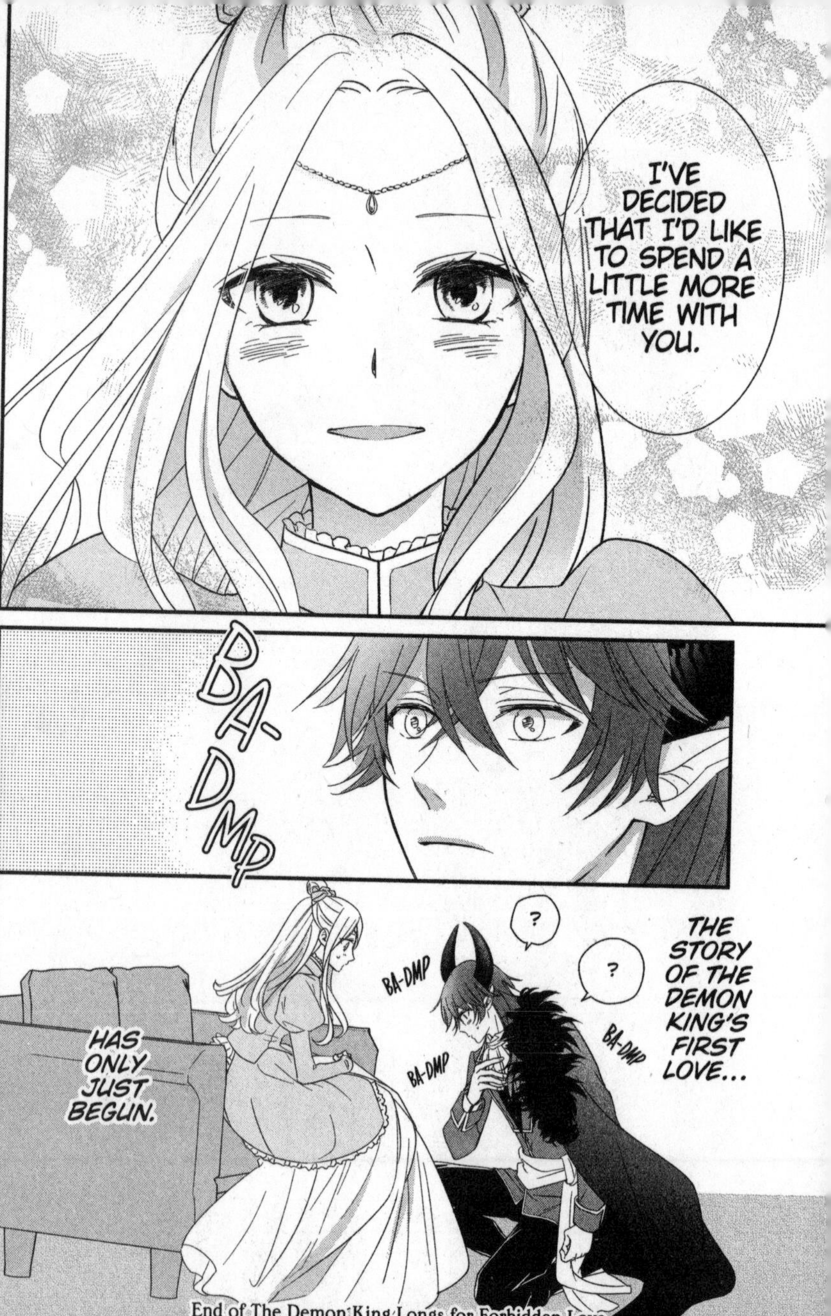
I'VE DECIDED THAT I'D LIKE TO SPEND A LITTLE MORE TIME WITH YOU.
BA-DMP
THE STORY OF THE DEMON KING'S FIRST LOVE...
?
?
BA-DMP
BA-DMP
BA-DMP
HAS ONLY JUST BEGUN.

End of The Demon King Longs for Forbidden Love

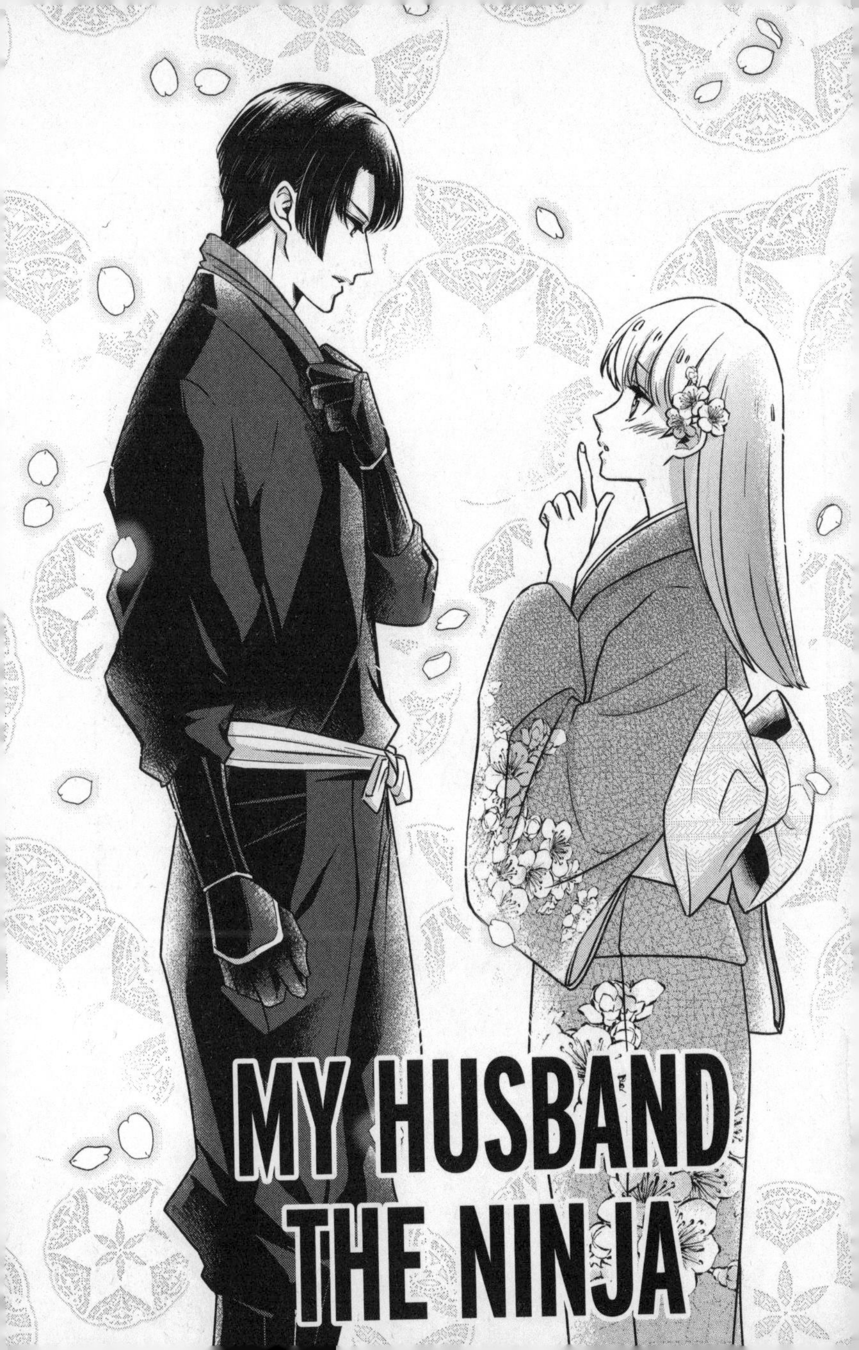
MY HUSBAND
THE NINJA

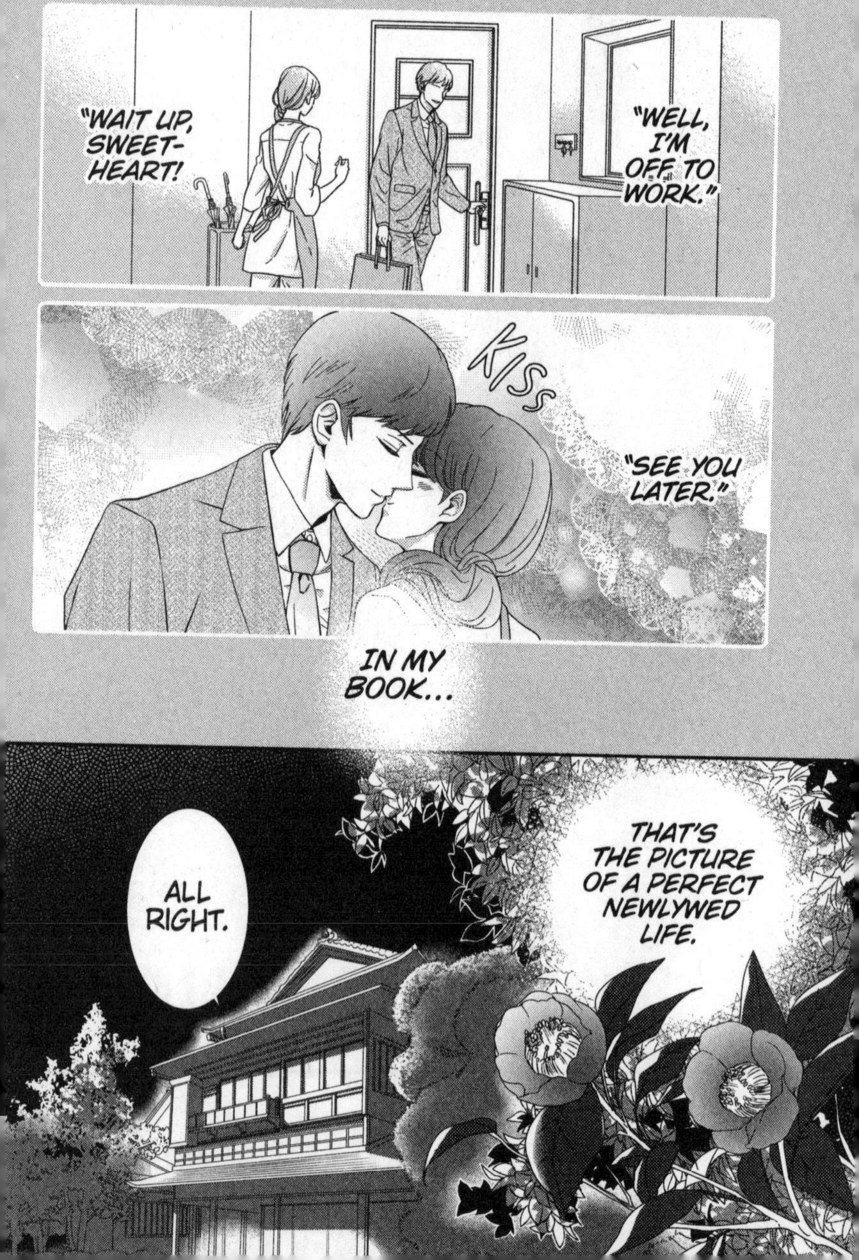
"WELL, I'M OFF TO WORK."
"WAIT UP, SWEET-HEART!
KISS
"SEE YOU LATER."
IN MY BOOK...
THAT'S THE PICTURE OF A PERFECT NEWLYWED LIFE.
ALL RIGHT.

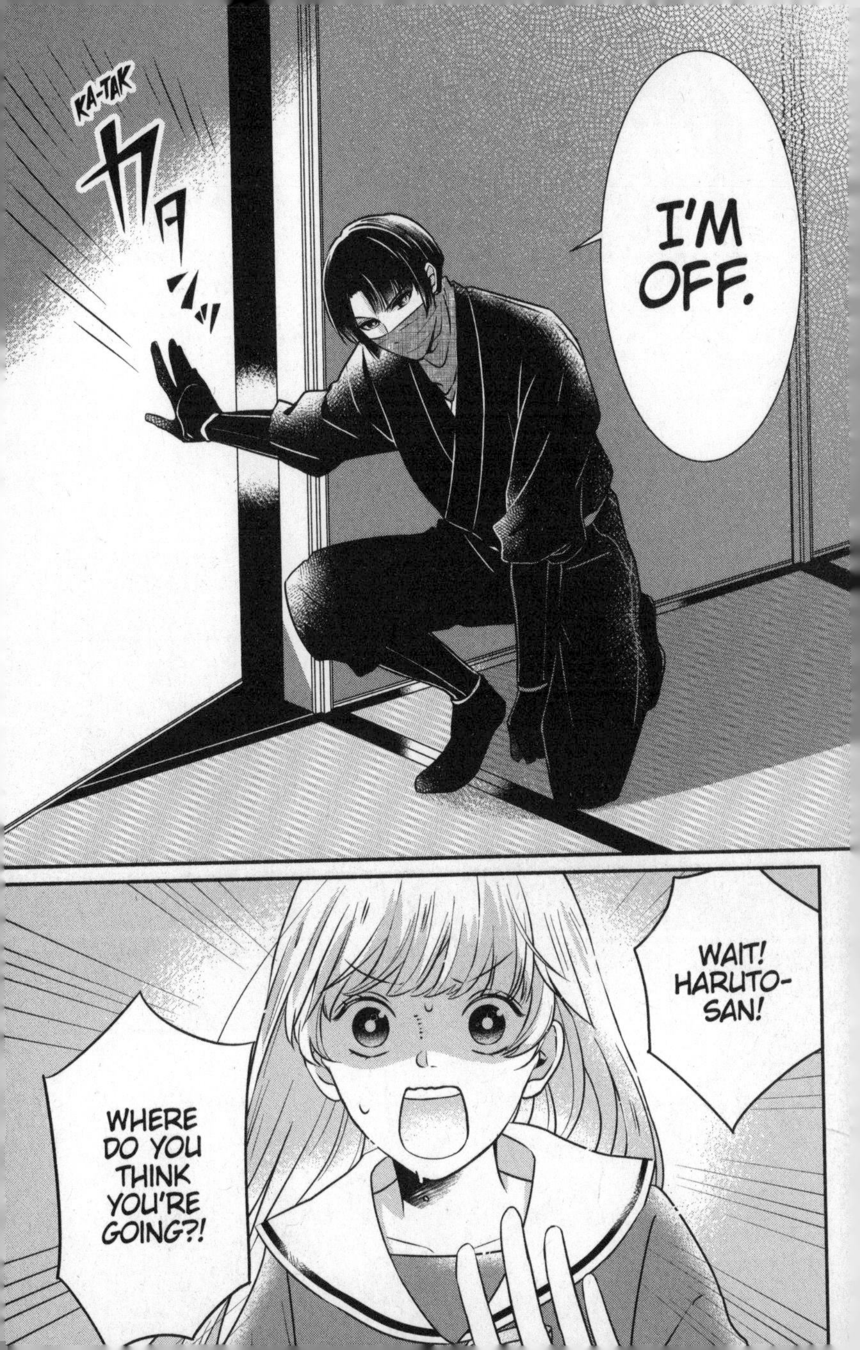
I'M OFF.
KA-TAK
カタッ
WAIT! HARUTO-SAN!
WHERE DO YOU THINK YOU'RE GOING?!

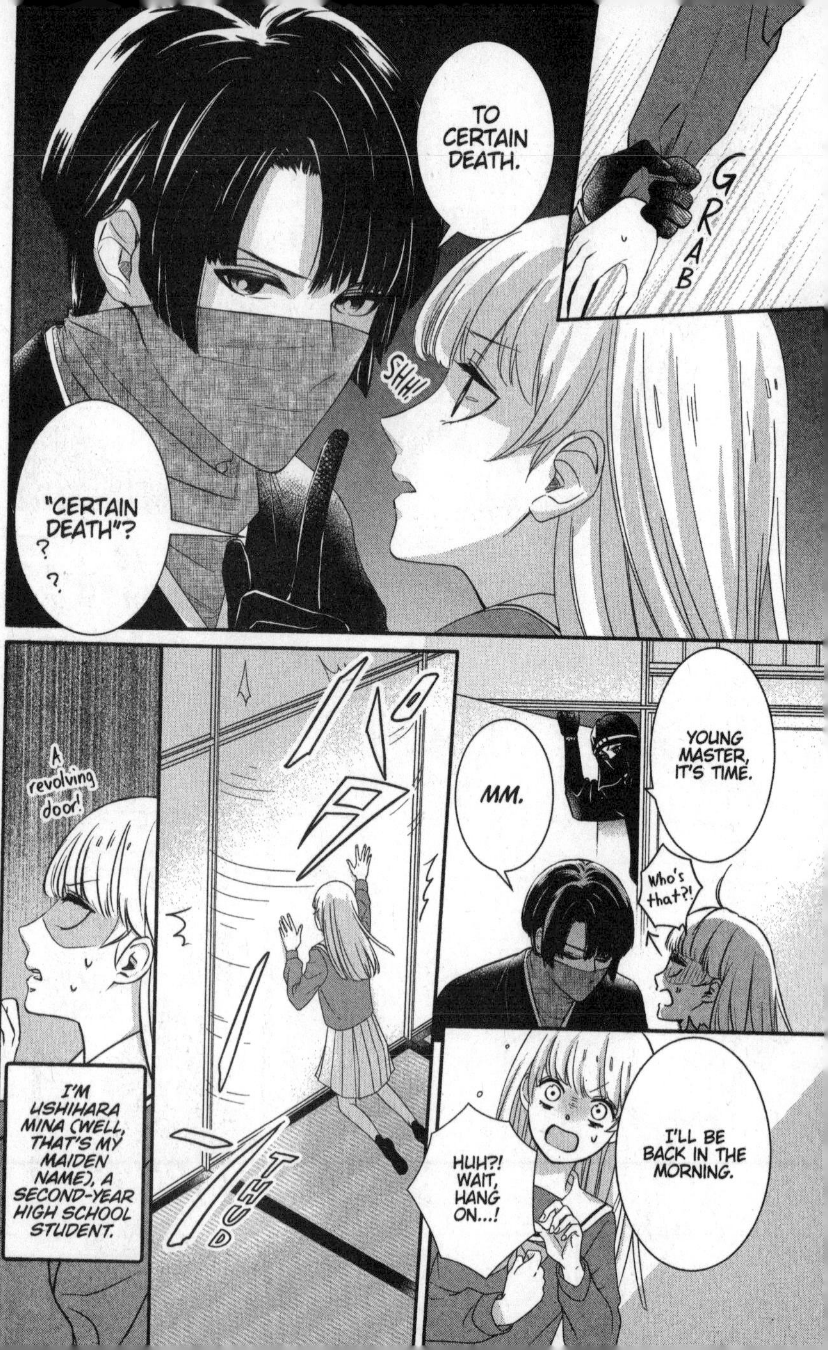
GRAB
TO CERTAIN DEATH.
SHH!
"CERTAIN DEATH"?
? ?
YOUNG MASTER, IT'S TIME.
MM.
Who's that?!
I'LL BE BACK IN THE MORNING.
HUH?! WAIT, HANG ON...!
THUD
A revolving door!
I'M USHIHARA MINA (WELL, THAT'S MY MAIDEN NAME), A SECOND-YEAR HIGH SCHOOL STUDENT.

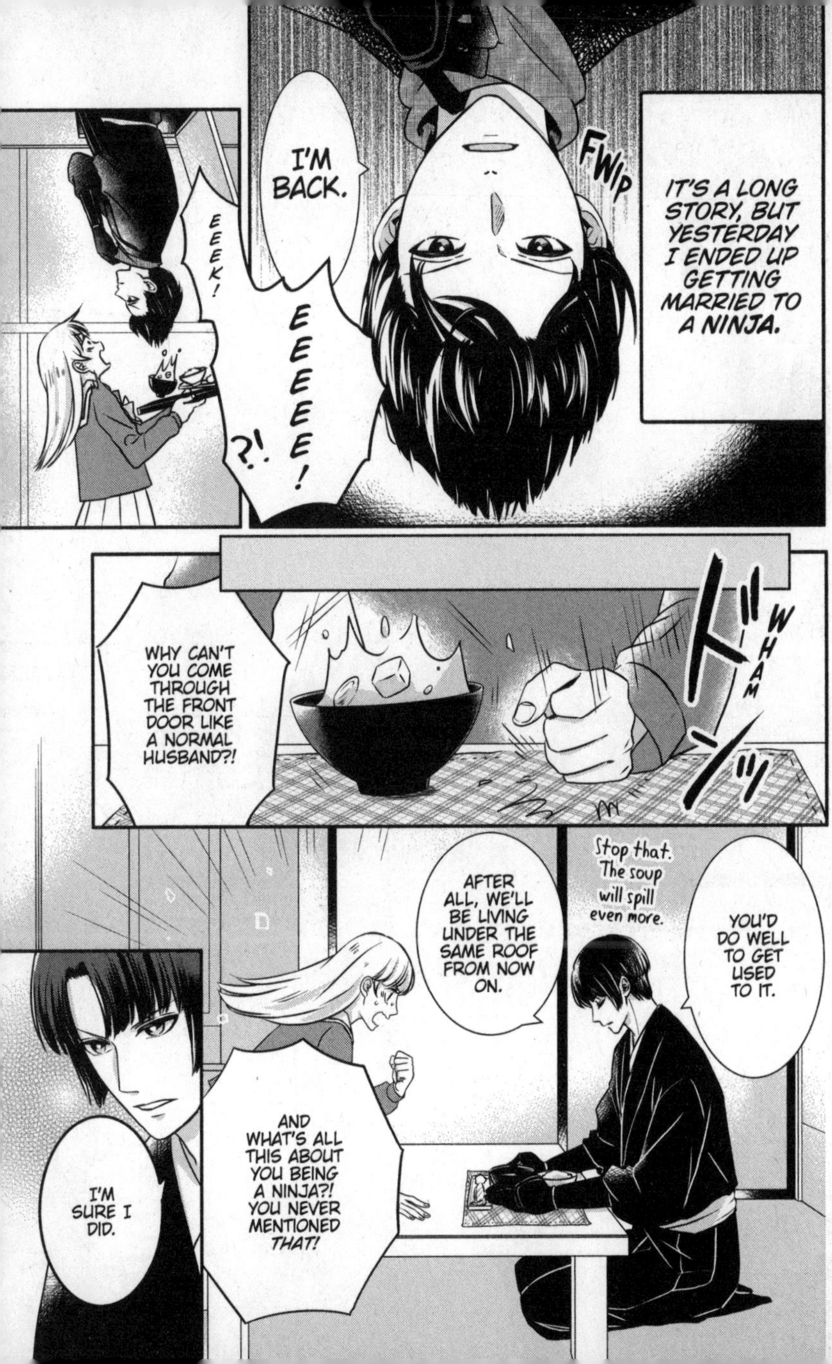
IT'S A LONG STORY, BUT YESTERDAY I ENDED UP GETTING MARRIED TO A NINJA.
FWIP
I'M BACK.
EEEK!
EEEEEE!
?!
WHAM
WHY CAN'T YOU COME THROUGH THE FRONT DOOR LIKE A NORMAL HUSBAND?!
Stop that. The soup will spill even more.
YOU'D DO WELL TO GET USED TO IT.
AFTER ALL, WE'LL BE LIVING UNDER THE SAME ROOF FROM NOW ON.
AND WHAT'S ALL THIS ABOUT YOU BEING A NINJA?! YOU NEVER MENTIONED THAT!
I'M SURE I DID.

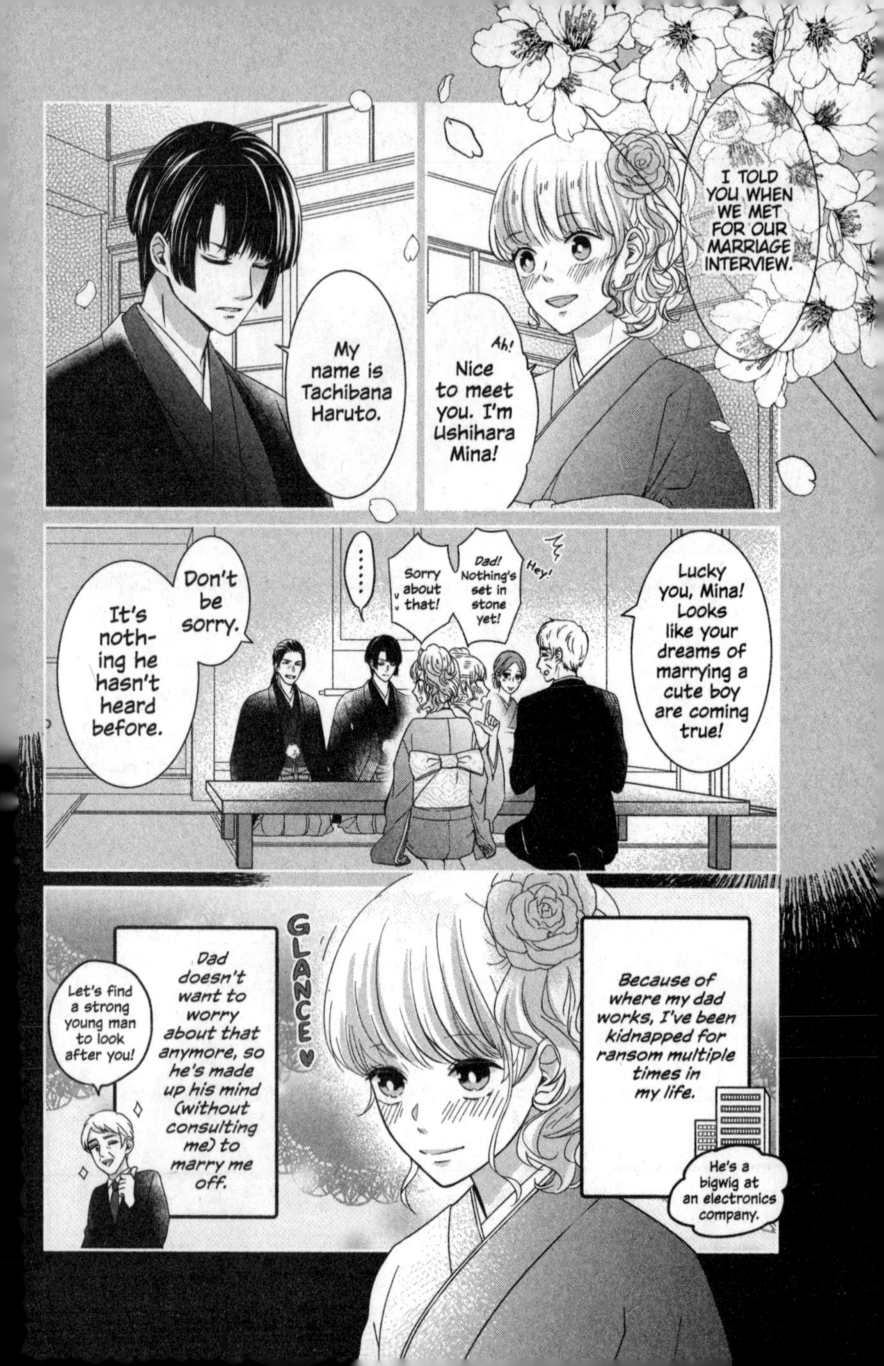
I TOLD YOU WHEN WE MET FOR OUR MARRIAGE INTERVIEW.
Ah!
Nice to meet you. I'm Ushihara Mina!
My name is Tachibana Haruto.
Lucky you, Mina! Looks like your dreams of marrying a cute boy are coming true!
Hey!
Dad! Nothing's set in stone yet!
Sorry about that!
......
Don't be sorry.
It's nothing he hasn't heard before.
Because of where my dad works, I've been kidnapped for ransom multiple times in my life.
He's a bigwig at an electronics company.
GLANCE
Dad doesn't want to worry about that anymore, so he's made up his mind (without consulting me) to marry me off.
Let's find a strong young man to look after you!

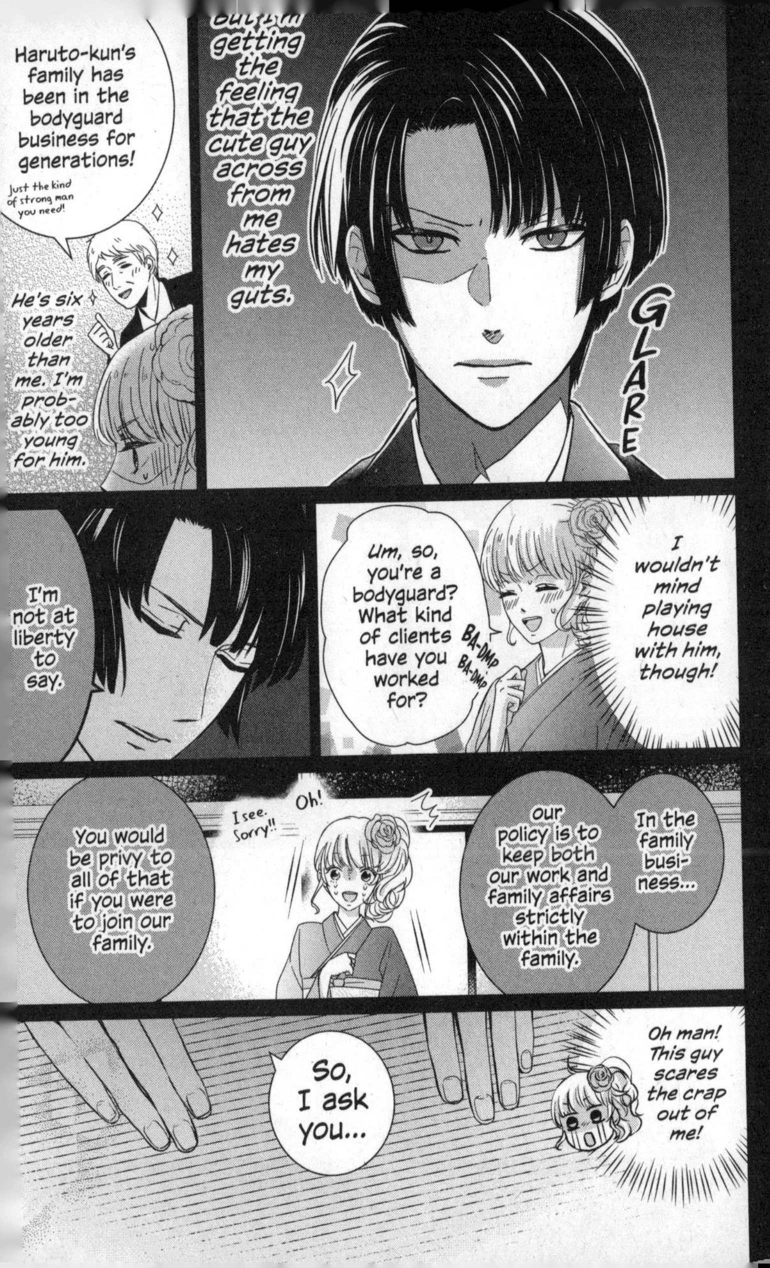
getting the feeling that the cute guy across from me hates my guts.
GLARE
Haruto-kun's family has been in the bodyguard business for generations!
Just the kind of strong man you need!
He's six years older than me. I'm probably too young for him.
I wouldn't mind playing house with him, though!
Um, so, you're a bodyguard? What kind of clients have you worked for?
BA-DMP BA-DMP
I'm not at liberty to say.
In the family business...
our policy is to keep both our work and family affairs strictly within the family.
Oh!
I see. Sorry!!
You would be privy to all of that if you were to join our family.
Oh man! This guy scares the crap out of me!
So, I ask you...

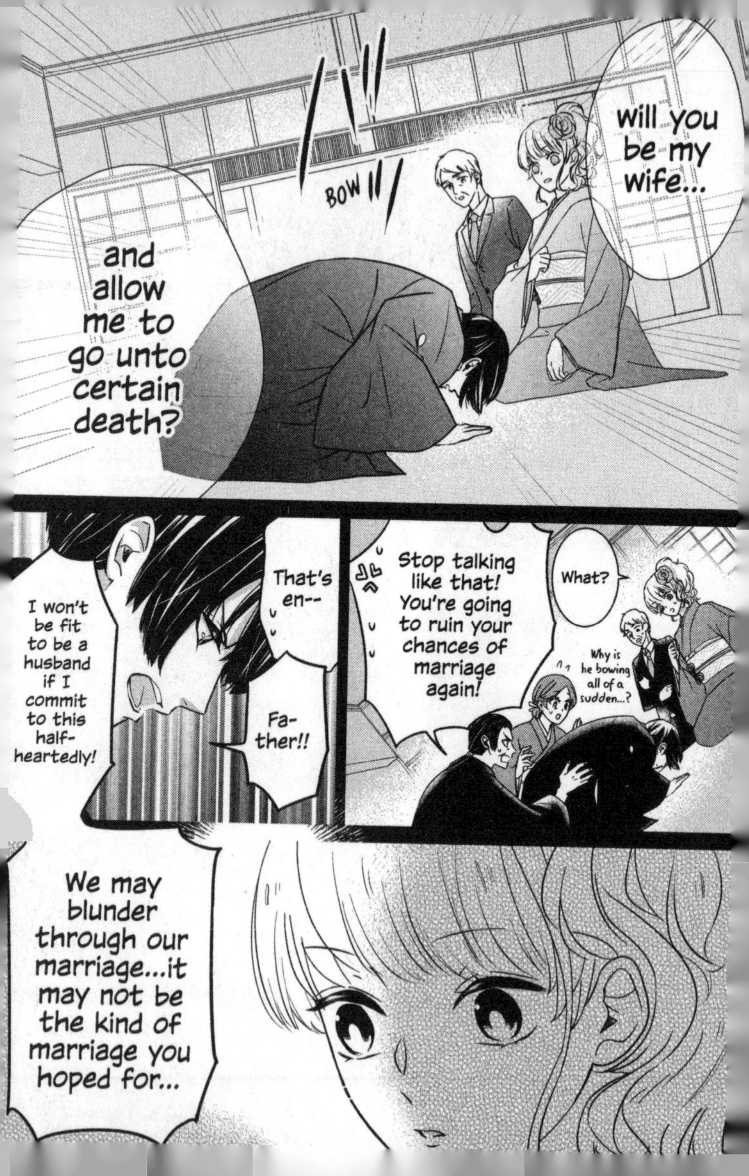
Will you be my wife...
BOW
and allow me to go unto certain death?
What?
Stop talking like that! You're going to ruin your chances of marriage again!
Why is he bowing all of a sudden...?
That's en--
Fa-ther!!
I won't be fit to be a husband if I commit to this half-heartedly!
We may blunder through our marriage...it may not be the kind of marriage you hoped for...

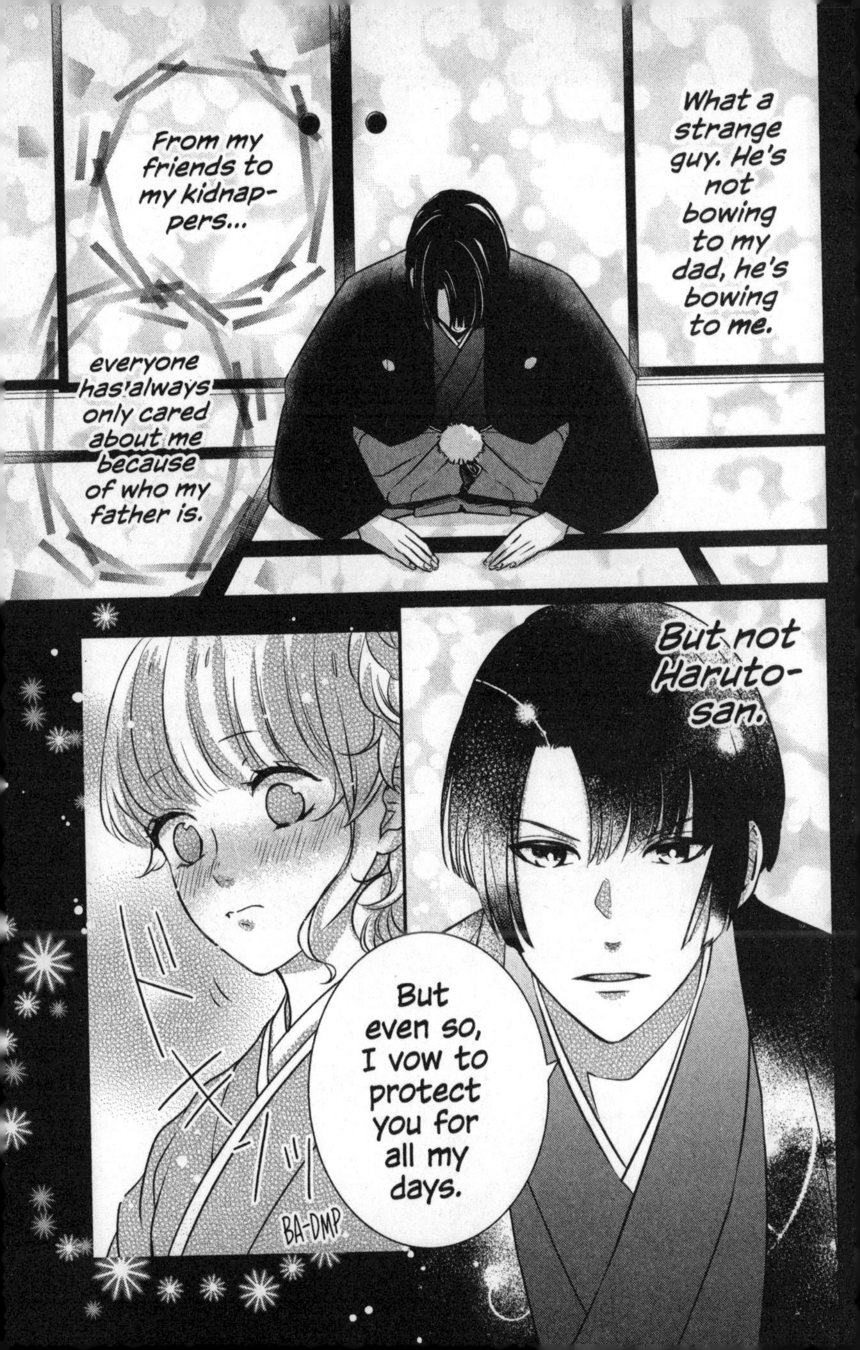
What a strange guy. He's not bowing to my dad, he's bowing to me.
From my friends to my kidnap-pers...
everyone has always only cared about me because of who my father is.
But not Haruto-san.
But even so, I vow to protect you for all my days.
BA-DMP

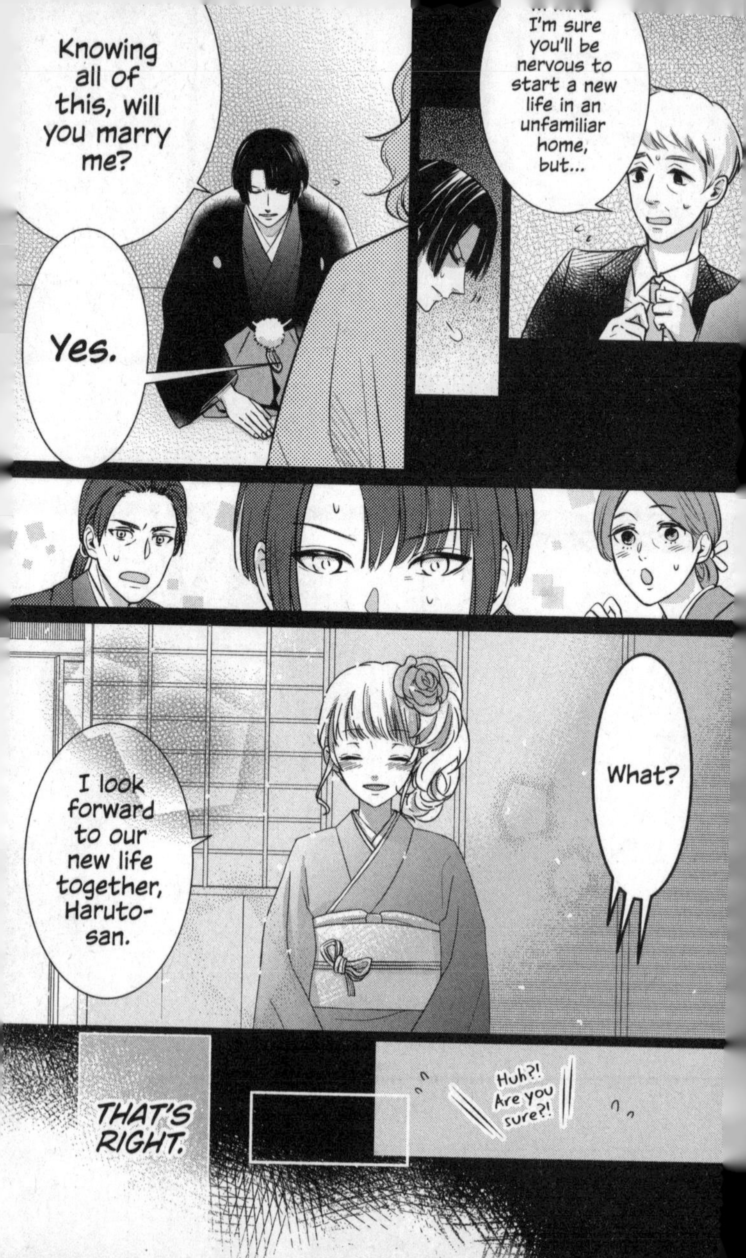
I'm sure you'll be nervous to start a new life in an unfamiliar home, but...
Knowing all of this, will you marry me?
Yes.
What?
I look forward to our new life together, Haruto-san.
Huh?! Are you sure?!
THAT'S RIGHT.

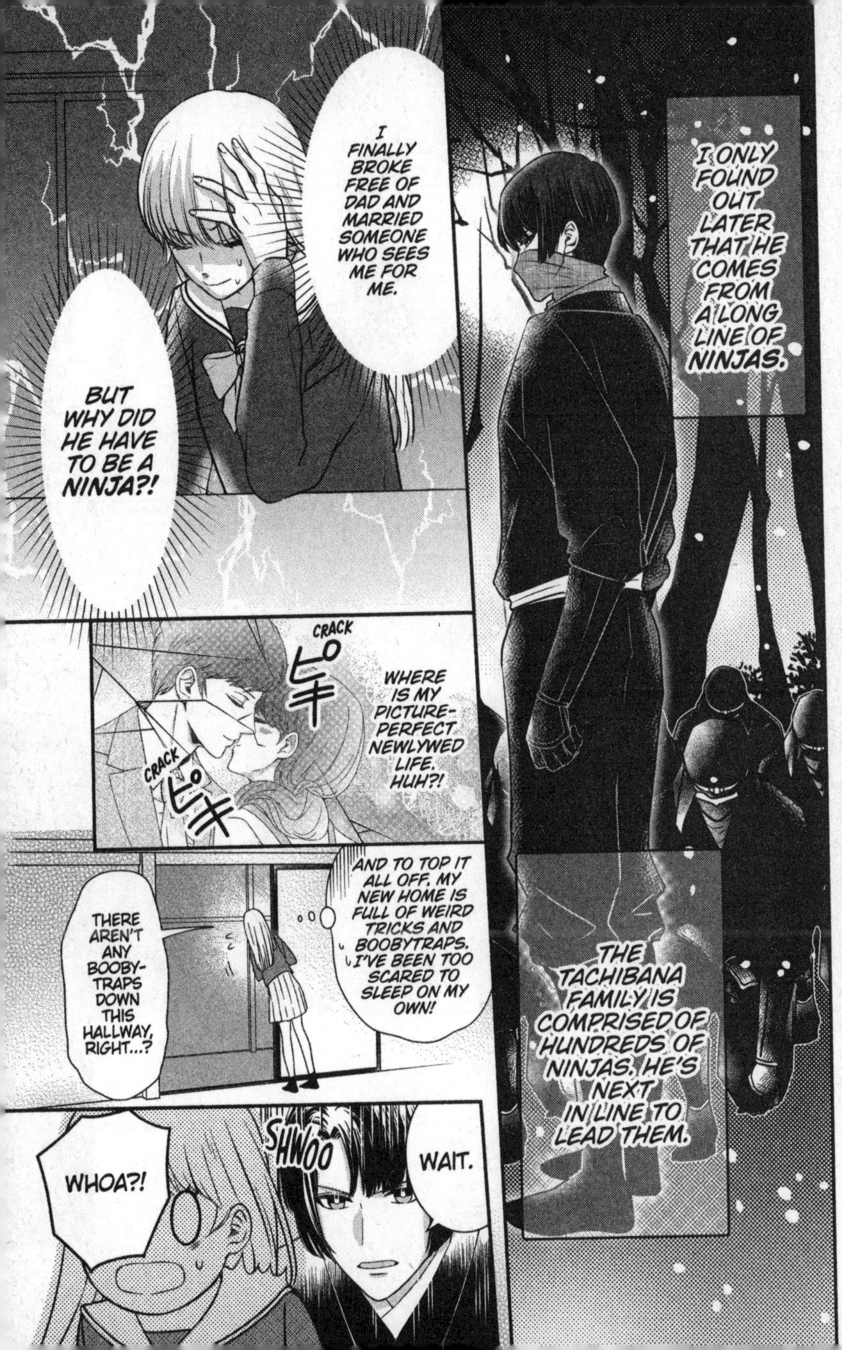
I ONLY FOUND OUT LATER THAT HE COMES FROM A LONG LINE OF NINJAS.
THE TACHIBANA FAMILY IS COMPRISED OF HUNDREDS OF NINJAS. HE'S NEXT IN LINE TO LEAD THEM.
I FINALLY BROKE FREE OF DAD AND MARRIED SOMEONE WHO SEES ME FOR ME.
BUT WHY DID HE HAVE TO BE A NINJA?!
CRACK
ピキ
WHERE IS MY PICTURE-PERFECT NEWLYWED LIFE. HUH?!
CRACK
ピキ
AND TO TOP IT ALL OFF, MY NEW HOME IS FULL OF WEIRD TRICKS AND BOOBYTRAPS. I'VE BEEN TOO SCARED TO SLEEP ON MY OWN!
THERE AREN'T ANY BOOBY-TRAPS DOWN THIS HALLWAY, RIGHT...?
WAIT.
SHWOO
WHOA?!

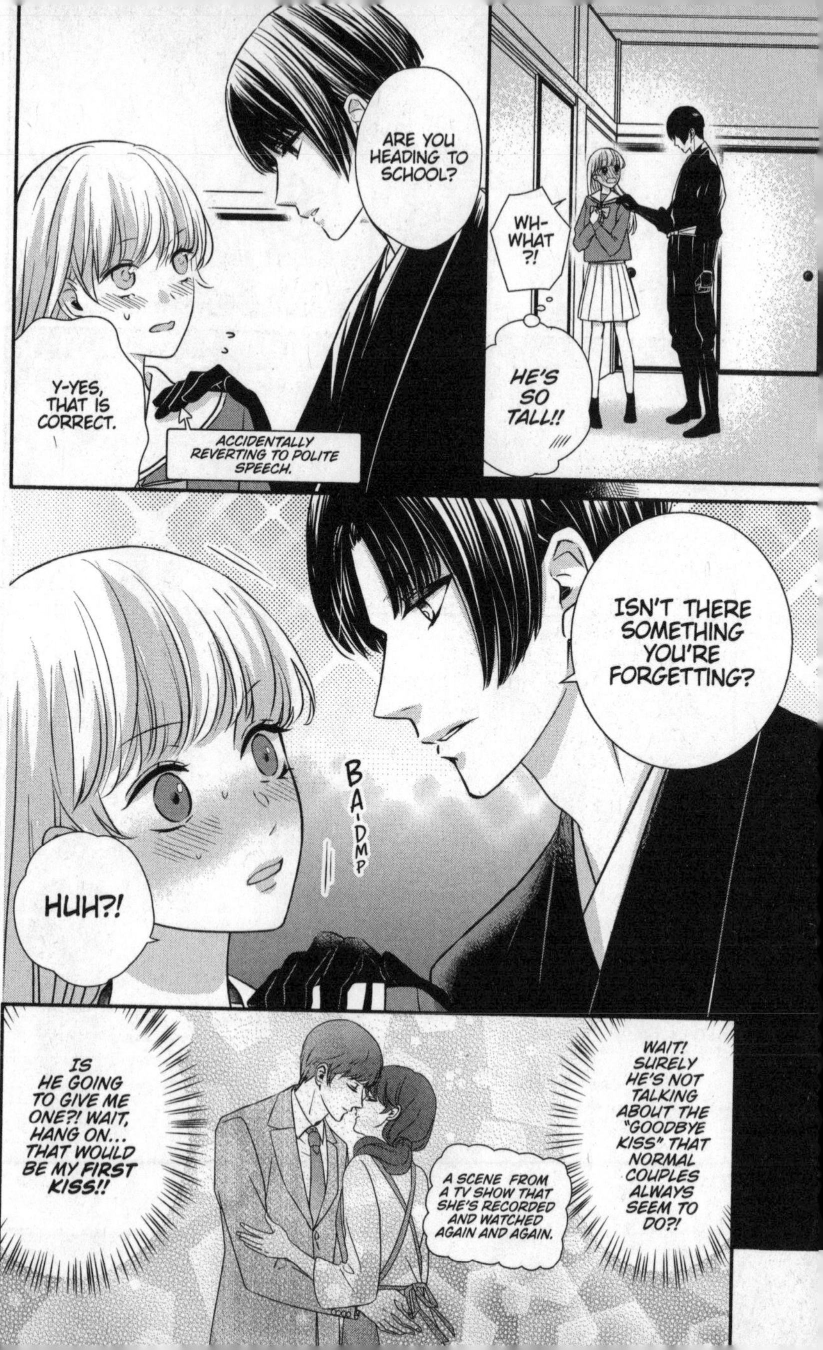
WH-WHAT?!
HE'S SO TALL!!
ARE YOU HEADING TO SCHOOL?
Y-YES, THAT IS CORRECT.
ACCIDENTALLY REVERTING TO POLITE SPEECH.
ISN'T THERE SOMETHING YOU'RE FORGETTING?
BA-DMP
HUH?!
WAIT! SURELY HE'S NOT TALKING ABOUT THE "GOODBYE KISS" THAT NORMAL COUPLES ALWAYS SEEM TO DO?!
A SCENE FROM A TV SHOW THAT SHE'S RECORDED AND WATCHED AGAIN AND AGAIN.
IS HE GOING TO GIVE ME ONE?! WAIT, HANG ON... THAT WOULD BE MY FIRST KISS!!

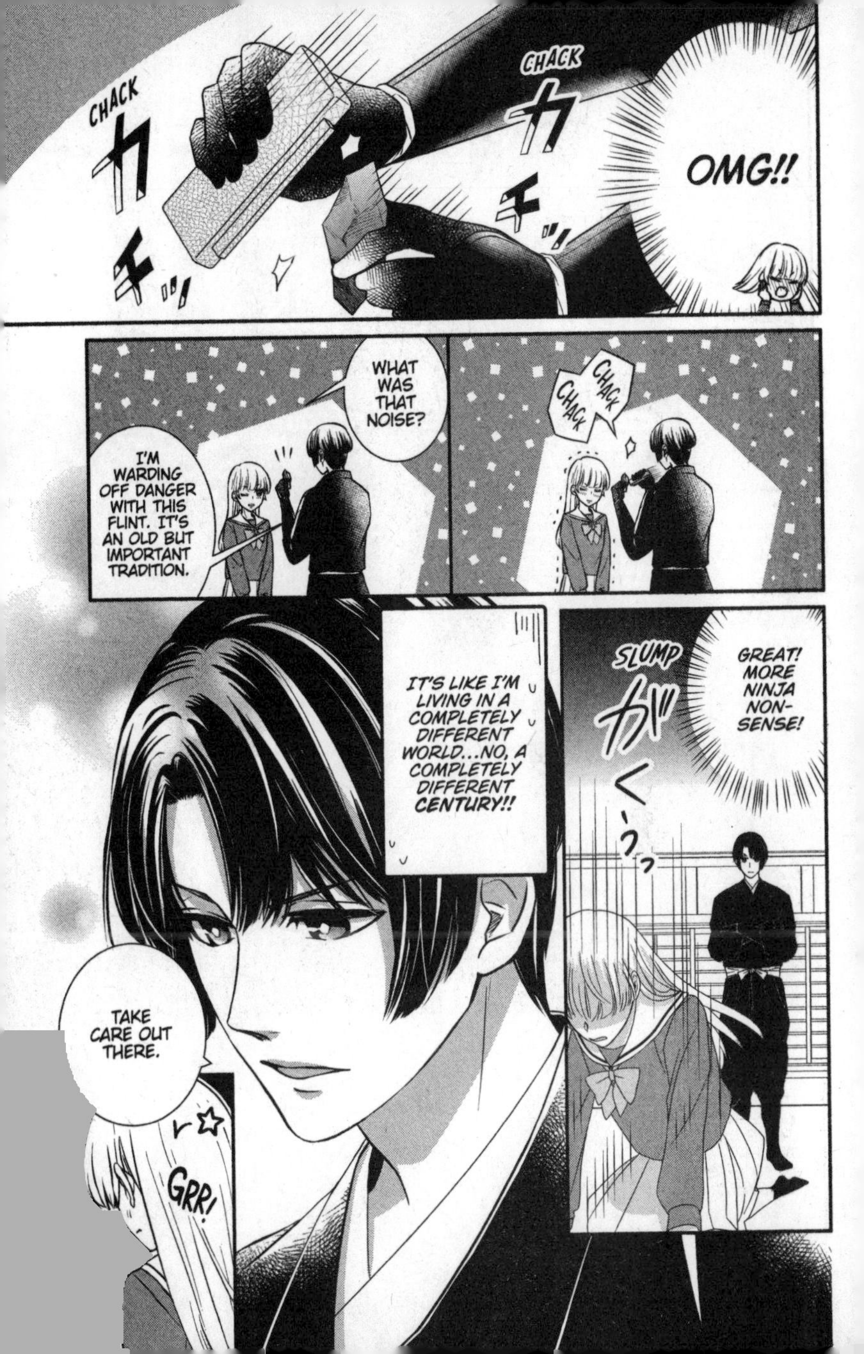
CHACK
カチッ
OMG!!
CHACK
カチッ
CHACK
CHACK
WHAT WAS THAT NOISE?
I'M WARDING OFF DANGER WITH THIS FLINT. IT'S AN OLD BUT IMPORTANT TRADITION.
GREAT! MORE NINJA NON-SENSE!
SLUMP
IT'S LIKE I'M LIVING IN A COMPLETELY DIFFERENT WORLD...NO, A COMPLETELY DIFFERENT CENTURY!!
TAKE CARE OUT THERE.
GRR!

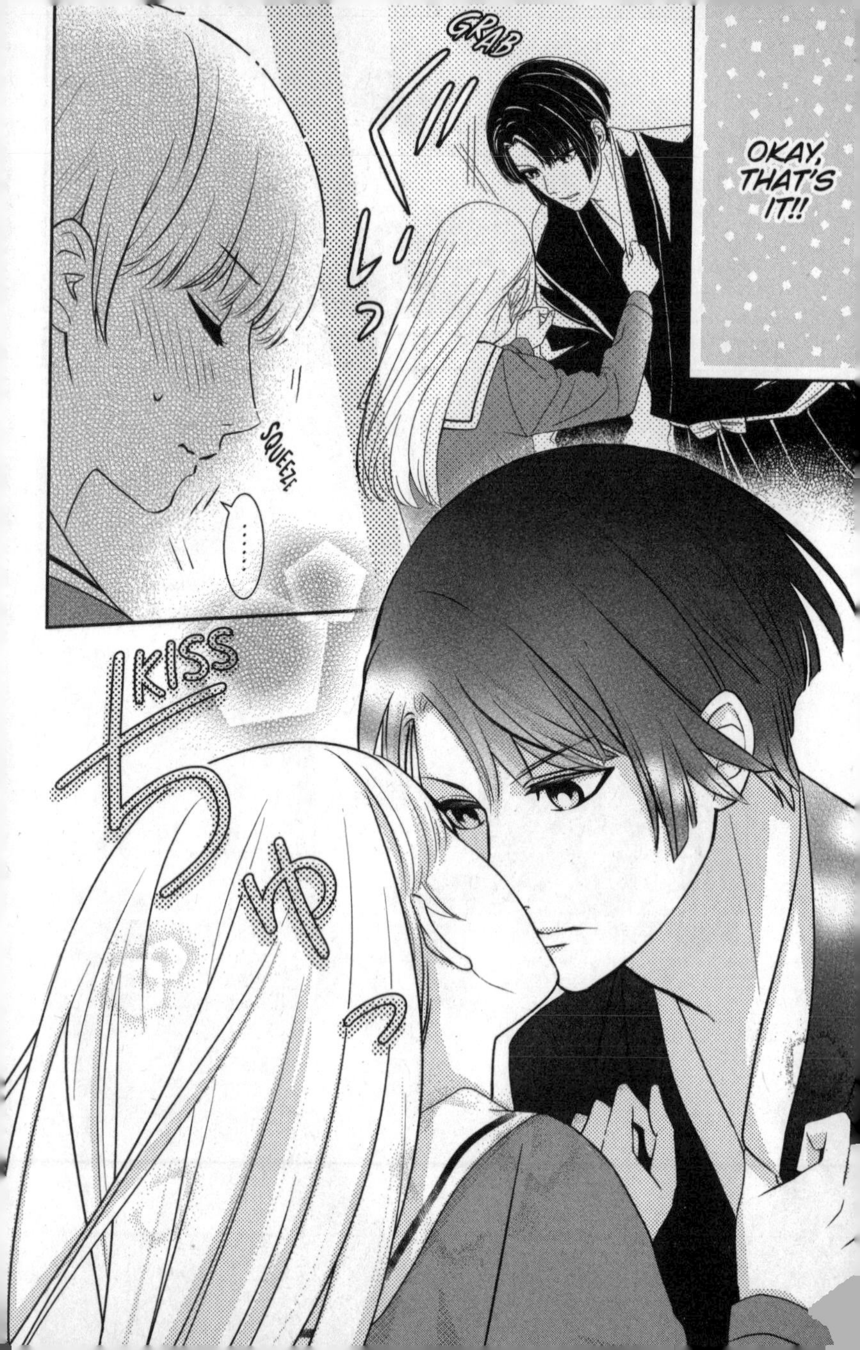
OKAY, THAT'S IT!!
GRAB
SQUEEZE
......
KISS

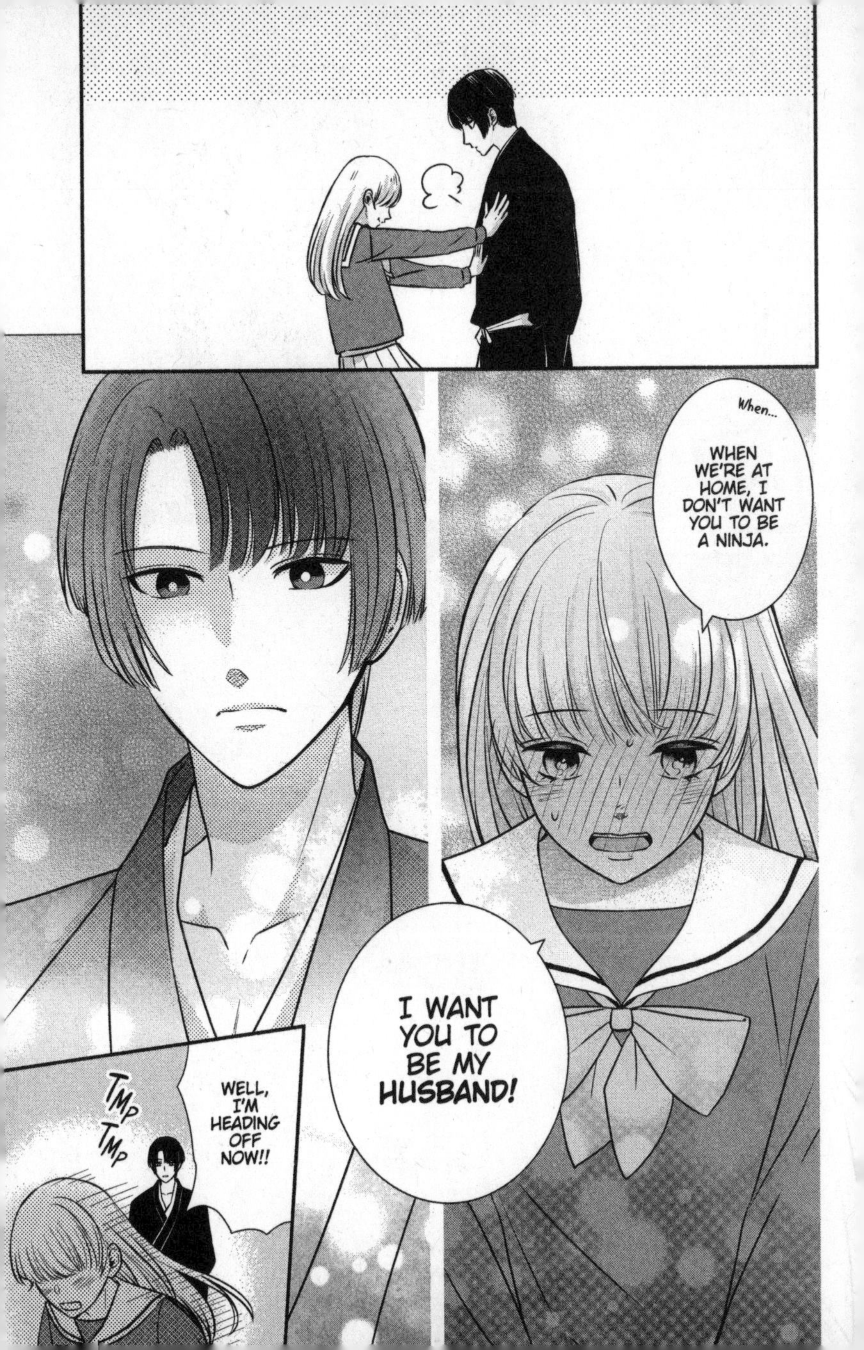
When...
WHEN WE'RE AT HOME, I DON'T WANT YOU TO BE A NINJA.
I WANT YOU TO BE MY HUSBAND!
WELL, I'M HEADING OFF NOW!!
TMP TMP

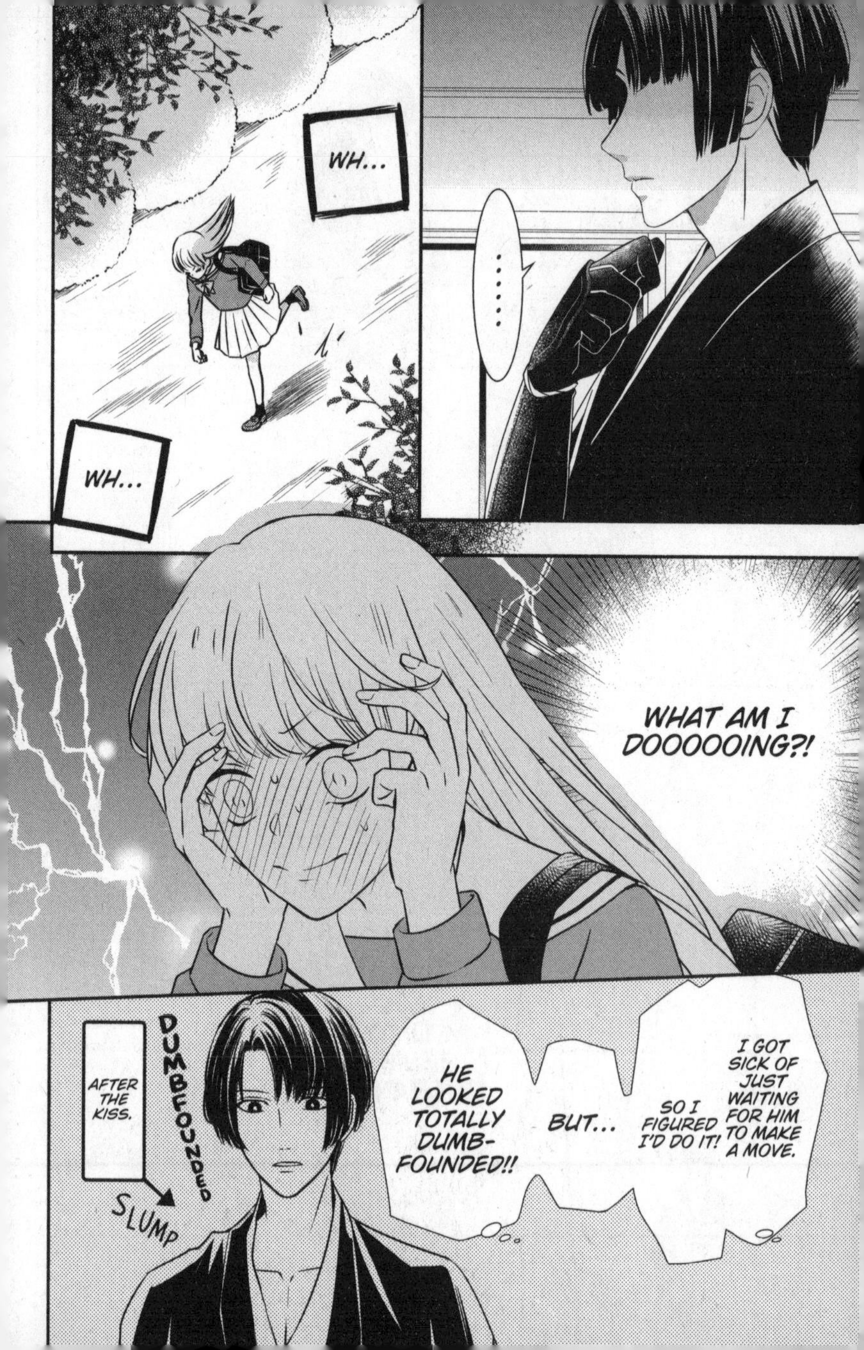
......
WH...
WH...
WHAT AM I DOOOOOING?!
I GOT SICK OF JUST WAITING FOR HIM TO MAKE A MOVE.
SO I FIGURED I'D DO IT!
BUT...
HE LOOKED TOTALLY DUMB-FOUNDED!!
DUMBFOUNDED
AFTER THE KISS.
SLUMP

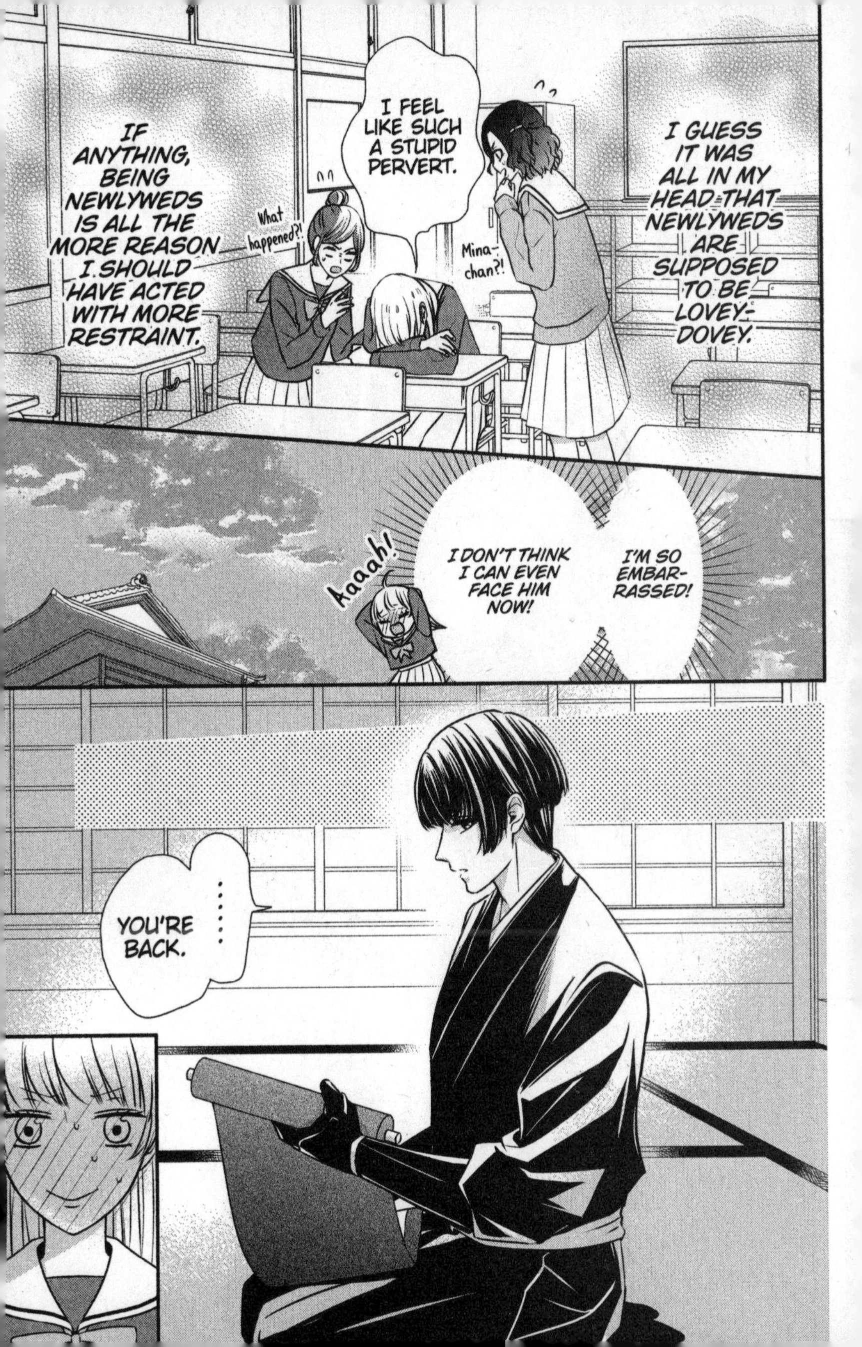
I GUESS IT WAS ALL IN MY HEAD THAT NEWLYWEDS ARE SUPPOSED TO BE LOVEY-DOVEY.
Mina-chan?!
I FEEL LIKE SUCH A STUPID PERVERT.
What happened?!
IF ANYTHING, BEING NEWLYWEDS IS ALL THE MORE REASON I SHOULD HAVE ACTED WITH MORE RESTRAINT.
I'M SO EMBARRASSED!
I DON'T THINK I CAN EVEN FACE HIM NOW!
Aaaah!
...... YOU'RE BACK.

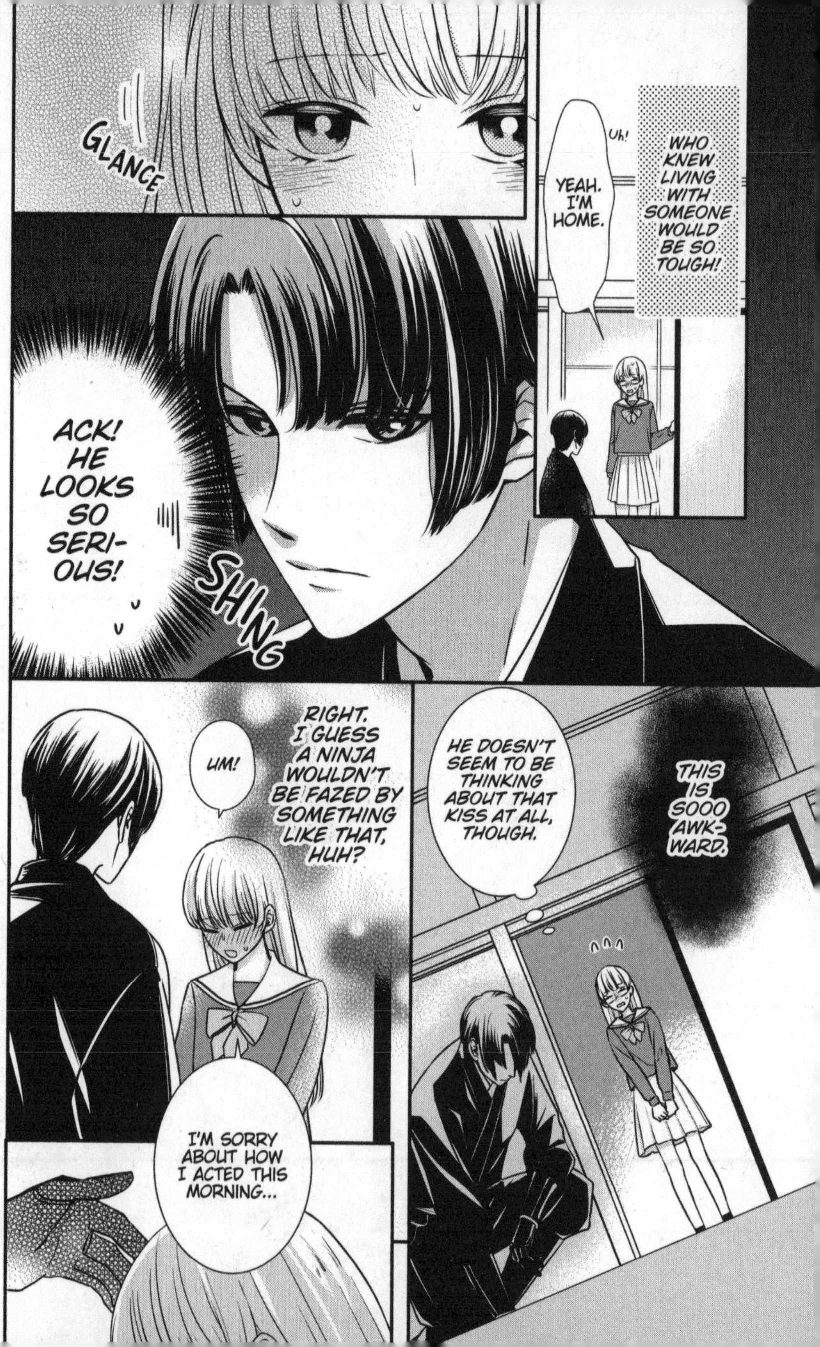
WHO KNEW LIVING WITH SOMEONE WOULD BE SO TOUGH!
Uh!
YEAH. I'M HOME.
GLANCE
ACK! HE LOOKS SO SERI-OUS!
SHING
THIS IS SOOO AWK-WARD.
HE DOESN'T SEEM TO BE THINKING ABOUT THAT KISS AT ALL, THOUGH.
RIGHT. I GUESS A NINJA WOULDN'T BE FAZED BY SOMETHING LIKE THAT, HUH?
UM!
I'M SORRY ABOUT HOW I ACTED THIS MORNING...

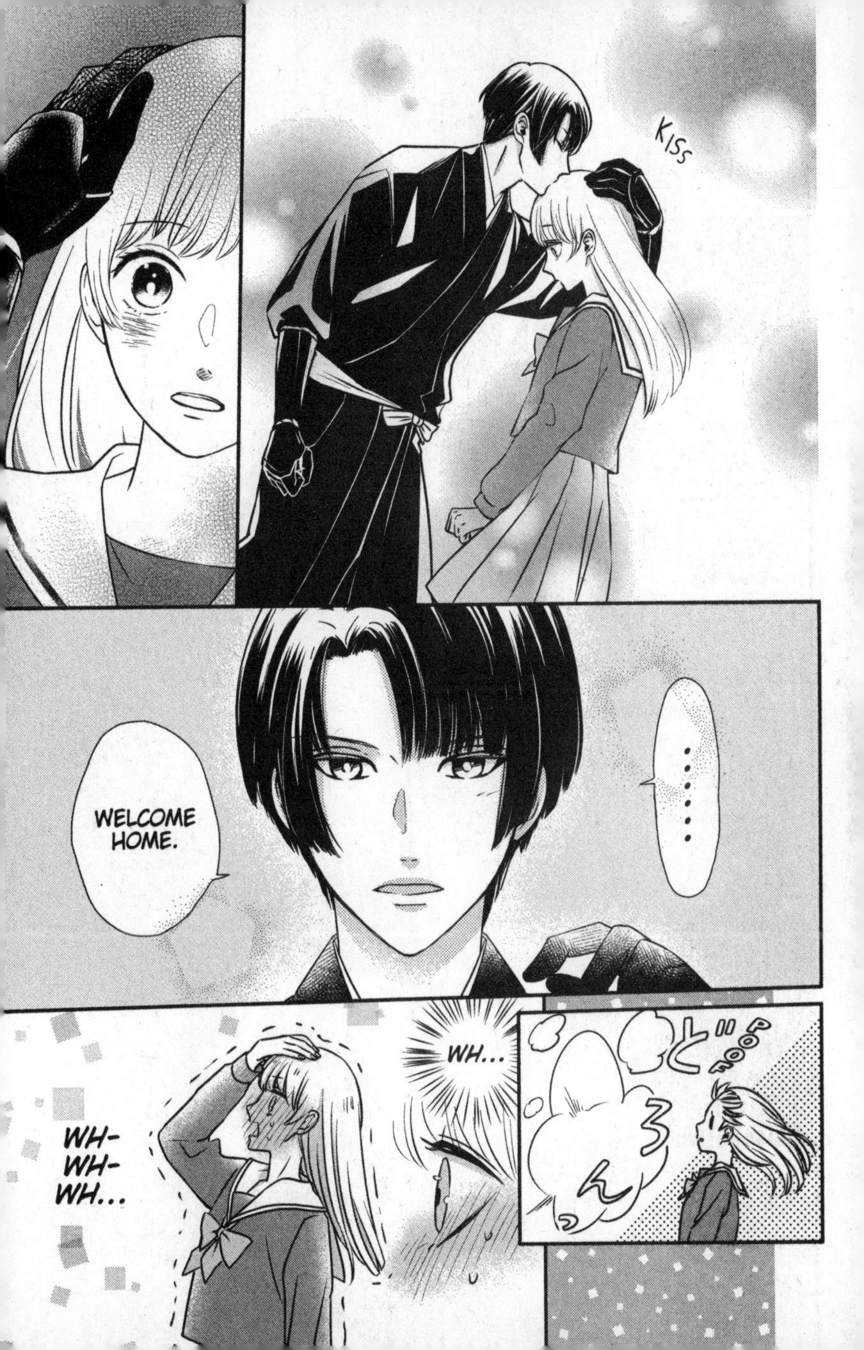
KISS
......
WELCOME HOME.
どろんっ
POOF
WH...
WH-
WH-
WH...

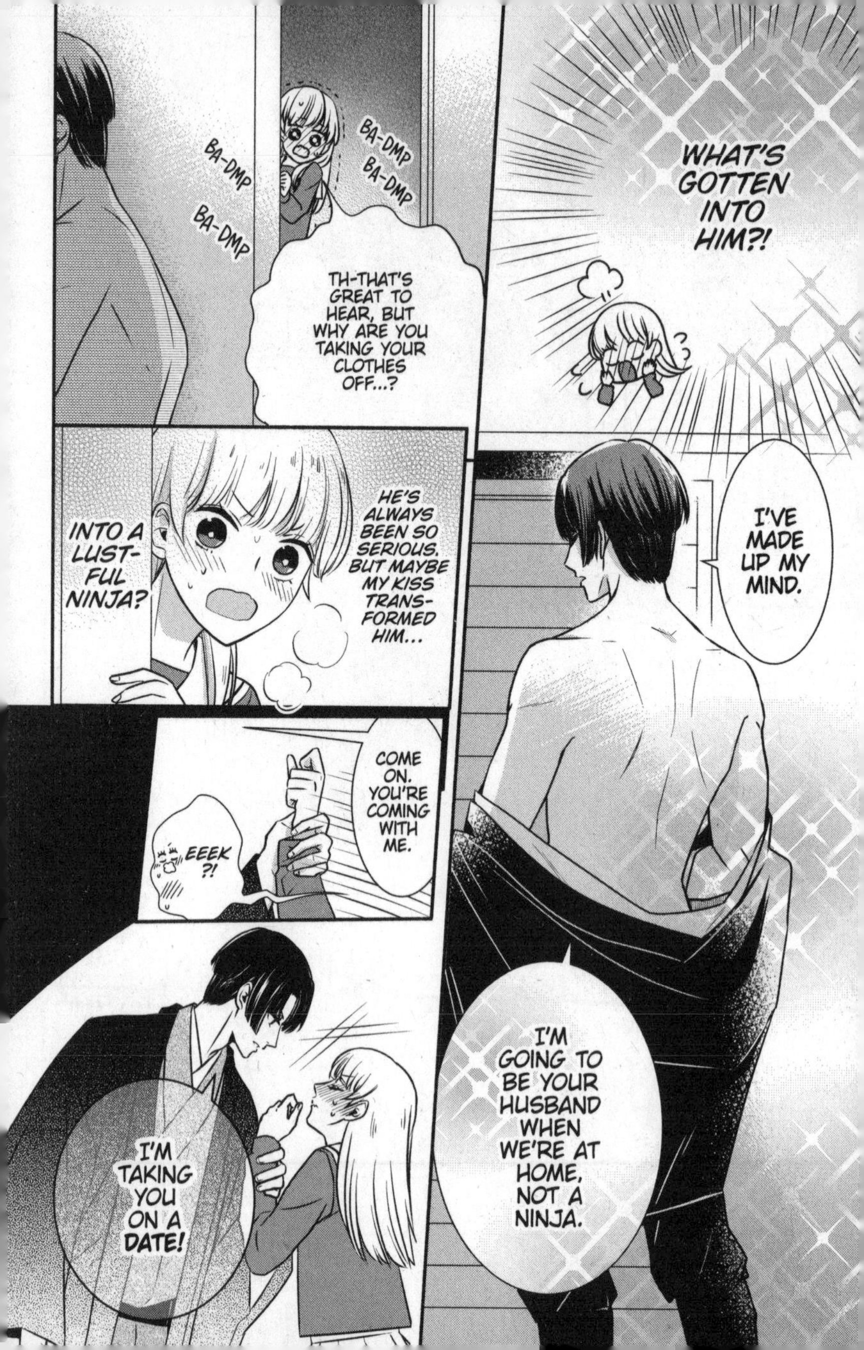
WHAT'S GOTTEN INTO HIM?!
I'VE MADE UP MY MIND.
I'M GOING TO BE YOUR HUSBAND WHEN WE'RE AT HOME, NOT A NINJA.
BA-DMP BA-DMP
BA-DMP BA-DMP
TH-THAT'S GREAT TO HEAR, BUT WHY ARE YOU TAKING YOUR CLOTHES OFF...?
HE'S ALWAYS BEEN SO SERIOUS. BUT MAYBE MY KISS TRANS-FORMED HIM...
INTO A LUST-FUL NINJA?
COME ON. YOU'RE COMING WITH ME.
EEEK ?!
I'M TAKING YOU ON A DATE!

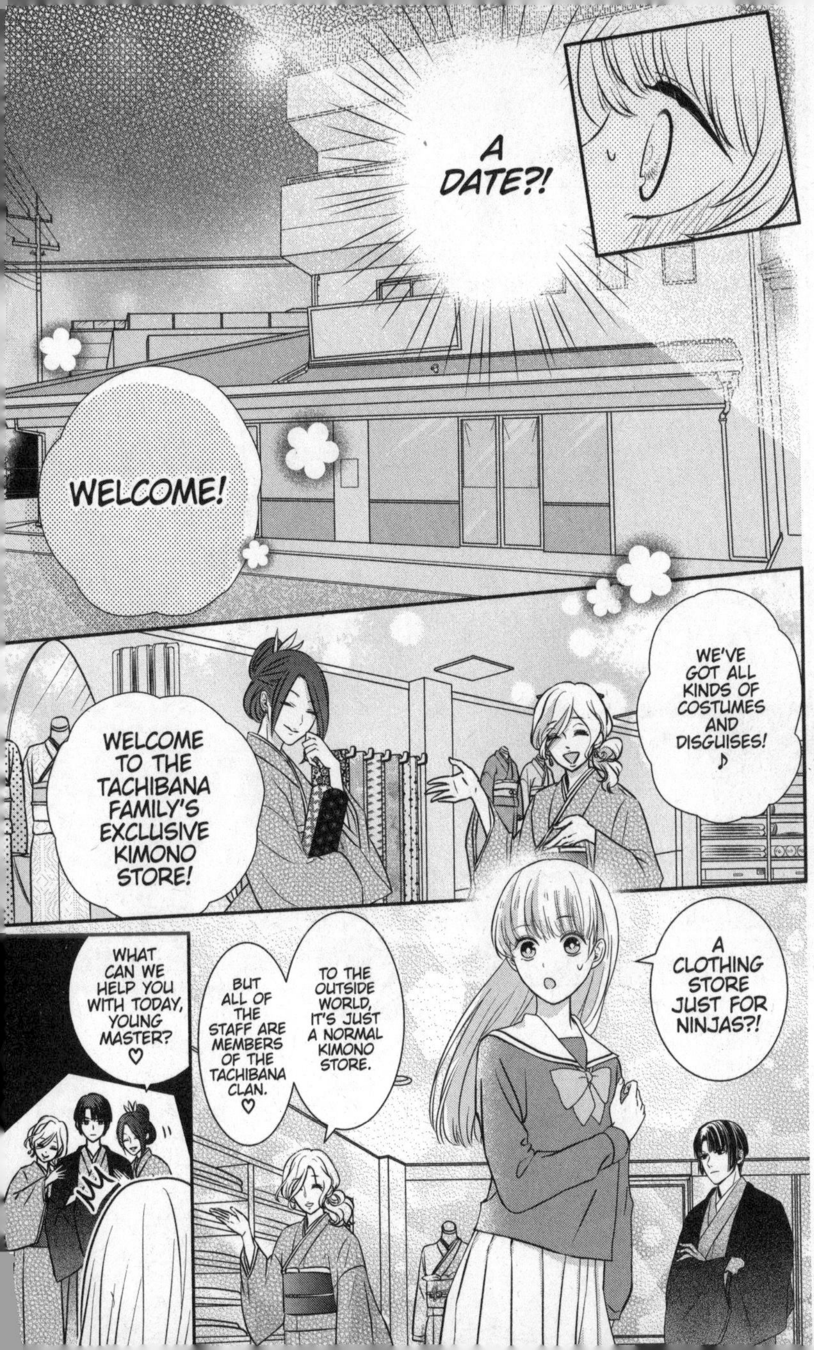
A DATE?!
WELCOME!
WE'VE GOT ALL KINDS OF COSTUMES AND DISGUISES! ♪
WELCOME TO THE TACHIBANA FAMILY'S EXCLUSIVE KIMONO STORE!
A CLOTHING STORE JUST FOR NINJAS?!
TO THE OUTSIDE WORLD, IT'S JUST A NORMAL KIMONO STORE.
BUT ALL OF THE STAFF ARE MEMBERS OF THE TACHIBANA CLAN. ♡
WHAT CAN WE HELP YOU WITH TODAY, YOUNG MASTER? ♡

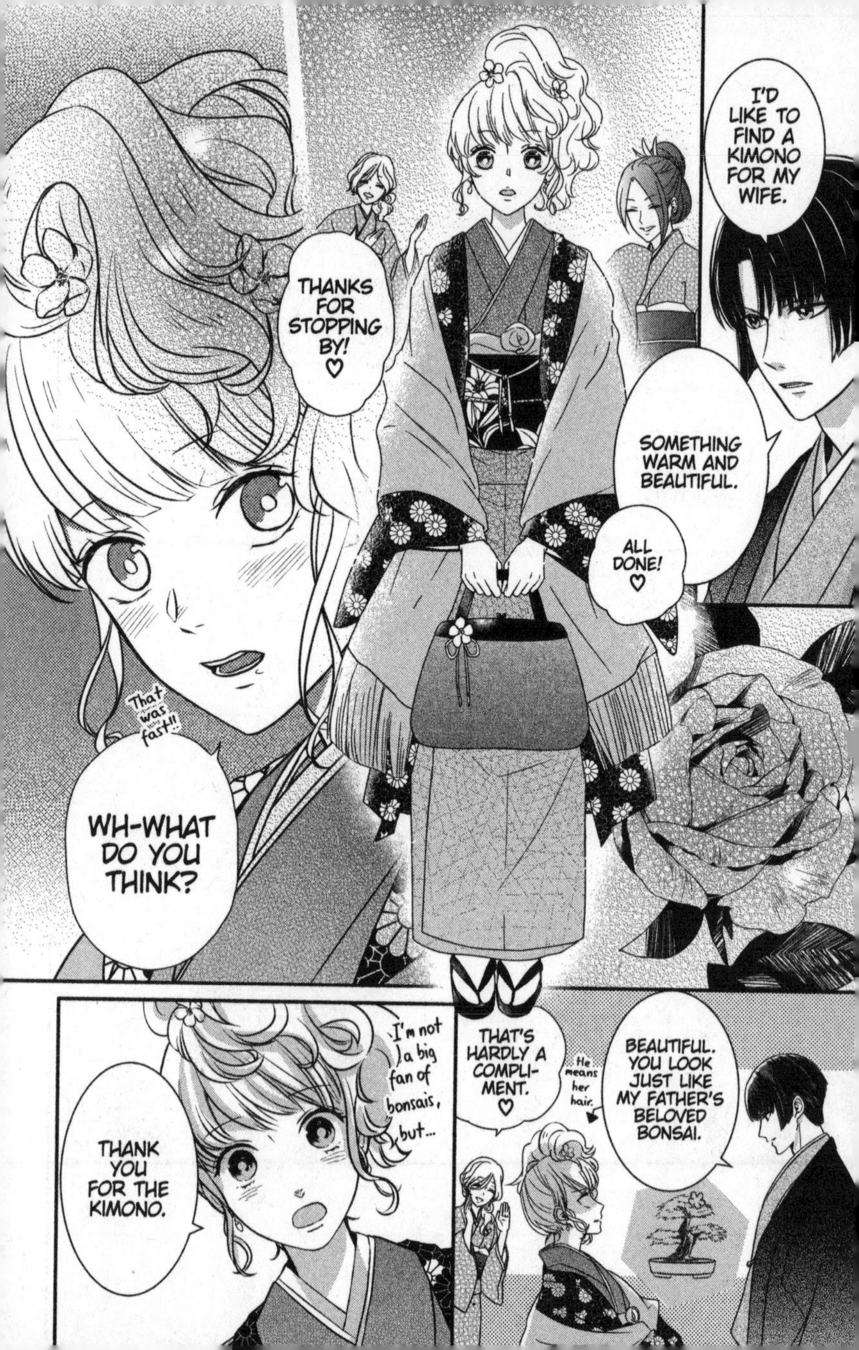
I'D LIKE TO FIND A KIMONO FOR MY WIFE.
SOMETHING WARM AND BEAUTIFUL.
ALL DONE! ♡
THANKS FOR STOPPING BY! ♡
That was fast!!
WH-WHAT DO YOU THINK?
BEAUTIFUL. YOU LOOK JUST LIKE MY FATHER'S BELOVED BONSAI.
He means her hair.
THAT'S HARDLY A COMPLI-MENT. ♡
I'm not a big fan of bonsais, but...
THANK YOU FOR THE KIMONO.

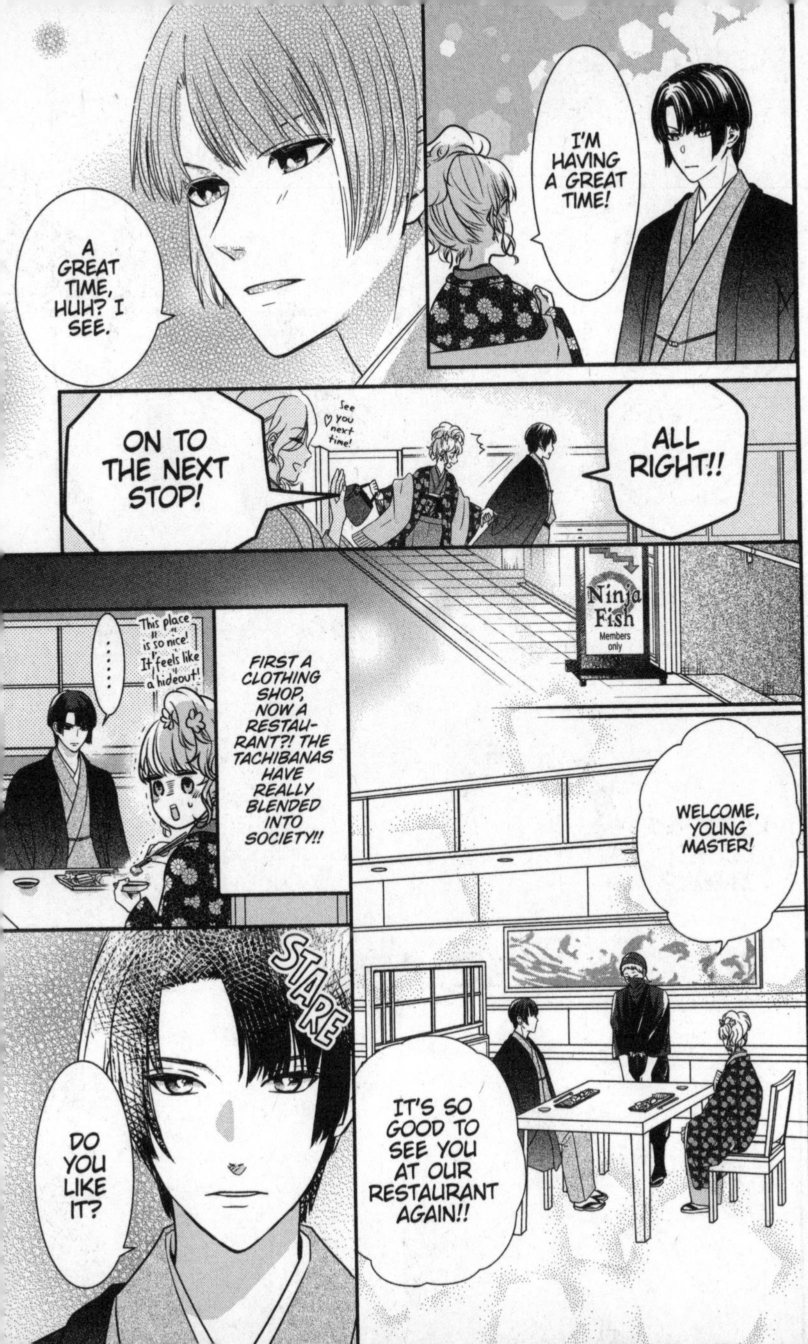
I'M HAVING A GREAT TIME!
A GREAT TIME, HUH? I SEE.
ALL RIGHT!!
See you next time!
ON TO THE NEXT STOP!
Ninja Fish
Members only
WELCOME, YOUNG MASTER!
IT'S SO GOOD TO SEE YOU AT OUR RESTAURANT AGAIN!!
FIRST A CLOTHING SHOP, NOW A RESTAURANT?! THE TACHIBANAS HAVE REALLY BLENDED INTO SOCIETY!!
This place is so nice! It feels like a hideout!
......
STARE
DO YOU LIKE IT?

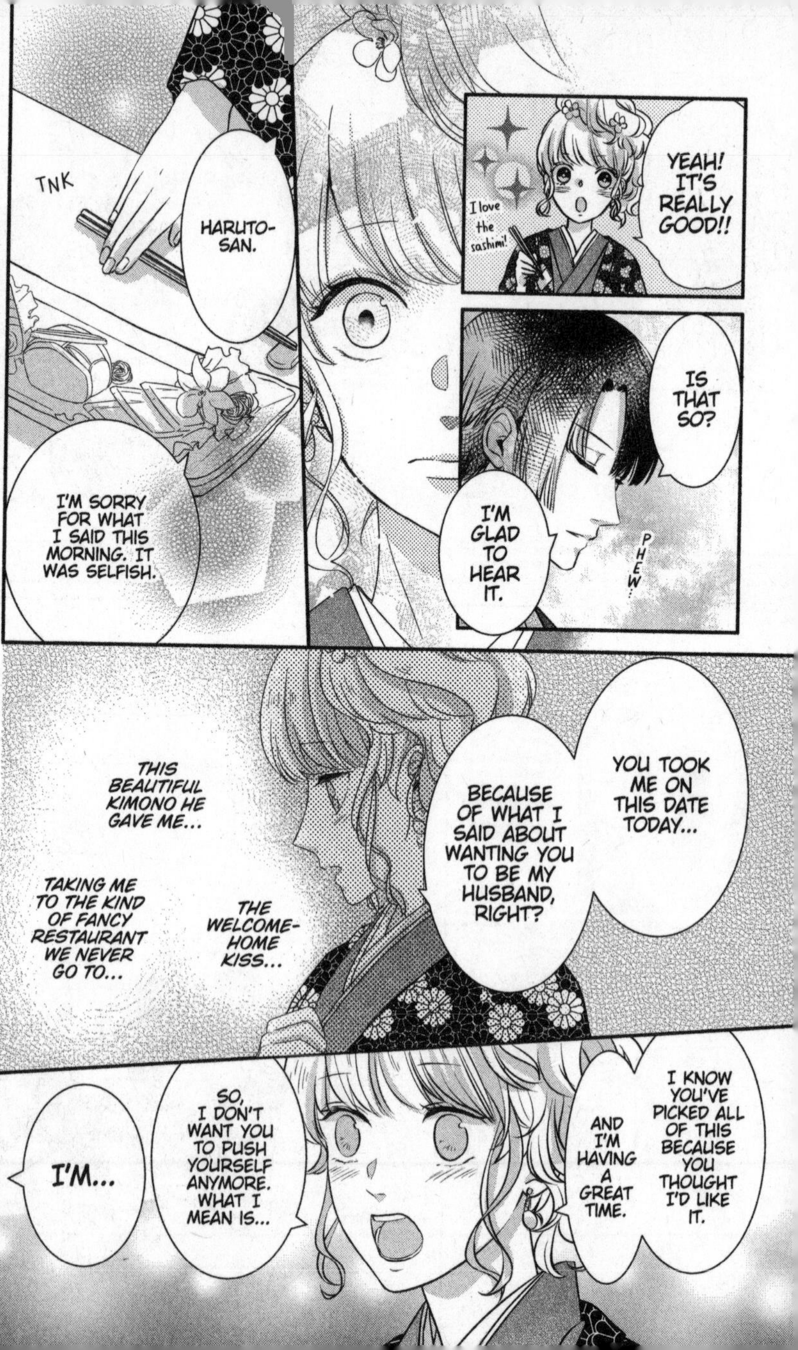
YEAH! IT'S REALLY GOOD!!
I love the sashimi!
IS THAT SO?
I'M GLAD TO HEAR IT.
PHEW...
TNK
HARUTO-SAN.
I'M SORRY FOR WHAT I SAID THIS MORNING. IT WAS SELFISH.
YOU TOOK ME ON THIS DATE TODAY...
BECAUSE OF WHAT I SAID ABOUT WANTING YOU TO BE MY HUSBAND, RIGHT?
THIS BEAUTIFUL KIMONO HE GAVE ME...
THE WELCOME-HOME KISS...
TAKING ME TO THE KIND OF FANCY RESTAURANT WE NEVER GO TO...
I KNOW YOU'VE PICKED ALL OF THIS BECAUSE YOU THOUGHT I'D LIKE IT.
AND I'M HAVING A GREAT TIME.
SO, I DON'T WANT YOU TO PUSH YOURSELF ANYMORE. WHAT I MEAN IS...
I'M...

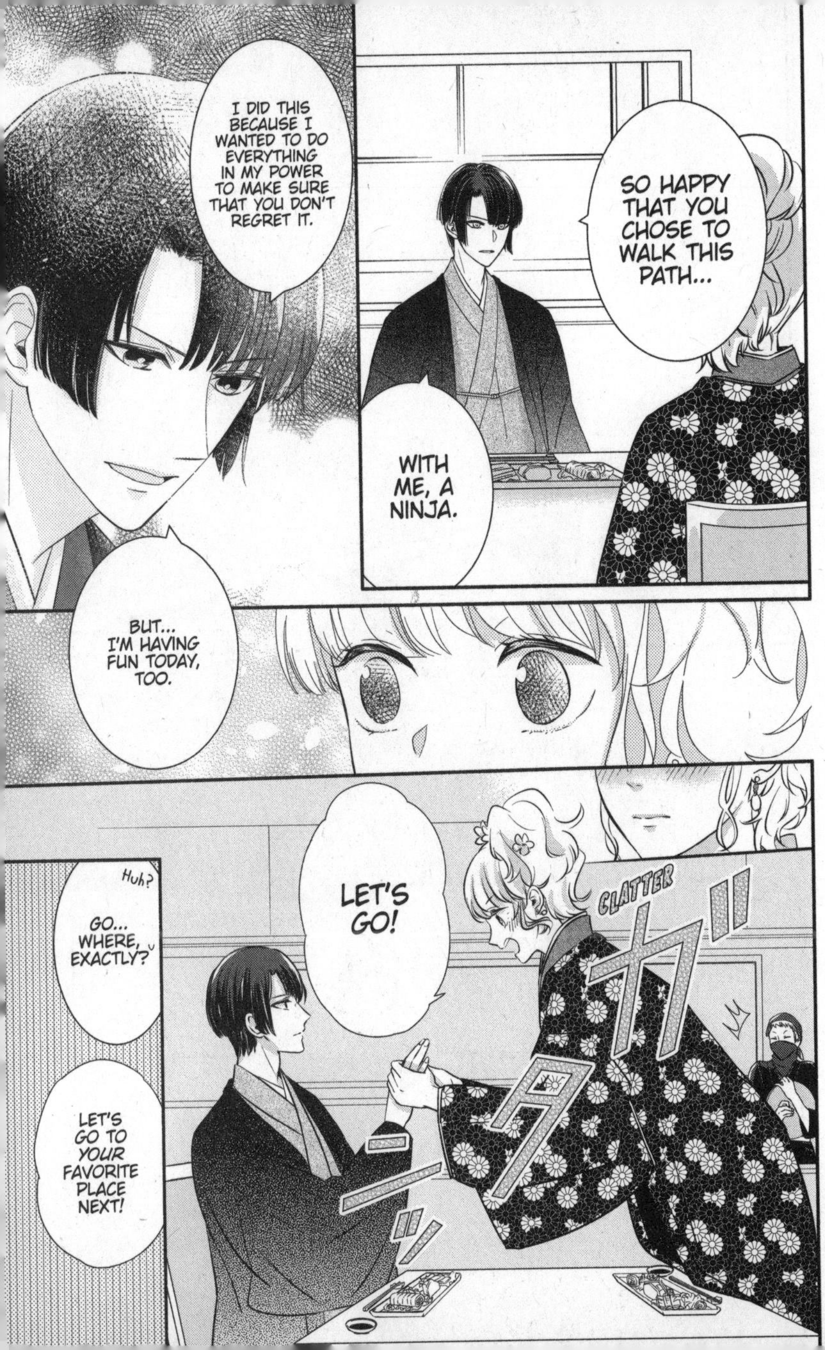
SO HAPPY THAT YOU CHOSE TO WALK THIS PATH...
WITH ME, A NINJA.
I DID THIS BECAUSE I WANTED TO DO EVERYTHING IN MY POWER TO MAKE SURE THAT YOU DON'T REGRET IT.
BUT... I'M HAVING FUN TODAY, TOO.
LET'S GO!
CLATTER
Huh?
GO... WHERE, EXACTLY?
LET'S GO TO *YOUR* FAVORITE PLACE NEXT!

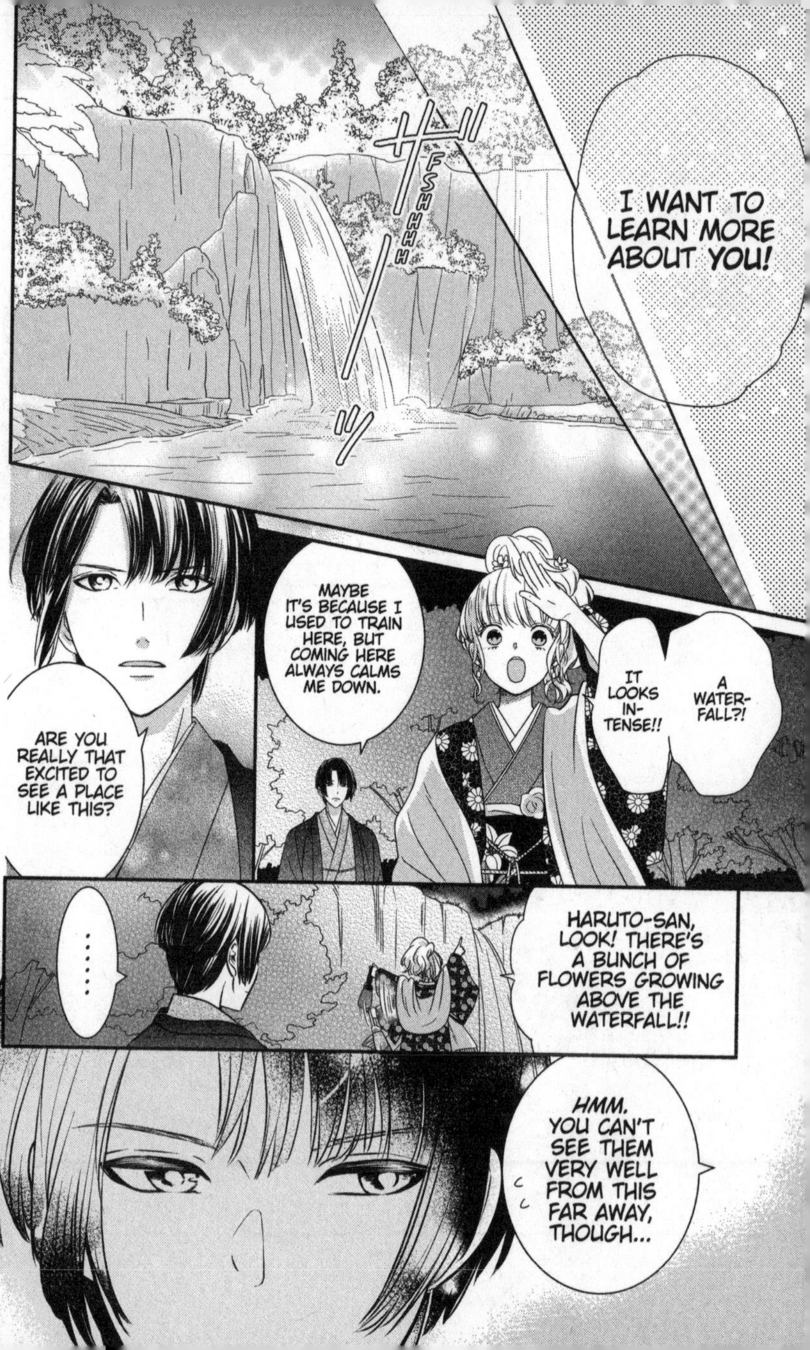
I WANT TO LEARN MORE ABOUT YOU!
FSHHHHH
A WATER-FALL?!
IT LOOKS IN-TENSE!!
MAYBE IT'S BECAUSE I USED TO TRAIN HERE, BUT COMING HERE ALWAYS CALMS ME DOWN.
ARE YOU REALLY THAT EXCITED TO SEE A PLACE LIKE THIS?
HARUTO-SAN, LOOK! THERE'S A BUNCH OF FLOWERS GROWING ABOVE THE WATERFALL!!
......
HMM. YOU CAN'T SEE THEM VERY WELL FROM THIS FAR AWAY, THOUGH...

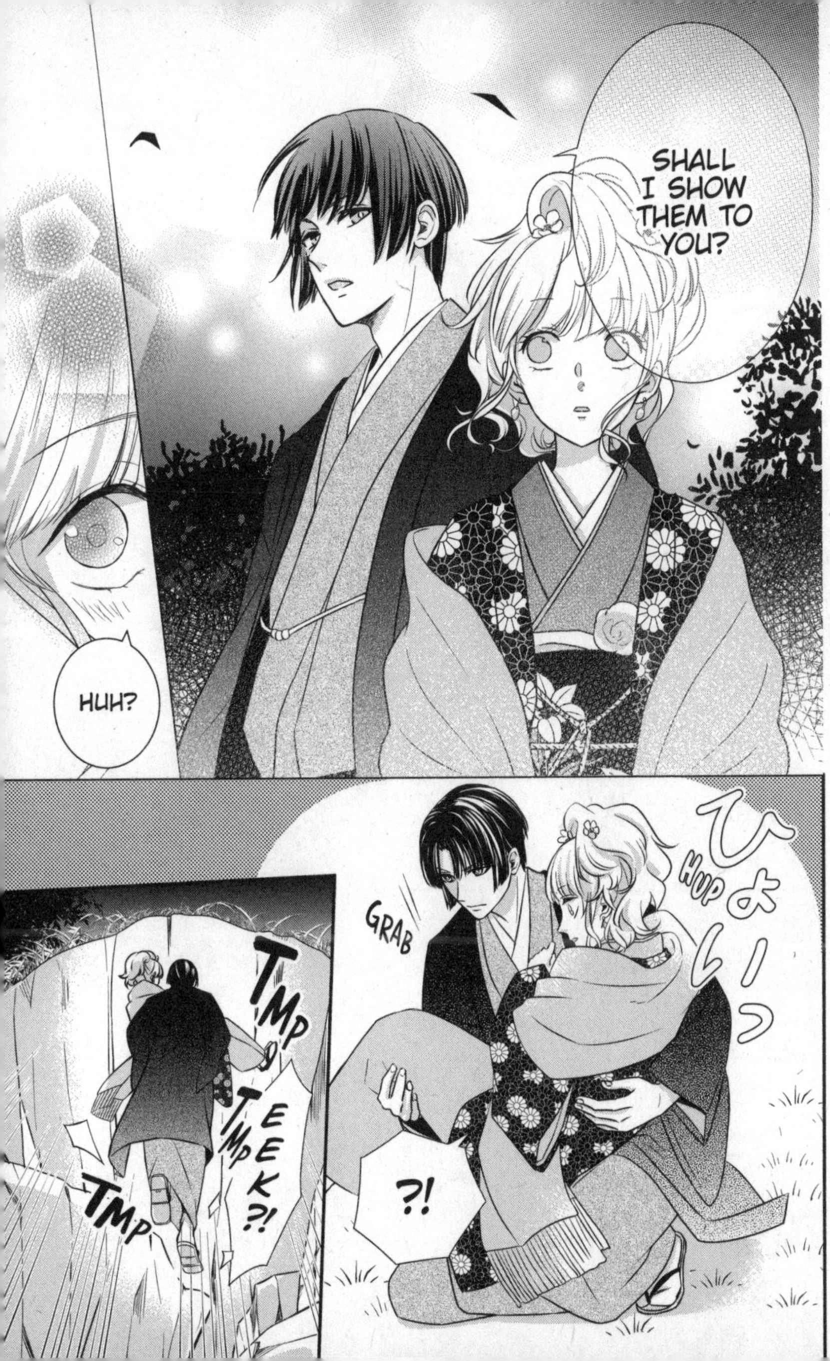
SHALL I SHOW THEM TO YOU?
HUH?
ひょいっ
HUP
GRAB
?!
TMP
TMP
EEK?!
TMP

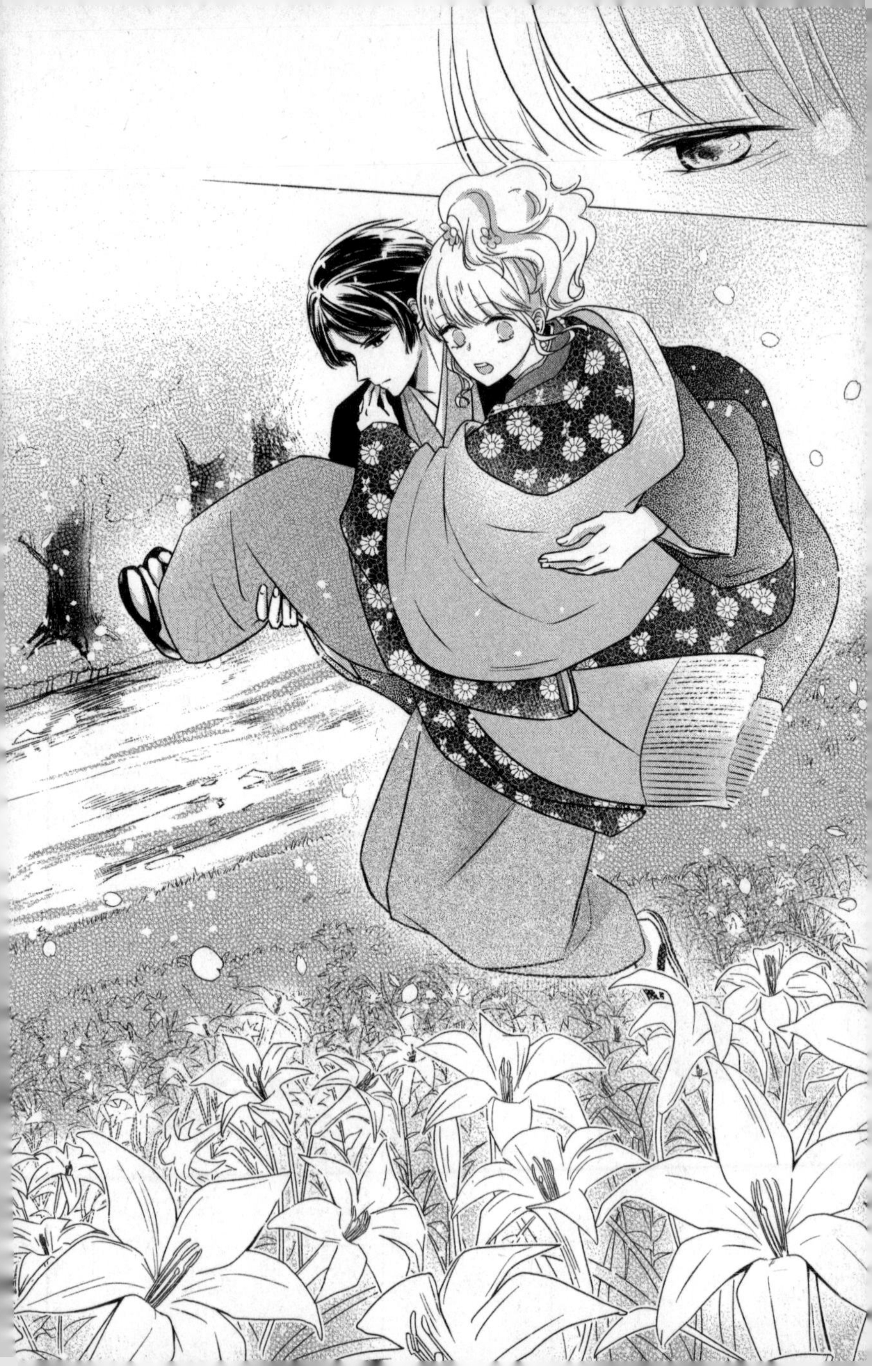

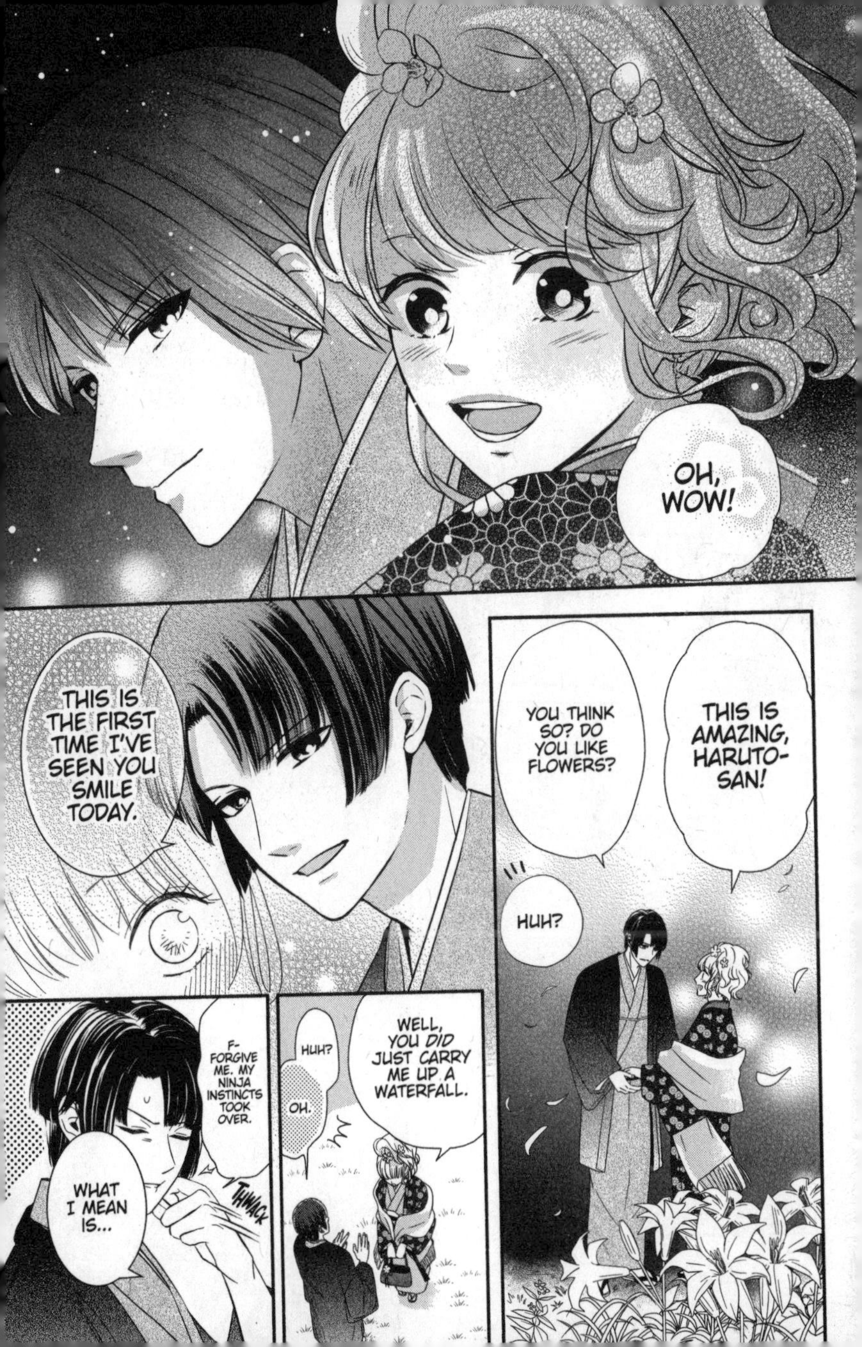
OH, WOW!
THIS IS AMAZING, HARUTO-SAN!
YOU THINK SO? DO YOU LIKE FLOWERS?
HUH?
THIS IS THE FIRST TIME I'VE SEEN YOU SMILE TODAY.
WELL, YOU *DID* JUST CARRY ME UP A WATERFALL.
HUH?
OH.
F-FORGIVE ME. MY NINJA INSTINCTS TOOK OVER.
THWACK
WHAT I MEAN IS...

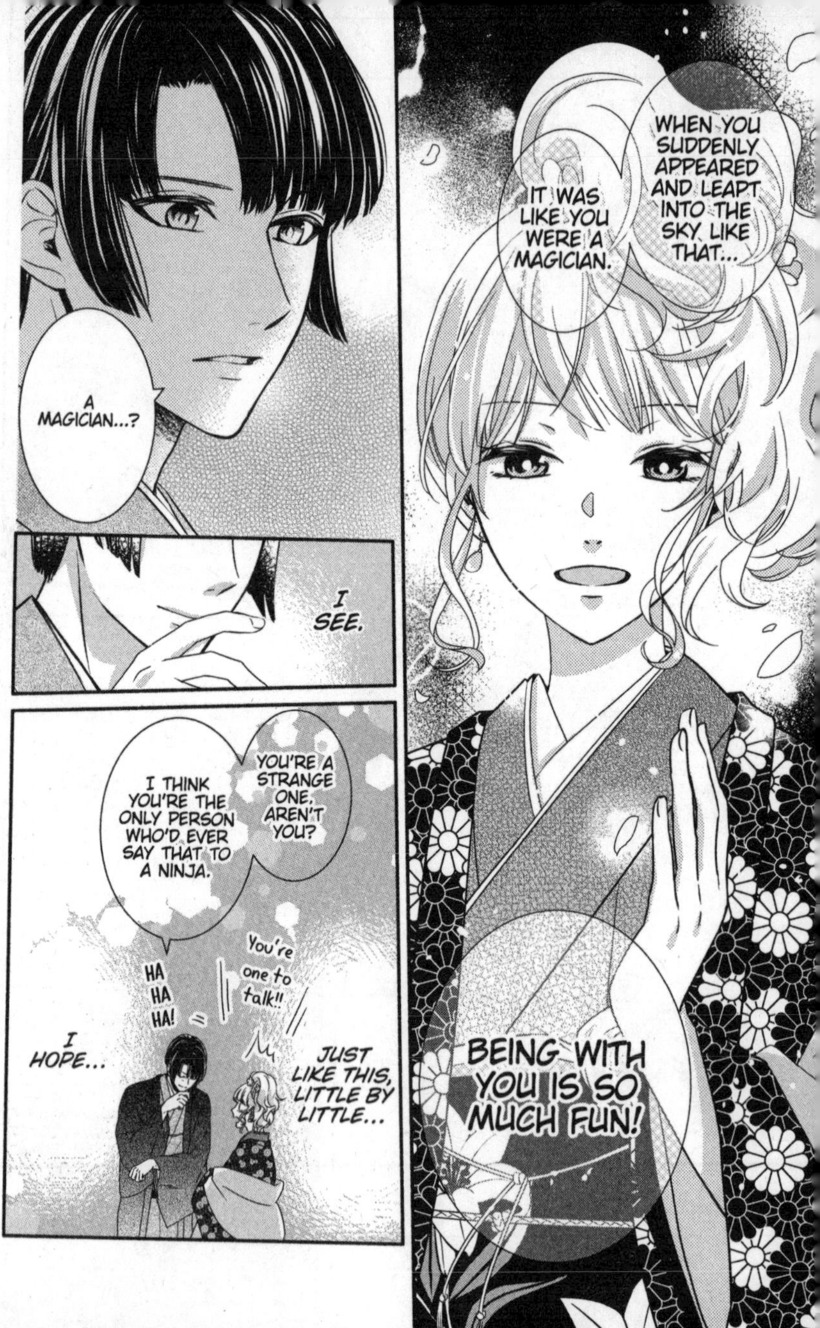
WHEN YOU SUDDENLY APPEARED AND LEAPT INTO THE SKY LIKE THAT...
IT WAS LIKE YOU WERE A MAGICIAN.
BEING WITH YOU IS SO MUCH FUN!
A MAGICIAN...?
I SEE.
YOU'RE A STRANGE ONE, AREN'T YOU?
I THINK YOU'RE THE ONLY PERSON WHO'D EVER SAY THAT TO A NINJA.
You're one to talk!!
HA HA HA!
JUST LIKE THIS, LITTLE BY LITTLE...
I HOPE...

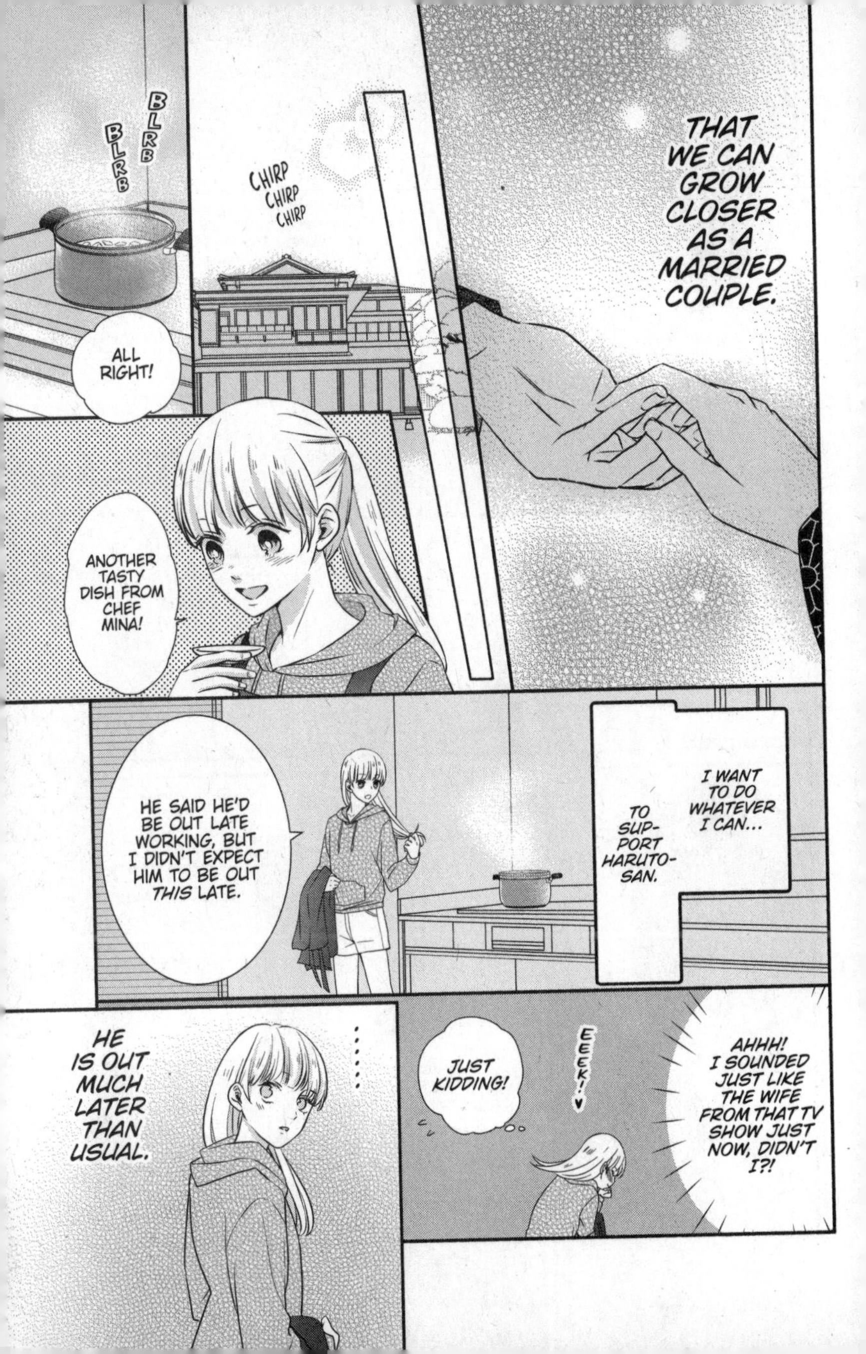
THAT WE CAN GROW CLOSER AS A MARRIED COUPLE.
CHIRP CHIRP CHIRP
BLRB BLRB
ALL RIGHT!
ANOTHER TASTY DISH FROM CHEF MINA!
I WANT TO DO WHATEVER I CAN...
TO SUPPORT HARUTO-SAN.
HE SAID HE'D BE OUT LATE WORKING, BUT I DIDN'T EXPECT HIM TO BE OUT THIS LATE.
AHHH! I SOUNDED JUST LIKE THE WIFE FROM THAT TV SHOW JUST NOW, DIDN'T I?!
EEEK!♥
JUST KIDDING!
......
HE IS OUT MUCH LATER THAN USUAL.

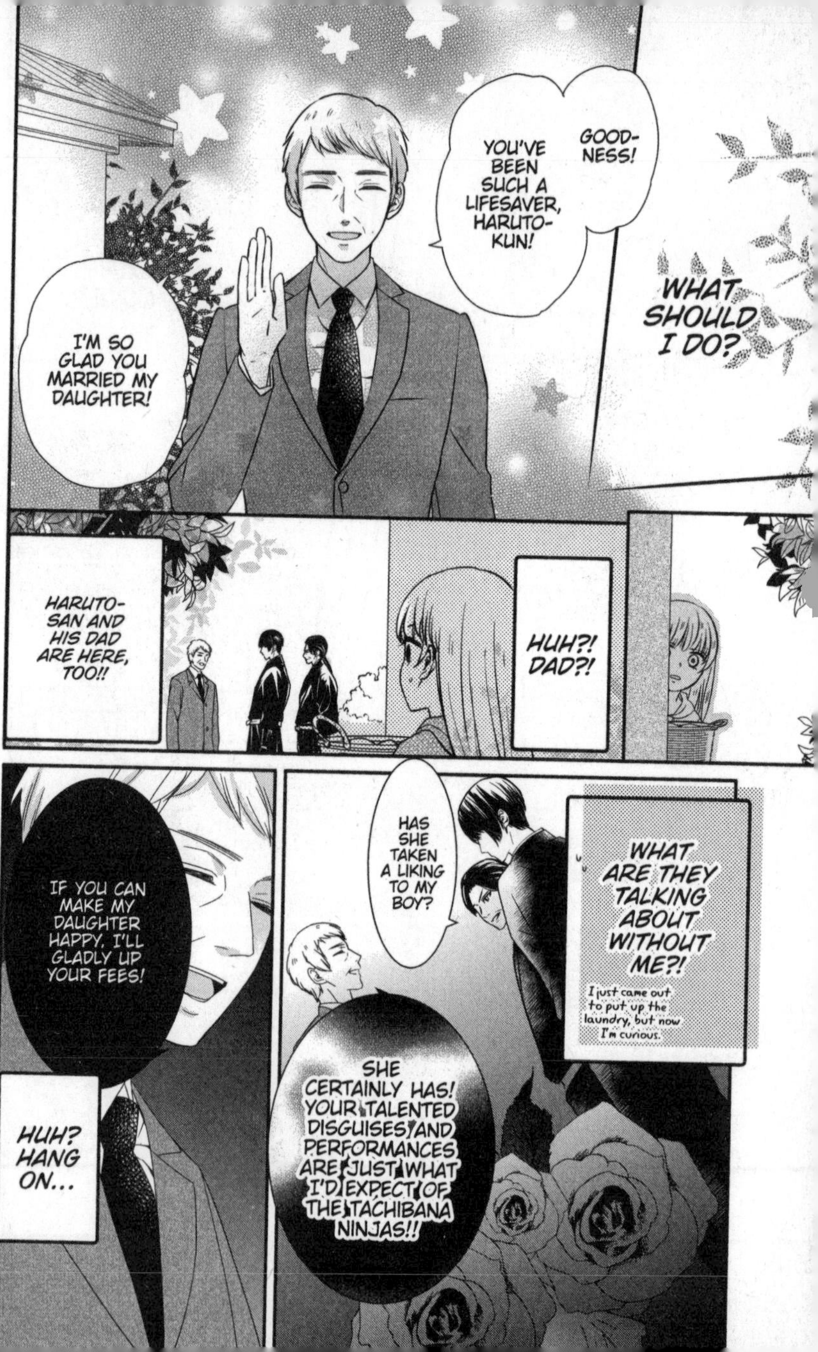
WHAT SHOULD I DO?
GOOD-NESS!
YOU'VE BEEN SUCH A LIFESAVER, HARUTO-KUN!
I'M SO GLAD YOU MARRIED MY DAUGHTER!
HUH?! DAD?!
HARUTO-SAN AND HIS DAD ARE HERE, TOO!!
WHAT ARE THEY TALKING ABOUT WITHOUT ME?!
I just came out to put up the laundry, but now I'm curious.
HAS SHE TAKEN A LIKING TO MY BOY?
SHE CERTAINLY HAS! YOUR TALENTED DISGUISES AND PERFORMANCES ARE JUST WHAT I'D EXPECT OF THE TACHIBANA NINJAS!!
IF YOU CAN MAKE MY DAUGHTER HAPPY, I'LL GLADLY UP YOUR FEES!
HUH? HANG ON...

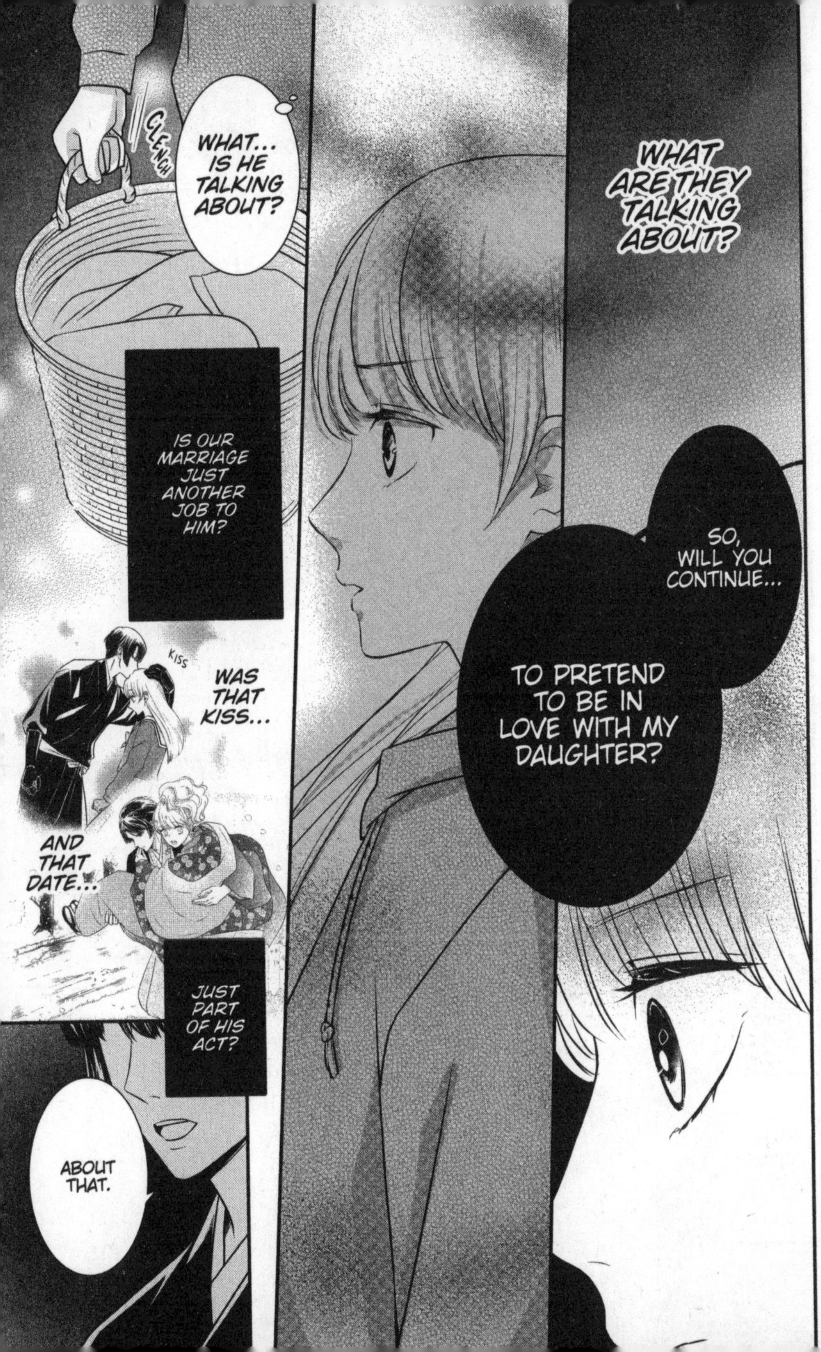
WHAT ARE THEY TALKING ABOUT?
SO, WILL YOU CONTINUE...
TO PRETEND TO BE IN LOVE WITH MY DAUGHTER?
CLENCH
WHAT... IS HE TALKING ABOUT?
IS OUR MARRIAGE JUST ANOTHER JOB TO HIM?
KISS
WAS THAT KISS...
AND THAT DATE...
JUST PART OF HIS ACT?
ABOUT THAT.

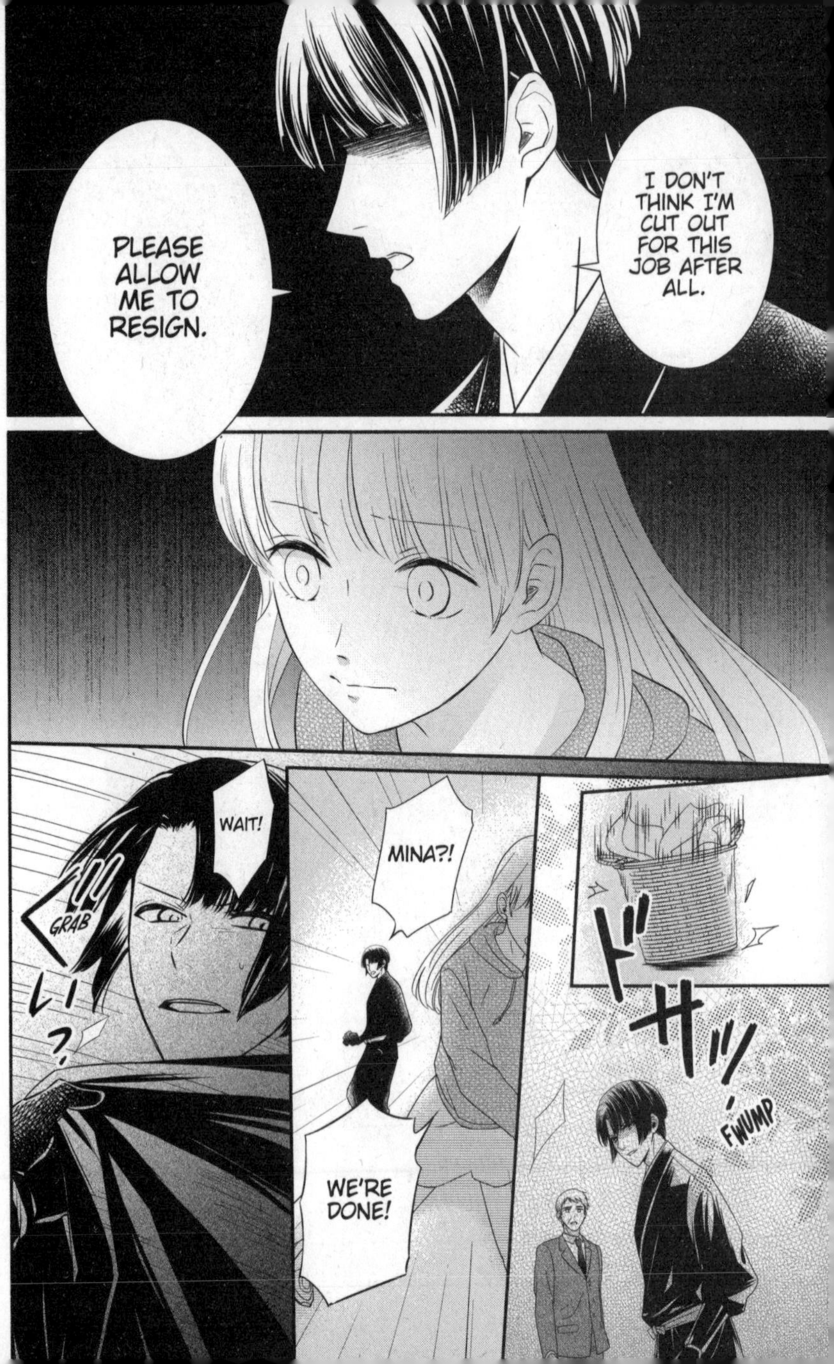
I DON'T THINK I'M CUT OUT FOR THIS JOB AFTER ALL.
PLEASE ALLOW ME TO RESIGN.
ドサッ
FWUMP
MINA?!
WE'RE DONE!
WAIT!
GRAB

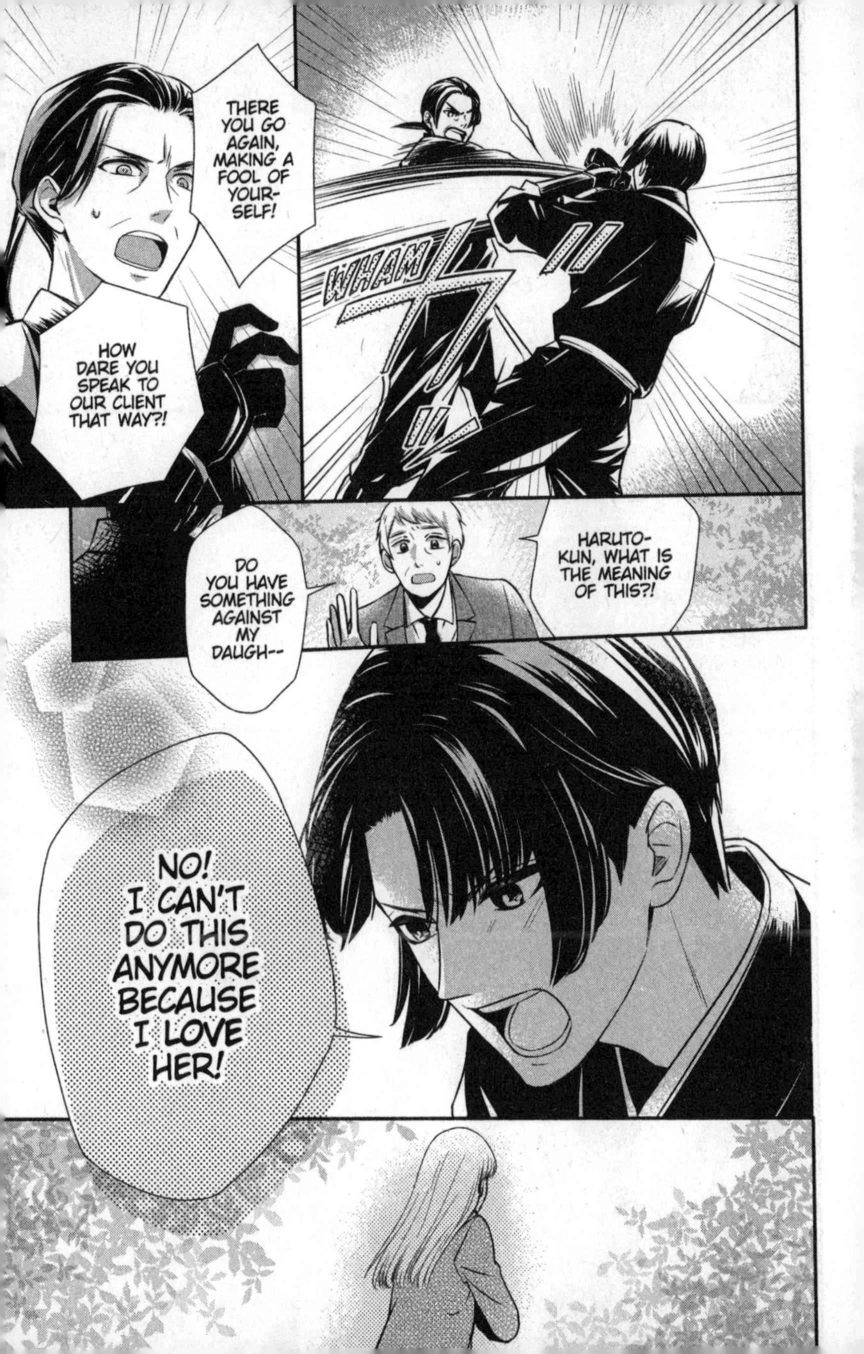
WHAM
THERE YOU GO AGAIN, MAKING A FOOL OF YOUR-SELF!
HOW DARE YOU SPEAK TO OUR CLIENT THAT WAY?!
HARUTO-KUN, WHAT IS THE MEANING OF THIS?!
DO YOU HAVE SOMETHING AGAINST MY DAUGH--
NO! I CAN'T DO THIS ANYMORE BECAUSE I LOVE HER!

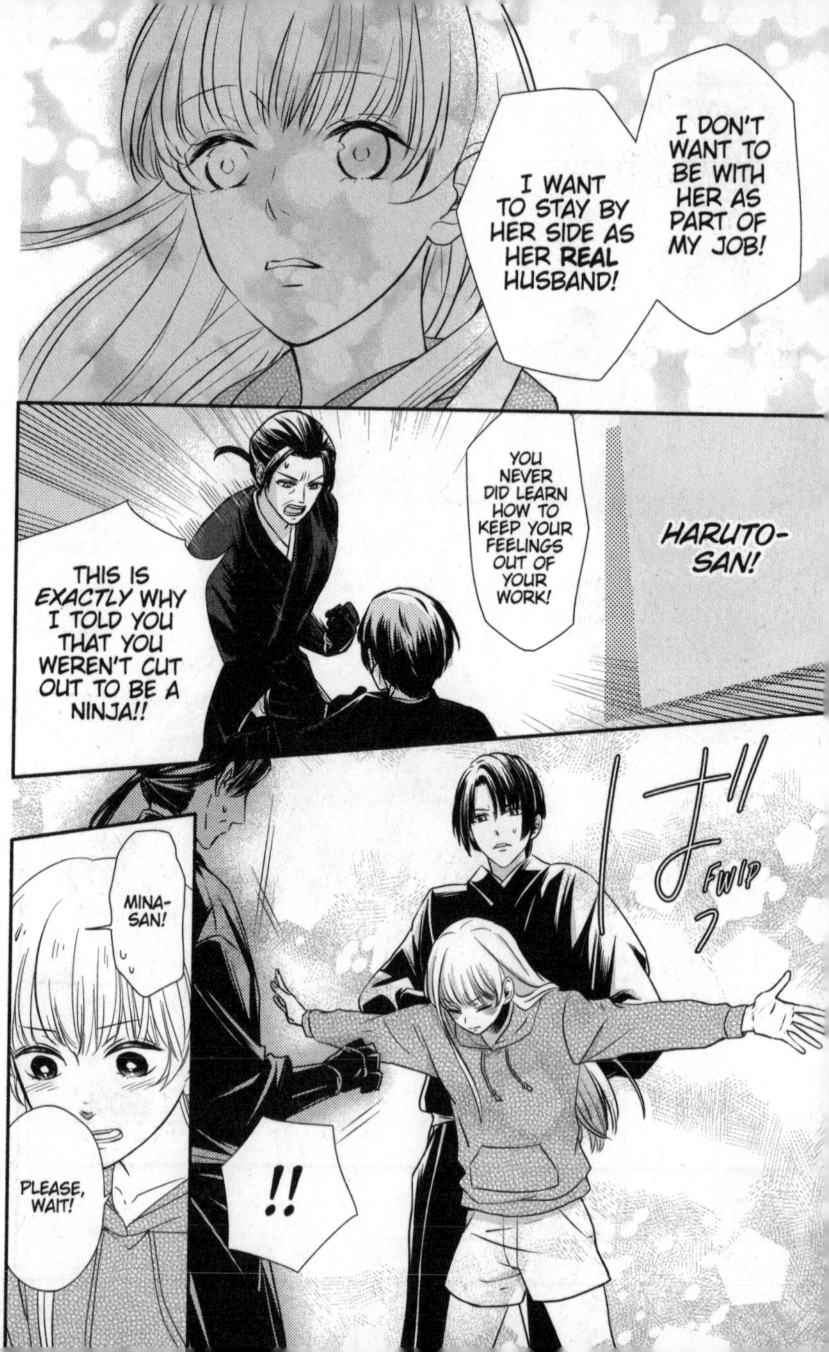
I DON'T WANT TO BE WITH HER AS PART OF MY JOB!
I WANT TO STAY BY HER SIDE AS HER **REAL** HUSBAND!
HARUTO-SAN!
YOU NEVER DID LEARN HOW TO KEEP YOUR FEELINGS OUT OF YOUR WORK!
THIS IS *EXACTLY* WHY I TOLD YOU THAT YOU WEREN'T CUT OUT TO BE A NINJA!!
FWIP
!!
MINA-SAN!
PLEASE, WAIT!

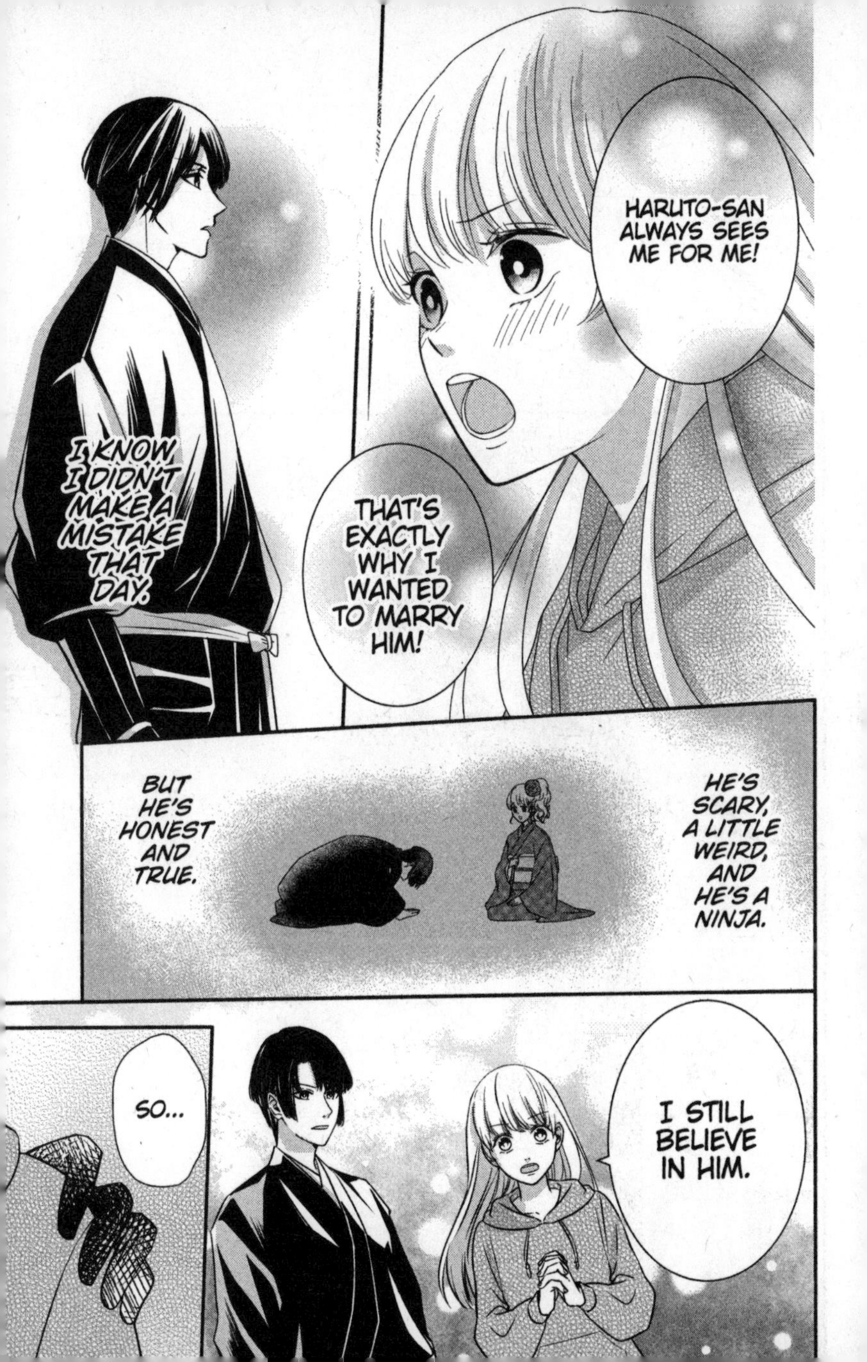
HARUTO-SAN ALWAYS SEES ME FOR ME!
THAT'S EXACTLY WHY I WANTED TO MARRY HIM!
I KNOW I DIDN'T MAKE A MISTAKE THAT DAY.
HE'S SCARY, A LITTLE WEIRD, AND HE'S A NINJA.
BUT HE'S HONEST AND TRUE.
I STILL BELIEVE IN HIM.
SO...

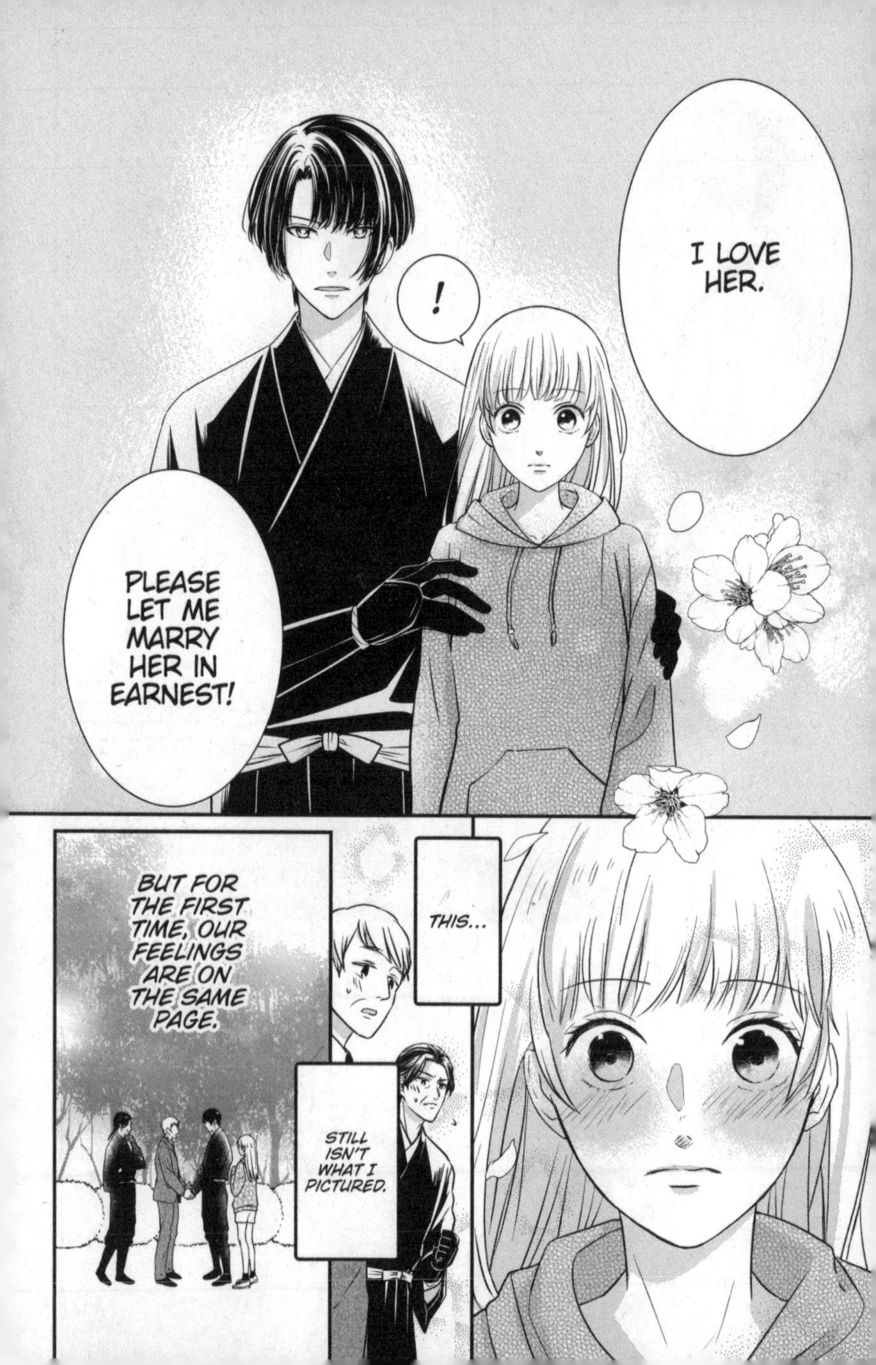
I LOVE HER.
!
PLEASE LET ME MARRY HER IN EARNEST!
THIS...
STILL ISN'T WHAT I PICTURED.
BUT FOR THE FIRST TIME, OUR FEELINGS ARE ON THE SAME PAGE.

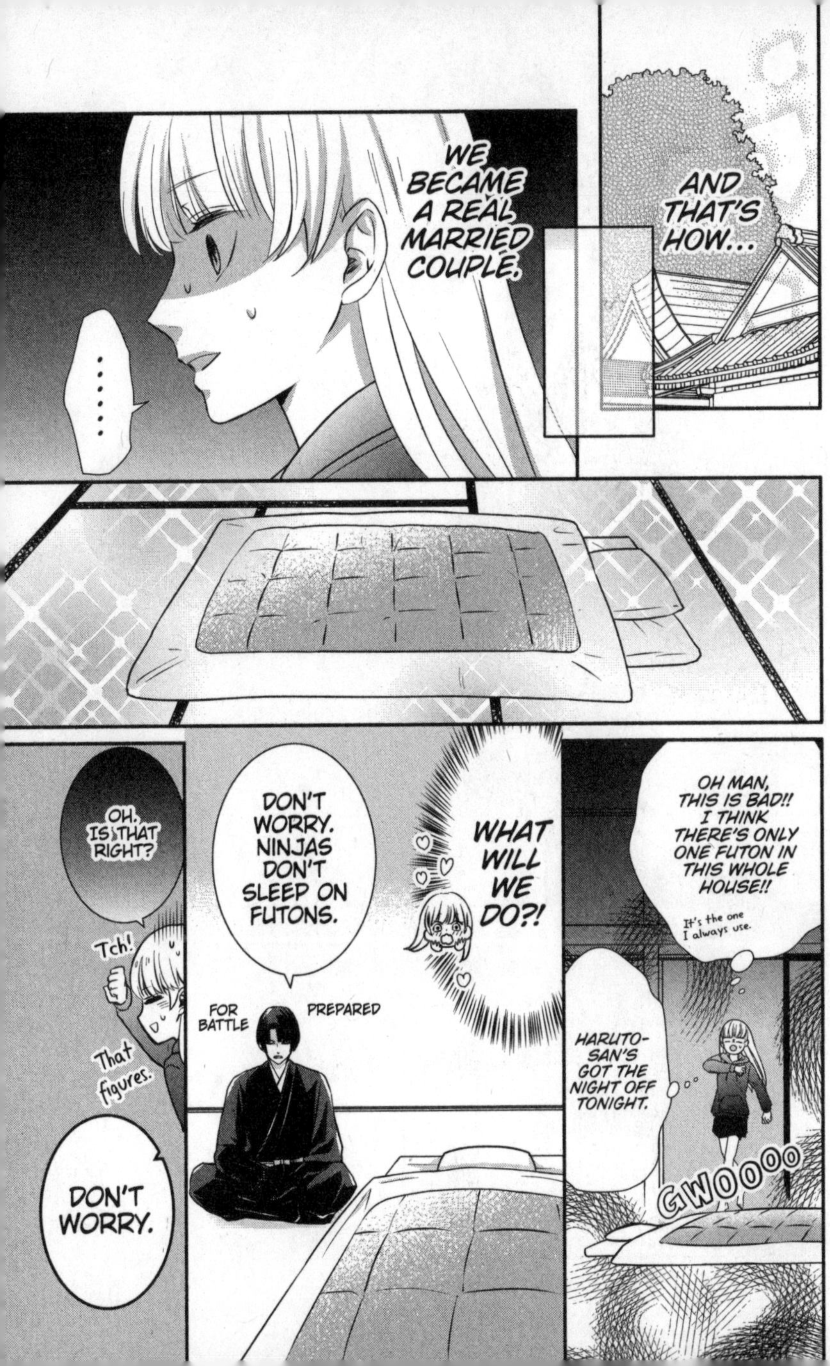
AND THAT'S HOW...
WE BECAME A REAL MARRIED COUPLE.
......
OH MAN, THIS IS BAD!! I THINK THERE'S ONLY ONE FUTON IN THIS WHOLE HOUSE!!
It's the one I always use.
HARUTO-SAN'S GOT THE NIGHT OFF TONIGHT.
GWOOOO
WHAT WILL WE DO?!
DON'T WORRY. NINJAS DON'T SLEEP ON FUTONS.
PREPARED FOR BATTLE
OH. IS THAT RIGHT?
Tch!
That figures.
DON'T WORRY.

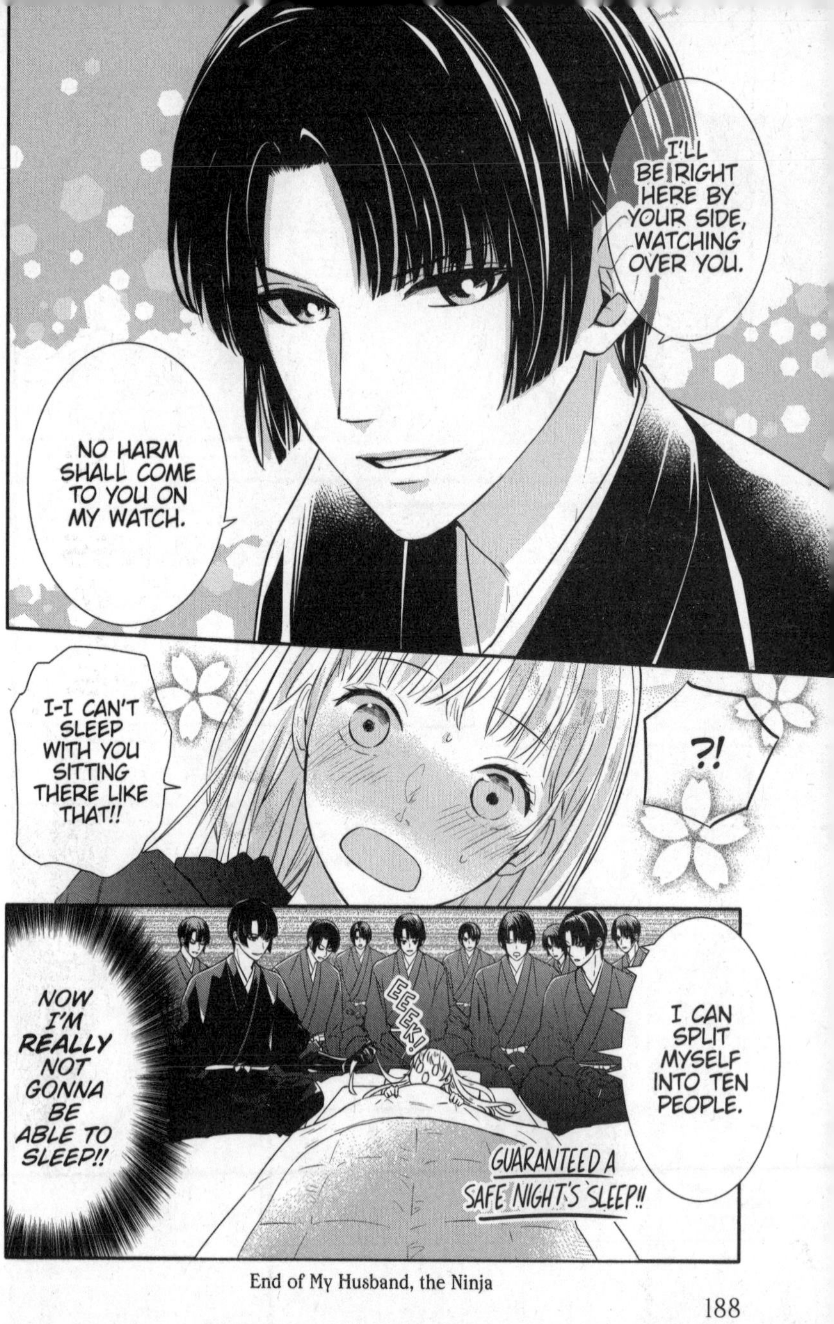
I'LL BE RIGHT HERE BY YOUR SIDE, WATCHING OVER YOU.
NO HARM SHALL COME TO YOU ON MY WATCH.
?!
I-I CAN'T SLEEP WITH YOU SITTING THERE LIKE THAT!!
I CAN SPLIT MYSELF INTO TEN PEOPLE.
EEEK!
GUARANTEED A SAFE NIGHT'S SLEEP!!
NOW I'M REALLY NOT GONNA BE ABLE TO SLEEP!!

End of My Husband, the Ninja

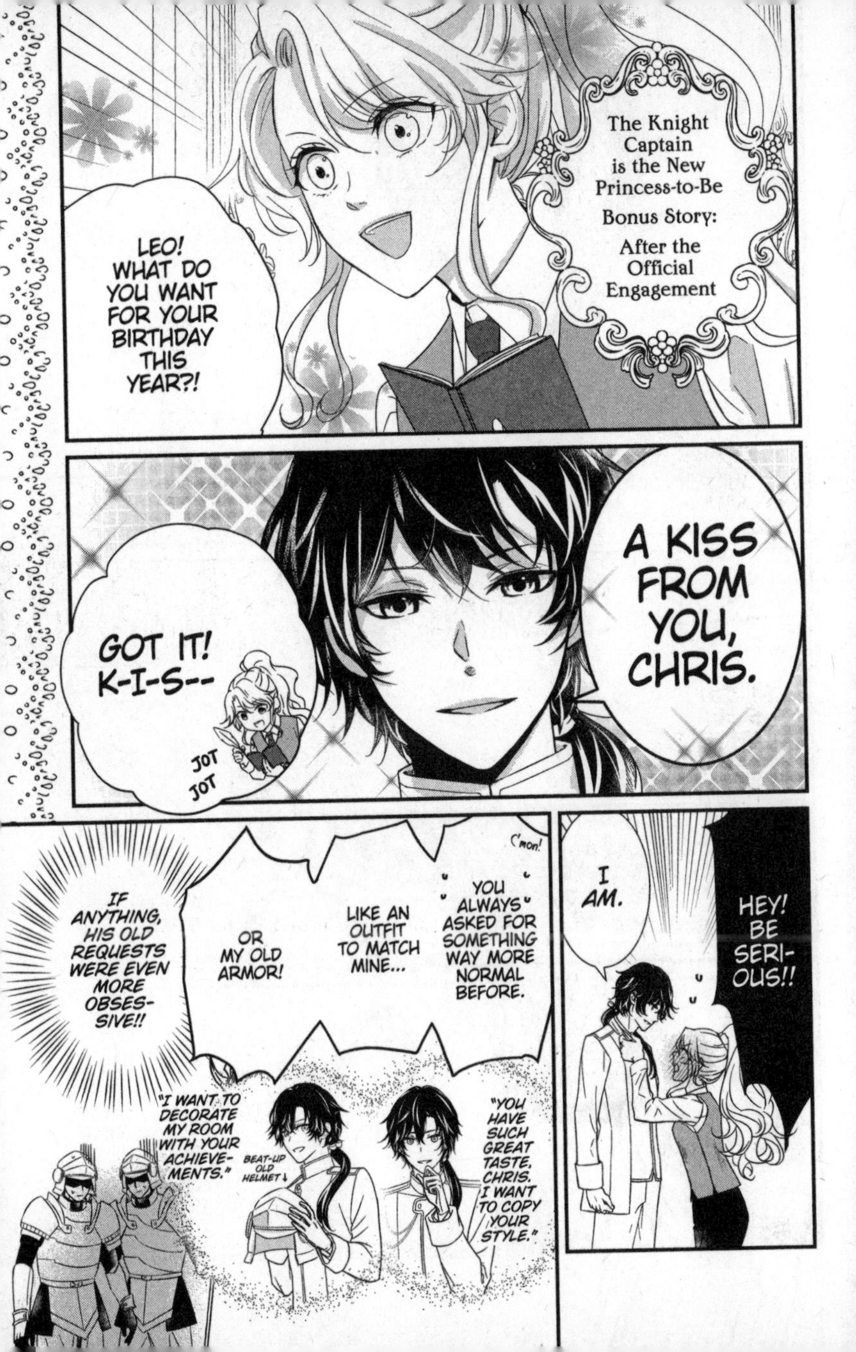
The Knight Captain is the New Princess-to-Be
Bonus Story:
After the Official Engagement
LEO! WHAT DO YOU WANT FOR YOUR BIRTHDAY THIS YEAR?!
A KISS FROM YOU, CHRIS.
GOT IT! K-I-S--
JOT JOT
HEY! BE SERI-OUS!!
I AM.
C'mon!
YOU ALWAYS ASKED FOR SOMETHING WAY MORE NORMAL BEFORE.
LIKE AN OUTFIT TO MATCH MINE...
OR MY OLD ARMOR!
IF ANYTHING, HIS OLD REQUESTS WERE EVEN MORE OBSES-SIVE!!
"YOU HAVE SUCH GREAT TASTE, CHRIS. I WANT TO COPY YOUR STYLE."
BEAT-UP OLD HELMET
"I WANT TO DECORATE MY ROOM WITH YOUR ACHIEVE-MENTS."

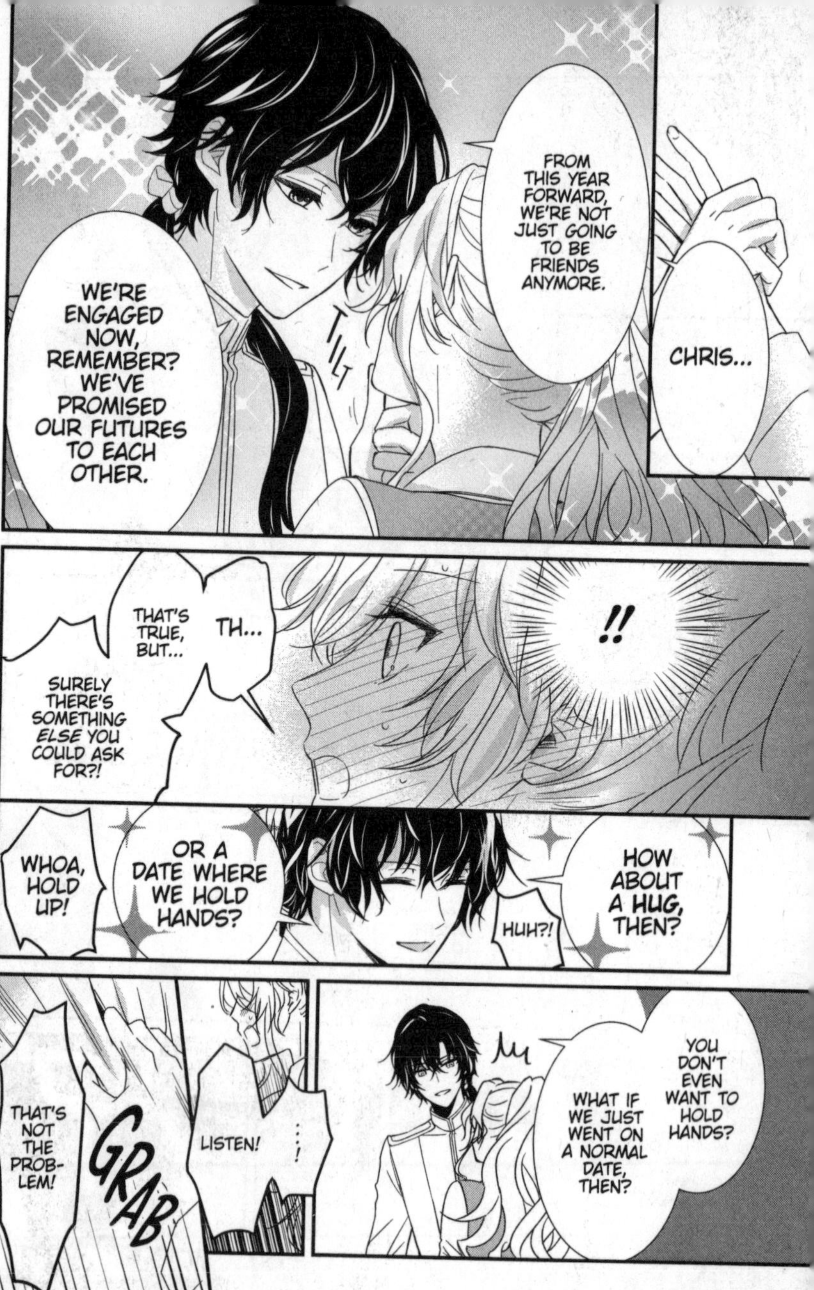
CHRIS...
FROM THIS YEAR FORWARD, WE'RE NOT JUST GOING TO BE FRIENDS ANYMORE.
TILT
WE'RE ENGAGED NOW, REMEMBER? WE'VE PROMISED OUR FUTURES TO EACH OTHER.
!!
TH...
THAT'S TRUE, BUT...
SURELY THERE'S SOMETHING *ELSE* YOU COULD ASK FOR?!
HOW ABOUT A **HUG,** THEN?
HUH?!
OR A DATE WHERE WE HOLD HANDS?
WHOA, HOLD UP!
YOU DON'T EVEN WANT TO HOLD HANDS?
WHAT IF WE JUST WENT ON A NORMAL DATE, THEN?
...!
LISTEN!
GRAB
THAT'S NOT THE PROB-LEM!